The Spatial Dimension of Risk

T0304027

Through its exploration of the spatial dimension of risk, this book offers a brand new approach to theorizing risk, and significant improvements in how to manage, tolerate and take risks. A broad range of risks are examined, including natural hazards, climate change, political violence and state failure. Case studies range from the Congo to Central Asia, from tsunami and civil war-affected areas in Sri Lanka to avalanche hazards in Austria. In each of these cases, the authors examine the importance and role of space in the causes and differentiation of risk, in how we can conceptualize risk from a spatial perspective and in the relevance of space and locality for risk governance. This new approach – endorsed by Ragnar Löfstedt and Ortwin Renn, two of the world's leading and most prolific risk analysts – is essential reading for those charged with studying, anticipating and managing risks.

Detlef Müller-Mahn is Professor of Social Geography and Director of ZENEB (Center for Natural Risks and Development Bayreuth) at the University of Bayreuth, Germany.

Earthscan Risk in Society series
Edited by Ragnar E. Löfstedt, King's College London, UK

The Spatial Dimension of Risk

How geography shapes the emergence
of riskscapes

Edited by
Detlef Müller-Mahn

LONDON AND NEW YORK

from Routledge

First published 2013
by Routledge
2 Park Square, Milton Park, Abingdon, Oxfordshire OX14 4RN

Simultaneously published in the USA and Canada
by Routledge
711 Third Avenue, New York, NY 10017

First issued in paperback 2014

Routledge is an imprint of the Taylor & Francis Group, an informa business

British Library Cataloguing in Publication Data
A catalogue record for this book is available from the British Library

Library of Congress Cataloging-in-Publication Data
The spatial dimension of risk : how geography shapes the emergence of riskscapes / edited by Detlef Müller-Mahn
p. cm. -- (The earthscan risk in society series ; 27)
Includes bibliographical references and index.
1. Human geography. 2. Spatial behavior. 3. Risk--Sociological aspects. 4. Risk perception. 5. Risk management. I. Müller-Mahn, Hans-Detlef.
GF95.S68 2012
304.2'3--dc23
2012019858

ISBN 978-1-84971-085-5 (hbk)
ISBN 978-1-138-90094-3 (pbk)
ISBN 978-0-203-10959-5 (ebk)

Typeset in Times New Roman by
Saxon Graphics Ltd, Derby

Endorsements

'*The Spatial Dimension of Risk* offers fresh, practical ways of seeing risk, governance and space. It combines previously separate approaches: sociology of risk, geography of hazard and politics of policy. The authors invite us to think about war, flood, disease and terrorism in new ways – changing our thought as profoundly as Beck's *Risk Society* 20 years ago.' – *Benjamin Wisner, disaster management consultant with 44 years of experience and author of* Disaster Risk Reduction: Cases from Urban Africa *(Earthscan 2009),* Handbook of Hazards and Disaster Risk Reduction *(Routledge 2011) and* Disaster Management: International Lessons in Risk Reduction, Response and Recovery *(forthcoming Routledge 2013)*

'The book gives the floor to a central dimension of risk, namely its spatiality. Spatiality comes in many different disguises, in the Global South as well as in the North, be it state border policies, propagation of contagious diseases, distribution of drought or landslide risk, or the question on which scale a risk should be managed in a most optimal way. With the concept of "riskscapes", the book provides an innovative and comprehensive frame for these widely diverse aspects of risk.' – *Jakob Rhyner, Director of the United Nations University Institute for Environment and Human Security and Vice Rector in Europe of the United Nations University*

Contents

List of figures and tables

Tables

List of contributors

Bernd Belina is Professor of Human Geography at Goethe University, Frankfurt am Main, Germany and research associate at the Leibniz Institute of Regional Geography, Leipzig, Germany. His main areas of interest include the policing of urban space, territorial borders, critical urban geography and historical-geographical materialism.

Martin Doevenspeck is Professor of Geographical Conflict Research at the University of Bayreuth, Germany. His research focuses on violent conflict and the political geography of climate change and risk in West and Central Africa.

Jonathan Everts works in the Department of Geography, University of Bayreuth. He is a member of the Population and Social Geography team headed by Professor Detlef Müller-Mahn. Jonathan Everts's earlier work focused on ethnic economy and corner shops. His current work concentrates on biosecurity and pandemic anxieties.

Sven Fuchs is Assistant Professor at the University of Natural Resources and Life Sciences, Vienna, Austria. His research interests are focused on mass movement processes, vulnerability to mountain hazards, environmental systems analysis, adapted risk management strategies and human–environment interaction.

Karl-Michael Höferl works in the Department of Urban Planning and Regional Development at HafenCity University in Hamburg.

Margreth Keiler is Associate Professor and head of the Geomorphology and Risk Research Group in the Department of Geography, University of Bern, Switzerland. Her research interests are focused on mass movement processes, complex systems research, risk assessment, risk evolution and coupled human–landscape systems.

Andreas Klinke is Associate Professor of Environmental Policy at the Environmental Policy Institute, Memorial University of Newfoundland. He was previously the head of a social science research group on governance at the Aquatic Research Institute within the ETH domain in Switzerland and lecturer in risk management at King's College, London.

Benedikt Korf teaches Political Geography at the University of Zurich, Switzerland. His research is concerned with the political economy of violent conflict, natural disasters and political protest in South Asia and the Horn of Africa.

Hermann Kreutzmann holds the Chair of Human Geography at the Institute of Geographic Sciences and is Director of the Centre for Development Research at Freie Universität Berlin. His research focuses on issues such as migration, conflict, development, water utilization, pastoralism and political geography in Central and South Asian contexts.

Fred Krüger is Full Professor of Geography at the University of Erlangen-Nuremberg, Germany. His research and teaching interests, committed to cross-disciplinary approaches, focus on Urban Studies and on Development Geography. He specializes in actor-oriented analyses of poverty, vulnerability, resilience, livelihood security, and concepts of risk, with a regional focus on southern Africa.

Julia Mayer is a PhD student in the Department of Geography, University of Bonn. Her research interests focus on social system theory and the interdisciplinary perspective on natural hazards and risks, particularly on risk prevention. She works as a consultant for the Federal Office of Civil Protection and Disaster Assistance (BBK), Germany.

Judith Miggelbrink is head of the research unit 'The production of space: state and society' at the Leibniz Institute for Regional Geography at Leipzig. Her current research interests focus on methodology of regional geography and social geography, territorial borders, and indigeneity and territoriality in northern Europe.

Detlef Müller-Mahn is Professor of Social Geography and head of the Center for Nature, Risk and Development at the University of Bayreuth, Germany. His current research interests focus on the constitution of risk in coupled social-ecological systems, adaptation to climate change, and water governance in Africa.

Jürgen Pohl is Professor of Social Geography at the University of Bonn. His main research fields are natural hazards and risk management with regard to spatial planning and human security. He focuses on perceptions and reactions of individuals, as well as of organizations.

Ortwin Renn is Professor of Environmental Sociology and Technology Assessment at the University of Stuttgart. He also directs the non-profit research institute Dialogik. His current research interests focus on risk governance and communication, citizen participation and sustainable energy systems.

Conrad Schetter is Research Fellow and Acting Director of the Center for Development Research (ZEF) of the University of Bonn. He received his habilitation in 'Development Studies' at the University of Bonn in 2009. His research focus is on local structures of power and violence, international intervention politics and collective identities. During the past few years, his main regional focus has been on Afghanistan, Pakistan and Central Asia.

Peter Weichhart is Professor of Human Geography at the University of Vienna, Austria. His main research interests are methodology and philosophy of geography, housing, migration and residential multilocality, social and economic geography, theory of man–environment relations, spatial planning, territoriality and place identity.

Barbara Zahnen is a postdoctoral research fellow at the Institute of Geography of the Humboldt University of Berlin, Germany. Her current research interests focus on the theory of geography, inspired by philosophical hermeneutics and phenomenology.

Swen Zehetmair is a postdoctoral research fellow in Social Geography at the Department of Geography, University of Bonn, Germany. His current research interests focus on risk communication, risk management and systems theory, with particular reference to flood risks.

Preface

Space plays an important role for risk production, but so far it has been paid relatively little attention in the theorizing of risk. The time dimension has occupied a more central position, since risk is essentially seen as a category that links the present with the future. This book is intended to make a contribution to the understanding of the intricate relationship between risk and space by discussing different conceptualizations of the two, and by exploring how they are related.

The examples of the relevance of space presented in the book are very diverse. In the case of natural hazards like floods, avalanches or landslides, the spatial dimension is obvious, because these risks can be localized and represented on maps. In the political geography of borders, conflicts and transboundary risk governance, risk is often related more or less directly to territorial units. Other types of risk, however, cannot so easily be associated with particular territories or places, as some recent experiences have shown: the Fukushima catastrophe for example was a local event with global consequences. Climate change is a global process with local consequences. Recent outbreaks of pandemic diseases like swine flu or SARS have been perceived as global threats, although their immediate impacts remained more or less locally confined. The production of risk in a local–global continuum can only be understood by taking into account different spatial levels, geographical settings and scalar effects. Space provides the arena for the overlapping of multiple risks in particular places and regions. The case studies in this book show that space may be addressed both as an analytical framework for the study of risk, and as an empirical tool for risk management, based on localizing, measuring, regionalization and mapping of particular risks.

Against this backdrop, the guiding question of the book is: 'What makes risk a spatial phenomenon, and what can Geography contribute to its study and management?' Of course, Geography does not hold any claim to exclusive competence in risk research, but the specific contribution of the discipline to the study of risk may be seen in its tradition of studying social and biophysical processes in spatial contexts, an interest in integrative approaches at the interface between science and social studies, and a professional sensitivity for questions related to space and scales.

The articles in this book mostly follow constructivist perspectives, which implies that risk is understood as an object of perception and negotiation within society. In this context, the concept of 'riskscape' is introduced to indicate how individual actors and social groups develop personal visions of risk and translate them into spatial settings. The notion of 'riskscape' has a metaphoric meaning that combines the idea of a territory or a landscape with that of risk. A landscape in this sense is a territorial unit that is characterized by mutual interactions between its elements, whereas risks are regarded as structuring phenomena that shape the landscape into a riskscape. The concept seeks to link materiality and meaning from an actor-oriented perspective. Similar to a landscape, the physical elements of a 'risky territory' form obstacles to and opportunities for the movement of people, and they are therefore part of their action frame of reference. The concept of the riskscape also allows the analysis of multiple risks and how people manage them. Riskscapes may therefore be understood as landscapes of multi-layered and interacting risks that represent both the materiality of real risks, and the perceptions, knowledge and imaginations of the people who live in that landscape and continuously shape and reshape its contours through their daily activities.

The chapters of the book present a wide range of conceptual approaches, case studies and riskscapes, but there are some similarities that can be explained by the fact that the authors – with the exception of Ortwin Renn who is a sociologist – are geographers based at universities in Germany, Austria and Switzerland. This has some influence on their thinking and the selection of empirical examples. Their shared interest is not simply their focus on territories or spatial containers, but the social constructedness of space, social practices of appropriation and formation of space, and the way individuals and societies give meaning to material objects situated in space. In other words, the shared geographical perspective in the contributions to this book lies in the duality of space as material structure and social construction.

Editing this book has been a long process and I wish to thank all who have contributed to it for their endurance. Special thanks go to Ragnar Löfstedt and four anonymous reviewers for their valuable comments, Sebastian Köllner and Sebastian Scholl for their help in formatting the texts, Michael Wegener for producing the maps, and Ruth Schubert for helping with proofreading and language editing.

Detlef Müller-Mahn, Bayreuth, April 2012

1 Space matters!
Impacts for risk governance

Ortwin Renn and Andreas Klinke

The first chapter of this edited volume conceptualizes the role of space and time in risk governance. The main objective is to integrate spatial dimensions into a systematic approach to organizational and policy learning in assessing, evaluating and managing risks. For this purpose, the risk governance model suggested by the International Risk Governance Council (IRGC) is expanded to include more spatial dimensions at the stages of pre-estimation, interdisciplinary risk estimation, risk characterization and evaluation, risk management, and monitoring and control. This new risk governance model also incorporates expert, stakeholder and public involvement as a core feature at the communication and deliberation stage.

Introduction

Deciding on suitable locations for hazardous facilities, setting standards for chemicals, making decisions about cleaning up contaminated land, regulating food and drugs, or designing and enforcing safety limits all have one element in common: these activities are collective endeavours to understand, assess and handle risks to human health and the environment. These attempts are based on two requirements. First, risk managers need sufficient knowledge about the potential impacts of the risk sources under investigation, and the likely consequences of the different decision options for controlling these risks. Second, they need criteria to judge the desirability or undesirability of these consequences for the people affected and the public at large (Rowe and Frewer 2000; Horlick-Jones *et al.* 2007; Renn and Schweizer 2009). Criteria in respect of desirability are reflections of social values such as good health, equity or efficient use of scarce resources. Both components – knowledge and values – are necessary for any decision-making process independent of the issue and the problem context.

Anticipating the consequences of human actions or events (knowledge) and evaluating the desirability and moral quality of these consequences (values) are the core elements of risk analysis. 'Crucial for these understandings is the idea that we are living increasingly in a world that changes, not according to what has happened, but according to what is anticipated, i.e. what may happen in the future [...]' (Everts, in this volume). Anticipating future events and judging their desirability poses particular problems if the consequences are complex and uncertain and the values contested and controversial. Dealing with complex, uncertain and ambiguous outcomes often leads to the emergence of social conflict relating to both epistemological as well as moral issues. Questions of how to deal with complex, uncertain and controversial risks demand procedures for dealing with risks that go beyond the conventional risk management routines. Numerous strategies to cope with this challenge have evolved over time. They include technocratic decision-making through the explicit involvement of expert committees, muddling through in a pluralist society, negotiated rule-making via stakeholder involvement, deliberative democracy or ignoring probabilistic information altogether (see reviews in Nelkin and Pollak 1979, 1980; Brooks 1984; Renn 2008: 290ff). The main thesis of this chapter is that risk management institutions need more adequate governance structures and procedures that enable them to integrate professional assessments (systematic knowledge), adequate institutional process (political legitimacy), responsible handling of public resources (efficiency) and public knowledge and perceptions (reflection on public values and preferences). These various inputs are not independent from space and time: they emerge in a specific spatio-temporal context and create, as Zahnen (in this volume) puts it, a feeling of spatio-temporal nestedness. The structures that evolve from the interactions of various actors in all phases of the risk-handling process are again related to spatial and time dimensions.

The way in which actors negotiate and construct 'landscapes' of risk or 'riskscapes' (Müller-Mahn and Everts, Chapter 2 in this volume) is subsumed under the term 'risk governance' (IRGC 2005; Renn 2008: 8). Hutter characterizes the move from governmental regulation to governance in the following manner:

> This decentring of the state involves a move from the public ownership and centralized control to privatized institutions and the encouragement of market competition. It also involves a move to a state reliance on new forms of fragmented regulation, involving the existing specialist regulatory agencies of state but increasingly self-regulating organizations, regimes of enforced self-regulation [...] and American-style independent regulatory agencies.
>
> (Hutter 2006: 215)

'Risk governance' involves the 'translation' of the substance and core principles of governance to the context of risk and risk-related decision-making (Hutter 2006). Based on our previous work on risk governance and risk evaluation (Klinke and Renn 2001, 2002, 2010; Klinke *et al.* 2006; Renn 2008; Renn *et al.* 2011), we will expand in this chapter on the spatial dimensions that underlie or even structure the risk governance process. We adopt a hybrid view on space in this chapter: space is, first, a reference to a physical entity to which humans can relate. This could be a specific landscape or a point on the map. Space in this sense provides an objective anchor for all actors. Second, it refers to a construction of associations that various actors link to space and its dimensions. Space in this sense is a social or mental construct that determines the boundaries of what is seen as inside vs. outside, as reasonable vs. unreasonable or as normal vs. distorted. Space in the

second sense interlinks diverse actors with similar mental models of reality, shapes their claims, structures the institutional means to process diverse inputs and determines to a large degree the individual and social capacity to cope with threats (Bickerstaff and Simmons 2009; see the chapters by Belina and Miggelbrink, Fuchs and Keiler, and Kreutzmann in this volume). Müller-Mahn has suggested a similar distinction between (i) space as principle of order and (ii) space as a projection of social meanings (Müller-Mahn and Everts, Chapter 2 in this volume).

In this chapter we first analyse the major characteristics of risk knowledge, and then address major functions of the risk governance process: pre-estimation, interdisciplinary risk estimation (including scientific risk assessment and concern assessment), risk characterization and risk evaluation, and risk management, including decision-making and implementation. Each of these stages is described in the light of the two meanings of space, drawing on the examples and ideas expressed in this volume. Furthermore, the chapter expands the spatial perspective to design an effective and fair institutional arrangement, including four different forms of public and stakeholder involvement for coping with the challenges raised by the three characteristics of risk knowledge. Finally, the chapter concludes with some general remarks about the relationship between space and risk.

Three characteristics of risk knowledge

Integrative risk governance is expected to address the challenges raised by three risk characteristics that result from a lack of knowledge and/or competing knowledge claims about the risk problem. Transboundary and collectively relevant risk problems, such as global environmental threats (climate change, loss of biological diversity, chemical pollution, etc.), new and/or large-scale technologies (nanotechnology, biotechnology, offshore oil production, etc.), food security or pandemics, are all characterized by limited and sometimes controversial knowledge with respect to their risk properties and their implications (Horlick-Jones and Sime 2004; see Korf in this volume). The three characteristics are complexity, scientific uncertainty and socio-political ambiguity (Klinke and Renn 2002, 2010; Klinke *et al.* 2006; Renn 2008).

Complexity

Complexity refers to the difficulty of identifying and quantifying causal links between a multitude of potential candidates and specific adverse effects (see Lewin 1992; Underdal 2009). A crucial aspect in this regard concerns the applicability of probabilistic risk assessment techniques. If the chain of events between cause and effect follows a linear relationship (as for example in car accidents, or an overdose of pharmaceutical products), simple statistical models are sufficient to calculate the probabilities of harm. But even such simple relationships may be associated with a high degree of uncertainty, for example when very few data are available, or the effect is stochastic by nature. Sophisticated models of probabilistic reasoning are required if the relationship between cause and effect becomes more complex (Renn and Walker 2008). The nature of this difficulty may be traced back to interactive effects among these candidates (synergisms and antagonisms, positive and negative feedback loops), long delay periods between cause and effect, inter-individual variation, intervening variables, and others. It is precisely these complexities that make sophisticated scientific investigations necessary, since the cause–effect relationship is neither obvious nor directly observable.

At first glance, complexity seems to be a universal and abstract term that is not related to time and location. However, all causal knowledge requires a concept of temporal sequence (A leads to B) as well as a concrete place where cause and consequence can be physically located. Non-linear response functions often result from interactions that depend on the spatial context in which they occur. Complexity therefore requires sensitivity to temporal and spatial factors relating to scale, as well as to the presence of intervening factors within the space in which the risk occurs. Space also refers to a multitude of exposure pathways and the composite effects of other agents that are present in the spatio-temporal context modelled by the scientists. Examples of highly complex risk include the diffusion of chemicals in air and water, synergistic effects of potentially eco-toxic substances on the environment, failure risk of large interconnected infrastructures and risks relating to critical loads in sensitive ecosystems. All of these examples require a spatial analysis as part of the process of knowledge acquisition in respect of impending risks.

Scientific uncertainty

Scientific uncertainty relates to the limitedness or even absence of scientific knowledge (data, information) that makes it difficult to exactly assess the probability and possible outcomes of undesired effects (see Rosa 1997; Aven and Renn 2009; Filar and Haurie 2010). It most often results from an incomplete or inadequate reduction of complexity in modelling cause–effect chains (see Marti *et al.* 2010). Whether the world is inherently uncertain is a philosophical question that is not pursued here. It is essential to acknowledge in the context of risk assessment that human knowledge is always incomplete and selective, and, thus, contingent upon uncertain assumptions, assertions and predictions (Functowicz and Ravetz 1992; Laudan 1996; Renn 2008: 75). It is obvious that the modelled probability distributions within a numerical relational system can only represent an approximation of the empirical relational system that helps elucidate and predict uncertain events. It therefore seems prudent to include additional aspects of uncertainty (van Asselt 2000: 93–138). Although there is no consensus in the literature on the best means of disaggregating uncertainties, the following categories appear to be an appropriate means of distinguishing between the key components of uncertainty:

- *Variability* refers to different vulnerability of targets such as the divergence of individual responses to identical stimuli among individual targets within a relevant population such as humans, animals, plants, landscapes, etc.

- *Inferential effects* relate to systematic and random errors in modelling including problems of projecting inferences from small statistical samples, from animal data or experimental data onto humans or from large doses to small doses, etc. All of these are usually expressed as statistical confidence intervals.
- *Indeterminacy* results from a genuine stochastic relationship between cause and effects, apparently non-causal or non-cyclical random events, or badly understood non-linear, chaotic relationships.
- *System boundaries* allude to uncertainties stemming from restricted models and the need for focusing on a limited number of variables and parameters.
- *Ignorance* means a lack of knowledge about the probability of occurrence of a damaging event and about its possible consequences.

The first two components of uncertainty qualify as statistically quantifiable uncertainty and can be reduced by improving existing knowledge, applying standard statistical instruments such as Monte Carlo simulation and estimating random errors within an empirically proven distribution. They include the spatio-temporal component in the first, physical sense. Space and time structure the analysis for characterizing and ideally calculating uncertainties. The last three components represent genuine uncertainty components and can be characterized to some extent by using scientific approaches, but cannot be completely resolved. This is the domain for spatial dimensions of the second kind: they mark boundaries between what humans believe 'could happen to them', what stakeholders claim as being significant or insignificant and what individuals feel as a justified cause for being concerned or not (Everts, in this volume). The validity of such uncertainty considerations (or 'bethinking' as Zahnen has phrased it in this volume) depends on the shared meaning of spatio-temporal experiences. Risk assessment and management agencies require additional information and input, such as a subjective confidence level in risk estimates, potential alternative pathways of cause–effect relationships, ranges of reasonable estimates, maximum loss scenarios and others. Examples of high uncertainty include many natural disasters, such as earthquakes, possible health effects of pandemics and long-term effects of introducing genetically modified species into the natural environment.

Socio-political ambiguity

While more and better data and information may reduce scientific uncertainty and cause a gradual overlapping of the two concepts of space, more knowledge does not necessarily reduce ambiguity. Ambiguity thus indicates a situation of ambivalence in which different and sometimes divergent streams of thinking and interpretation about the same risk phenomena and their circumstances are apparent (see Feldman 1989; Zahariadis 2003). We distinguish between interpretative and normative ambiguity which both relate to divergent or contested views regarding the justification, severity or wider 'meanings' associated with a given threat (Stirling 2003; Renn 2008: 77). Entering the realm of ambiguity opens the dimensions of space towards a whole set of subjective interpretations and meanings. This range is often associated with a different understanding of spatial and temporal dimensions. For example, Kreutzmann (in this volume) explores the meaning of boundaries in risk perception and conflict assessment, while Everts (in this volume) demonstrates that distance has a variety of meanings when applied to the threat of pandemics.

Interpretative ambiguity denotes the variability of (legitimate) interpretations based on identical observations or data assessment results, e.g. an adverse or non-adverse effect. Variability of interpretation, however, is not restricted to expert dissent. Lay people's perception of risk often differs from expert judgements because it is related to qualitative risk characteristics such as familiarity, personal or institutional control, assignment of blame, and others. Moreover, in contemporary pluralist societies diversity of risk perspectives within and between social groups is generally fostered by divergent experiences of space and location. Some people view themselves as world citizens who extend their concerns to all areas of the world; others expand their home space to all people who have similar life experiences or worldviews. They may care for all people who live in Catholic communities or who have been victims of car accidents. The virtualization of space has widely expanded the number and structure of options that demarcate the line between us (home space) and the others (foreigners or intruders). One interesting example of high interpretative ambiguity is concern about the impact of alien species on natural environments. Crucial questions are: is home defined by physical locality or familiarity? Have alien species a right to move to places that provide better living conditions even if they reduce the species that already inhabit the respective eco-space? How far should I go back in time to determine which species is alien and which domestic?

This leads us to the aspect of *normative ambiguity*. It alludes to different concepts of what can be regarded as tolerable, referring for instance to ethics, quality of life parameters, distribution of risks and benefits, etc. Ambiguity emerges where the problem is agreeing on the appropriate values, priorities, assumptions or boundaries to be applied to the definition of possible outcomes. Normative ambiguities can be associated, for example, with exposure to noise, aquaculture in sensitive areas, pre-natal genetic screening or genetically modified food. As Belina and Miggelbrink point out (in this volume), tolerability and acceptability are not properties of a risk object but products of power and social attribution. Appropriation of space is a means used by powerful actors to influence social judgements about what is tolerable and what is not. A good example of this is the use of phthalates in toys. All analysts are aware that this substance is potentially carcinogenic, but given the known exposure and the dose–response functions there is hardly any possibility of young children being negatively affected (Wilkinson and Lamb 1999). Yet the mere idea of having a carcinogenic substance in children's toys (home territory) has incited a fierce debate about the tolerability of such an ingredient in rubber toys.

Most risks are characterized by a mixture of complexity, uncertainty and ambiguity. Passive smoking may be a good example of low complexity and uncertainty, but high ambiguity. Nuclear energy may be a good candidate for high complexity and high ambiguity, but relatively little uncertainty. The massive emission of aerosols into the atmosphere to combat the effects of greenhouse gases might be cited as an example of high complexity, uncertainty and ambiguity.

Towards an inclusive risk governance model

The ability of risk governance institutions to cope with complex, uncertain and ambiguous consequences and implications has become a central concern of scientists and practitioners alike. In 2005, the International Risk Governance Council suggested a process model of risk governance (IRGC 2005; Renn 2008). This framework structures the risk governance process in four phases: pre-assessment, appraisal, characterization and evaluation, and risk management. Communication is conceptualized as a constant companion to all four phases of the risk governance cycle. The framework's risk process, or risk-handling chain, is illustrated in Figure 1.1.

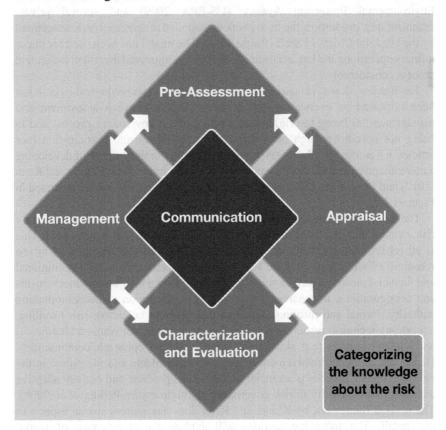

Figure 1.1 The Risk Governance Framework

Since its publication in 2005, the IRGC Risk Governance Framework has been applied to diverse risk governance issues in various case studies. Publications of these case studies are available on IRGC's homepage (www.irgc.org/publications. html). The case studies deal with emerging risks such as air quality, bioenergy, carbon capture and storage, critical infrastructure, nanotechnology, pollination services and synthetic biology. Furthermore, the IRGC has commissioned several case studies as tests of the applicability, efficacy and practicability of the Risk Governance Framework (Renn and Walker 2008). The applications have shown that the framework can be used as broad conceptual guidance on the critical elements of the risk governance process. To date, the IRGC risk framework has been discussed and partially applied to a number of institutions and organizations, including most prominently the European Food Safety Authority (Vos and Wendler 2009) and the Health Council of the Netherlands (2006). Reports using the framework have been given by the German Occupational Health and Safety Committee (Bender 2008), the International Occupational Safety Association (Radandt *et al.* 2008), the UK Treasury (HM Treasury 2005a), the US Environmental Protection Agency (US-EPA 2009) and several private organizations. In addition, the framework was applied to strategic risk management by the US Joint Chiefs of Staff (Rouse 2011). The model has been used for major military operations and has, according to the source, improved the risk management process considerably.

The framework was primarily developed to deal with technological risks. It has been criticized as overstating the demarcation line between assessment and management, as being too rigid in its phasing of the governance process and in being not specific enough on stakeholder involvement and participation (see articles in Renn and Walker 2008; van Asselt 2005). For the purpose of developing a more adaptive and inclusive version of the IRGC framework, Klinke and Renn (2012) and Renn *et al.* (2011) suggest a slightly modified version as illustrated in Figure 1.2.

The modified framework consists of the steps: pre-estimation, interdisciplinary risk estimation, risk characterization, risk evaluation and risk management. This is all related to the ability and capacity of risk governance institutions to use resources effectively (see Figure 1.2). Appropriate resources include institutional and financial means as well as social capital (e.g. strong institutional mechanisms and configurations, transparent decision-making, allocation of decision-making authority, formal and informal networks that promote collective risk handling, education), technical resources (e.g. databases, computer software and hardware) and human resources (e.g. skills, knowledge, expertise, epistemic communities). Hence, the adequate involvement of experts, stakeholders and the public in the risk governance process is a crucial dimension to produce and convey adaptive and integrative capacity in risk governance institutions (see Pelling *et al.* 2008). The revised framework by Klinke and Renn does not address spatial aspects in any detail. The following sections will explore the significance of spatial dimensions for each stage of the risk governance process.

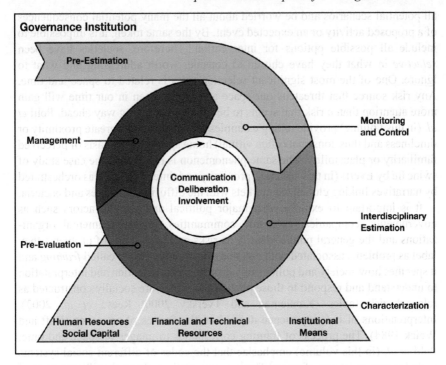

Figure 1.2 inside image includes labels: Governance Institution, Pre-Estimation, Monitoring and Control, Management, Communication Deliberation Involvement, Interdisciplinary Estimation, Pre-Evaluation, Characterization, Human Resources Social Capital, Financial and Technical Resources, Institutional Means

Figure 1.2 Adaptive and integrative risk governance model

Pre-estimation

Risks are not straightforwardly objective phenomena. They are based on the observation of hazards, i.e. the inherent potential for causing harm. Kreutzmann (in this volume) refers to this understanding of risk as representing the first level of analysis, i.e. potentiality of contingent changes in system behaviour. His third level of analysis refers to potentiality according to the contingency of ways of defining, dealing with or being involved in this potentiality of harmfulness. This corresponds in our analysis to the conception that risks are also mental constructions that reflect how people perceive uncertain phenomena and the ways in which their interpretations and responses are determined by social, political, economic and cultural contexts and judgements (see Luhmann 1993; OECD 2003; IRGC 2005). In this sense, both risks and space have an objective and a subjective component (see Weichhart and Höferl in this volume).

The introduction of risk as a mental construct is contingent on the presumption that human action can prevent harm in advance. The conceptualization of risk as a mental construct has major implications for how risk is considered. Risks are created and selected by human actors. What counts as a risk for one person may be seen by another as a destiny explained by religion, or even as an opportunity by a third party. Although societies have over time gained experience and collective knowledge of the potential impacts of events and activities, one cannot anticipate all potential scenarios and be worried about all the many potential consequences of a proposed activity or an expected event. By the same token, it is impossible to include all possible options for intervention. Therefore, societies have been *selective* in what they have chosen to consider worth addressing and what to ignore. One of the most significant selection rules is related to space and time. Any risk source that threatens our space and will happen in our time will gain more attention than a risk that seems to be far away or a long way ahead. Pohl *et al.* (in this volume) provide telling examples of how the media create proximity or timeliness and thus construct (often virtual) home spaces on the basis of perceived familiarity or plausibility. The same phenomenon is reported in the case study of swine flu by Everts (in this volume): proximity and time presence was orchestrated by narratives linking globalized markets with the diffusion of viruses and bacteria.

It is important to explore what major political and societal actors such as governments, companies, epistemic communities, non-governmental organizations and the general public identify as risks and what types of problems they label as problems associated with risk and uncertainty. This is called *framing* and it specifies how society and politics rely on schemes of selection and interpretation to understand and respond to those phenomena which are socially constructed as relevant risk topics (Kahneman and Tversky 2000; Reese *et al.* 2003). Interpretations of risk experience depend on the frames of reference (Daft and Weick 1984). The process of framing corresponds to images of space and time. Pohl *et al.* (in this volume) emphasize that the codes of different social systems include representations of space. These representations shape specific concepts of risks and dangers. Stakeholders with narrow space definitions are often more risk prone than those who prefer wider concepts of space, thus acknowledging more uncertainty and ambiguity. For example, Merad *et al.* (2008) were able to prove that managers of hazardous sites were more often convinced that stringent risk management actions were necessary the more they felt that a disaster could affect people outside of the disaster zone. Conversely, those who held the conviction that accidents in their facilities could only affect people living directly in the neighbourhood had little doubt that the risk assessment numbers were correct and reliable. Another issue is variety among the actors. What counts as a serious risk may vary among different actor groups. Whether an overlapping consensus evolves about what requires consideration as a relevant risk depends on the legitimacy of the selection rule. For example, the risks and benefits of biomass conversion for energy purposes can be seen under the frame of energy security, national independence, climate protection or economic development opportunities for rural areas. Depending on the frame, different types of risks and benefits may emerge; furthermore some benefits under one frame (for example national independence) may be a risk for another frame (economic opportunities for developing countries). One should note that all these frames make explicit reference to space: in particular, the frame of national independence (not dependent on energy imports) as well as the development frame (opportunity for local farmers to co-produce food and energy) rely on a definition of what space is considered relevant and significant for policy-making.

Interdisciplinary risk estimation

For politics and society to make reasonable decisions about risks in the public interest, it is not enough to consider only the results of (scientific) risk assessment. In order to understand the concerns of the people affected and various stakeholders, information about both risk perceptions and the further implications of the direct consequences of a risk is needed and should be taken into account by risk management.

Interdisciplinary risk estimation thus includes scientific assessment of risks to human health and the environment and assessment of related concerns, as well as social and economic implications (IRGC 2005; Renn and Walker 2008). The interdisciplinary estimation process should be clearly dominated by scientific analyses, but, in contrast to traditional risk regulation models, the scientific process includes both the natural sciences and engineering as well as the social sciences, including economics. This view corresponds with the two underlying concepts of space and risk: the physical orientation context and the social construction context.

The interdisciplinary risk estimation comprises two stages:

1 *Risk assessment:* experts from the natural and technical sciences produce the best estimate of the physical harm that a risk source may cause.
2 *Concern assessment:* experts from the social sciences, including economics, identify and analyse the issues that individuals or society as a whole link to a certain risk. For this purpose, the repertoire of the social sciences, such as survey methods, focus groups, econometric analysis, macro-economic modelling or structured hearings with stakeholders, may be used.

There are different approaches and proposals regarding how best to address the issue of interdisciplinary risk estimation. The German Advisory Council on Global Change (WBGU) has developed a set of eight criteria to characterize risks beyond the established assessment criteria (Klinke and Renn 2002; WBGU 2000). Some of the criteria have been used by different risk agencies or risk estimation processes (for example HSE 2001). These criteria include a space and a time component:

- *Extent of damage:* adverse effects in natural units, e.g. death, injury, production loss, etc.
- *Probability of occurrence:* estimate of relative frequency, which can be discrete or continuous.
- *Incertitude:* how do we take account of uncertainty in knowledge, in modelling of complex systems or in predictability in assessing a risk?
- *Ubiquity:* geographical dispersion of damage (*space dimensions*).
- *Persistence:* how long will the damage last (*time dimension*)?
- *Reversibility:* can the damage be reversed?
- *Delay effects:* latency between initial event and actual damage.

- *Potential for mobilization:* the broad social impact. Will the risk generate social conflict, outrage, etc.?
- *Inequity and injustice* associated with the distribution of risks and benefits over time, space and social status.
- *Psychological stress and discomfort* associated with the risk or the risk source (as measured by psychometric scales).
- *Potential for social conflict and mobilization* (degree of political or public pressure on risk regulatory agencies).
- *Spillover effects* that can be expected when highly symbolic losses have repercussions on other fields, such as financial markets or loss of credibility in management institutions.

The last four aspects of the criteria list reflect many factors that have been proven to influence risk perception. The 'appraisal guidance' published by the UK Treasury Department in 2005 recommends a risk estimation procedure that is similar to this proposal and includes both the results of risk assessment and the direct input from data on public perception and the assessment of social concerns (HM Treasury 2005b).

Risk evaluation

A heavily disputed task in the risk governance process relates to the procedure for judging a given risk and justifying an evaluation of its societal acceptability or tolerability (see Figure 1.2). In many approaches, risks are ranked and prioritized on the basis of a combination of probability (how likely is it that the risk will occur) and impact (what are the consequences, if the risk does occur). In the so-called traffic-light model (see Figure 1.3, here shown in black and white), risks are located in the diagram of probability versus expected consequences, and three areas are identified: green (white), yellow (grey) and red (black) (Klinke and Renn 2002; Renn 2008: 149ff). A risk falls in the green (white) area if the occurrence is highly unlikely and the impact is negligible. No further formal intervention is necessary. A risk is seen as tolerable when serious impacts might occur occasionally (yellow/grey area). The benefits are worth the risk, but risk reduction measures are necessary. Finally, a risk is viewed as intolerable when the occurrence of catastrophic impacts is very likely (red/black area). Possible negative consequences of the risk are so catastrophic that in spite of potential benefits it cannot be tolerated.

Drawing a line between 'acceptable', 'tolerable' and 'intolerable' risk is one of the most controversial tasks in the risk governance process. The UK Health and Safety Executive has developed a procedure for chemical risks based on risk–risk comparisons (Löfstedt 1997). Some Swiss cantons such as Basle County have experimented with round tables as a means to reach consensus on drawing the two demarcation lines, where participants in the round table represented industry, administrators, county officials, environmentalists and neighbourhood groups. Irrespective of the means selected to support this task, the judgement concerning

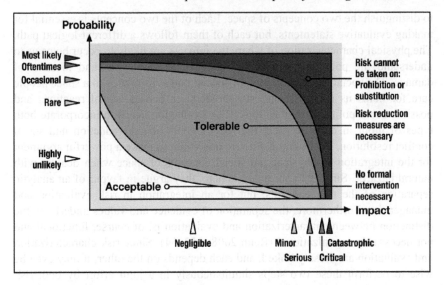

Figure 1.3 Risk areas

acceptability or tolerability is contingent on making use of a variety of different knowledge sources. It is important to include all data and insights resulting from risk assessment activities, and additional data from the concern assessment.

Risk evaluations in general rely on causal associations and moral judgements about the desirability of anticipated consequences (see Goldstein and Keohane 1993). Causal associations refer to the scientific evidence from risk assessment, whether, how and to what extent the hazard potential causes harm to the environment or to human health. This dimension emphasizes cause–effect relations and provides factual guidance as to which strategy is appropriate to achieve the goal of risk avoidance or reduction. However, the question of what is safe enough also implies a moral judgement about the acceptability of risk and the tolerable burden that risk producers can impose on others. The results of the concern assessment can provide insights into what kind of associations are present and which moral judgements people would prefer in a choice situation. Of major importance is the perception of just or unjust distribution of risks and benefits. How these moral judgements are made and justified depends to a large degree on cultural values and worldviews. They affect personal thinking and evaluation strategies and are shaped by collectively shared ontological and ethical convictions. The selection of strategies for risk handling is, therefore, understandable only within the context of broader worldviews. Hence, society can never derive acceptability or tolerability from looking at the evidence alone. Likewise, evidence is essential if we are to know whether a value has been violated or not (or to what degree).

Spatial analysis is crucial to this step of characterizing and evaluating risks. People distinguish between identical risks happening in their area versus another area, or in their time versus some future time (Boholm 1998). It is important here to distinguish the two concepts of space. Each of the two concepts is essential for making evaluative statements, but each of them follows a different logical path. The physical characterization of where the impacts are likely to occur helps us to understand the potential hazards, exposure routes and types and location of damage. The social characterization of special concerns related to a space people care for helps us to understand stakeholders' responses, social reactions and possible socio-political ramifications. Risk evaluation needs to incorporate both types of input in order to meet the requirements of risk reduction and social conflict resolution. Fuchs and Keiler (in this volume) make a powerful argument for the integration of physical and social concepts of space when dealing with natural hazards. Similar to our analysis here, they argue in favour of an analytic separation of the two concepts, but for an integration in risk evaluation and management. Furthermore, the separation of evidence and values underlying the distinction between characterization and evaluation is, of course, functional and not necessarily organizational (Renn 2008: 153–54). Since risk characterization and evaluation are closely linked, and each depends on the other, it may even be wise to perform these two steps simultaneously in a joint effort by both risk assessment experts and risk management decision makers (Frewer and Salter 2007). The US regulatory system tends to favour an organizational combination of characterization and evaluation, while European risk management tends to maintain the organizational separation, e.g. in the food area (Löfstedt and Vogel 2001). The US Food and Drug Administration (FDA) is responsible for both risk assessment and management, whereas the European Food Safety Authority (EFSA) has only a mandate to perform risk assessments. Risk management tasks are reserved for the EU Commission. Similarly in Germany, the Federal Institute for Risk Assessment (BfR) is authorized to assess food risks, while the Federal Office of Consumer Protection and Food Safety has the responsibility for risk management.

Risk management

Risk management starts by reviewing all relevant data and information generated in the previous steps of interdisciplinary risk estimation, characterization and risk evaluation (Figure 1.3). The systematic analysis of risk management options focuses on tolerable risks (yellow/grey area) and those where tolerability is disputed (light and dark grey transition zones). The other cases (green/white and red/black areas) are fairly easy to deal with. Intolerable risks demand prevention and prohibition strategies aimed at replacing the hazardous activity with another activity leading to identical or similar benefits. The management of acceptable risks is left to private actors (civil society and economy). They may initiate additional and voluntary risk reduction measures, or seek insurance to cover for possible minor losses. If risks are classified as tolerable, or if there is a dispute as to whether they are in the transition zones of tolerability, public risk management needs to design and implement actions that make these risks either acceptable or at least tolerable by introducing reduction strategies. This task can be described in terms of classical decision theory (see Aven and Vinnem 2007; Klinke and Renn 2010):

- identification and generation of generic risk management options;
- assessment of risk management options with respect to predefined criteria;
- evaluation of risk management options;
- selection of appropriate risk management options;
- implementation of risk management options and;
- monitoring and control of option performance.

Again it is obvious that space is an important criterion for selecting and evaluating risk management measures. It is not enough to demonstrate that a risk reduction option is able to perform what it promises to do but that these effects can be traced in space and time. First, the effect of interventions can only be measured when time and space are specified. Second, people may have different concerns about spatial and temporal distribution. They may not be alarmed if the measures reduce the risks in their home space but increase the risk in foreign spaces (such as reducing acid rain by building higher stacks that transport pollutants to neighbouring countries). They may not care if impacts are going to happen in a distant future (such as raising ocean temperatures until the Gulf Stream collapses). An interesting example is the introduction of geo-engineering as the impacts are likely to affect different areas and human livelihoods in very diverse ways.

Turning to the social construction of space, the emphasis in risk management will be on the integration of different frames and conceptualization of space and other crucial factors. Weichhart and Höferl (in this volume) have created a convincing link between space perceptions and discourse types concerning risks. This link is based on the dominant meaning associated with space in different social contexts and the need to define discourse forms according to spatial contexts. In our risk framework we have classified such discourse types on the basis of complexity, scientific uncertainty and socio-political ambiguity (Klinke and Renn 2002).

The first category refers to linear risk problems: they are characterized as having low scores regarding the dimensions of complexity, uncertainty and ambiguity. They can be addressed by *linear risk management* because they are normally easy to assess and quantify. Routine risk handling within risk assessment agencies and regulatory institutions is appropriate for this category, since the risk problems are well known, sufficient knowledge of key parameters is available and there are no major controversies about causes and effects or conflicting values. The management includes risk–benefit analysis, risk–risk comparisons or other instruments for balancing pros and cons. Here, space plays a major role in its physical sense. Regulators will ask: who and what is affected and how can one protect the home space by introducing protective rules and behaviour? An example might be requiring that cyclists should wear helmets.

If risks are ranked high for complexity but low for uncertainty and ambiguity, they require the systematic involvement and deliberation of experts representing the relevant epistemic communities in order to produce an accurate estimate of the complex relationships. It does not make much sense to integrate public concerns, perceptions or any other social aspects in the resolving of complexity, unless specific knowledge from the concern assessment helps to untangle complexity. Complex risk problems therefore demand *risk-informed management* that can be offered by scientists and experts applying methods of expanded risk assessment, determining quantitative safety goals, consistently using cost-effectiveness methods, and monitoring and evaluating outcomes. Again spatial considerations are mostly focused on physical location and time. However, complex relationships tend to be misinterpreted by many stakeholders and the public. It is therefore essential to investigate perceptions and positions with respect to the risk source and initiate either risk communication or risk modification programmes to address these concerns.

Risk problems that are characterized by high uncertainty but low ambiguity require *precaution-based management*. Since sufficient scientific certainty is currently either not available or unattainable, expanded knowledge acquisition may help to reduce uncertainty and thus move the risk problem back to the first stage of handling complexity. If, however, uncertainty cannot be reduced by additional knowledge, risk management should foster and enhance precautionary and resilience-building strategies and decrease vulnerabilities in order to avoid irreversible effects. Appropriate instruments include containment, diversification, monitoring and substitution. Uncertainty is also a major indicator of spatial flexibility. One area might be affected or not. The same is true for social spaces. It is not clear whether they are under threat or not. This situation of uncertainty contributes to personal anxiety and social constructions of threats (Everts, in this volume). It is therefore essential to initiate a major communication and involvement process for finding common strategies to handle uncertain outcomes.

Finally, if risk problems are ranked high for ambiguity (regardless of whether they are low or high for uncertainty), *discourse-based management* is required, demanding participative processing. This includes the need to involve major stakeholders as well as the affected public. The goal of discourse-based risk management is to produce a collective understanding among all stakeholders and the concerned public on interpretative ambiguity or to find legitimate procedures of justifying collectively binding decisions on acceptability and tolerability. It is important that a consensus or a compromise is achieved between those who believe that the risk is worth taking (perhaps because of self-interest) and those who believe that the impending consequences do not justify the potential benefits of the risky activity or technology.

Communication, deliberation and involvement of non-governmental actors

The effectiveness and legitimacy of the risk governance process depends on the capability of management agencies to resolve complexity, characterize uncertainty and handle ambiguity by means of communication and deliberation.

Instrumental processing involving governmental actors

Dealing with linear risk issues, which are associated with low scores for complexity, scientific uncertainty and socio-political ambiguity, requires hardly any changes to conventional public policy-making. The data and information regarding such linear (routine) risk problems are provided by statistical analysis; law or statutory requirements determine the general and specific objectives; and the role of public policy is to ensure that all necessary safety and control measures are implemented and enforced. Traditional cost–benefit analyses including effectiveness and efficiency criteria are the instruments of political choice for finding the right balance between under- and over-regulation of risk-related activities and goods. In addition, monitoring the area is important to help prevent unexpected consequences. For this reason, linear risk issues can well be handled by departmental and agency staff and enforcement personnel of state-run governance institutions. The aim is to find the most cost-effective method for a desired regulation level. If necessary, stakeholders may be included in the deliberations as they have information and know-how that may help to make the measures more efficient. As mentioned above, space issues will enter the discourse mainly in the form of information about physical distribution of impacts.

Epistemic processing involving experts

Resolving complex risk problems requires dialogue and deliberation among experts. The main goal is to scan and review existing knowledge about the causal connections between an agent and potential consequences, to characterize the uncertainty of this relationship and to explore the evidence that supports these inferences. Involving members of various epistemic communities which demonstrate expertise and competence is the most promising step for producing more reliable and valid judgements about the complex nature of a given risk. Epistemic discourse is the instrument for discussing the conclusiveness and validity of cause–effect chains relying on available probative facts, uncertain knowledge and experience that can be tested for empirical traceability and consistency. The objective of such a deliberation is to find the most cogent description and explanation of the phenomenological complexity in question as well as a clarification of dissenting views (for example, by addressing the question of which environmental and socioeconomic impacts are to be expected in which areas and in what time frame). The deliberation among experts might generate a profile of the complexity of the given risk issue on selected intersubjectively chosen criteria. The deliberation may also reveal that there is more uncertainty and ambiguity hidden in the case than the initial appraisers had anticipated. It is advisable to include natural as well as social scientists in the epistemic discourse so that potential problems with risk perception and different space associations can be anticipated. Controversies would then be less of a surprise than is currently the case.

Reflective processing involving stakeholders

Characterizing and evaluating risks, as well as developing and selecting appropriate management options for risk reduction and control in situations of high uncertainty, poses particular challenges. How can risk managers characterize and evaluate the severity of a risk problem when the potential damage and its probability are unknown or highly uncertain? Scientific input is, therefore, only the first step in a series of steps constituting a more sophisticated evaluation process. It is crucial to compile the relevant data and information about the different types of uncertainties to inform the process of risk characterization. The outcome of the risk characterization process provides the foundation for a broader deliberative arena, in which not only policy makers and scientists, but also directly affected stakeholders and public interest groups ought to be involved in order to discuss and ponder the 'right' balances and trade-offs between over- and under-protection. This reflective involvement of stakeholders and interest groups pursues the purpose of finding a consensus on the extra margin of safety that potential victims would be willing to tolerate and potential beneficiaries of the risk would be willing to invest in to avoid potentially critical and catastrophic consequences. If too much precaution is applied, innovations may be impeded or even eliminated; if too little precaution is applied, society may experience the occurrence of undesired consequences. The crucial question here is how much uncertainty and ignorance the main stakeholders and public interest groups are willing to accept or tolerate in exchange for some potential benefit. This issue has direct implications for space and time. A reflective discourse implies that affected stakeholders can be identified.

The boundary between affected and non-affected public is, however, fuzzy under the condition of effect uncertainty. Often one relies on the subjective images of those who believe they are affected. Determining a demarcation line between affected and non-affected publics demands an excellent knowledge and a prudent handling of the physical and social concepts of space. The perception of space extensions and boundaries and the belief that one is inside or outside a specific space co-determines the range of groups that feel affected and demand to be involved. Space relationships also affect the procedures appropriate for debating how decisions should be made in the light of the uncertain distribution of effects over time and space. The reflective involvement of policy makers, scientists, stakeholders and public interest groups can be accomplished through a spectrum of different procedures such as negotiated rule-making, mediation, round-table or open forums, advisory committees, and so on (see Rowe and Frewer 2000; Beierle and Cayford 2002; Klinke 2006; Stoll-Kleemann and Welp 2006).

Participative processing involving the wider public

If risk problems are associated with high ambiguity, it is not enough to demonstrate that risk regulation addresses the public concerns of those directly affected by the impacts of the risk source. In these cases, the process of evaluation needs to be open to public input and new forms of deliberation. This starts with revisiting the question of proper framing. Is the issue really a risk problem or is it an issue of lifestyle or future vision? Often the benefits are contested as well as the risks. The debate about 'designer babies' may illustrate the point that observers may be concerned not only about the social risks of intervening in the genetic code of humans but also about the acceptability of the desired goal to improve the performance of individuals (Hudson 2006). Thus the controversy is often much broader than dealing with the direct risks only. The aim here is to find an overlapping consensus on the dimensions of ambiguity that need to be addressed in comparing risks and benefits, and balancing pros and cons. High ambiguity would require the most inclusive strategy for involvement because not only directly affected groups but also those indirectly affected should have an opportunity to contribute to this debate.

Resolving ambiguities in risk debates necessitates the participatory involvement of the public to openly discuss competing arguments, beliefs and values. Participatory involvement offers opportunities to resolve conflicting expectations through a process of identifying overarching common values, and to define options that will allow a desirable lifestyle without compromising the vision of others. Critical to success here is the establishment of equitable and just distribution rules when it comes to common resources and a common understanding of the scope, size and range of the problem, as well as the options for dealing with the problem (Renn and Schweizer 2009). Unless there is some agreement on the boundaries of space and time, there is hardly any chance for a common solution. Such a common agreement will touch upon the physical dimensions of space (and seek 'objective' clarification of the impacts on a defined region) but focus more intensely on the various social constructions of space and time that the participants associate with the problem at hand. The set of possible procedures for involving the public includes citizen panels or juries, citizen forums, consensus conferences, public advisory committees and similar approaches (see Rowe and Frewer 2000; Beierle and Cayford 2002; Hagendijk and Irwin 2006; Klinke 2006; Abels 2007; Renn 2008: 284ff).

An overview of the different participation and stakeholder involvement requirements with respect to linear, complex, uncertain and ambiguous risks is displayed in Figure 1.4. As is the case with all classifications, this scheme shows a simplified picture of the involvement process and it has been criticized for being too rigid in its linking of risk characteristics (complexity, uncertainty and ambiguity) and specific forms of discourse and dialogue (van Asselt 2005). In addition to the generic distinctions shown in Figure 1.4, it may, for instance, be wise to distinguish between different types of risks and different types of regulatory cultures or styles (Löfstedt and Vogel 2001; Renn 2008: 358ff). It also does not address the spatial context in which the deliberations take place. To conclude these caveats, the purpose of this scheme is to provide a general orientation and to make a generic distinction between ideal cases rather than to offer a strict recipe for participation.

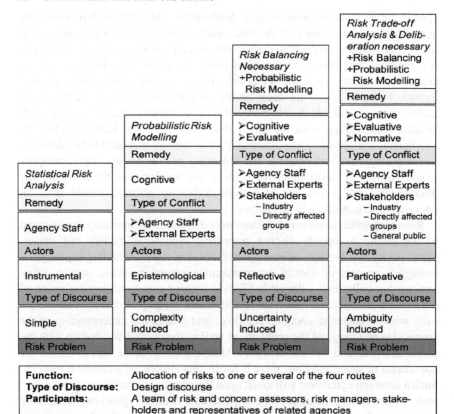

Function:	Allocation of risks to one or several of the four routes
Type of Discourse:	Design discourse
Participants:	A team of risk and concern assessors, risk managers, stakeholders and representatives of related agencies

Figure 1.4 The risk escalator: a guide to inclusive risk governance

The classification in Figure 1.4 offers a taxonomy of requirements for stakeholder and public inclusion based on the characteristics of risk knowledge. These general guidelines can be further specified by looking into each phase of the risk governance cycle (Renn 2008; Renn and Walker 2008: 356–57).

Conclusions

The aim of this chapter has been to illustrate the significance of space and also time for risk governance, including all stages from pre-assessment to management and communication. For this purpose, both terms, space and risk, were regarded as hybrids of physical entities and social constructions. The idea was not to define a strict demarcation line between the physical and social concepts, since both depend on methods of generating human knowledge and interpreting signals from the environment. Yet they are based on different epistemic questions: (i) where and when will the impacts of activities or events affect those targets that we value? And (ii) what do people associate with 'where' and 'when' in the context of the likely impacts of activities or events? Several chapters in this volume echo this distinction. Weichhart and Höferl distinguish between four conceptual and two theoretical meanings of space, highlighting the variability between realist and constructivist versions of space definitions. Pohl *et al.* focus on the systems-driven conceptualization of space but also emphasize the role of physical location for inter-systems interaction. Korf introduces the term of 'certainty of uncertainty' to the debate and demonstrates that while people can get used to high-risk situations, they still have an intrinsic reference for what they would frame as normality. Finally, Müller-Mahn points out the main difference between physical space as a principle of orientation (that is or at least appears to be intersubjective) and space as the projection of a diversity of meanings.

The analytic distinction of risk characteristics – complexity, uncertainty and ambiguity – helps to facilitate an integrated approach to risk governance and space. Whereas the analysis of simple and – to some degree – complex problems is better served by relying on the physical understanding of space and risk, uncertain and ambiguous problems demand the integration of social constructions and mental models for both understanding and managing these problems. The distinction of risks according to risk characteristics not only highlights deficits in our knowledge concerning a risk issue, but also points the way forward for the selection of management options. Thus, the Risk Governance Framework attributes an important function to public and stakeholder participation, as well as risk communication, in the risk governance process. The framework suggests efficient and adequate public or stakeholder participation procedures. The concerns of stakeholders and/or the public are integrated in the risk appraisal phase via concern assessment. Furthermore, stakeholder and public participation are an established part of risk management. The optimum participation method depends on the characteristics of the risk issue. In this respect, space and time enter into the various discourses through the images that the participants bring into the discussions. The need for finding an agreement on the respective time and space boundaries underlines the necessity to understand and comprehend the various space concepts and images.

2 Riskscapes

The spatial dimensions of risk

Detlef Müller-Mahn and Jonathan Everts

On 11 March 2011, the combined earthquake–tsunami–nuclear disaster in Fukushima came as a total surprise, considering that Japan has one of the world's most sophisticated early warning and disaster preparedness programmes. The catastrophe had a devastating impact, killing almost 20,000 people and leaving three nuclear reactors struggling with a meltdown. Moreover, its consequences reached far beyond the place of destruction. It sent shockwaves around the globe, leading to unexpected side effects in places far away from the immediately affected areas. In Germany, for example, people demonstrated in the streets only a few hours after the tsunami had hit the Japanese east coast and proclaimed 'Fukushima is everywhere' (*Spiegel* online 11 March 2011). Under the impression of the dramatic events in Japan, the German federal government decided in favour of an immediate temporary shutdown of the seven oldest of 17 operating reactors in the country. Only a few days later, the German government even changed its overall national nuclear energy policy and decided to opt out of the production of nuclear power entirely.

The example of the Fukushima disaster leads to three observations important for an understanding of the relationship between risk and space. First, the catastrophe was a local *and* global event. It involved material damage in a clearly defined territory and, at the same time, engendered worldwide political and social responses. The event may truly be called 'cosmopolitical' (Schillmeier 2011). It reached a degree of global significance and exceptionality by which it was able to 'disrupt, question and alter common and taken for granted modes of ordering social life' (Schillmeier 2011: 514). The geography of the disaster and the responses it evoked around the world shed light on the multifaceted spatial dimensions of risk which were an inherent trait of sites such as Fukushima long before the disaster occurred. Risk is not isolated or restricted to one place and one moment in time. Rather, risk is always multiple. There is not only one risk but multiple risks entwined with other risks – such as the combined risks of the earthquake–tsunami–nuclear meltdown. Furthermore, no matter how widely distributed and dispersed they may seem, risks are connected over space and time; in the case of Fukushima, the earthquake led to revised energy policies elsewhere.

Second, through disasters such as that associated with Fukushima, different notions of risk become clearly visible; notions that either apply to the same place with different conclusions, or to the same risk in different places. The worldwide communication of cosmopolitical events accelerates the disentanglement of physical co-presence and the feeling of being at risk, a psycho-social disposition which Beck (1999) has identified as a characteristic of the emergence of new, ubiquitous types of 'world risk'. Beck argues that the anticipation of a catastrophe may become politically more influential than the 'real' catastrophe and the damage caused by it, because it undermines people's sense of safety. Interestingly, this happens regardless of how directly people are affected. Risks experienced as relevant to one's own life do not necessarily depend on spatial proximity. Rather, risk awareness connects far-away places, although in contradictory ways. In Germany, many citizens realized that the Fukushima disaster was not caused by technological failures or careless engineers. On the contrary, it was a consequence of the existing risk management system in Japan. When the reactors were built on the shore, the probability of a mega-tsunami had been calculated, but was assumed to be low enough to justify smaller seaward defences, thereby keeping construction costs within reasonable limits. In other words, the catastrophe was neither totally unforeseen, nor was it caused by negligence or violation of safety standards. It was deliberately taken into account by planners and politicians, but in a way that ensured the profitability of nuclear energy. Adopting a critical stance toward the official notion of risk in Japan, German notions of risk were revised with long-lasting effects on the landscape of energy production facilities.

Third, and following up on the last two points, Fukushima is an example of the growing significance of contingency in increasingly complex settings of risk. It demonstrates that the overlapping of multiple risks and possible cross-reactions cannot be calculated and are difficult to control. Confronted with multiple risks, we do not know to what extent potentially disastrous events are going to affect our lives in the future. Even more so, we realize that there will always be an area of unpredictability. We begin to understand that we do not even know what we don't know. The fear of the unknown is often harder to bear than calculated risk, as many authors have pointed out (Aven and Renn 2009; Renn 2008; Slovic 2000; Stirling 2007; Zinn 2008, to name a few). The problem of uncertainty is aggravated by an erosion of public confidence in the competence of experts and the trustworthiness of politicians. The civil unrest that followed the events in Fukushima may be considered as symptomatic of what Löftstedt (2005) calls the 'post-trust society'. What is most needed in this situation of uncertainty is orientation. The awareness of more risks and new ways of anticipation and prediction, such as incident-tailored preparedness planning and exercises, seemingly offer orientation. But if it is true that risks are not isolated and cannot be countered in isolation, the same must hold true, and even more so, for those who feel 'at risk' (Slovic 2010; Wisner *et al.* 2004). Every human being faces multiple risks, during their whole life course as well as on any ordinary day. Only if we begin to analytically connect these risks and the landscapes they inhabit, will we be able to understand how these 'riskscapes' shape lives and spaces in various, at times contradictory and competing, ways.

Among the number of risks that are currently receiving wide attention in public debates, the spatial dimensions of risk are of growing importance. While many risks appear 'global' by their very definition, they are still embedded in particular landscapes and produce locally discernible effects. For instance, we may consider the spatial dimensions of climate change and global food sufficiency, the financial crisis and the future of the Euro, epidemic diseases like swine flu, avian flu, SARS and EHEC, the demographic challenges of ageing and shrinking societies, the unknown consequences of genetic engineering, the future problems of ozone depletion and the threats of terrorism to public security. Each of these risks occupies, not just metaphorically, a specific territory and presents a particular landscape of risk. However, they do not exist in isolation from one another. Although risks might differ, they need to be analysed within a common framework in order to understand how they collectively shape life and place. In the following section, we propose the term 'riskscapes' as a conceptual tool for contributing to such an agenda. This is followed by a case study on competing riskscapes in relation to a part of Eastern Africa. We conclude by discussing the implications of riskscape analysis for current and future research.

Riskscapes

In this chapter, we seek to develop the concept of 'riskscapes'. We are aware of different uses that have already materialized around this term within environmental health (Morello-Frosch *et al.* 2001) and multi-hazard mapping tools (www. riskscape.org.nz). However, our approach to riskscapes comes from a social science perspective and is, among others, indebted to the works of the anthropologist Arjun Appadurai, the social theorist Theodore Schatzki and the human geographer Valerie November. A similar approach is followed by Sutherland *et al.* (2012: 48) who argue that 'citizens carry the history of their place and their narratives with them, and that these in turn shape notions of risk and "riskscapes"'. They develop their concept of riskscape from Soneryd's (2004) work on 'soundscapes'. We agree with the idea that 'people respond to risk in relation to their broader experiential and synthetic knowledge about the place they live in' (Sutherland *et al.* 2012: 48). Nevertheless, we want to broaden the theoretical basis of the concept and include riskscapes that are not necessarily tied to living in a particular place. The way we understand riskscapes differs from other conceptualizations of '-scapes', which are primarily related to particular territories. Instead, we propose to relate riskscapes to risks and the way they emerge through practice. This means riskscapes always have to be understood from the perspective of individuals or groups, and they may overlap in space and time, although they do not necessarily and do not always do so. Thus, we are able to visualize and explain contradictions that arise from (partially) overlapping riskscapes.

In his well-known piece 'Disjuncture and difference in the global cultural economy' (Appadurai 2006 [1990]), Appadurai contends that we need to acknowledge the loss of importance of place and the increased prevalence of global cultural flows. Instead of (only) studying how people dwell in and relate to one place, we should look at the deterritorialized and border-crosscutting movements of people, things and ideas. Departing from Benedict Anderson's analysis of *Imagined Communities* (2006 [1983]), Appadurai asserts that today we live not only according to what we believe our local or national community is, but also according to what kind of worlds we believe we are part of. Thus, he proposes to analyse deterritorialized 'Imagined Worlds' rather than geographically bounded 'Imagined Communites'. To illustrate this point, Appadurai introduces five '-scapes' as pre-eminent instances of imagined worlds – or building blocks, as he calls them – in which we situate ourselves; ethnoscapes, mediascapes, technoscapes, financescapes, ideoscapes. The term -scapes itself is deliberately chosen to produce variations of the metaphorically understood term 'landscape'.

> The suffix *-scape* allows us to point to the fluid, irregular shapes of these landscapes, shapes that characterize international capital as deeply as they do international clothing styles. These terms with the common suffix *-scape* also indicate that these are not objectively given relations that look the same from every angle of vision but, rather, that they are deeply perspectival constructs, inflected by the historical, linguistic, and political situatedness of different sorts of actors: nation-states, multinationals, diasporic communities, as well as subnational groupings and movements (whether religious, political, or economic), and even intimate face-to-face groups, such as villages, neighborhoods, and families. Indeed, the individual actor is the last locus of this perspectival set of landscapes, for these landscapes are eventually navigated by agents who both experience and constitute larger formations, in part from their own sense of what these landscapes offer.
>
> (Appadurai 2006 [1990]: 628)

Transferring Appadurai's ideas on -scapes to our own project on riskscapes, we would like to emphasize two aspects.

First, landscapes, as Appadurai contends, correspond to points of view. It might be the same stretch of land, but what is perceived and actively apprehended depends on the viewpoint or perspective of the observer. It is never one landscape, which is the same to all observers, but multiple landscapes depending on the range of possible perspectives. The same holds true for riskscapes; there is not one riskscape but multiple riskscapes depending on the range of perspectives and the risks highlighted.

Second, Appadurai makes an argument for an analysis of the social rather than the individual. Although it is individuals who 'navigate' the various -scapes, they are social beings and belong to larger groups. Their agency (or acts of navigation for that matter) is bound up with and nestled into the fabric of social groups and societies and their ways of collectively making sense of the world. While we could argue that there are at least as many riskscapes as there are individual perspectives, in terms of spatial impact and political relevance, it makes sense to analyse the -scapes that have become meaningful to a larger group or social formation. In analogy to Appadurai's concept of -scapes we may conclude that riskscapes, viewed from different perspectives and by different actors, are partially overlapping, intrinsically connected and at the same time often controversial socio-spatial images of risk.

Acknowledging the inherently social character of -scapes points us to another crucial aspect of riskscapes. Riskscapes are practised and constituted in practice. According to Schatzki, a contemporary theorist of social practice (Schatzki 1996, 2002), the analysis of all social phenomena – to which, we argue, riskscapes also belong – has to foreground human activity. Things, spaces or societies are not just given or pre-existing items, but they are made and remade through an intricate set of practices. In our view, riskscapes are such a social phenomenon. They are not just representations in the minds of actors or 'imagined worlds'. Rather, they are created and enacted in practice. Crucially, practices do not occur on the head of a pin; they are bound up in time and space and their full scope can only be brought to the fore by considering the spatial and temporal dimensions of practice. For this reason, Schatzki suggests that we take into account the 'timespaces' of human activity and analyse (at least partially) practices by the particular place-path arrays through which they transpire:

> As a person goes through her day, her actions bear futures and pasts and occur at places and paths that are parts of place-path arrays. She also thereby carries on this and that practice. Some of her futures, pasts and places will be common to and shared with the lives of other participants in the same practices. The organization, regularities and settings of a practice engender a net of interwoven timespaces, a net of interwoven jointly instituted futures-presents-pasts and place-path arrays. This net, incidentally, is a property of the practice. The activities of individual people are what possess futures and pasts and are performed at particular places and paths. *As a whole,* however, the net of interwoven timespaces that a practice's organization, regularities and settings engender is a property of the practice and not of individual lives. In sum, the social character of timespace consists in the dependency of (1) the timespace of a person's life and (2) the common and shared temporalspatial features of people's lives on the social practices they carry out.
>
> (Schatzki 2009: 40)

Transferring this argument to the concept of landscape, Schatzki argues that landscapes are 'temporalspatial phenomena' that exist in relation to practice (Schatzki 2010: 99–106). Landscapes exist through a host of activities such as looking or viewing, visually inspecting and assembling selected features of that landscape, finding clues to past or future activities and encountering the material stuff among which our present activity permeates. Landscapes are not given networks of material objects but they are experienced and made sense of through practice. Since the practices carried out in relation to landscapes are plural, landscapes in turn are plural, too. This is not just the case in the sense of finding different landscapes in different places. Various practices can relate to the 'same objective spatial expanse of the world' (Schatzki 2010: 106). Depending on the kind of activities and their particular place-path arrays, different landscapes emerge in the same place.

In terms of riskscapes, we find the same processes at work. Depending on the viewpoint, the practices carried out and the risks attuned to, riskscapes can vary considerably, although they might refer to the 'same objective spatial expanse'. To give but one example, an informal settlement near a large city in the global South may represent a riskscape to local authorities in terms of crime, whereas it could be another riskscape for the inhabitants with regard to soil erosion and polluted drinking water.

Moving on from our discussion of -scapes to risk, we also need to emphasize the practised and plural character of risk. Of course, academic accounts of 'risk societies' are impregnated with the diversity of risks we are facing, from nuclear power plants to climate change and the financial system (Beck 1999; Löfstedt and Boholm 2009). There exists a very elaborate understanding of how these risks develop according to human activity or how they are related to human lives (Slovic 2010). However, there has been less focus on the multiplicity of risks relating to the same topic and/or the same place (Bickerstaff and Simmons 2009), as human geographer Valerie November has repeatedly pointed out. By exploring the various spatial dimensions of risk and the ways in which these are construed and acted upon by different experts, November shows how the variety of risks depends on the variety of practices. For example, the risk of fire in a city changes its contours, definition and nature depending on which expert practices are concerned with the risk of fire, which might be the practices of firefighters, planners or architects (November 2004).

Second, November demonstrates how various risks coexist in one place (November 2008). Fire, pathogens or flooding might affect the very same area and the very same people. Nevertheless, different practitioners are concerned with different risks. To use our own terminology, they have each established their own riskscapes. However, these riskscapes are not only representational or 'in the minds' of experts. Each riskscape is related and attuned to some feature of that particular part of the world, which makes it appear as 'risky territory'. There are a host of 'signposts' (November *et al.* 2009, 2010) that are used by practitioners to guide their perception of a particular riskscape, be they fire-prone activities, incidences of influenza-like illnesses or past high-tide levels. November concludes that we need to study space 'considering all the risks it faces', and risk by 'taking all its spatial dimensions into account' (November 2008: 1525). We should not study risks in isolation but attend to 'cross-cutting issues affecting different categories of risk and ... their interrelationships ...' (ibid.: 1526). In effect, we should analyse how 'each risk situation generates its own process of arguments, strategies, calculations, alliances, and procedures, which may lead to the subsequent adoption of preventive measures, with their respective spatial effects' (ibid.: 1526).

This task, we argue, is facilitated by the concept of riskscapes. Riskscapes focus our attention on the intricate relationships of particular concerns, places and practices. In addition, different riskscapes are interwoven and need to be analysed in relation rather than in isolation. Finally, each riskscape is tied to unique acts of navigation (cf. November *et al.* 2010). Practising riskscapes includes assembling the riskscape from various clues or 'signposts', making interpretations and estimates, or advocating changes in spatial practice.

In the following section, we demonstrate how riskscapes are produced, lived and interwoven, by way of an example. Our case study centres on Eastern Africa, especially Ethiopia and Somalia. We wish to underline that our territorial focus is much more than an illustrative but arbitrary example for our conceptual ideas. Rather, in grappling empirically and theoretically with problems endemic to this particular region of Eastern Africa, the concept of riskscapes has proved to be a powerful analytical tool. People living in this region continually face serious challenges and the lives of millions are recurrently at stake – in fact, thousands have died already. There is a multitude of ways of explaining this miserable state of affairs (Bloemertz *et al.* 2012). However, they all fail to take into account the diversity of riskscapes encountered, and the effects resulting from their partial overlap. As our own analysis reveals, at the heart of ongoing conflict and misery, there are different riskscapes producing different struggles in the same region.

Riskscapes of drought, conflict and famine in Eastern Africa

Regional riskscapes in Eastern Africa are shaped by different social groups and their divergent risk perspectives and practices. Parts of Eastern Africa are affected by numerous overlapping risks with potentially disastrous consequences for local populations. 'Risk' in this context may indeed refer to a matter of life and death. Experts consider local livelihoods as highly vulnerable, because they are exposed to risky environments. However, even under exceptional conditions, people are not only exposed to risk. People also deliberately take risks and actively shape their riskscapes.

Against this backdrop, our case study highlights three aspects of the constitution of riskscapes. First, any riskscape is a combination of material aspects that can be located in a physical landscape, and the ways in which individuals or communities make sense of them in and through everyday practices. Second, although dealing with the 'same objective spatial expanse of the world' (Schatzki 2010: 106), different riskscapes are enacted, depending on the diverse ways in which people make sense of 'signposts' and navigate through their riskscape. Different riskscapes can interfere with each other and influence or change paths and places. Third, we contend that any external intervention for the sake of risk management has to take the diversity of riskscapes into account in order to understand particular agencies and dependencies.

In the light of our case study, we distinguish between two bundles or sets of practices; one set can be labelled 'expert practices', while the other set pertains to the everyday life of people living permanently in the area. In our case, expert practices involve people from diverse backgrounds, such as global science forums, international organizations, the donor and development community, and government administrations at national and regional levels. The second set of practices are those of the local population, which primarily consists of peasant and pastoralist communities. Expert and local practices of risk management exhibit different interests, knowledge resources and capacities. While local populations are confronted with risks in their everyday life, risk is important for experts in connection with numerous research, aid and relief activities. Both sets of practices overlap and influence each other through their shared spatial focus. However, they differ in scale, motivation and awareness of particular risks. Consequently, both sets of practices constitute a 'space' of tensions.

In the practices of climate change science, Eastern Africa belongs to the global riskscape of climate change. Climate scientists consider climate change as a decisive driver in a process that adversely affects local ecosystems and puts livelihoods at risk (Boko *et al.* 2007). Their scenarios present rather pessimistic outlooks for most of the African continent. The fourth Intergovernmental Panel on Climate Change report (IPCC 2007) expects that by 2020 up to 250 million people will be affected by increasing water stress, a decline of arable land and agricultural productivity, with ensuing food shortages and famine. The authors of the report conclude that 'Africa is one of the most vulnerable continents to climate variability and change because of multiple stresses and low adaptive capacity' (ibid.: 65). Taking the number of risks and development indices as important signposts, the African continent features prominently in the global climate change riskscape. The IPCC and other expert councils plead for intensified efforts regarding adaptation to climate change. They do so despite the fact that models of future climate change are generally constrained by fundamental and irreducible uncertainties (Adger *et al.* 2009: 343). With respect to the African continent, these uncertainties are particularly high and difficult to assess (Conway 2009). In Ethiopia, for example, the available models of climate change produce quite different projections with regard to temperatures and rainfall patterns (Conway and Schipper 2011: 231). It is often not clear what kind of climate risks local populations will have to face, and what type of conditions they should adapt to. However, thanks to global climate change negotiations, large amounts of money are currently being made available for national adaptation programmes. In turn, government administrations and international development agencies invent new projects that fit the expectations of donors. In Ethiopia, for example, money dedicated to adaptation to climate change is used for the development of large-scale irrigation schemes, and the policy that supports a shift from pastoralism to irrigated agriculture is 'relabelled' as adaptation to climate change. The downside of this project is that it has little to do with the needs of local people who live in the development areas. As a matter of fact, it has already resulted in the eviction of thousands from their land (Müller-Mahn *et al.* 2010). In this case, the climate change riskscape derived from expert practices has produced new risks. The reconfiguration of space, meant to minimize risks produced by climate change, has increased the risk of local people, who now face the loss of basic components of their livelihoods and food safety.

Hunger and famine are indeed problems endemic to the Horn of Africa. However, like the effects of climate change expertise, expert practices operating within the riskscapes of famine are equally debatable. In the summer of 2011, disaster scenarios projected by the IPCC seemed to occur sooner than expected. Large parts of the Horn of Africa were struck by one of the worst droughts in 60 years, followed by a severe food crisis. In July 2011, the United Nations declared a famine. Up to 13 million people were estimated to be at risk of starvation. In Somalia, UN sources said that 'what was an "emergency" has now tipped into a "catastrophe"' (*The Telegraph* 20 July 2011). Aid was made available, although unevenly distributed, leaving large parts of the affected area untouched. To understand the uneven geography of relief activities, the particular riskscape of famine requires closer inspection.

The riskscape of famine is powerfully articulated through the representational format of the map. Maps are important tools of risk communication and risk management in a state of emergency. They are produced on the basis of satellite image interpretation and information from the ground by the UN Food and Agriculture Organization (FAO) Famine Early Warning Systems Network and the United Nations Office for the Coordination of Humanitarian Affairs (UN OCHA). The way they compile and visualize the available data takes the form of a risk-based regionalization. They allow a quick grasp of the situation and serve as navigational platforms for decision-making. The map in Figure 2.1 is a spatial

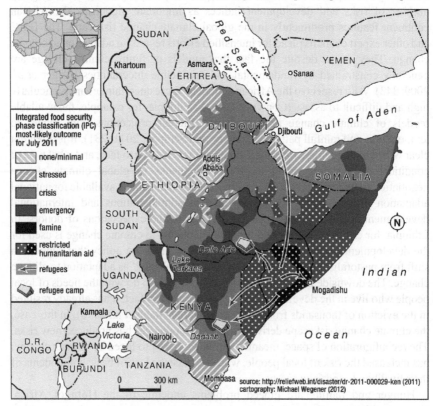

Figure 2.1 Spatial dimension of food crisis at the Horn of Africa as projected by UN OCHA

representation of the riskscape in which international humanitarian aid agencies operated during July 2011. By then, the space in which people were affected by famine already encompassed all of southern Somalia and was expanding to Ethiopia, Kenya and nominally independent Somaliland. The cartographic view of the riskscape focuses on two categories that constitute risk. One category distinguishes between areas with different degrees of food shortage and need, and the other highlights the inaccessibility of Somali territories due to the current political situation.

In the terminology of the United Nations, the situation had reached the level of a 'complex emergency' (Keen 2008), with a large area of the Horn of Africa being affected by a humanitarian crisis. Political instability and violent conflict in Somalia made large parts of the territory virtually inaccessible for relief operations. Hundreds of thousands abandoned their Somali home, trying to reach the relative safety of camps in Kenya and Ethiopia. The infamous camp at Dadaab in Kenya was already overcrowded, with more than half a million Somali refugees depending on food aid and support by foreign agencies. Yet, people still kept coming in their thousands day by day. A press release issued on 20 July 2011 by the Food Security and Nutrition Analysis Unit of the FAO and the Famine Early Warning Systems Network of the United States Agency for International Development (USAID) and other donors described the situation in Somalia as follows:

> Evidence of severely reduced food access, acute malnutrition, and crude mortality indicates that a famine is currently ongoing in two areas of southern Somalia: the Bakool agropastoral livelihood zones and all areas of Lower Shabelle. A humanitarian emergency currently exists across all other regions of the south, and current humanitarian response is inadequate to meet emergency needs. As a result, famine is expected to spread across all regions of the south in the coming 1–2 months. An immediate, large-scale, and comprehensive response is needed and tens of thousands of lives can be saved, but the window of opportunity to do so is extremely limited. Preliminary estimates are that 3.7 million people are in crisis nationwide; among these 3.2 million people need immediate, lifesaving assistance (2.8 million in the south). Assistance needs will remain extremely high through at least December 2011.
>
> (FSNWG 2011)

In addition, the UNICEF (undated) website pointed out the demographically uneven distribution of risk: 'The risk of dying is 10 times higher for a child with severe malnutrition, which reduces a child's ability to fight deadly diseases. Disaster is imminent for children in the Sahel if appropriate emergency relief efforts are not started now.'

The map and both quotes demonstrate how organizations involved in relief operations experienced and made sense of the riskscape of famine. The humanitarian crisis of the Horn of Africa appears as a regional problem caused by natural forces. Like an infectious disease, famine is expected to 'spread' from one affected area to another. Similar to other natural hazards, response is advocated on a grand scale exceeding the local. Suggested response activities are based on local demographics. The 'complex emergency' is interpreted as a riskscape in want of management. This understanding of risk results from a spatial focus on drought, food shortage and famine. However, this spatial perspective homogenizes the Horn of Africa as a riskscape of famine. With respect to the diversity of local situations and social practices, famine-centred riskscapes risk silencing other perspectives.

As an example, we present some aspects of a case study[1] in the Afar region in Ethiopia. The region lies on the western edge of the area highlighted by the riskscape of famine. Most of the approximately 1.5 million Afars are nomadic pastoralists, although they are increasingly being pressurized to settle down and shift from mobile animal husbandry to agro-pastoralism. Nevertheless, land and pasture remain the essential resources in the Afar production cycle. The case study area, near Gewane and Lake Yardi on the Awash river, once used to be one of the more fertile lands in the territory inhabited by the Afars. But today, even in this area the people are suffering from recurrent droughts and food shortages, and many of them have become dependent on food aid supplied by foreign donors. Local government officials and aid workers view the disastrous drought cycles of recent years and the insufficient food supply as key problems in the area.

However, the local clan members themselves frame the current livelihood crisis quite differently from 'experts'. Despite mentioning drought and food shortages as serious problems, they do not consider them as the most pressing issues. Instead, they place drought and issues of food safety in the context of a differentiated and locally relevant riskscape. Among a multitude of risks and hardships, drought is considered as a condition they are used to and with which they can cope. As many of the interviewed pastoralists said, they have age-old experience of living in the arid environment of the Awash valley, collecting wild fruits and roots from the bushland when there is nothing else to eat. The key driver of vulnerability, however, is seen in the loss of control over land and water resources (Rettberg 2009).

Figure 2.2 gives an impression of the situation that an Afar elder described desperately in the following words: 'If you put a flea between two of your thumbs like this, it would have nowhere to go. We are just like that' (quoted in Rettberg 2009: 147). The quote refers to a continuous process of reduction of pasture lands and herd mobility. It is caused by three ongoing processes of encroachment that have resulted in a disastrous loss of resources for the pastoralists. First, the Afars are involved in a violent conflict with neighbouring clans that belong to Issa ethnic groups. The conflict has been going on for decades, and it has resulted in a gradual and often very violent push-back of the Afars in which they have lost large parts of their grazing lands. Second, the loss of land is aggravated by the aforementioned expansion of large irrigated farms owned by the government, and by national and foreign investors along the course of the Awash River which flows through the Afar territory. And third, the Afars are losing grazing land because of an invasive plant (*Prosopis juliflora*) that is spreading rapidly in the Awash valley (Rettberg and Müller-Mahn 2012). The Afar explicitly view these three processes in conjunction with each other. Together they constitute the complex riskscape relevant to Afar everyday life. The loss of land and of mobility reduces their flexibility and ability to react to seasonal and spatial variations in rainfall, and makes them more vulnerable to recurrent droughts.

In this case, different practices and perspectives result in different riskscapes. These riskscapes are, however, not isolated from one another. Through their shared spatial focus, they come to interact. In the case of Eastern Africa, the interaction of different riskscapes may even lead to controversy and conflict. In our case, experts tend to isolate particular risks and, as a consequence, follow a risk-specific path of related practices, whereas the local population perceives and

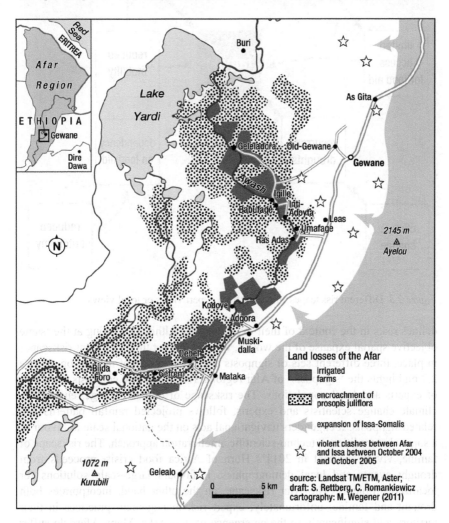

Figure 2.2 Land losses of the Afar due to multiple stresses

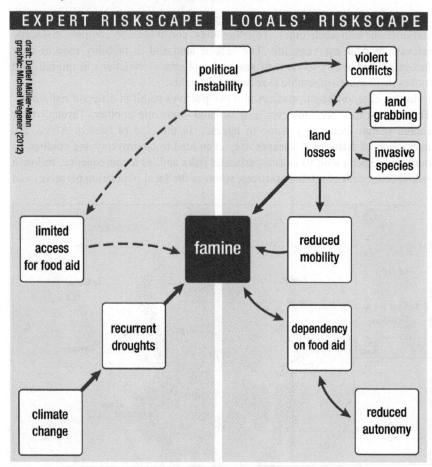

Figure 2.3 Different riskscapes emerging from expert views or local views

defines risks in the context of their everyday life. Although looking at the 'same objective spatial expanse of the world', we find at least three different riskscapes in place, three different sets of signposts and discrete acts of navigation. Figure 2.3 highlights the 'signposts' of Afar regional riskscapes and contrasts the views of experts and local populations. The riskscape of climate change, enacted by climate change scientists and experts, follows projected rainfall patterns and related signposts. It engenders navigational acts on the national scale in favour of a somewhat traditional, techno-scientific amelioration approach. The riskscape of famine, vividly present in 2011's Horn of Africa food crisis, proceeds from drought events and local demographics. It favours large-scale solutions for localized problems. The Afar riskscape, on the other hand, incorporates both drought and famine; unfortunately, expert risk management practices in their territory add significantly to the emergence of new risks. Many Afars do suffer from food shortages and malnutrition, but quite astonishingly, they consider famine as only one risk among many. The Afar riskscape is mainly characterized by loss of land, be it through national and commercial irrigation schemes, violent ethnic conflict or invasive plants. The increasing risk of famine is seen in this context as one of the consequences of a complex set of processes that erode the autonomy of clan groups and make them dependent on food aid.

Conclusion

We began this chapter by outlining three facets of contemporary risks. Many risks are both local and global. Disaster still occurs in one place, but its effects can be widely distributed. The 'cosmopolitical' aspect of disaster events is tied to negotiations of different notions of risk. While certain risks are deemed acceptable in one place or by one group of experts, the same risks exceed tolerable thresholds for others by far. The sense of uncertainty appears to be heightened in our 'post-trust societies'. People feel alienated from politicians and experts, who claim to calculate, control and manage risk. The Fukushima disaster and ensuing tragedy brought all of these facets of risk vividly to the fore. The spatial dimensions of risk are dispersed and far more complex than any focus on disaster sites would reveal.

Nevertheless, as we have argued, risk is still embedded in the physical world through and amid which human life transpires. Place and space matter, not just metaphorically. Risks occupy territories that are made as much of meanings and 'imagined worlds' as they consist of tangible material stuff. Anything specific to one place – be it extreme rainfall, temperature variations or highly uneven distribution of wealth – can be read as a signpost for a particular risky territory, or, as we prefer to call it, 'riskscape'. Riskscapes emerge when particular dangers are highlighted pertaining to a given territory. This encompasses the global scale as apparent in the riskscape of climate change, and the local scales of everyday life. Depending on the practices engendering the riskscape, the 'same objective spatial expanse of the world' is likely to be part of different riskscapes. In that sense, riskscapes overlap, interact and often produce conflict. We have shown how the Horn of Africa is such a territory, occupied by different and competing riskscapes. Riskscapes of climate change and famine are often in conflict with riskscapes in the everyday life of local people.

In our case study, risk management strategies have clearly not resulted in a safer environment for the local people. Issue-centred riskscapes, presented mainly through expert practices on climate change and famine, operate on a large-scale understanding of problems. Downscaling of such understandings has not taken the complexity of everyday life and the multiplicity of risks into account: the riskscapes encountered at the 'local' level. Likewise, upscaling has not taken place either – yet. We hope that our research will contribute to a more nuanced understanding of how conflicting riskscapes emerge, and how expert practices need to attune to a wider variety of risks relevant to local populations, including risks emanating from expert riskscapes. Further research into the intricate relationships between local–global risks and overlapping riskscapes should yield more insights into the spatial dimensions of risk and reveal further strategies so that we can engage critically with contemporary patterns of risk exposure and risk taking.

Notes

1   The study was carried out between 2004 and 2012, financially supported by the Deutsche Forschungsgemeinschaft. For details, see Rettberg (2009) and Müller-Mahn *et al.* (2010).

3 A place for space in risk research

The example of discourse analysis approaches

Peter Weichhart and Karl-Michael Höferl

In everyday language and everyday communication processes, the meaning of words seems to be quite easy to grasp. In most cases, the exact definition of a term is not necessary. We just 'know' their meaning in the context within which they are communicated. The language of science and scientific thinking, however, requires a precise handling of terms. They have to be accurately defined and used according to their accepted definitions. Otherwise, intersubjective comprehensibility cannot be ensured.

Yet, we are faced with the problem that there is no such thing as 'true' or 'correct' definitions and it is impossible to prove the absolute correctness of a specific definition. The usage and meaning of a term depend on a complex framework of thought and scientific practice, which is related to the specific scientific discipline, the explicit (or implicit) epistemology, the paradigm applied, the specific school of thought, the theoretical background and even to the 'national' (language-dependent) tradition of research within a specific scientific approach. Thus, misunderstandings and confusions are bound to occur, especially in interdisciplinary fields of research.

As an interdisciplinary and multiparadigmatic field, risk and hazards research is highly susceptible to such confusions. In discussions relating to a theory of risk, doubt is frequently expressed about specific definitions of basic terms, which are criticized as being either 'too narrow' or 'too wide', 'reductionist' or 'too comprehensive', depending on the different standpoints. We have come to realize that there is an intense desire to develop 'the' ultimate and best definition of basic concepts in this field of research.

In the present chapter, we will critique such attitudes and analyse some of the specific relationships between the conceptual, theoretical and epistemological frameworks applied in risk and hazards research, and the specific and different meanings of basic terms used. We aim to demonstrate that differences in the definition of basic terms should not be rated as weaknesses of this field of research, but rather as specific strengths. Detailing the relationship between a particular concept and its specific framework will allow us to pinpoint the viability of the concept for solving specific problems – while others will remain unconsidered.

In the first part, various concepts of space and risk and their potential relationships will be discussed, using a constructivist, pragmatic perspective. We will scrutinize the following questions: which definition of risk may be linked to which concept of space, and what are the epistemic and theoretical frameworks that are necessary to make such a combination viable? In a second step, we will focus on the influence of these concepts of space and risk and their relationship to a specific framework of hazards research from a socio-geographical perspective. By choosing a discourse theory approach as the framework of interest, this step will be structured by the question as to how the construction of risks and the construction of space are interrelated to each other. Furthermore, we will discuss the interplay of *communicative constructions* of space and risk (related to Popper's World 2 of mental objects and World 3 of theories; Popper 1973: 188) and the *material construction* of space and risk (related to Popper's World 1 of physical objects) in this approach (because both modes are aspects of everyday regionalization in the sense proposed by Werlen 1997).

Space and risk – two ambiguous and 'difficult' terms

The term 'space' is as difficult for scientists in various disciplines as the term 'time' for Saint Augustine: 'If you do not ask me what time is, I know it; if you ask me, I do not know'. This is also true for geographers, although in geography space is assumed to be a constitutive principle of the discipline. Most geographers will claim that 'space' constitutes the core concept of their discipline and that anybody working in this field has absolutely no doubt about the meaning of the term. Reflections on its meaning tend to seek an obvious correspondence between the term (signifier) and the specific entity that is denoted by the term (signified). And hence, it is common to ask 'What *is* space?' We want to avoid this kind of question and employ a pragmatic approach. We do not think that it is possible to formulate an absolute and ultimate definition that comprises exactly that 'thing' called 'space'. We do not even believe that space *is* a 'thing' or an 'entity' that may be distinguished from other entities in the 'real world'. We propose that 'space' should be conceived of as a specific *perspective*, a specific way of looking at the 'real world' – whatever that may be.

Thus, we are able to avoid a questioning attitude which, in the manner of linguistic realism, at best leads to metaphysical speculations. Reconstructing the different usages of the term is a task which has already been undertaken by various authors. Among others, we would like to mention Bartels (1974), Massey (1985, 1999), Reichert (1996), Curry (1996), Zierhofer (1999), Weichhart (1999), Sturm (2000), Miggelbrink (2002) and Blotevogel (2005). The following short inventory of concepts related to the term 'space' refers to Weichhart (2008: 75–93 and 326–29).

In its primary meaning, the word 'space' implies a specific location or address. It denotes a specific section of the earth's surface. Thus, we talk about 'the Alps' (in German: 'Alpenraum', English: 'Alpine region'), the Mediterranean region ('Mittelmeerraum'), or the 'Greater London area' ('Großraum London', 'Londoner Zentralraum'). 'Space' (area, region) is used as a vague and shortened label to indicate a specific part of the earth's surface whose boundaries are either not precisely defined and remain more or less fuzzy, or are conventionally or pragmatically specified. On the other hand, this version of 'space' also designates areas of the earth's surface that are characterized by specific *dominant* attributes. We speak, for instance, of 'mountain areas/regions' ('Gebirgsräume'), of 'agglomerations' ('Ballungsräume'), or of 'peripheral regions' ('Peripherie'). This usage is related to areas that may be regarded as characteristic in respect of specific phenomena found there. They are referred to as 'space$_1$',[1] which corresponds (more or less) to terms like 'gegenständlicher Raum' (objective space), as used by Blotevogel (2005), or 'Realobjektraum', as employed by Lichtenberger (1998) or Fassmann (2004).

A second meaning of 'space' refers to the kind of 'thing' that will remain if, putting it bluntly, we extract the mountains from a mountain area. According to Newton, this concept of space must be regarded as a sort of three-dimensional container in which all material things are embedded. It is an 'empty' space, an autonomous ontological structure or entity, which exists independently from its material equipment. This concept – let us call it 'space$_2$' – represents an infinite three-dimensional extension in which objects and events occur that are characterized by a specific position and/or direction. Space$_2$ is a key construct of the 'spatial approach' in geography, especially when it comes to formulating 'spatial laws'. Viewed from the perspective of social theory, however, this 'container space' is a problematic concept.

A third usage of the term 'space' is quite common and can be found in nearly any scientific discipline. 'Space$_3$' stands for immaterial relations and refers to a logical structure which allows localization of the defined elements of a system of thought. 'Colour spaces' or 'terminological spaces' (Swartout and Neches 1986) may serve as examples here.

A fourth, and rather important, concept of space was introduced by the German philosopher Gottfried Wilhelm Leibniz: 'spatium est ordo coexistendi' (Inertia rerum mathematicarum metaphysica III). This 'space$_4$' refers to the *relationship between material things and bodies*. It is a relativistic concept that does not require the idea of an 'empty space' or container. It is based on the notion that 'space' is constituted exclusively by the relations between material things, and it is developed by the positional relationship of elements of the material world (e.g. beside, distant, near, over, under, left, right, neighbouring). Space$_4$ is conceived not as an autonomous ontological structure or 'thing', but as an attribute of material things and bodies. Therefore, when referring to this concept, we should rather speak of 'spatiality' and not of 'space' (cf. Massey 1985, 1999 or Weichhart 1999, 2008). We need this concept every time we deal with the *material aspects* of social phenomena.

Another use of the term 'space' refers to the subjective and group-specific perception and cognition of space$_1$. It is the experienced 'space$_{1e}$', which is closely related to a specific space$_1$, but in terms of content it includes a lot more than a site-specific address, as it is loaded with subjective and/or group-specific meanings and significance. Space$_{1e}$ is seen as a cognitive concept that signifies a specific emotional interpretation of some spatially defined part of the subjective or collective life-world. In human geography, space$_{1e}$ is called a 'place'.

For the sake of completeness, we have to mention a further concept of space which goes back to the philosopher Immanuel Kant. He interpreted space as a kind of perception that helps organize the human vision of the world. Kant's 'space$_5$' is (like time) not a thing, and not only a form of perception, but also a *necessary precondition* for the mere possibility of conceiving the world.

Space as a *social construct* ('space$_{6s}$') is probably the most important version of the concept. Space$_{6s}$ is a very complex entity that emerges through the practice of social attribution, appropriation and production. It refers to the concepts of space$_1$, space$_{1e}$, and – in many, but not in all cases – to space$_4$. Such spaces are produced and constituted by cognitive processes and by the actions of individual or collective human actors. According to Werlen (1997), space$_{6s}$ is the outcome of the process of *everyday regionalizations*. It is very important to realize that on the one hand such a production of spatial entities results in cognitive constructs that are expressed by means of language and articulated as toponyms. In this case, space$_{6s}$ is an element of Popper's Worlds 3 and 2. On the other hand, social and economic practice produces specific configurations of things within the material world. Constructing dams or buildings, or establishing a specific system of land use must be regarded as constructions of social space in Popper's World 1. Space$_{6s}$ is reflected in the material world by the resulting space$_4$ and produces specific spatial relations of things and material objects. Before discussing the relevance of the various concepts of space for risk research, it seems necessary to take a closer look at the diverse concepts of risk.

The terms 'risk' and 'space' are both used with a fair amount of nonchalance, as if they were self-evident. Apparently, everybody knows what 'risk' means, and the only problem seems to be to find a comprehensive definition that comprises the intentions and requirements of all the disciplines involved. Yet, if we look at the word from the perspective of language pragmatics, we will realize that the difficulties in handling this term are even greater than those associated with 'space'. Whereas 'space' may be conceived as a *categorical* concept, 'risk' has to be regarded as a *relational term*. When talking about risk, it is necessary to include *multiple relations with other entities or concepts* that are absolutely indispensable in order to provide 'risk' with an assignable meaning. Nobody would ever think of using 'risk' in an absolute sense, meaning 'risk per se'. There is no risk 'as such'. Speaking of 'risk' indicates that someone or something is exposed to a potential and harmful event. Furthermore, this implies that we must define the attributes or aspects of existence of the entity involved. We must also figure out which entities or processes are 'responsible' for this exposure to a hazard, and determine the probabilities connected with the potential occurrence of an incident that will mean realization of the threat implied by the specific risk. So far, a variety of approaches has been developed to conceptualize this relational character of risk. Reviews of these approaches have been provided, amongst others, by Thywissen (2006), Renn (2008a, 2008b) and the International Risk Governnance Council – IRGC (2005).

In order to consider the term 'risk' in its relational aspects we must expand the pragmatic perspective employed so far. As one way of doing so, we propose to introduce the *logic of distinctions*, developed by the sociologist Rodrigo Jokisch (1996, 1999), as an analytical tool. According to the theory of distinctions, it is assumed that the processing of information, mental processes and observations is only possible if we are capable of realizing the *differences* between the 'things' or mental constructs we are talking about. 'Such a theory of distinctions allows us to make any identity observed in everyday life scientifically accessible as a form of distinction' (Jokisch 1999: 83).[2]

Niklas Luhmann's (1995) theory of social systems is also marked by a basic orientation towards the theory of distinctions. Such approaches are – explicitly or implicitly – related to ideas developed in the book *Laws of Form*, written by the mathematician George Spencer-Brown (1969). His basic theorem reads as follows: 'Draw a distinction and a universe comes into being' (Spencer-Brown 1969: 98). Conversely, this means that nothing comes into being without a distinction and it remains existent as long as this distinction is sustained. 'The term "form" denotes the unity of the difference of the two sides which are differentiated by a distinction' (Egner 2006: 98). By using our productive capacity to define a distinction, we indicate a boundary by means of which a specific object, an idea or a concept 'comes into being'. Only due to our observation, that is the distinction of something by means of something else, do we produce formally constitutive categories of narratives and, thus, the world as we conceive it.

We suggest combining the pragmatic approach to reconstructing the different meanings of 'risk' with an analysis of form in the sense of the theory of distinctions (cf. Weichhart 2007). The starting point is the hypothesis that ambiguous and relational terms like 'risk' *have different valences of distinction*. Therefore, the meaning of 'risk' is exclusively constituted by the respective antonym, the term from which 'risk' is distinguished. An analysis of meaning has to comprise the entire form: 'risk', boundary and the antonym by which 'risk' is differentiated. The specific understanding of risk 'comes into being' only in the context of the whole form. This reconstruction of the different versions of distinction within different scientific discourses appears to be highly convenient to elucidate the dimensions of the term and its usefulness for specific research issues. Such an 'analysis of form' may also be applied to the attributes that are assigned to the various concepts of risk.

A first concept of risk can be found in economic discussions. The specific meaning of the term becomes explicit by means of its counterpart 'chance'. In this context, 'risk' indicates the fact that the economic consequences of actions are *uncertain*. 'Risk' denotes the possibility that any entrepreneurial decision may result in a deviation of the factual profit from the expected profit (cf. Holzheu 1987: 12; Kyrer 2005: 105). This may yield a loss, but also an added profit. 'Risk' characterizes the possibility of a disadvantage which, however, is accepted in order to achieve a potential revenue or benefit. As a general rule, we have to accept the fact that more profitable economic actions bear greater risks. Risk reduction, on the other hand, implies the abandonment of potential gains. The respective benefit or loss may be measured in terms of money, but also in terms of non-material values.

In mainstream risk research, as well as in the insurance or engineering industries, discussions focus on another dimension of distinction. In these fields the meaning of the term 'risk' is constituted by the antonym 'safety'. 'Risk' denotes the fact that someone or something may be exposed to a potential threat; 'safety', on the other hand, indicates the absence of danger. It should be mentioned that 'certainty' and 'safety' are empty concepts and social constructions.[3] Both concepts are mere illusions because of the contingency of history.

A third dimension of distinction was introduced by Niklas Luhmann (1990, 1991). He emphasizes the process of active and conscious calculations that may produce potential risks and distinguishes between decision makers and the persons affected. This dimension of distinction produces yet another constellation of problems. In this context, the relevant antonym of 'risk' is 'danger'. 'Danger' means any potential threat to a person resulting from actions for which the person is *not directly responsible*. In contrast, 'risk' denotes any threat which is a direct consequence of an actor's conscious decision. In this usage, 'risk' is an aspect of active decision-making, a consequence of the decision maker's own choice, which has to be taken into account by them (cf. Luhmann 1997: 327). Let us assume that a powerful decision maker is taking a risk in order to achieve potential gains. Yet it is not the decision maker who bears the potential negative consequences, but other people involved. Thus, risk is transformed into danger. Situations like these are quite common in the present age of second modernity (cf. Beck 1986).

By analysing and differentiating the diverse meanings of space and risk, we have attempted to demonstrate that scientific endeavours in the field of risk research should consciously take into account the whole spectrum of meanings of these concepts, and use their combined potentials to describe and explain the risk-related phenomena of our world. We may distinguish three different valid and viable approaches to defining 'risk', and each of them may be related to the various concepts of 'space'. Apart from $space_5$, all the varieties of the concept of space mentioned above are relevant and useful for risk research. $Space_1$ is necessary for describing the distribution of the occurrence of a harmful event and its consequences. Even $space_2$, which is not appropriate for modelling spatiality and spatial relations, is needed in risk research and is indispensable for making statements concerning the amount of damage caused by a specific catastrophic event, as any form of census is necessarily related to the concept of $space_2$. In the context of risk research, the concept of $space_3$ was used, for instance, by Klinke and Renn (2006, illustration 1, n.p.) to classify systemic risks.

In the field of risk research, particular importance must be attributed to the concepts of $space_4$ and $space_{6s}$. Whenever we refer to relational aspects of harmful events, we need to use the concept of $space_4$ (take the friction and accumulation zones of avalanches, for instance). $Space_{6s}$ is necessary to understand the social construction of the material and immaterial aspects of 'secure' and 'insecure' areas in spatial planning policies. In the following discussion, we will try to demonstrate the usefulness of the diverse variants of risk and space through the example of a discourse analysis approach to risk research.

Language pragmatics in action: discourse analysis in hazards research

As a strand of the anti-essentialist 'new cultural geographies', discourse analysis approaches do not focus on the efforts of an agent to achieve something and on the intentions that have triggered these endeavours. From a discourse analysis perspective, attention shifts to the practices which (re-)produce and transform 'ensemble[s] of ideas, concepts, and categories through which meaning is given to social and physical phenomena' (Hajer 1993: 45). In other words: discourses can be regarded as constant processes of drawing distinctions, thus offering patterns of interpretation to structure our perceived reality and guide our actions. The anti-essentialist bias of a discourse analysis perspective is based on the idea that the meaning of social as well as physical phenomena, including the identity of subjects, is socially constructed. At the same time, the notion of an extra-discursive meaning of phenomena 'as such' is rejected. This anti-essentialist bias allows us to ask questions about the inner mechanics of structuring concepts and categories, how they are legitimated, how they are connected with certain interests and, finally, how such concepts and categories are combined with causal narratives to form extensive story lines, such as 'integrated flood management'.

From the mid-1990s on, discourse analysis approaches made their way into various disciplines, among them environmental politics and human geography. In these two disciplines, discourse analysis has been applied in various fields of interest ranging from environmental problems (Hajer 1993; Keller 1998; Feindt and Oels 2005) to the construction of sustainable (Bauriedl 2007) and (in)secure places in cities (Glasze 2005), and to planning theory (Flyvbjerg 1996; Sharp and Richardson 2001; Flyvbjerg and Richardson 2002).[4] In the past decade, discourse analysis approaches have also been applied to risk and hazards research, in connection with topics such as providing and improving knowledge about climate change and its harmful consequences (Stehr and von Storch 2000; Boykoff 2008; Boykoff *et al.* 2010), the debate about harmful effects of nuclear power (Bickerstaff *et al.* 2008), the legitimization of risky situations (Davidson 2003; Collins 2009), the uncertainties associated with diseases like BSE (Kewell and Beck 2008), the coverage and interpretation of natural hazards in newspapers (Ashlin and Ladle 2007), or the use of scientific arguments on climate change in prevention strategies (Lange *et al.* 2005; Lange and Garrelts 2007).

In the following discussion, however, we will scrutinize discourse as a spatially and temporally contextualized arrangement for assigning meaning to social and physical phenomena. According to Foucault's (1972) interpretation of discourse, it is the individual speech act that forms the analytical starting point. Such speech acts may be documented in newspaper articles, meeting minutes, books, reports, scientific papers or plans. These speech acts are interpreted as the effects of unspoken rules governing the formation of terms, objects, identities and strategic interests (Diaz-Bone 1999). Therefore, a collection of such materials – the so-called 'corpus' – forms the starting point for studies using a discourse analysis perspective. In the subsequent analysis of this corpus, the methodological spectrum ranges from quantitative lexicometric approaches to code-based ones, following the principles of grounded theory (Glaser 1992; Strauss and Corbin 1998).

Which are the potential insights this perspective may contribute to our discussion of the concept of risk and its relations to space? To illustrate how these issues are dealt with in practice, we have chosen the management of flood hazards through the spatial planning system of Lower Austria, one of the Austrian federal states, in the period from 1990 to 2009 (Höferl 2010).[5]

Following the anti-essentialist bias of discourse analysis approaches, we make the following assumption: a discourse analysis perspective cannot provide an analytical definition of risk that will help evaluate the concepts of risk found in the textual and graphical corpus, or assess their degree of 'correctness'. What are the reasons for this? Discourse analysis perspectives do not recognize extra-discursive ways of reasoning, which implies that all the concepts of risk discussed so far must be accepted as possible ways of constructing the meaning of risk. This said, we might conclude that, once 'constructivist randomness' has been assumed, discourse analysis is just an intellectual warm-up for accepting that 'anything goes'. This conclusion, however, is based on a common misconception, namely on the confusion of deconstruction and randomness. It is a major benefit of discourse analysis perspectives that they serve as useful instruments to deconstruct the meaning of a specific risk in its spatial, temporal and thematic context. Instead of randomness, two dimensions of giving meaning to risk, depending on each other, move into focus: one of the dimensions involves the reconstruction of the periods of time when the meaning assigned to a specific risk was produced by one or several dominant and stable sets of ideas, concepts and categories. On the other hand, these homogeneous periods can only be determined by cracks and gaps between them. These cracks and gaps are the stage on which new arrangements of ideas, concepts, identities and categories challenge the hegemonic ones and change the meaning applied to that risk so far.

Flood hazard management through the Lower Austrian spatial planning system

In order to check whether this methodological assumption can be verified empirically, let us take a closer look at the discourses on flood management through the spatial planning system of Lower Austria. According to Höferl (2010), three dominant discourses on the management of floods, comprising ensembles of ideas, concepts, identities and categorizations, may be reconstructed for the period from 1990 to 2009 (see Table 3.1).

The discourse of ecological (self-)endangering started in the 1980s, and its dominant conception of flood risk was embedded in a story line focusing on the general ecologization of society and planning. In this narrative, the decline of biodiversity in floodplain forests was causally linked to the channelization of rivers. Due to industrialization, this connection had been legitimized by society's general ignorance of ecological relationships. To solve these problems, a number

Table 3.1 Selected patterns of interpretation in discourses relating to the management of floods in Lower Austrian spatial planning from 1990 to 2009 (adapted from Höferl, 2010: 182)

	Discourse of ecological (self-) endangerment *1990——1996*	*Discourse of consequentialism in planning policy* *1997——2002*	*Discourse of mitigating losses through spatial planning* *2003——2009*
Concept of safety	Absolute safety ('risk vs. security')		Relative safety ('risk vs. chance')
Concept of nature	Technically controllable forces of nature, functionally independent from society		Technically uncontrollable, socialized nature
Concept of ethics	Ecological ethics of conviction	Ethics of responsibility within an ecological narrative	Ethics of responsibility due to risks of participation
Thematic key concept	Renaturalization	Tolerability	Residual risks

of strategies were applied: an ecologically structured ethics of conviction served as a last resort for the ecologization of society and planning. Due to the enhanced knowledge of ecological relations, the ecologization of rivers was combined with the concept of renaturalization, defined as the dismantling of channelized rivers, to re-establish a 'natural' interaction between rivers and their floodplain forests. In this context, the development of settlements within 'natural' floodplains was conceived as a marginalized instance of society's insufficient knowledge of ecological relations. By conceptualizing ecologization in a rather linear, modernistic way, such self-endangering of society and endangering of natural resources was sought to be avoided by enhancing the stock of ecological knowledge. Accordingly, floods were regarded as 'natural' ecological events that could be forecast by ecology specialists. This development triggered the establishment of a key distinction, namely the distinction between the producers of knowledge about rivers – in our case, the Federal Water Engineering Administration (FWEA) – and the recipients of information. Thus, the integration of ecological knowledge about rivers, especially about their inundation lines, in local spatial planning was eventually linked to the distinction between unsafe 'inundation areas' and safe areas suitable for settlement. Yet the powerful community organizations succeeded in weakening regulations on flood-specific land use and the right to decide which specific annuality should determine the local inundation areas was surrendered to the communities. In other words, the authority to define the boundary between risk and security in spatial planning lay within the competence of the individual community. The strategic dualism of basing zoning on 'ecological facts', and at the same time allowing communities to define the border between risky inundation areas and safe non-inundation ones represents a remarkably persistent inconsistency in Austrian planning policies.

Relating to the discourse of consequentialism in planning policy, the ethics of responsibility was employed to reveal the communities' conceptualization of risky inundation areas as self-serving and as caught in political dependencies.

Legitimized by this set-up, authority to define the boundaries of inundation areas was withdrawn from the communities by the Lower Austrian parliament. Based on the principles of the ethics of responsibility, it was decided that inundation areas – being the key concept for deciding on areas suitable for settlement – had to be more directly linked to the 'ecological facts' as provided by the FWEA. These inundation areas were then generally defined as the runoff areas of a 100-year event.

Although this concept of inundation areas had also been part of the discourse of mitigating losses through spatial planning, it was no longer regarded as a viable concept to distinguish safe settlement areas from unsafe ones. The reason for this change in attribution must be seen in the abandonment of the concept of absolute safety in favour of relative safety. Due to floods that exceeded the 100-year event, the definition of inundation areas as applied by spatial planning so far proved to be outdated, as it had not proved suitable for avoiding the flooding of settlements. 'Mother Nature' had demonstrated that she could evade technical control in the shape of dams and other preventive strategies. The conceptualization of nature as being beyond technical controllability becomes even more evident in a sub-narrative that attributed intensified flooding to the effects of man-made climate change. This concept of a socialized nature beyond control formed the background of the distinction between risk and chance. Since society was not able to avoid being exposed to risk, chance was positioned as a viable counterpart to reflect the benefits of being at risk. In this framing, the identification of new settlement areas was directly related to the identification of a specific risk–chance relation that was regarded as socially acceptable. Based on the unchallenged safety standards for a 100-year event, as defined by the FWEA, this risk–chance relation was constituted as the 100-year event in Lower Austrian spatial planning provisions. At the same time, the framing of residual risks as general participatory risks was legitimized by the inability of spatial planning to exercise any influence on the material building stock. This lack of competence rendered any consideration of residual risks useless, since it was only this material building stock that might be negatively affected by residual risks.

If we focus on the cracks between these three temporally stabilized discourses, two questions arise: where are these cracks, and, more pressingly, why have these discourses changed at all? Projected against the history of flood events in Lower Austria, the genealogy of discourses may be illustrated as shown in Figure 3.1.

At first glance, we may conclude that the flood events with the highest economic losses correlate with changes in flood perception and their management. Another finding is that the geo-deterministic view of flood management, interpreting it as a 'disaster-driven' process, may run into trouble when trying to explain why the floods of 1991 or 2006 had no impact on the relevant discourse.

Therefore, we must ask whether it is really the monetary impact of a flood event that determines a change in the discourse on flood management. Trying to answer this question from a discourse analysis perspective requires a reformulation: how can we link the material flood event and its interaction with other material entities, such as houses, cars or humans, to the discursive production of meaning?

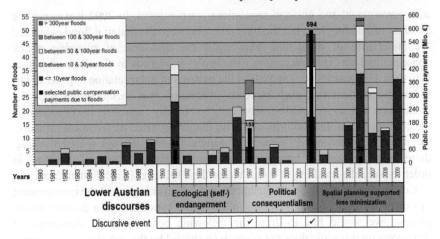

Figure 3.1 Lower Austrian discourses on flood management and their temporal
development (adapted from Höferl, 2010: 96)

Let us interpret material flood events as discourse-external events that will occur
no matter whether a society is willing to engage in discourses of assigning meaning
to these events or not. The moment we start categorizing a flood event as a 100-
year event, a) we assign a discursive ensemble of ideas and concepts to a selected
material flood event, and b) we establish a relationship between this ensemble and
the material flood event, as well as its consequences. The nature of this relationship
mirrors the structuring and yet proliferating aspects of discourses. If the hegemonic
ensemble of ideas and concepts can place the material flood event in a coherent
context of meaning, it will be difficult to find starting points for counter-discourses
to challenge the predominant way of producing meaning. In this situation, the
material flood event does not leave its imprint on the discourse; on the contrary, it
becomes structured by the dominant discourse. Failure to embed a material flood
event in a coherent context of meaning results in contradictions, which may be
more or less obvious, between the material flood event and the meaning assigned
to it. This is the starting point for breaking up the hegemonic ensemble of ideas
and concepts, and the search for a new dominant ensemble begins. In this case the
material flood event challenges and resists the assignment of meaning by the
dominant discourse. Such material flood events take the position of 'discursive
events' (Jäger 2006: 100ff), which exercise influence on, as well as marking the
transformation of a discourse. By tracing back the specific meaning assigned to
each material flood event, Höferl (2010) revealed that from 1990 to 2009 only two
flood events managed to prevail over the dominant production of discursive
meaning.[6] In the case of the floods of 1997, the excessive flooding of non-built-up
areas, which, however, had been designated for development a few years earlier,
triggered a discussion about the communities' competence to define 'unsafe'
inundation areas. In the following discourse of planning policy consequentialism,
the authority to define inundation areas was transferred to the Lower Austrian

state government and uniform regulations were enacted. In 2002 it was not the flooding of building lots, but the interaction between the material flood event and the materiality of dams that challenged the discourse of planning policy consequentialism. This interaction – the spillover of dams by floods much higher than their 100-year levels – surpassed the patterns of interpretation applied so far: it became evident that such material interaction was incompatible with the assumption that nature could be completely technically controlled. In consequence, the concept of absolute security could no longer be based on technical measures like dams. In the following discourse of mitigating losses through spatial planning, these former patterns of interpretation were transformed into their opposites in order to place the breaking of dams and/or their spillover in a coherent narrative.

Concerning the question of whether the (strategic) changes in flood management in Lower Austrian spatial planning followed the hypothesis of a disaster-driven process, we would like to draw the following conclusion: the genealogy of discourses on this topic does not seem to be shaped by the question as to whether nature drives societal adaptation or vice versa.

By accepting a non-human co-agency in discourse analysis, society and processes in ecosystems may be read as 'actants' (Latour 2005) in the ongoing process of giving meaning to social and material phenomena. In this equitable socio-ecological interaction, it is the ability of discourses to put material processes and entities in a coherent context of meaning that drives development.

This notion that the meaning of material entities is not independent from discursive attributions and that these attributions themselves are not independent from material entities (Bauriedl 2007) leads to a significant conclusion: if the way in which we assign meaning to a material entity or process, such as the flow of water, is discursively produced, the same must apply to the meaning of spatial concepts (for instance inundation areas) that refer to these material processes or entities. This reasoning implies that inundation areas, defined as the spatial manifestation of flood risk, may be interpreted as a discursively constructed social space$_{6s}$.[7] Such spaces may be understood as a particular, locatable form of narrative that fulfils two interdependent essentials: on the one hand, it provides an ontological blueprint – including a normative assessment – for the inundation areas. To meet the requirements of a locatable narrative, there must also be a sub-narrative focusing on the way this blueprint can be connected to different arrangements of material entities (space$_4$) in space$_1$. This sub-narrative serves to legitimize a specific way of projecting the text-based constitution of an inundation area (space$_{6s}$) into space$_1$.

In the case of Lower Austria, the discourse of ecological (self-)endangerment allowed a twofold production of inundation areas as space$_{6s}$. As the spatial planning authorities and communities were regarded as the recipients of scientifically based knowledge about the river ecosystem, the competence to conceptualize the material event of water runoff resided with the FWEA. On the grounds of an FWEA-internal discourse, this knowledge was manifested in the spatial projection of 30- and 100-year events. In parallel, and to satisfy diverse strategic interests, the 'insecure' inundation area was conceptualized as a definitional black hole in spatial planning. This was aimed at granting communities the right to individually decide on the location of inundation areas in accordance with the knowledge provided by the FWEA. Within this frame, the free choice between the 30-year or the 100-year event, or any other one, allowed communities to modify the definition of inundation areas and, thus, their space$_4$ spatiality in accordance with their development policies. With the start of the discourse of political consequentialism, an entirely different definition of inundation area became obvious. Once again it was the FWEA that provided the knowledge basis, but now the authority to define inundation areas was entirely attributed to the Lower Austrian parliament and its spatial planning authorities. This shift was legitimized by the above-mentioned communities' inability to efficiently designate inundation areas, and was aimed at coherently assigning meaning to the massive flooding of newly zoned building areas during the 1997 floods. By using productive power, inundation areas were generally related to the 100-year event.

To sum up, the discursive understanding of social space may be read as an ensemble of formation rules, permitting a specific geometry of relations between concepts,[8] identities, strategic interests, practices, and material things or processes, which, at the same time, excludes other potential geometries. Being the result of these relations, social spaces do not have a given and fixed meaning and may become part of the dominant way of producing meaning via discursive cracks. Höferl (2010: 121ff and 146ff) has demonstrated how retention areas became an integral part of the discourse of planning policy consequentialism, whereas residual risk areas became an integral part of the discourse of mitigating losses through spatial planning. In accordance with Massey's (1991) idea of a relational understanding of social space, it is not the line on a piece of paper that defines phenomena such as inundation areas, retention areas or residual risk areas in space$_{6s}$. Regarded from a discourse analysis perspective, these lines and areas – as entities in space$_1$ – are effects of discursively structured practices that are based on locatable narratives. These lines and areas – in other words, site-related inscriptions of the discourse in space$_1$ – are symbols of someone's power of definition.

Conclusion

Using 'inundation area' as an example, we have tried to show that a phenomenon may simultaneously exist in more than one space. Although the same signifier, in this case 'inundation area', is used, the representation of such an area in space$_1$ (a line on a map) differs widely from its representation in space$_{6s}$ (a discursive set of rules for assigning meaning to an 'inundation area'). Therefore, we conclude that different conceptions of space offer different epistemic perspectives of phenomena. Furthermore, this offers the opportunity to examine different dimensions of these phenomena (see Figure 3.2).

Following this line of argumentation, we may state that there is no right or wrong concept of space in risk research. Each of the concepts of space discussed above offers a unique epistemological perspective, a unique way of looking at

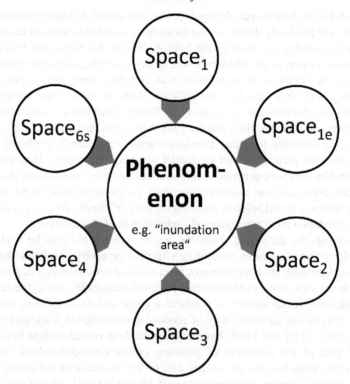

Figure 3.2 Concepts of space as different epistemological perspectives of phenomena (created by the authors)

phenomena. Research interests focusing on the geodetic delineation of inundation areas may be most closely associated with the space$_1$ concept. In contrast, the space$_{6s}$ concept may be applied to issues dealing with the productive powers of assigning meaning to the signifier 'inundation area'.

Utilizing this plurality of space concepts as epistemic perspectives in geographic contributions to the risk research debate may sound confusing. On the other hand, such plurality offers an opportunity for interdisciplinary triangulation of phenomena in the field of risk and hazards research. Last but not least, such a triangulation may help overcome the dichotomy between human and physical geography.

Acknowledgement

We are very grateful to Angelika Weichhart for correcting our English.

Notes

1 The abbreviations for the different concepts of space using subscripted numbers follow the conventions introduced by Weichhart (1999, 2008).
2 Translated by the authors. This interpretation of distinction which is based on formal epistemology and language analysis must not be confused with the concept of distinction elaborated in Bourdieu's theory of habitus (1984).
3 Cf. Taleb (2007).
4 More detailed reviews of the adoption of discourse analysis perspectives in environmental politics and human geography have been provided by Hajer and Versteeg (2005), and Glasze and Mattissek (2009).
5 It should be noted that each of the nine federal states of Austria is in charge of its own spatial planning policy. In consequence, each of them has developed its own approach to the meaning assigned to floods and the ways planning practice is structured by this meaning (Kanonier 2005).
6 In this context, 'flood event' refers to the sum of single flood events along various rivers within a period of some days.
7 It should be noted that this is not the only way to integrate space into discourse analysis. A more detailed discussion of this methodological topic can be found in Bauriedl (2007, 2009), Schreiber (2009), Huffschmid and Wildner (2009), and Glasze (2009).
8 According to Foucault (1978), such a specific geometry of relations may be termed a dispositif (apparatus), which means a processing arrangement of discursive rules, practices and material artefacts fulfilling a specific need (Caborn 2007; Agamben 2008).

4 Risk, space and system theory
Communication and management of natural hazards

Jürgen Pohl, Swen Zehetmair and Julia Mayer

Introduction

'Risk' is closely linked to human decisions. Decisions are necessary to stay alive, to move on and to develop society. By taking decisions, we reduce our options for the future and create constraints. Our actions may have unexpected consequences, i.e. we produce risks. If we think of the risks of an investment, the risks of the world finance system, the risks of global warming and so forth, it seems clear that risk is closely bound to time. However, damages – as realized risks – have a spatial dimension, too, for instance the size of the affected area, the accessibility of the region under stress and its specific 'spatial structure'. This chapter looks at risk as an aspect of decision-making in relation to both its chronological and spatial dimensions.[1] Of course, different perspectives on risk and space are possible. Fuchs and Keiler (in this volume) describe the idea of coupling the different concepts for a deeper understanding of the spatial dimensions of hazard and risk: a positivist view of risk, on the one hand, and constructivist approaches on the other hand, with their different roots and scientific methods. We want to take a look at spatial aspects of risk management (in a broader sense). We especially want to regard the link between risk and space from the position of system theory according to Niklas Luhmann. Space and place are important elements of different kinds of social systems like the political system, the scientific system or the system of the mass media and organizations. So we will not start by discussing the spatial aspects of hazardous events, but by introducing the role of space and place within social systems. We especially want to look at the 'administrative space' in flood management, the perception of the spatial dimension in an early warning system and the meaning of places in the mass media when reporting on disastrous events.

Our approach is closely related to a constructivist notion of space. Of course, there is a wide range of different constructivist positions. We compare constructivist and naturalistic positions of space in a general manner. We will start with some illustrations of different relations between risk and space. Before exploring the concept of 'space', we will explain some basic concepts of Luhmann's theory. In the final section we try to outline potentials for efficient risk management, taking spatial aspects of risk into account.

Risk and different concepts of space: some examples

The examples presented below result from our studies of flood protection management in the Elbe area, and our research on the development of an integrated early warning system for landslides in the Swabian Alb.

'Spatial fit': natural and administrative territories

Hazardous events always occur within a certain spatial extension. They follow natural rules, for instance the laws of gravity. A downhill debris flow affects the owners of land and buildings, and therefore the owner or tenant holds a form of ownership of the risk, as long as he or she has some property in the affected space. Risks are thus the concern of individual people. They have to evaluate the risk, consider precautions and, in the case of damage, handle the consequences. The tenant is also dependent on his neighbours' behaviour in that situation. So, already on the individual level, there is a spatial dimension of risk.

The question of 'ownership' of a particular risk may become more complicated when organizations get involved. Whose tenure is the risk of a river flooding? Does the responsibility lie with the Ministry of the Interior? Can it be attributed to an industry or subordinate institutions in any way? Are the administrations for spatial planning, for the environment or for water resources management in charge?

'Problems of spatial fit' (Young 1999, 2002; Moss 2004; Fichter and Moss 2004) often occur in cases of public risk management concerning spatially fixed natural risks (e.g. floods, landslides, volcano eruptions). The term points at the incompatibility of institutional arrangements and biophysical conditions. Natural risks of this kind are based on the spatial concept of (geo-)ecosystems, which is not compatible with the concept of a region – and therefore the administrative space of the administration. Problems of spatial fit are often discussed in the context of flood risks: rivers pass through different states, and do not stop at political, national or any other territorial borders.

This may have important consequences. In the German federal system for example, it is impossible for central authorities to carry out risk management effectively as long as more than one federal state is involved. The Ministries of the Interior of the respective federal states (regions) hold full responsibility for their territory, but their competence ends strictly at the state's border. Thus, in the Rhine valley it is not allowed to flood retention areas in Baden-Wuerttemberg in order to prevent the flooding of cities in North Rhine-Westphalia. Only if a disaster alarm is issued by the government of Baden-Wuerttemberg is it allowed to open the polder.

Problems of spatial fit not only create problems in risk management, because administrative boundaries are not compatible with the spatial extension of a particular hazard, but they may even create new risks. The lack of a coordinating, superordinate institution leads to a situation in which each administrative unit (in Germany: the federal state) can set its own threshold values for protection. In

2005 this led to a situation in which the state of Brandenburg unilaterally determined a new design flood ('Bemessungshochwasser') and elevated its Elbe dikes accordingly. For the downstream riparian states (Lower Saxony and Schleswig-Holstein), this led to an additional flood risk (Zehet mair 2012). Regarding flood risk management, the competences are not only spread across the horizontal level of the different federal states, but also vertically in the different sectoral administrative departments, which in turn have different spatial layouts (e.g. the administrative spaces of regional planning) (see Figure 4.1).

The situation differs according to the size of the areas and political conditions. In China, a top-down structure allows the central state to make decisions concerning flood management and controlled inundation that will cause the least overall damage (or spare a politically important province) (Shen 2009). But the general problem exists as long as administrative units do not follow natural units like river basins, earthquake areas or hurricane regions. It is not possible to rearrange administrative borders to fit natural entities. The incompatibility of natural space and administrative space often results in major difficulties, especially in public risk management.

'Landslide early warning' as a prevention measure with different space–time concepts

Landslides are local phenomena which can materialize within different time and space frames, ranging from a few centimetres per year to sudden and rapid events. Sometimes the affected area is very small, and sometimes large regions are involved. Landslide early warning needs to acknowledge the different space–time dimensions of the different phases of prevention.[2] At the least a distinction

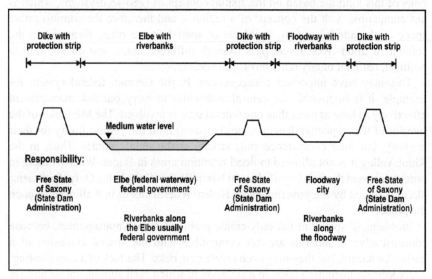

Figure 4.1 Responsibilities at the Elbe River (modified after DKKV 2003: 31)

between mitigation and preparation as distinct phases of prevention is necessary. In the case of early warning, mitigation refers to the development, long-term establishment and testing of an adjusted early warning system, whereas preparation refers to the application of the warning system: the warning process itself (Dikau and Weichselgartner 2005: 127).

There are different space–time dimensions, reproduced by the stakeholders' discourses that prevent collective action in risk prevention. The differences between the two phases concerning their space–time dimensions take on the forms shown in Figure 4.2.

The mitigation phase temporally precedes the phase of preparation. The focus lies on long-term measures, referring to an event in the future. The possibly harmful event can only be anticipated, with a high level of uncertainty concerning the general occurrence of damage and its potential magnitude. The phase of mitigation is the time for technological development of the early warning system itself. That is also the time when the identification and participation of the various social systems concerned (mainly organized social systems) and their forms of communication ought to take place. Plenty of decisions need to be taken in this phase, relating to the functioning of the early warning system (Is it a monitoring system, an expert system or an automatic alarm system?), the warning itself (How does the warning take place? Who ought to express the warning? Who should receive the warning?), the localization of responsibility and competency (legal framework, administrative regulations, factual and political competencies), but

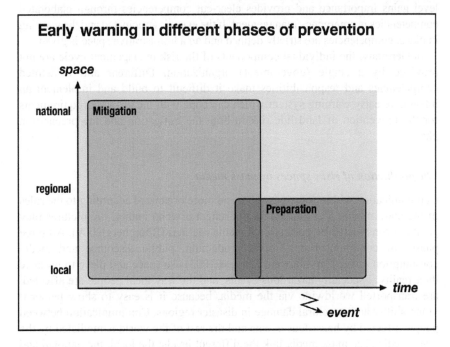

Figure 4.2 Early warning in different phases of prevention (own illustration)

also the attendance and supervision of the system (competencies, absorption of operating costs). Prevention measures in this first phase of mitigation take effect only in an uncertain future. So there is great uncertainty with regard to the hazard (probability of loss occurring) and with regard to the risk, in terms of decisions, responsibility and accountability. People and organizations have the tendency to neglect such a risk in the face of everyday problems and decisions. Problems often arise from the fact that no organization claims responsibility for the coordination of the different social systems in this phase. As landslides are phenomena that happen locally, they are often dealt with exclusively on a local level. Mitigation measures, however, need to be established on a local, regional and national scale. There is a lack of responsibility and competency on the higher regional and supra-regional level, although this is the level on which they should ideally be situated. Administrative organizations have not yet been established to tackle the problem of landslide risks in low mountain ranges. As a consequence, it is impossible to establish a local administrative body with clear-cut competencies and responsibility for early warning in the mitigation phase. The lack of these structures leads to considerable difficulties in the implementation of an early warning system: the necessary steps for successful warning cannot be taken (questions of attendance, financing and responsibility).

In the preparation phase, which is discussed below, emergency management becomes essential. The warning is the basis for the following steps. On the time axis, the warning is seen as very close to the event. On the spatial scale, the local level gains importance and provides clear-cut competencies through elaborated competencies in emergency management. If the event is anticipated and the warning in place, competencies are strictly defined and an administrative space is given.

In Germany, the individual components of the risk management cycle are not provided by a single (government) organization. Different and ill-defined competencies and responsibilities make it difficult to build and implement an integrative early warning system which can cope with the growing requirements for the prevention of landslide risk in both the mitigation and the preparation phases.

The production of risky spaces by mass media

Communication within society is more and more organized according to the rules of the mass media. Mass media do not reflect or echo reality, the pictures they paint are constructed by professional media routines (Rhomberg 2009). All three phases of communication – news production, public discourse and media consumption – (see Carvalho and Burgess 2005) use space and place to produce their reality. Especially hazardous events, and the way local people are affected, are transported worldwide via the media, because it is easy to show personal vulnerability and structural damage in disaster regions. Communication between people affected by hazardous events and the rest of the world is mediated by the mass media. The mass media link the different levels: the local, the national and the global.

Abstract and theoretical information about risks comes in conjunction with pictures, and sometimes even sounds and smells. This combination is highly attractive for modern mass media. For the mass media, selection goes by the rule 'only a visible risk is a good risk'. This visibility is usually attributed to a particular spatial entity or place. The best conditions for media coverage are presented by dynamic risks, generating vivid and spectacular pictures: a flood, its water flowing around cars or possibly even bringing down bridges; an oil spill leading to birds sticky with oil, spreading across the ocean and coast; or a bushfire raging through the woods and destroying houses. A little less convenient are cases of realized risks, showing damage and destruction in the aftermath of the event: a house buried by an avalanche or a building in ruins after an earthquake are examples of this second type. On the other hand, 'abstract' risks like the extinction of a species or the completely invisible phenomenon of nitrification do not sell very well in the media.

Such visible risks and the resulting damage can easily be localized by the media. In the process of localization, space becomes an integral component of social perception and communication. It thus not only serves as a stage for the reported event, but as an authentic synonym for the catastrophic event itself. The mass media apply ten criteria to the selection of news: surprise, conflicts, quantities, local relevance, norm violations, difference of good and bad (moral dimension), interest in particular people, topicality, expression of opinions and organizational aspects of the newspaper or TV station (Luhmann 2000: 28–35). These selection criteria are also applied to the coverage of a catastrophic event. The selection criterion 'local relevance' is prominent for the coverage of risks. Distance is a decisive element: while hundreds of people died in a flood in Eastern India in 1997, newspapers in Germany were only concerned with the far less destructive Oder flood in Germany. Small but nearby calamities and accidents make it into the local news, whereas catastrophes that take place farther away will only be mentioned in the media from a certain size and number of casualties upwards.

The mass media – as the name indicates – are mediators. This also includes mediation between society and risk. In that context, space takes the position of an assistant. Risks only become an element in the mass media, if they are palpable. Risks, or rather the realized damage, accidents or catastrophes, need to trigger a personal relation, they need to appear as a certain image in order to be recognized and comprehended. This image may consist of an inundated dike, a house covered with cracks, or a person who escaped the flood by climbing onto his or her roof.

This image of catastrophe includes additional people, beyond those immediately hit by the catastrophe: politicians are often part of the picture at the scene of the catastrophe. The presence of politicians – on the dike or at least in a helicopter circling over the place – is not only widely noticed; the pictures in the mass media transform their attention into a part of society's communication, which mostly takes place in the mass media. Due to the sensitive and critical situation, there is a special interest in their presence.

The news and reports in the mass media are closely linked to a political awareness of risks and damage, and they do not offer alternative frameworks for the communication of risks (Carvalho and Burgess 2005; Olausson 2009). There is also a strong interrelation between the media and politicians with respect to the role of space and place.

The simple conjunction of high-level politicians and the place of the realized risk symbolizes a clear responsibility and signals that political action is being taken. The presence of politicians at the disaster zone should not be seen as a mere substitute for action. It is a means of representing and visualizing the invisible, but nevertheless effective, actions of the government.

System theory as an analytical framework for the spatial dimensions of risk

A possible analytical framework for the observation of the spatial dimensions of risk is Niklas Luhmann's theory of social systems. It is a general theory of society, which aims to address every aspect of social life within its universal theoretical framework (Luhmann 1984: 33). Luhmann's theory is on a highly abstract level, encompassing an enormous number of topics. System theory places risk at the centre of modern society by regarding it as a form of observing society (Japp and Kusche 2008: 78). Accordingly, risk is a system category inherent in any social system (Japp 1996). Risk in system theory thus concerns space and time dimensions.[3]

The difference between system and environment is the starting point of any analysis based on system theory (Luhmann 1995: 16). A system can never exist without an environment, because it is generated by *demarcation*, assigning all there is either to the system or to its environment. Social systems are autopoietic, which means that the elements of the system are reproduced by the elements itself. Autopoiesis does not mean that the system is autonomous. The closed nature of the system is a condition for its openness, in that the system itself determines the intake of environmental contacts (Luhmann 1984: 63–64).

For our observation of the relation of risk and space, the focus will be on social systems, which are reproduced on the basis of communication. This switch from action to communication is the essentially new idea Luhmann promoted (Egner 2008: 423). But his concept of communication differs significantly from traditional understandings of communication. The crucial moment of communication is the connectivity of communicative moments. Luhmann dismisses the idea of communication as a sender–receiver relationship with successful or unsuccessful transmission, and defines communication as an emergent occurrence which is a unity of three selections (information, utterance and understanding). The structures of social systems are expectations of communicated themes (Seidl 2005: 31). If the expectations concerning the communicated topics are met, the connectivity of new communication rises, thus enabling the self-preservation of the system. Social systems can be differentiated into three subtypes: interactions, organizations and societies. They are generated by different modes of demarcation and selection. With regard to our observations on the spatial dimensions of risk, organizations play a decisive role, as well as function systems. The term function system describes systems in a functionally differentiated society, where we find several societal subsystems specialized in providing certain societal functions (e.g. politics, law, economy, science, mass media).

The way system theory deals with the topic of risk bears upon general assumptions about structures and processes of modern society within the social system theory. Thus, system theory develops a concept of risk which differs fundamentally from other theoretical approaches in risk research. In a constructivist view, risks are not seen as objectively given dangers, but as social constructions. Probably the most important conceptual change Luhmann suggested in his works on risk concerns the distinction between *risk* and *danger* (Japp and Kusche 2008: 87). Risk implies that the cause of possible loss or damage is attributed to the system itself, whereas danger refers to an external cause of possible damage. With regard to this definition, we abandon the term 'safety' as the counterpart of 'risk' and substitute it with 'danger'. Thus we acknowledge that total security never exists, and the only relevant distinction is whether interference can avert an impending disaster or not. Due to the essential distinction between risk and danger, 'attribution' becomes the focal point. Whether we regard something as a risk or a danger is a question of attribution. Consequently, we use the distinction between 'decision makers' and 'affected persons'. This distinction derives from the question of whether the possibility of loss or damage is voluntarily accepted, being the result of an individual's own decision, or if the cause of the damage is attributed to an external system in the environment and therefore an external danger. The important thing is that it depends on the mode of observation which is held to be a decision maker or which is the affected system (Luhmann 1993). Only a second-order observer, who observes the distinctions of a first-order observer, can analyse how risks are constructed, perceived and attributed, while a first-order observer identifies risk as an object. This concept of risk and danger demonstrates that the distinction between risk and danger is not objectively given, but is a second-order distinction (Japp and Kusche 2008: 89).

In our functionally differentiated society, risk plays an important role (Luhmann 1993). Risk research from a system theory perspective analyses the communication of function systems and decisions by organizations, the central issue being how they deal with risk, how they construct risk, how they attribute risk decisions and which spatial dimensions underlie these constructs. We will specify the concept of function systems by giving two examples, the mass media and the political system. In modern society, all communications refer to one of several distinct forms. In terms of binary coding, each form belongs to one societal subsystem. Any communication of the autopoietic system is orientated towards this code, for example power/non-power (political system) or information/non-information (mass media). This binary code is the basic distinction shaping observations of the function systems. Communications in the environment are perceived as perturbations with regard to their intrinsic logic (Luhmann 1997a: 748ff). References to the environment of a function system are always internally constructed and therefore dependent on the structure and the binary code of the system itself (Japp and Kusche 2008: 77).

The mass-media function system is a means of self-observation for the societal system (Luhmann 1996: 173) and contributes to the construction of reality in society by producing a continuous self-description of the world (Luhmann 1996: 183). The mass-media system observes risks referring to its information/non-information code, and contributes to the construction of risks in society by coverage of these risks. 'Whatever we know about our society, or indeed about the world in which we live, we know through the mass media' (Luhmann 2000: 1). The mass media can give an account of risks, if the system itself refers to them as information. The more catastrophic, visible and dreadful the information, the more media attention is directed towards the event (see above).

From the perspective of system theory, the public leads us from the mass media to the political system and its organizations, on which we focused above. For the political system, 'public opinion' is the internal environment of political organizations and interactions, and plays an important role in the handling of risks within the political system. The political system may thus observe itself through the medium of 'public opinion', and can use this observation to adjust its communication (Luhmann 2000: 110ff). System theory assumes that there is no centre to a functionally differentiated society, not even the political system. The political system has the function of taking collectively binding decisions (Luhmann 1990). Within the political system, risks are only referred to in terms of its own code, which in the spatial dimension is restricted to the respective state's territory (see above). Essential organizations concerned with risk management in the political system are administrative bodies that design threshold values (e.g. setting flood areas, assessing threshold values for water levels or volcano ash). Even so, the political organizations cannot cross the system's border with their decisions, but must adhere to the internal logic of the political system.

Spatial concepts in geography and their reference to risk

The question of the relation between risk and space can be answered in different ways, depending on how a risk is identified and what kind of risks are considered. In this chapter, we focus on the differences in the concepts and notions of space that are applied when talking about risk and space. It is necessary to complete the system theory viewpoint with different concepts of space, because a wide range of these concepts are applied in societal communication on risks and in risk management.

How is space conceptualized in system theory? Luhmann himself does not see space as an essential category of social systems. Social systems are not bounded by space (but by meaning) (Luhmann 1997a: 76), and they do not rely on space and time for their designation (Luhmann 1997a: 30). Nevertheless, in German debates there is a variety of different approaches to finding the spatial dimension in system theory, to introducing space into it, or at least to discussing it (see Baecker 2005; Bahrenberg and Kuhm 1998; Hard 1986; Klüter 1986; Kuhm 2000; Lippuner 2007; Lippuner and Lossau 2004; Pohl 1993b; Pott 2007; Stichweh 1998, 2001, 2003, 2008).

Pott summarizes that, even though the approaches of the diverse authors arguing in system theory terms still appear as a *search movement* ('Suchbewegung'), the contours of a system theory notion of space are becoming more and more distinct, and with it a conceptualization of the relationship between society and space that is grounded in system theory. Against the background of a system theory of Social Geography, Klüter addressed space as a construct of social communication as early as 1986. Based on this view, he assigned different spatial abstractions to different social systems and social codes. Pohl denotes space as an important code of the second order (Pohl 1993a: 53ff). Probably the most widely known conceptualization of space in system theory was proposed by Stichweh (1998): In his view, spatial differences in the environment of society may have causal implications for social systems. Stichweh develops an 'ecology of society', in which the causal dependencies within society are derived from the conditions of the material environment. Furthermore, he suggests that space should be treated as an additional meaning dimension (next to the fact dimension, temporal dimension and social dimension), but drops this idea after coming to the conclusion that space no longer plays an important role today. Kuhm (2000: 333) considers arranging all objects according to the criterion of 'closeness and distance'. In addition, he sees space as a medium of communication. In this context, Pott (2007: 59) suggests treating space as a medium of perception and of communication, building on the important system theory distinction of medium and form. According to this, system theory does not describe any objective space behind the forms that are built by the medium of space. Spaces are system-internal products (Pott 2007: 61). Thus, our focus is on observation of the communicative generation of spaces and the question of how these spaces are communicatively produced and applied.

The container space is only one concept of space that is discussed. The wide range of different concepts of space – in geography as well as in other disciplines – has been much discussed since the 1970s. In particular, the emergence of linguistic and constructivist approaches in geography stimulated these debates, following the concept of space developed by the famous geographer and philosopher, Immanuel Kant (Gedan 1905), who defined space as an epistemological but not as an ontological phenomenon. Later on, in the context of post-modern thinking and post-structural epistemological ideas, the discussion has moved to a more differentiated view. It is now possible to categorize different concepts of space (Bartels 1974; Soja 1989; Lefebvre 1991; Thrift 2004). As a consideration of each concept would lead too far from the subject, we will focus on two classifications to discuss the relationship between risk and space. Both Hard (2003) and Wardenga (2002) give a list of concepts of space. The advantage of these classifications is that they try to integrate and arrange all forms of spaces in chronological order of appearance in the academic discourse. We discuss different references to risk in each concept (see Table 4.1).

Although there is a reference to risk in each of the mentioned concepts of space, we focus in our further study on three of these concepts. The second concept of space characterizes space as a 'region' with different administrative units and risk

Table 4.1 Concepts of space according to Hard and Wardenga

Spacial concepts modified after Hard 2003	Spatial concepts according to Wardenga 2002	Reference to risk
Concept 1: Entity of perception, 'landscape'	Container space	'classical' hazard research: risk as an element of spatial structure and as an object of its analysis
Concept 2: Region	**Relational space**	**administrative units: places and locations as objects of operative risk management**
Concept 3: Nature as opponent of man, Environment	**Container space (partially also relational space)**	**e.g. river basins as 'natural space' of the man-environment paradigm (Mensch-Umwelt-Paradigma)and paradigm of culture ecology**
Concept 4: (Geo-) Ecosystem	Relational space	often base for physical geographic risk and hazard research (process research)
Concept 5: 'mental map'	Perception space	'areas of risk' in the perception of (potentially) affected people, stakeholders, decision-makers etc. applied for research on environment and risk perception
Concept 6: 'communicated map'	**Constructed place**	**Communicated 'areas of risk'**
	Place as an element of communication and action	**Place as communicated by the mass media**
Concept 7: 'Space' as metaphor for social issues, 'social space'	Constructed space and constructed places	'areas of risk' in the collective memory: e.g. Atlantis/Santorini, Bermuda Triangle, (earthquake of) Lisboa, New Orleans, Ground Zero

refers to places and locations, especially as objects of operative risk management (see the early warning system example above). Space as 'environment' refers to 'natural spaces', such as river basins, and the natural risks that arise from these natural spaces, like floods, earthquakes or landslides. Concepts 2 and 3 collide in the 'problem of spatial fit' (see discussion of flood prevention management above). The 'communicated map' is a constructed space: space is related to social constructs and appears as an element of communication. Examples of such communicated maps are 'areas of risk' as communicated by the mass media (see above). This communicated map is closely linked to the concept of place in the sense of '*chora*' as a specific place where everyday life is experienced and embedded (Derrida 1990: 42–43; Pohl 1993b: 263).

A comparison of the above concept of space with the system theory understanding of space leads us first of all to the understanding of space as communicated space (concept 6), and thus as an element of communication. Beyond this, the space abstraction of interaction systems can also be described as perception space (concept 5), since interactions are dependent on the coexistence of communication partners and their perceptibility (Luhmann 1975; Kieserling 1999). Hence, system theory applies the constructivist spatial concept 6. Within communication, however, all of these spatial concepts described by Hard and Wardenga may emerge. Communication may refer to a landscape and all its features, just as much as to an ecosystem or a specific region. They are then, however, a topic within communication, and not a system theory concept of space.

In his work, Klüter (1986) assigned individual spatial abstractions to the different types of systems (interaction, organization, society). Accordingly, interactions operate with scenery ('Kulisse'), organizations with specific programme spaces ('Programmraum'), for instance the administrative space ('Administrativraum') for state organizations, and societies with linguistic spaces ('Sprachraum').

Application of spatial concepts and risk management

Spatial concepts and empirical risk management

This last section contains some reflections concerning the relation between the described spatial concepts and empirical risk management, especially as carried out by governmental organizations. We will consider organization systems on the one hand, and the specific communication of the political function system on the other hand.

According to the basic assumptions of system theory, the term 'control signal' does not mean control in the sense of a direct mechanism that causally connects impulse and impact. It means the system-internal influence of risk-related decisions within the organization. This can be seen clearly in the case of the so-called administrative spaces: the examples presented above deal with programme spaces, especially administrative spaces which, according to Klüter (1994: 161), form programme spaces of the administrative units and which have evolved as strategies of spatial arrangement. This form of spatial arrangement determines the communication of the systems that handle risk: communication and thus also system structures (as expectations and expectations about expectations) are limited to these spaces. Which implications do these thoughts on space and risk have for risk management by state organizations? In order to observe risk management, it is highly important to analyse the different system levels involved. Which systems are involved? Which type of system (interaction or organization) and, connected to that, which system operations (such as decisions in organizations) are considered? Which function does this communication have in respect of the primary differentiation of society (function system level)? Each of these system types possesses independent mechanisms of system generation and demarcation. They operate in entirely different structures and have different functions for society. Even if the focus is placed on organizations in what follows, it should be noted that the possibility of analysing different system types presents an additional benefit for the observation of risks and their spatial dimensions.

One part of risk management is the definition of protection targets. From the content side, these targets are the result of political and scientific communication, which has a strong normative influence. The protection targets determine the actions of the state organizations. One field of action is the calculation of threshold values. Luhmann describes threshold values as a special type of political risk management (Luhmann 1997b: 210). They are seen as a kind of result and performance of the political system (Luhmann 1997b: 200). For this purpose it is only of minor importance if the threshold values are merely estimated. The important thing is that the political system can get rid of the problem by this form of regulation. The political system avoids a transformation of all risks into political risks, and a situation where all social risks are attributed to politics (Luhmann 1997b: 210).

Threshold values can be observed as a special form of decision programme in organizations, namely as conditional programmes. They separate conditions and consequences. By contrast, we distinguish purposive programmes that determine the goals to be achieved in the future, and differentiate them from the means to be applied (Luhmann 2006: 265). Conditional programmes are unproblematic to deal with for organizations, because they are a special type of uncertainty absorption. The identification of an assessment threshold for 100-year flood discharge levels, for example, appears to a state organization (administration) as clearly defined if it has previously been verified by science or politics, or by another system-external authority.

Risk management concepts like the use of threshold values as conditional programmes often apply spatial concepts. On the one hand, they always refer to the programme space of the organization (for administrative organizations these are the administrative spaces), while on the other hand there are explicitly spatial elements. These include areas, lines and locations:

1   *Land use designation and priority areas*
    Areas are especially suitable for risk prevention if the risks are spatially fixed and their extension well predictable, as is the case for floods, volcanoes or accidents in industrial facilities. In these cases, protection areas can be designated that imply limitations of utilization, ranging from adjusted building techniques to total interdiction of any utilization. Area designations are usually set up in Germany by the competent sectoral administration and adapted by the spatial planning authorities.

2   *Borderlines, 100-year flood discharge level (lines)*
    Not only areas, but also lines are applied in risk management. They are used to determine the 'borders' of the expansion of a hazard. In the case of flood risks, a line is drawn, up to which a flood will expand to the left and right of its riverbed with a certain probability. Often these lines form the borders of the prevention areas mentioned above. Linear elements are also used for technical protection measures, e.g. for dikes for flood prevention.

3   *Locations for control structures*
    The third form of spatial element in state risk management is constituted by locations in the form of spots. Barriers for the protection of landslides or

retaining dams that fulfil the function of flood protection can be counted in this category. These facilities are usually small-scale and are built at appropriate locations. They can be conceptualized as a supplementation of existing linear and laminar elements or as independent structures.

Operational state risk management always refers to administrative spaces. We have said earlier that programme spaces refer to the respective organization, in this case state organizations. This generates limits to risk management, in which administrative spaces are not communicatively existent, or do not match the expansion of the natural phenomenon (floods do not stop at political borders). This fact can easily be pilloried from a scientific point of view. However, from the system theory perspective it is obvious that any change, from introducing different spatial demarcations (upstream/downstream riparian states) to a new concept of action (purposive programming), can only succeed if it is initiated inside the system. In other words, adaptation to scientific (or any alternative) methods of risk management can only be carried out system-internally, due to the operational closedness of the systems. A change in the decision programmes is mandatory, and this can only be carried out through internal decisions in the organization.

Our examples in the context of spatial concepts and system theory

System theory helps us to observe the role of space in societal communication about risks. Each risk is a result of decisions within a social system. It results from and is part of system-internal evolution. Risk is just a (new) situation for the communication of elements within a system and can produce differentiation and further decisions (and of course new risks) in an autopoietic way. These developments may derive from events outside of the system, such as an earthquake. But these events are not directly responsible for developments within the system; they can only irritate the internal operation of the system.

At the heart of system theory lies communication. So risk communication is part of an integrative risk management concept. Traditional concepts of risk communication see risk communication as information about risks and dangers with the objective of clarification of given facts and education of lay people. With system theory premises, the successful transmission of any given (risk) information depends on the system itself. Due to the autopoietic operations of the system, the handling of the information depends on the internal structures of the system. The crucial moment of communication is 'understanding' within the system (see above). What does the system theory concept of risk mean for effective risk management? First, the general assumption that risk is a social construction has to be the premise of any effort to manage risk. Consequently, risk management has to analyse which social systems are involved, with special regard to the different types of social systems and their different kinds of communication. Risk management needs the perspective of a second-order observer to analyse who is the decision maker, and which other systems are affected. Thus, does the system construct something as a risk or a danger? Willingness to accept disadvantages and possible loss, as well as willingness to invest in adequate prevention measures, follow from this intrasystem attribution. There is no such thing as risk by itself. Risk always refers to one particular system, or to systems in the environment of a system.

In this view, all concepts of space mentioned in Table 4.1 are part of the communication within a function system, or within an organization. It should be remembered that 'naturalistic' concepts of space are just notions used in communication, even when they are described as 'natural areas', '(holistic) landscape' and so forth. When people talk about L'Aquila, Port-au-Prince, the Gulf of Mexico, the Dust Bowl in the Great Plains, the Mangroves of Myanmar, etc., all these places, areas and regions are just elements of communication.

With the theoretical background of the previous sections, we can summarize our empirical studies as follows:

- *'Spatial fit':* political organizations communicate with the help of the spatial concept 'administrative space'. As we have pointed out above, the decisions of the administration refer to their respective administrative space. 'Region' is the normal concept of space in this context. The administration has no other option than to operate in this spatial category. The administrative space is a special form of programme space and is therefore incorporated in their organization programme. Normally, however, these administrative spaces are strictly bound to the internal rationality of the administration. If there is a risk which crosses the administrative border of an organization, whether criminals or floods or volcanic ash, new administrative spaces are needed – the creation of which might well take years. Of course, the organization knows that it cannot force the flood to stop at the borders of the administrative unit. The only chance for applying their organization programme to the entire affected area is to create new organizations with a special spatial fit, or to switch to informal arrangements agreed on by the parties affected. However, creating a new administrative space is not the preferred option for organizations.
- *Prevention measures and different space-time concepts:* examples of spaces as media of communication are programme spaces. These can give guiding incentives to different social systems and generate spatial abstractions that are socially relevant, meaning that they refer to more than one specific interaction system. Such programme spaces in connection with risk are obvious in recovery programmes: Haiti, the city of L'Aquila, the riparian states of the Gulf of Mexico and other areas affected by disasters are the addressees of aid (infrastructure, money, etc.) donated by national governments, international organizations and NGOs. Furthermore, the opposite case also exists: spatial fit is necessary, but somehow ignored. With reference to our section on landslide early warning, it is obvious that different phases of risk management need well-defined competences and responsibilities. Administrative spaces as programme spaces of state organizations, produced and reproduced by these very state organizations, have not been developed for giving early warning of landslides in low mountain ranges (Swabian Alb).

Thus, there are no administrative spaces for the design and implementation of landslide early warning systems in the mitigation phase. Different or even non-existent programme spaces for the individual phases make installation of the necessary conditions for successful early warning impossible. These findings are important for the application of risk management: spaces can be formed by communication. It would thus be the task of risk management to form an administrative space for the mitigation phase, with development, installation and implementation of an early warning system, which defines clear-cut legal and political competencies, responsibility structures and decision trees. According to the assumptions of system theory, this can only happen within the system, through the state organizations themselves. Organizations need decision programmes through which they can orientate their operations and constitute their programme spaces. These decision programmes cannot be changed by any other system, but only by the organization itself. Other systems, such as science and scientific organizations, which are important for analysing risk management and trying to reform it, may irritate the state organizations (while hoping for a response), and may result in bringing about changes in their decision programmes.

- *The production of risky places:* the role of man in changing or even destroying nature (concepts 3 and 4) is part of scientific communication and is connected with the mass media. The mass media use and create places for their own purposes. Identifying a specific place where things happen lends authenticity to the messages of the mass media. Furthermore, they need landscapes as visual background and scenery for the presentation of their messages and the people they present (hungry children, boat people, politicians in rubber boots). The mass media are especially important for the formation of public opinion. Public opinion is the internal environment of the political system, shaping all political organizations and interactions.

Notes

1 The verb 'to risk' is derived from late Latin and Italian and means 'to sail around a cliff' ('resecum' means 'cliff', cf. also the Greek word 'rhisikon'). Risk as the decision of the sailor (in general: of a subject, of an organization, a system or a society) to take a particular route is related to spatial circumstances (Hubig 1994: 311; Luhmann 1993: 8–14).
2 These two phases of early warning as a prevention measure were analysed in the context of the Integrative Landslide Early Warning Systems (ILEWS) project dealing with early warning of landslide risks in the low mountain range of the Swabian Alb.
3 Unfortunately most of the literature by Luhmann and about Luhmann's system theory, and particularly the academic debate on the conception of space in system theory, has so far been published only in German.

5   The certainty of uncertainty

Topographies of risk and landscapes of fear in Sri Lanka's civil war[1]

Benedikt Korf

Introduction

'Warscapes' are landscapes saturated with the blood and destruction of violence, military combat, and guerrilla warfare. What does it mean to inhabit such a landscape of warfare? And what does this have to do with risk and uncertainty (and the theory thereof)? These two questions puzzled me in writing this chapter on living 'ordinary' lives in Sri Lanka's warscape: how can one live an 'ordinary', i.e. not unusual, exceptional, life in extraordinary, exceptional times, such as war? As Rebecca Walker reminds us: perhaps the paradox of living ordinary lives in extraordinary conditions involving daily experiences of violence and fear is that while such a life becomes an everyday experience, it does not necessarily become 'normal' (Walker 2010: 13): 'Given that it is regular, usual, and unexceptional in this particular context, it might be seen as ordinary. Yet, at the same time, it appears to exceed the limits of "ordinariness".' While the question of the ordinary is interesting by itself, in this chapter, I will explore the (extra-)ordinariness of inhabiting warscapes through the landscapes of risk and uncertainty that have shaped 'ordinary' living in this context.

The term 'warscape' was first proposed by Caroline Nordstrom (1997) to describe the fluid landscapes of warfare and the lifeworlds 'ordinary' people develop. Nordstrom, of course, built her neologism on Arjun Appadurai (1996: 33) who used the suffix 'scape' to refer to 'the fluid, irregular shapes of [...] landscapes [...] which are eventually navigated by agents who both experience and constitute larger formations'. Appadurai identified a number of such 'scapes', e.g. ethnoscapes or mediascapes. Appadurai's 'scapes' were mostly de-territorialized, imagined, communicated 'landscapes' in a broader sense. Warscapes, in turn, are clearly (re-)territorialized 'scapes' – battlefields, terrain, territories, borders – which produce risk, uncertainty and fear.

When Ulrich Beck wrote his influential *Risikogesellschaft* and later *Weltrisikogesellschaft* (Beck 1986, 2007), he mainly discussed the risks of natural disasters and human-made disasters, and concluded that risks do not know boundaries any more, that we share a world risk society. Beck's account fits into a wide array of studies which discuss the link between modernity and risk. Here, the conceptual distinction between risk that is calculable, and uncertainty that is not, is a central tenet (Bonss 1995; Jaeger *et al*. 2001; O'Malley 2004; Renn 2008). Risk is conceived as a strategy for transforming unmanageable contingency into manageable complexity (Zinn 2006). Uncertainty, these studies suggest, is an everyday experience that seems to be ubiquitous; it is not confined to specific societies. And yet, experiences of uncertainty vary across contexts, societies and landscapes, and require an approach that is closer to what Zinn (2006) has framed as a 'socio-cultural approach to risk' (e.g. Tulloch and Lupton 2003) or 'risk culture' (Lash 2000), both of which aim at describing the complex and dynamic process of risk issues in everyday life.

The globalizing risks of modernity that influence most of the sociology of risk literature are quite different to the micro-geographies of risk and uncertainty that shape everyday experiences, and the ordinariness and extraordinariness of living in warscapes. In the analysis of warscapes as landscapes of risk and uncertainty that this chapter proposes, the distinction between risk and uncertainty is analytically important. In *Risk, Uncertainty and Profit* (1921), Frank Knight famously proposed the conceptual distinction between 'risk' (randomness with knowable probabilities) and 'uncertainty' (randomness with unknowable probabilities). Uncertainty, write Mehta *et al*. (2001: 2), 'describes a situation where we don't know what we don't know. This is [...] distinct from risk, where probabilities of outcome can be calculated.' But how far is life in a warscape simply a risk or rather an incalculable gamble? What is certain in warscapes is the 'certainty of uncertainty' (Hoffmann and Lubkemann 2005: 318):

> In a context in which the certainty of uncertainty has become a fundamental
> reality in the lives of social actors, the relationship between the unpredictable
> moment and the predictable one have been normatively inverted. Inasmuch
> as instability has become the norm, unpredictability has become unremarkable,
> and the predictable moment the one marked as exceptional. Such 'event-full'
> lives challenge [...] the subjects who must live them.

One could also say: people live with a higher level of 'alertness'. Living in warscapes is stressful, it bears risks, fears, vulnerabilities – and at the same time, warscape inhabitants have to learn to live with this alertness – to live some kind of normalcy, some kind of ordinary life. When Hoffmann and Lubkemann talk about the certainty of uncertainty, they provide a semantic connotation of this level of alertness, of fearing 'to be at the wrong place at the wrong time'. It is here that the (extra-)ordinariness comes into play: landscapes of risk and uncertainty combine 'ordinary' – in the sense of usual, known – elements of risk and extraordinary levels of alertness that have become an everyday experience (the alertness, the certainty of uncertainty), but certainly not 'normal'. In this way, landscapes of risk and uncertainty are also landscapes of fear. When Yi-Fu Tuan wrote his classic humanistic study on *Landscapes of Fear* (1978), he defined the latter as cognitive landscapes, as mental processes of imagined geographies, which he found in children's stories, for example. Tuan's constructivist approach is suggestive, but misses out on the material production of such landscapes of fear:

landscapes of fear are not only internalized imaginaries, they are also the product of a material re-working of the physical landscape, in the case of warscapes through destruction or military confinement and enclosure (e.g. through the barbed wire of checkpoints).

Warscape as landscape of risk and uncertainty

In this chapter, I will investigate the landscape of risk and uncertainty in the former Sri Lankan civil war, and the landscape(s) of fear that emerge out of the geographies of violence this particular warscape produced. This warscape is of particular interest as we can identify the spatialization of risk and uncertaintyscapes in different war dynamics: in the first empirical period discussed here, the war had resulted in a kind of low-intensity equilibrium between the two military adversaries, the Liberation Tigers of Tamil Eelam (LTTE) and the Sri Lankan military forces. This is the Sri Lankan civil war prior to the ceasefire agreement in 2002. During this period, a very specific geography of risk and uncertainty developed that shaped the everyday practices of the inhabitants of this warscape. The second empirical period that will be discussed is the post-ceasefire period after 2002, where, paradoxically, uncertainty *increased*, as there was a proliferation of militant parties and shadow zones of crime, intimidation and killings.

The Sri Lankan civil war, fought between the Sri Lankan security forces and the LTTE, developed a very specific guerilla geography in the east. This was also the result of the military strategies of the two parties, as the main theatre of conflict was in the north (in Jaffna), and both conflict parties had limited armed personnel on the ground in the more peripheral territories outside of this main theatre. The Sri Lankan security forces mainly controlled the major towns and the main roads during daylight, but large parts of the rural areas were under the full control of the LTTE. These areas were called 'uncleared' areas – in the language of the Sri Lankan military, those territories not (yet) cleared of the LTTE. But the semantics of cleared vs. uncleared areas give the impression of two pure, distinct spaces, each being under the control of one party. That was certainly not the case. The discourse of 'cleared/uncleared' obscured the fact that the realities of control were much more fluid: the armed forces controlled the so-called 'cleared' areas only during daytime; at night, they largely withdrew to their camps (to minimize their combat risk) and left the floor open for the LTTE to infiltrate and do their business (taxation, intimidation of anti-LTTE elements).

When I conducted fieldwork in 1999–2001 (period one), military combat in Trincomalee only took place on a low-intensity scale, with occasional small skirmishes and battles between LTTE cadres and security forces, but no major offensive from either side. A kind of power equilibrium with a demarcated spatial separation between 'cleared' (i.e. government controlled) and 'uncleared' (i.e. LTTE controlled) areas had developed. Cleared versus uncleared territories were materially demarcated by checkpoints, barbed wire and a mental boundary, although this borderline, as I have pointed out, was not impermeable, either for the

LTTE or for civilians, who often lived in uncleared areas but travelled to cleared areas for work, trade or other business.

What interests us here are the two elements in the landscape of risk and uncertainty that emerged from this guerilla geography: inhabitants of the warscape faced (1) an element of risk, those aspects of a more or less settled equilibrium of territorial control, of hotspots of risk, of the cleared/uncleared dialectic, which they could accommodate into their livelihood strategies, and (2) an element of uncertainty, an incalculable possibility of sudden attacks and fighting where they could become trapped in the middle, especially as their spaces of livelihood production (e.g. paddy fields, the sea) often also constituted the border zone between LTTE and the army in which skirmishes were most likely to take place. While a person could develop a risk strategy to deal with the first aspect, the certainty of uncertainty was more difficult to tackle. Although there were several known 'risky' places, often places at the borderline between areas controlled by the two parties, which one could try to avoid, a place could suddenly become dangerous, for example by the presence of an army convoy which could become the target of an attack. As a result, the topography of risk and uncertainty developed very specific spatial and temporal characteristics, and helped form a landscape of fear where certain places were inscribed with imaginaries of uncertainty and fear, while others could become sources of refuge (see Table 5.1).

What imaginary a place could hold was not fixed, but subject to change in time and space, again depending on changing battlefield geographies and particular events. Following the logic of the cleared/uncleared equilibrium, a particular place could be a source of security, e.g. one's own village, while the space outside it, such as the jungle, the sea or the paddy fields, could be filled with imaginaries of fear and uncertainty. Following the logic of attack, a place could be a prime source of risk as a target of attack (e.g. Sinhalese border villages), and the outside space, the jungle or the fields, could become a place of refuge, a place to hide, to withdraw from the place of attack. These different connotations of imaginaries of threat, fear, refuge, risk and uncertainty are fluid, they are not fixed in space and time. Similarly, responding to elements of risk and uncertainty requires a re-working of spatial practices of livelihood production and everyday movements across space (Korf and Fünfgeld 2006: 394).

Table 5.1 Risk, uncertainty and ordinariness

Risk	Uncertainty
calculable	escapes calculability
'ordinary'	'extraordinary'
marked places	diffuse space

Living with the certainty of uncertainty

In this section, I will explore empirically what it means to live with the certainty of uncertainty by travelling with different persons who live 'ordinary' lives in warscapes. This exposition will show how farmers, fishing folk and local traders managed their livelihoods in the midst of the ongoing military combat between the Liberation Tigers of Tamil Eelam (LTTE) and the Sri Lankan armed forces. I will trace the movements and strategies of different agents in the landscape of war. While there is a certain danger of producing homogenizing or generalizing accounts of 'Tamil farmers' or 'Muslim traders' doing this or that, sharing a particular set of aspirations, fears, hopes or strategies, some generalizations can be made. When discussing 'a Tamil farmer's landscapes of risk and uncertainty', for example, this is an analytical abstraction: I will not narrate the personal life histories of specific individuals, but rather indicate rough maps of landscapes of risk and uncertainty that would affect similar agents in similar ways. In other words, most Tamil farmers living in the same place, though each having their own distinct life histories, would nevertheless have similar risk and uncertaintyscapes as produced by the geographies of violence. And this was so, both in the material sense that certain places were, indeed, more risky, and in the sense that there were shared imaginations of specific places being risky or otherwise.

Henrik Vigh (2006, 2009) has used the terminology of 'social navigation' to encompass 'instability' and movement in our understanding of action in warscapes, while building on an awareness of both individual will and social forces (Vigh 2006: 135). Vigh's concept underlines, *first*, how actors concomitantly steer through their immediate and imagined lifeworld, both in relation to their current placing within a given order and to their imagined future placing, and *second*, how actors behave in relation to other actors, to a given predominant social order, and to intricate interactions between actors, events and the shifting constellations of these social orders (Korf *et al.* 2010). This is also relevant for navigating in landscapes of risk and uncertainty. Vigh particularly emphasizes that with increasing navigation experience, tactics and strategies employed by people living in warscapes become ingrained in everyday practice. Arguably, while people largely incorporate risk tactics, dealing with the certainty of uncertainty, with the level of doubt that is omnipresent, is more difficult to internalize in everyday social practice, as it constantly calls these practices into doubt.

Let us now look at some of these navigation strategies. All the situations and contexts described here are taken from places located within a relatively small territory, and yet their landscapes of risk and uncertainty were very different (Korf 2004). These people lived in a jigsaw of different ethnic communities, livelihoods and political–military boundaries (those between cleared and uncleared, see Figure 5.1). Mutur and Seruvila, the two sub-districts where these people were living, are characterized by a rural economy largely based on paddy cultivation and fishing. Mutur is a Tamil–Muslim mixed territory, while Seruvila is a predominantly Sinhalese sub-district. In Mutur sub-district, Tamils and Muslims mostly live in mono-ethnic localities (with the exception of the market town of

Mutur and a few other places, where both ethnicities lived in the same town, though mostly in separate quarters), but these different localities are positioned side by side like pieces of a jigsaw. A substantial part of Mutur sub-district (D.S. division) was controlled by the LTTE and demarcated as an 'uncleared' area. When a person wanted to enter or leave these areas, he or she had to pass military checkpoints. Seruvila, in turn, is largely a Sinhalese settler colony that was brought into the area after 1950 with the establishment of a large irrigation scheme, the Allai Extension Scheme. Since the ethnic conflict became aggravated in the 1980s, these settlements were increasingly militarized to make them defensible against LTTE attacks. While Tamils' and Muslims' livelihoods were entangled through trade, land use and other things, the Sinhalese largely lived separately from the Tamils and Muslims in their daily life, as well as being physically separated by checkpoints and military defence infrastructure.

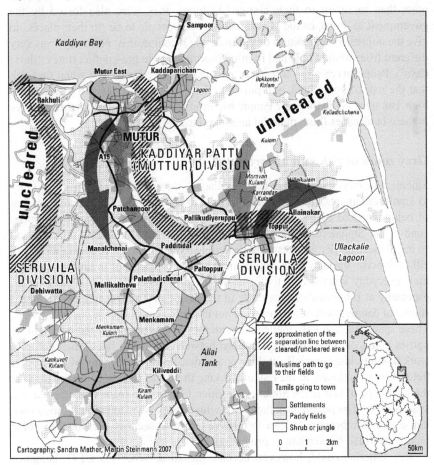

Figure 5.1 Warscape Sri Lanka – a landscape of risk and uncertainty

The relationship between the three communities has not been an easy one since the ethnic conflict escalated after 1983. In the 1980s, there were several massacres where militants attacked villagers from another ethnic group. Often, when the LTTE attacked and killed Sinhalese villagers, the army would retaliate by displacing, killing and torturing Tamil villagers. But a number of violent incidents also occurred between Tamils and Muslims, pitting against each other the two communities who were living side by side. While these mass killings were predominant in the 1980s, in the early stage of the ethnic conflict, the 1990s saw periods of relative calmness alternating with more violent periods. Most people now living in these places have been displaced at least once in their lives, and many have been displaced several times (Gaasbeek 2010). While some, often the more affluent urban elite, moved outside the war zone, those whose livelihoods were based on local natural resources, or who had little wealth, had few options other than to return to their homes. At times, they were also forced by the government to do so, as the government needed people to be 'in their places' to give the impression of a return to 'normalcy'. Of course, this 'normalcy' was very different from what people had in mind (normalcy as in pre-conflict times: 'those days'). People were often forced or 'encouraged' to return, even when they felt that the risk of going back and pursuing their livelihoods was still significantly high. But what could they do? People had little other choice than to return and live in these landscapes (both material and imagined).

Grey zones of risk and uncertainty

Sinhalese farmers living in the 'border villages', those locations in close proximity to Tamil settlements, lived with the certainty of uncertainty, with the constant fear of being attacked by the LTTE. These 'border villages' had become a frontier zone of the Sinhalese-dominated state against the Tamil militants. The farmers living in these border villages were becoming 'frontiersmen' (Thangarajah 2003), either directly, through their employment as home guards, or indirectly, through their everyday situation of living at the edge of rebel territory. Paddy fields, especially at the outside edges close to the jungle or Tamil localities, became a source of danger, as these spaces were not under the control of the security forces. These spaces were highly malleable, with lots of movements of the two fighting parties going on. One could get trapped between the battle lines when going to work in the fields, especially at dusk or at dawn. As a result, many of these outer fields were abandoned, as the risk of working there was seen as being too high. In the landscape of fear at the Sinhalese frontier, this outside space was mapped as a space of risk. The people saw their own village, their own community, their own house as a safe heaven, at least in relative terms, as security personnel or home guards provided some sense of protection.

This situation could, however, become unsettled. When the LTTE launched attacks on such border villages, the safe heaven became hell. The village, the house, then became a target, a high-risk place, where it would not be safe to stay. When attacks happened, villagers often fled to the jungle, to the outside space, away from their homes. In these terrible moments, the outside space, although normally considered as a space of risk, became a safer location to go to, to hide, to wait and see, than the village and the home. Those who fled the village stayed in these outside spaces as long as they were afraid or unsure about the situation in their village. What had been inscribed as a space of risk in the everyday landscape of fear became, for the moment of attack, temporarily a safer place. At the same time, people would leave that outside space to return to their homes as soon as they thought it to be safe and possible. The safer place outside was only a temporary refuge.

Many Tamil farmers lived in LTTE-controlled areas, the so-called 'uncleared areas'. These areas were clearly demarcated by army control points on one side of the border and LTTE checkpoints on the other side. In 'those' areas, many Tamil farmers depended on resources that were located outside uncleared areas. Some farmers had to cross the border in order to access their fields, which were located in cleared areas. This was the case especially for a number of better-off farmers who owned land in the Allai Extension Scheme. Other Tamils crossed the border in search of wage labour in the fields of Tamil or Muslim farmers who lived and had their fields in the cleared areas. Again, other Tamil farmers cultivated paddy or vegetables inside the uncleared areas, but had to cross the border in order to sell their produce to mainly Muslim traders in the nearby market town of Toppur.

Whatever their livelihood portfolio, most of these Tamil farmers had in common the risky task of having to pass the military checkpoints that controlled the borders. These material landscapes of barbed wire also visibly marked the border as a dangerous boundary. For military personnel, any Tamil coming from the LTTE-controlled areas was under suspicion: he could be an LTTE cadre hiding under the disguise of an 'innocent' farmer pursuing his daily business. Most vulnerable were those among the Tamils who were at an age where they would be likely to be recruited by the LTTE or to be an LTTE cadre. An elderly man would probably pass the checkpoint much more easily than a young one. Women were less likely to be put into custody, tortured or just harassed, although also women had some doubts in their minds as they were vulnerable to sexual harassment.[2] Crossing the materially and militarily marked border between the two territories meant passing through a high-risk space. But people were ready to take that risk as they had to secure their livelihoods.

The border was militarily fortified as it was also a prime theatre of military battle. Therefore, crossing the boundary could also mean becoming trapped in a sudden attack from one side or the other. The LTTE might attack a military post, or the military might attack the territories adjacent to cleared areas, often in retaliation for attacks by the LTTE. Or one could get trapped in some operation by deep penetration units, which were small government troops encroaching into rebel-held territory. The space that became dangerous was not only confined to the military checkpoint as such, but encompassed a much wider space situated in the 'grey zone' between the two territories. Similarly to the frontier between Sinhalese and Tamil settlements (within government-controlled areas), this grey zone was often abandoned, i.e. fields would be left uncultivated, and houses vacated, as these grey zones were spaces of high risk. Those passing by would do so with an element of doubt, of fear, with the certainty of uncertainty that just at the very moment when they had to pass through these grey zones, something terrible *could* happen. Therefore, the border area and the adjacent grey zones had two elements – the element of daily risk involved in passing through the checkpoint, experiences of low-level harassment, or possibly being arrested, and the element of uncertainty that an attack could happen any moment. The element of risk could to some extent be handled, tactics could be developed, for example by developing a relationship with security personnel, or by sending less vulnerable members of a household to go to cleared areas (e.g. women or elderly people), but the second element of uncertainty was more difficult to deal with. Of course, when tensions arose, when there were rumours of imminent attacks, people could try to avoid or postpone a journey across the border, but this was not always possible, and while there were rumours anticipating attacks for all sorts of reasons, it was difficult to make any prediction as to when an attack was really imminent. Sometimes, as Timmo Gaasbeck (2010) describes in some detail, inhabitants fled from a particular place in anticipation of violence, i.e. in the expectation of an attack, or a violent incident, based on some sort of information or rumour, before such an incident had taken place (if it did at all).

Another example shows the vulnerability of living trapped between the lines. Muslim fishermen in a small village called Vattam lived at the frontier zone between the army and the LTTE. Their village on the outskirts of Mutur town bordered the uncleared areas; it ended in no-man's land. The basis of the livelihood of many villagers, the local fishing grounds, had become the theatre of regular military skirmishes, and their place of living a pathway for LTTE cadres. The security forces restricted fishing and imposed bans for certain locations and times. Coming back late from the sea could be very dangerous, as the navy suspected small vessels on the sea during the times of ban as being 'sea tigers', cadres of the LTTE trying to infiltrate government territory or attacking navy boats. Going out to sea was risky, but necessary as there was no other way of earning an income (other than migration).

But these Muslims also had to live with the imminent threat, the certainty of uncertainty, of becoming the target of an attack by the LTTE – as they were an easy target. Their location at the border, on the outskirts of town, on the coast, made them vulnerable to attacks from both land and sea. Vattam also had a physical geography that made it an easy target for the attackers: it is situated on a narrow peninsula bounded on three sides by water: the sea, the mouth of the Kattaiparaichchan river and a lagoon. An attacker could quickly return to uncleared areas, as a lagoon separated the village from the town and other military checkpoints. And in fact, Vattam has experienced a history of being attacked. One of the worst is described in Timmo Gaasbeck's PhD dissertation: at the height of Tamil–Muslim riots in April 2003, the LTTE and a mob orchestrated by them entered Vattam and looted the village 'to teach the Muslims a lesson' (Gaasbeek 2010). Vattam was probably one of the easiest targets for such an attack. Living at the border, in the grey zone, trapped between the lines, meant being exposed to the certainty of uncertainty, living in a landscape of fear that was not manageable, not calculable.

Also, many Muslims were engaged in farming. Many of them lived in one of the local market towns (Mutur, Toppur), but their fields were located in the rural landscape that was dominated by Tamil villages. Fields belonging to Muslims and Tamils lay side by side. Historically, Tamils and Muslims had a highly integrated rural economy, and at times Muslims had bought land from Tamils (when these sold it to finance dowries, education etc.); at other times, Muslims sold land to Tamils when they became afraid to come to these locations in times of heightening tension (especially when the fields were located in Tamil-inhabited areas, see Gaasbeek 2010). During relatively calm periods, Muslim farmers would travel to their fields, passing by Tamil villages and fields owned by Tamils, or they would hire wage labourers or lease out their land to tenant cultivators, often Tamils, to do the cultivation, but came for supervision, wage payments or to collect their share of the crop. This fragile equilibrium, however, could always break down as soon as the security situation deteriorated. When fighting became intense between security forces and the LTTE, travel along the major roads would be considered as dangerous or even prohibited in case of curfews.

This situation became more uncertain after the war had officially ended (only temporarily, as we now know) with the ceasefire agreement in 2002. Inter-communal relations between Tamils and Muslims became more strained and several incidences of Tamil–Muslim riots and violence emerged. This made the situation for Muslim landowners even more delicate. Often, they were afraid or unable to go to the fields, when inter-ethnic tension was in the air or when roadblocks were erected. What had been a risky, but calculable enterprise, to go to the fields, became impossible. The territory of the ethnic other became a no-go area. Tamil farmers were then unable to go to a Muslim market town to sell their products.

The fragility of normalcy

Paradoxically, when a kind of 'normalcy' was installed after the ceasefire agreement in 2002, the risk and uncertainty for Muslims and Tamils rather *increased* compared to prior to the ceasefire. For Muslim farmers, the risk involved in going to their fields *increased* after the ceasefire of 2002 as the two former fighting parties (the Sri Lankan army and the LTTE) were frozen into their distinct territories (although the LTTE continued its infiltration into cleared areas) and open military combat was constrained. But this created opportunities for Tamil–Muslim riots and violence to come to the fore, this often being politically orchestrated in the difficult politics of gaining political supremacy over the multi-ethnic east. The LTTE had an interest in teaching the Muslims a lesson about who was the boss in town, and the Muslims tried to rally their forces to withstand this threat. But this meant that the warscape became an even more complex landscape of risk and uncertainty: before the ceasefire, the two military parties were the main power holders and their power was materially re-inscribed in the landscape of barbed wire, checkpoints and security regulations. After the ceasefire, the equilibrium of cleared/uncleared became shaken up. It became much less clear who was in control when and where, who were the different actors involved in trying to impose their rule, and what this meant for the daily risk of going to distant places. While prior to the ceasefire, there was a dominant element of calculable risk, the certainty of uncertainty came more to the fore *after* the ceasefire – a situation emerged where things were much less calculable, where dangers loomed constantly in the background.

'You only open your mouth to eat' a Tamil friend told me when I met him in Batticaloa, the district town in the neighbouring district of Trincomalee, in 2005. What he described was the paranoia that had developed among Tamils in the east after the split-up of the LTTE that occurred in 2004.[3] At that time, the then local commander of the LTTE in the east, known as Colonel Karuna, split from the LTTE and sought refuge among the security forces. What followed was a 'cleaning-up' campaign by both sides, Karuna and the LTTE. Killings and abductions took place on a daily basis, and the 'white vans' which appeared and took people away, even in daylight, became a permanent presence in Batticalo. This friend told me: 'You can't trust anybody, not even your wife! You just don't know which side someone is on.' Saying a wrong word could be dangerous, meaning that one suspected someone of supporting the other camp. As little was known about who supported who, talking politics became impossible. Those who did often paid with their lives.

In this case, we see another landscape of fear, one that is increasingly unsettled by a rising level of uncertainty. Calculable risk has somehow vanished from everyday life, the certainty of uncertainty has become the prime experience. And all this was taking place, although technically there was still 'peace', for a ceasefire was in force. But the ceasefire was between the army and the LTTE, not the LTTE and the Karuna group. The situation became even more complicated after there were also splits within the Karuna group, and the number of militants, gangs and thugs multiplied, in particular after the security forces had successfully 'cleared' the east of the LTTE and restored 'normalcy'. A strange kind of 'normalcy', indeed. The certainty of uncertainty had taken the upper hand; life was no longer a calculable risk.

The paradox is that this situation emerged after the end of military combat. What this also indicates is the malleability of landscapes of risk and uncertainty, their fragility. Perhaps, though, this is not surprising. Another Tamil friend explained to me that what she was afraid of were moments when things were changing, e.g. a ceasefire had collapsed, and in the immediate aftermath of renewed fighting, the rules of the game and the power balances were not clear to 'ordinary' people. When the civil war was ongoing, the situation was difficult, but nevertheless more stable, more manageable: some expectations about the behaviour of the major players, their local presence at specific moments, their spatial movements and spaces of control were at least roughly known. This gave some stability to the everyday experiences of risk and uncertainty, but this stability vanished completely with the disintegration of authority, the fragmentation of Tamil militancy and the breakdown of public order.[4]

Transgressions[5]

Whenever there are borders, these will be crossed, and possibly transgressed. Someone has to keep communication flows going across borders, between different camps or military parties. In situations where borders have become almost impermeable lines, or risky places due to intensified battlefield dynamics, who can cross these borders in order to communicate across the lines? The challenge of crossing borders was that as soon as someone became too noticeable as a local (civic) leader, as someone who might challenge the rule of either of the two combat parties, he or she became extremely vulnerable, a target of attack, arrest and torture. For the neighbouring district of Batticaloa, Goodhand *et al.* (2000) noted a kind of leadership vacuum, as becoming too noticeable meant exposing oneself to possible retaliation. Only a few actors would qualify under such conditions to take over functions as travellers across borders.

In many places of Sri Lanka's east, Catholic (Jesuit) priests played a dominant role in keeping up communication between cleared and uncleared areas, in delivering relief across borders, even in turbulent times. Historically, the Catholic Church had developed a stronghold in the east. The Jesuits derived their position from their recognized role as religious leaders; they were also highly visible and distinguishable in a crowd through their special habit and they had the intellectual capacities to defend the position of vulnerable people. Also, through the global network of the Catholic Church, they had excellent connections to the wider world which they could use if needed. Most Jesuits were Tamils (although a few old foreign missionaries still lived in Batticaloa), and while they tended to sympathize with Tamil nationalism, some were critical of the LTTE, while others may have been quite close to them. When, after 2006, the security forces started a military offensive against the LTTE in Batticalo and Trincomalee, where more than 200,000 people became temporarily displaced, and where civilians were often trapped between the lines, Jesuits were often the only agents who could cross from government-controlled areas to grey zones or even LTTE-controlled areas.

The Catholic church compounds often became places of refuge for Tamils, both Christians and Hindus, when a situation deteriorated, when attacks took place, or inter-communal tension arose. The church compound was clearly demarcated, and the priests were considered as strong and powerful brokers who could keep militants out of that compound. Therefore, in times of imminent threat, of gross danger, when fear was abundant, these compounds became little islands of refuge for Tamils. Their status as priests gave the Jesuits a tacit untouchability, something civic leaders, local politicians or elders did not have to the same extent. In the landscape of fear, the church compounds became a place of refuge and the Jesuits a symbol of protection.

But this protection did not always work. In a few places these islands were invaded, the boundary of the compound violated and people or priests killed. This indicates that traversing borders is a fragile, delicate affair and requires the willingness to take political risks. Also, the manoeuvering space for religious brokers was limited in scope: they could not change politics or military dynamics. They could deploy tactics of transgression that would not challenge the overall political order, but they had to stay outside politics proper. While the clergy played a role in keeping communication channels open to civilians trapped in the crossfire between security forces and the LTTE, they had little chance to change these battlefield dynamics or to interfere in internal LTTE politics.

Toward a grounded theory of risk, uncertainty and space

A warscape like the one in Sri Lanka can be described as a place where everyday life is a *constant* struggle with risks and with the certainty of uncertainty, where a high level of alertness has become normal. But contrary to many vague imaginations of such warscapes as hours of darkness, as 'culture in chaos' (Lubkemann 2008), as places of barbaric disorder, Stephen Lubkemann reminds us that war is not a matter of 'all terror all the time' (Lubkemann 2008: 13). Warscapes are sites of 'a complex and multi-dimensional agenda of social struggles [...] and life projects' that take shape in a context in which 'the certainty of uncertainty has become a fundamental reality in the lives of social actors' (Lubkemann 2008: 13). I concur with Lubkemann's argument – and have tried to spatialize his important point: by emphasizing that warscapes are also landscapes of risk and uncertainty, I have suggested that war is not a matter of 'all terror all the time *all over the place*' (Korf *et al.* 2010: 4). Jonathan Spencer (2003: 12) writes that 'those who live in the war zone both adapt themselves to the social and spatial contexts, and transform space to suit their own needs and practices'. This is true – but up to a certain point only, as far as the geography of risk and uncertainty allows them to do so.

In this chapter, I have sketched a grounded theory of risk, uncertainty and space to study warscapes. I have drawn an analytical distinction between risk as calculable and uncertainty as that which escapes calculation. The first is a kind of calculable risk that allows spatial movement in a circumscribed territory and a material landscape of barbed wire, boundary drawing and the mental landscape of fear that people inscribe into these material landscapes. The second layer is the certainty of uncertainty that Lubkemann describes – the level of doubt, of alertness, of knowledge that any time a terrible event could happen. And still, this event is more likely to happen in some places than in others, at some times more than others (for example during the night, or on certain dates when the LTTE celebrated past glories, battles and deaths and used those dates to mark their presence by attacks). Of course, in the messy realities of living in warscapes, these two elements of risk and uncertainty are often blurred.

Warscapes are *landscapes* of risk and uncertainty – landscapes in a territorial as much as an imaginary sense. Places, spaces, territories are associated with connotations of fear, of safety, of home, of alienness, of immanent threat, etc. But the production of these landscapes of fear has a material basis: which place, space or territory has which connotations depends on the geography of violence, the spaces of terror and confinement (Oslender 2007), the material production of a landscape of war with its barbed wire, destroyed houses, decapitated palm trees, armed soldiers and rebels. Analytically, the geography of risk and uncertainty entails both their material production and their geographical imaginations, their landscapes of fear. These landscapes are created by war, and they are imagined, filled with meaning and re-appropriated in the everyday practices of their inhabitants.

This begs the question: when people live in a situation of certainty of uncertainty, of high levels of alertness, do they get used to chronic levels of uncertainty? To some extent, this may be true in the case we studied. People became used to the sound of shelling, to the everyday practices of getting by, but never would they describe this situation as 'normal'. The certainty of uncertainty, the everyday awareness that 'something could happen', or just the fact that after 6pm one avoided travelling, being outside the home, were situations that were not taken as normal, were not internalized, not purely routinized, as Vigh (2006) seems to imply. 'Normal' were 'the old days' – the time before the conflict started, before 1983 (the Tamil pogrom in Colombo), and even the government used the rhetoric of 'restoring normalcy' to the war-affected areas by defeating the LTTE and clearing the northeast of the 'terrorist' elements. In this sense, most actors would have some imagination of 'normalcy', although these might differ according to ethnic affiliation, class, caste and gender.

Uncertainty and risk and their spatial dynamics, the certainty of uncertainty, become engrained in everyday practices, but never become 'normal' or ordinary, as Rebecca Walker reminds us (2010: 13). The high level of alertness, the doubt that looms in the background of everyday life that something terrible could happen here and now, is never considered as ordinary. People living in warscapes – and this is the key fact that emerged from studying their everyday practices and imaginations – can always say what is 'normal' and what is not, and war always remains something exceptional, extraordinary, in these imaginations and practices.

Notes

1 I would like to thank Sarah Byrne, Martin Doevenspeck, Timmo Gaasbeck, Pia Hollenbach and Bart Klem for comments on previous drafts of this paper. Funding for fieldwork is gratefully acknowledged from the following sources: Deutsche Gesellschaft für Technische Zusammenarbeit mbH (GTZ), Zentrum für Entwicklungsforschung, Bonn (ZEF), the Non-Governmental Public Action Programme (NGPA) of the British Economic and Social Science Research Council (ESRC, grant no. RES-155-25-0096) and the Swiss National Science Foundation (grants no. PDFMP1-123181/1 and no. 100013_124459/1).

2 See Hyndman and de Alwis (2004) for more details on the geographies of checkpoints in Sri Lanka's warscape, from a feminist perspective.

3 For a description of life in these circumstances, see Rebecca Walker's excellent article (2010) and her PhD thesis *Enduring Violence and the Question of the Ordinary in Contemporary Sri Lanka* (2012).

4 This post-2004 situation was organized anarchy: the state had an interest in the multiplication of Tamil militant groups, of the fragmentation of Tamil militancy. It was a formidable weapon of the state against the LTTE. And the state orchestrated this by giving weapons and money to some militants and letting them operate, even though the military could have easily stopped them. They could only operate under the protection of the security forces (otherwise, the LTTE would have exterminated them).

5 This section builds on joint work with Jonathan Goodhand, Bart Klem, Shahul Hasbullah and Jonathan Spencer in Batticaloa and Amparai (e.g. Goodhand *et al.* 2009).

6 Anxiety and risk

Pandemics in the twenty-first century

Jonathan Everts

Introduction: anxiety and risk

The terms anxiety and risk seem to stem from two different conceptual worlds. The first one is tied to personal experiences of distress and concern, and is rooted in the body as the primary site of these experiences (cf. James 1983 [1884]). The second one emerged from early capitalistic calculations of probabilities of loss and gain, and has to do with rational practices of managing and assessing uncertainties (Bernstein 1998). Anxiety, like its conceptual siblings such as fear or angst, invokes the emotional side of being human. Anxiety as an individual state of fear seems to stand for irrationality. This, as some of the risk literature suggests, has to be overcome by rational risk analyses that assess the likelihoods and probabilities in respect of those events that people are most worried about (for an overview, see Zinn 2006; Renn 2008). But considering the challenges of global threats such as pandemics, terrorism or climate change, the concepts of risk and anxiety share more than the accidental dichotomy of the rational and the irrational.

The 'risk society' approach and similar interpretations of reflexive modernity have all stressed the significance of anxiety-inducing events or the anticipation of these (Van Loon 2002; Beck 1992; Giddens 1991). From various environmental disasters (real and imagined) to the technological production of risks to anxieties about the health and shape of the individual body, these concerns have been placed centre-stage in explaining the forces that shape and change the late modern world. Crucial for these understandings is the idea that we are living increasingly in a world that changes, not according to what has happened, but according to what is anticipated, i.e. what may happen in the future (Beck 2008). The anticipation of a catastrophe, or put less starkly, the anticipation of a distressing future event, is therefore the first commonality shared by the concepts of risk and anxiety. Both are linked to the ways in which the future is imagined, and subsequently to how the present needs to be organised in order to prevent or deal with that future.

The second commonality is the occupation with events that may or may not happen. Whereas risk analysis assesses the probability that an event will happen in the future, often expressed through statistics and downplaying the more severe possibilities, anxiety or fear usually revolve around the worst-case scenario and the inevitability of its happening (Svendsen 2008). Having said that, this distinction is only a subtle one, whereas the notion of the event as something bad that could happen is intrinsic to the concepts of risk and anxiety alike. Such an event is usually one that is projected into the future but has roots in the past (cf. Anderson 2010). There may be direct links to the past in the sense that something happened elsewhere or a long time ago (such as pandemics, plane crashes, terrorist attacks) and it is believed that it may happen again in the future, perhaps on an even grander scale. And there may be indirect links to the past, such as fearing that an anticipated event could be worse than anything that has happened before, or the gathering of more or less insignificant events as evidence for something bigger that could eventually lead to disaster.

The third connection between risk and anxiety is the attention the anticipated event raises and the immediate calls for action or reaction it sparks. When a risk is 'selected' (Douglas and Wildavsky 1983), it needs to be assessed, categorised and subsequently managed. The same holds true for anxieties that urge the anxious body to do or leave certain things, to go to or avoid specific places, people or objects and to organise and arrange the present in order to prevent unwanted futures (cf. Barbalet 1998: 149–69). Both therefore have the power to inflict change. They are active agents that direct attention towards what seem to be the most pressing dangers or uncertainties.

The fourth connection is a more philosophical one, but one that explains the power of both risk and anxiety. Both terms point not only towards something potentially harmful that may happen, but also to the possibility of 'nothingness'. Within the taken-for-granted realities that maintain everyday life, and the expectation that things will go on smoothly and can be done again and again, risk and anxiety make us aware of the possibility that all this is contingent and could be interrupted at any second. All that seems stable could end, and all that exists could become nothing. What is meaningful in life, and for those alive in this world, is no longer meaningful in the face of anxiety. As Heidegger exclaims:

> *the world as such is that in the face of which one has anxiety*. The utter insignificance which makes itself known in the 'nothing and nowhere', does not signify that the world is absent, but tells us that entities within-the-world are of so little importance in themselves that on the basis of this *insignificance* of what is within-the-world, the world in its worldhood is all that still obtrudes itself.
>
> (Heidegger 2008 [1927]: 231, emphasis in the original)

On a less metaphysical level, economic (and more traditional, according to Beck 1997) risk analysis often deals with the likelihood of nothingness – what will happen if we lose all the goods that are being shipped from one harbour to another, what will happen if all the money invested is lost, what will happen to the airline if one of their planes crashes. In all cases, risk analysis conducted by, say, insurance companies or investment bankers considers what will happen if something that was there or was expected to run smoothly or to grow 'naturally' is suddenly not there anymore.

In the case of pandemics and epidemiology, risk 'is most often used to express the probability that a particular outcome will occur following a particular exposure' (Burt 2001: 1007). Again, the 'particular outcome' points to the event of healthy bodies becoming ill and potential deaths. Something that was supposed to run smoothly (e.g. the state or the economy) is interrupted and meaningful lives could literally turn into nothing. Moreover, infectious diseases in particular are an interesting example of interwoven instances of risk and anxiety and how they play out in space and time. Presupposing healthy, geographically and economically more or less stable societies, microbial travel seems to threaten populations and economies alike (cf. Ali 2010). Emerging space–time extensions of microbes are intertwined with the spread of expert knowledge about the impending pandemic, interspersed with anxiety-laden representations of death (which will be explained in more detail below). The diffusion of these materials of anxiety create global risks – i.e. an increasing awareness across borders that we live in an interdependent world of 'manufactured uncertainties' (Beck 1997).

In sum, anxiety, in this chapter, is the way we understand and grasp that 'some-thing' could turn into 'no-thing'. On this level, both risk and anxiety inform us about how to understand the uncertainty of the future. They are both neither rational nor irrational, but two – if different – forms of knowing the future. Departing from these preliminary conceptual thoughts, I will discuss the interdependencies of globalised risks and anxieties by looking especially at the threat of pandemics. The recent so-called swine flu pandemic (2009 H1N1/A) will provide some empirical material to exemplify my theoretical agenda.

The concept of social anxiety

In contemporary English usage, the word 'anxiety' has at least four separate meanings: a state of agitation, troubled in mind, a solicitous desire to effect some purpose, and uneasiness about a coming event (Tyrer 1999: 3–4). According to this definition, anxiety is an embodied state involving mental and emotional distress, combined with a more diffuse sense of uneasiness about a coming event. Following from this, the social sciences tend to treat anxiety as an individual pathological state rather than a social condition. For example, Iain Wilkinson states that 'feelings of anxiety can only be experienced uniquely as our own' (Wilkinson 1999: 453).

But Wilkinson himself makes a difference between the anxieties believed to be most widespread and powerful within late modernity, as suggested by Beck or Giddens, and the individual anxieties that people have to deal with in their everyday lives. That some issues gain the extraordinary attention of the news media, and that surveys reveal the awareness of these issues within the public, does not necessarily mean that people experience anxiety or fear in relation to these issues (Wilkinson 1999: 459–62). The surveys reveal the awareness and therefore the knowledge people have, but that is not the same as the experience of individual emotions. Seen from another angle, without making any claims about the intensity of emotional involvement, social historian Alan Hunt suggests distinguishing between individual and social anxiety for analytical reasons:

An individual anxiety has no social significance unless it is a shared social anxiety and, additionally, it results in some discernible action by significant numbers. If I and others cancel vacations in Egypt because of fear of attacks by 'fundamentalists' this shared anxiety has social and economic consequences.

(Hunt 1999: 510)

The distinction made classifies some anxieties as social because they are shared with a significant number of other people, whereas those that affect individuals alone (e.g. claustrophobia) are seen as more isolated phenomena. While this distinction may be difficult to sustain (see Davidson and Smith 2003, on the treatment of various phobias), an even more radical conceptual move would bring all the merits of the concept of social anxiety to the fore. What if social anxieties are those anxieties that can only exist within social interactions and connections? Social anxieties could be seen as the various phenomena that we commonly explain within the framework of anxiety and fear, but that do not come from, or end with, individual experiences of that feeling (Jackson and Everts 2010). To be sure, I am not saying that people are not afraid of terrorism, illnesses, climate change or crime, and do not experience emotional distress in relation to these issues. Rather I contend that personal feelings about these issues do not have any substantial bearing on how social anxieties are generated, circulated and collectively dealt with.

The case of swine flu is instructive here. Notwithstanding the emotional distress that people may or may not have experienced, the global measures proposed by various health agencies, the actions taken by governments, and the threatening tone of the news media assumed the existence of frightened individuals without any evidence. It was sufficient to assume a shared state of anxiety. It is in the light of this assumption that the heightened concern expressed by various organisations and institutions makes sense. This could also be seen as the difference between risk and anxiety. Whereas health agencies assessed the risk of an emerging infectious disease and governments made plans that would reduce the risk of infection, the converting of these assessments and plans into statistics, maps, bans or public campaigns recreated the global risk as social anxiety.

How does this conversion happen? I suggest that the conversion of risk to anxiety takes place within two important processes: the framing of an event as an event to be feared, and the subsequent effects of this on the everyday experience of the present, that becomes populated by new subjects and objects of anxiety.

Events, subjects and objects of anxiety

Events that give rise to social anxiety often involve the death of people. This does not always mean that people have already died, but fear can be due to projection of the event onto the future such as an environmental disaster. This differs from work on disaster that distinguishes pre-disaster from post-disaster, attributing to a disaster the power either to accelerate change or to contest the power geometries in place (Pelling and Dill 2009). Social anxiety blurs the boundary between pre- and post-disaster, since change and contestation are equally likely to arise from the projection of a future disaster (i.e. in the pre-disaster phase). Thus, in the case of social anxiety, we do not have to look for disaster events but anxiety events, that is the emergence of knowledge and awareness of unfolding or future disasters – in short, the production of risk.

Similar to disasters, the emergence of social anxiety occasions a rupture in the fabric of everyday life when the experience of one's being-in-the-world collapses into subjects and objects of anxiety, i.e. who needs to be afraid and what are the entities that subjects should be afraid of (see Jackson and Everts 2010). For example, the reported deaths of 113 people from December 2003 to April 2006, especially the accelerated diffusion of cases in late 2005 (see World Health Organization 2006), arc related to the social anxiety now known as 'bird flu' (avian influenza) (cf. Davis 2006). The framing of the event implied that more or less everyone in the world could become subject to the highly pathogenic H5N1 virus. Notably, scientists suggested in October 2005 that the lethal 1918 H1N1 virus, which is commonly held responsible for up to 50 million deaths worldwide, shares many of its characteristics with contemporary H5N1 (Taubenberger *et al.* 2005). Newspaper coverage is a good indicator for the spatio-temporal waxing and waning of this social anxiety with its tipping point in early 2006 (Ungar 2008). Alongside these events, the object of anxiety – the virus and the birds – was established and monitored closely (Hinchliffe and Bingham 2008). Still in a pre-disaster phase, actions were taken to stop the further spread of subjects and objects of anxiety; the objects (infected and vulnerable birds) were annihilated in a very literal sense, so that people were – at least subjectively – no longer exposed to the virus. In this case, the subjects of anxiety disappeared together with the object, and the topic retreated from public discourse, though the virus is still virulent and in 2010 human cases were reported from Egypt, Indonesia, Vietnam, Cambodia, and China (World Health Organization 2010). It seems that from early 2009 the issue lost much of its 'public potency' and gave way to other topics, such as economic crisis, climate change and swine flu. While the risk of H5N1 transmission remains a challenge to health agencies, the social anxiety known as bird flu became history, leaving its traces in individual and corporate practices of hygiene and pandemic preparedness (Nerlich *et al.* 2009; Fielding *et al.* 2005).

In work on the geographies of fear, a similar argument is developed. Lawson (2007: 335) encourages researchers to investigate the 'expansion of fear' that seems to arise from many sources, such as threats of natural disasters, global climate change and health pandemics, alongside geopolitical fear-mongering and apprehensions about social injustice. Pain and Smith (2008: 12–13) observe that fear is a 'collective experience' and 'that there are tracks and traces between the different lives of those who seek to control fear and those whose lives are pervaded by it'.

The decidedly 'material' actor-network theory dimension of this approach is mirrored in November's (2008) call to analyse risk from the practitioners' point of view as reconfigurations of human–non-human relationships, as *actants* that can transform the collective. By drawing on the examples of fire risk in Geneva, pandemic risks and how the WHO deals with them, and flooding risks, she demonstrates 'the spatiality of risk'. In each case, changing spatial perspectives change the concept of risk and likewise the practices of risk assessment, management, and so on. Thus, she concludes, 'categories of risk are not fixed, but rather move in relation to events' and 'risks transform affected areas, help to raise awareness of new dangers and lead to new meetings between stakeholders' (November 2008: 1525).

Risk, anxiety and emotive knowledge

The various risk strategies that frame the anxiety-invoking event leave material tracks and traces as much as they rely on representations. This is especially true of the 'new' risks identified by Beck and others, which are on levels beyond individual human perception. These are global risks, or invisible agents, like radiation, pollutants or microbes, which need various elaborate representational practices to establish the presence of these risks in the first place. In the case of swine flu, it needed the laboratory, and the assertion that the particular microbe was new, which was confirmed with its naming as H1N1 (A) 2009. It needed an origin, which was established partly through a territorial background (Mexico), and partly by distinguishing between the human and the non-human world ('swine' flu). Once its presence and geographies of origin became acknowledged, its spread and genealogy were mapped, and its connection to historical forerunners was shown. To a certain extent, all of these practices can be viewed within the framework of risk assessment, which relies significantly on the practice of mathematical modelling.

For example, the national framework for responding to an influenza pandemic, issued by the UK's Department of Health in 2007, describes the importance of this practice.

> Mathematical modelling provides an adjunct to previous experience to help inform both strategic and operational planning for a future pandemic. The models enable current circumstances and the likely impact and effectiveness of interventions to inform plans. However, models are only as good as the data fed into them and the assumptions made in their design. In the case of new influenza viruses, there are few data, and a wide range of plausible assumptions can be made. The main role of modelling in advance of a pandemic is to map out the range of possible risks and to investigate which responses are robust over the range of uncertainties. It is therefore important to emphasise that all impact predictions are estimates – not forecasts – made to manage the risks of a pandemic, and that the actual shape and impact may turn out to be very different. Impact predictions will therefore be compared against emerging data as the pandemic develops.
>
> (Cabinet Office (Department of Health) 2007: 20–21)

88   *Jonathan Everts*

In the case of pandemic risk, there are a number of questions health officials and experts need to answer. Documents from health agencies in Germany (STIKO), the UK (Department of Health), the USA (CDC) and the European Union (ECDC) show that the central questions in relation to the emerging 2009 H1N1 (A) pandemic were as follows:

- How dangerous is it? Answer: Very, because it is new.
- Where did it come from and who is to blame? Answer: Various origins, inter-species mixing of swine, birds, and humans connecting various viral strains from around the world but having materialised for the first time in Mexico and in the USA.
- What's it going to do to the world? Answer: Judging from its spread and compared to similar infectious diseases, such as the so-called Spanish flu pandemic in 1918–19, it will kill a substantial number of people worldwide and potentially lead to massive disruptions of everyday life with drastic economic consequences.

These seemingly neutral assessments found in various statements, documents and images that circulate through the channels of the news media and the internet are important mediators of social anxiety. Without any knowledge of the virus, anxiety is conceivable before the pandemic happens. In order to explain globalised anxieties, it is therefore crucial to look at the material representations of risk and the specific emotive knowledge they create.

Drawing on William Reddy, I want to introduce the concept of emotives, which can be useful in explaining what links the representations of risk to social anxieties. According to Reddy, emotives are a distinctive set of utterances that seek to convey emotions and thereby change how one feels oneself and how others feel:

> I propose to call emotion statements [...], in which the statement's referent changes by virtue of the statement, 'emotives'. [...] Emotives are themselves instruments for directly changing, building, hiding, intensifying emotions.
>
> (Reddy 1997: 331)

The connection between risk and anxiety becomes more visible if we take this idea a little further and consider as emotion statements not only utterances such as talk or gestures, or utterances that are obviously meant to convey something emotional, but also all kinds of artefacts and other things that can be considered as potential emotives, in the sense that they can be read and understood as a source of emotion or as pointing towards something emotional. Figures such as estimated fatality rates can be read as a threatening entity. A pure number without any context such as 75,000 does not convey much. But within the context of a headline such as 'flu pandemic will kill 75,000 Britons and 50 million worldwide',[1] it becomes an emotive that plays on social anxiety.

So how does the emotive such as a map of the spreading disease, or the number of expected fatalities, become powerful? The point is that human beings are capable of empathy and make sense of the present by drawing on past experience. Anxiety is not foreign to human beings but something that has been experienced by most people. Thus, there is a way of empathising with those who feel anxious, and there are 'experiential meanings' (Taylor 1971) (in this case: knowing how it feels to be anxious from experience) that enable the identification of potentially threatening entities. But identifying something as potentially threatening is not the same as being anxious. It is merely the recognition, based on experience, that there is something that could be seen as harmful, and which could thus cause emotional distress in some people. I propose to call this knowledge 'emotive knowledge'. It is the ability to decipher certain entities – be it words, gestures, figures, headlines, maps, places, practices, or objects such as facemasks – within particular arrangements as emotives. Strategies of risk assessment and related practices produce a significant amount of these. They can be circulated on a global scale and they resonate with localised emotive knowledge.

As the terms experience and knowledge suggest, social anxieties flourish on understandings and conceptions that precede the anxiety-invoking event. In order to understand what, when, where and how something becomes an object of anxiety – an emotive – we need to trace some of the collective imaginations that make emotives meaningful in the first place. In what follows, I will discuss three processes of boundary making that can explain how emotive knowledge becomes activated in the case of pandemics.

The geographies of globalised anxieties

Mapping the disease

In her excellent book on the emergence of the 'outbreak narrative', Priscilla Wald (2008) explains in her chapter 'Imagined Immunities' how the conceptualisation of the pandemic threat rests on various boundaries that construct dichotomous relations involving an inside that is threatened from the outside. At the heart of this dichotomy, she identifies the concept of herd immunity, a term coined in the 1920s:

> The biological aspect of community articulated in the idea of herd immunity makes any catastrophic illness a communally transformative event at the deeply conceptual (and psychological) level as well as, more explicitly, in social terms.
>
> (Wald 2008: 53)

Maps are a central tool for the imaginative work that brings the community into being. Tracing the routes of microbes across the globe and administrative boundaries reinforces the territorialised perspective of geographically bounded communities, as much as it subverts these seemingly separate spatial entities by depicting their interconnectedness with other places and their proneness to infiltration from 'other', 'non-local' entities (see Figure 6.1). No wonder then, as Wald (2008: 42) suggests, that the virus often becomes framed within the metaphors of unwelcome immigrants and strangers and vice versa. Moreover, anxieties about globalisation, and an increasingly interactive and interconnected world, are not just about exclusion, but about the difficulties of balancing a fear of strangers with the need for them and the necessary flux in a globalised world.

This is where ever more sophisticated means of surveillance (the map is an obvious one) meet with the imagined geographies of blame and stigmatisation. On the one hand, the (Western and modern) nation state is imagined as a fragile place where people's health and lives are subject to foreign threats (for a genealogy in the US context see Collier and Lakoff, 2008). On the other hand, these threats are not just from anywhere in the outside world but connected to the imagined, pre-cultural past of the undeveloped parts of the world:

> Cultural analysts have noted the anxieties about globalization expressed in these accounts in which diseases almost invariably emerge from Africa, occasionally from Asia or South America. Charting the one-way course of such diseases, accounts of emerging infections turn space into time, threatening to transform a contemporary 'us' into a primitive 'them'.
>
> (Wald 2008: 45)

The process of folding time into space is not new to geography. One recent example is the elaboration of absencing/presencing strategies of people exposed to technological risks (Bickerstaff and Simmons 2009). But a genealogy of today's

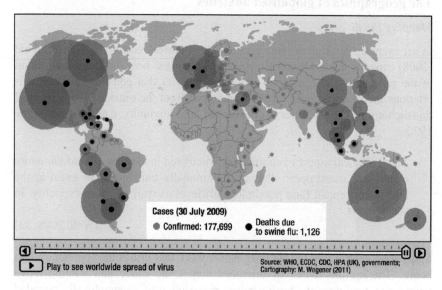

Figure 6.1 Swine flu cases worldwide: exemplary reproduction of interactive online maps during the H1N1/A pandemic 2009

'untimely' geographical imagination needs to foreground the legacy of modernisation theory that put the USA and other states of the Western hemisphere into the driving seat of development and modernity, foreshadowing the paths which other countries will enter sooner or later. From this followed that those 'undeveloped' other states are living in the past of modern states. As the outbreak narrative has it, the interaction between these different temporalities is imagined to be dangerous, because it is the modern and civilised world that encounters a forgotten and 'natural' past, that can no longer be coped with.

The implicit fears of 'thirdworldisation' can become very explicit, for instance when HIV/AIDS is imagined as a Third World problem that threatens First World health services. Alan Ingram (2008a) shows how immigration and health politics intersect in the UK when immigrants who suffer from AIDS are blamed as the cause of shortages in the national health service, thus fuelling fears that a promised 'world-class' health service is turning into a 'Third World' health service. Discrimination on the basis of race and ethnicity is never far away when pandemics happen. In Canada, for instance, there was a racialisation of SARS 'through the association of the disease with things Chinese' (Keil and Ali 2006: 43).

Another form, not mentioned by Wald, of mapping in a less literal way is the construction of risk groups as a way of managing the arrival of new microbes. In the event of swine flu, sophisticated lists were published defining several groups of people as 'risk groups' who should be treated preferentially. The German commission for vaccination, for instance, defined risk groups according to known complications within a predefined group in relation to the whole of the society (examples from Britain or the USA are similar). Thus, certain risk groups were singled out for vaccination in the following order: professional staff within the health services, people with chronic illnesses, pregnant women and those that had given birth recently, those who live in the households of people that cannot be vaccinated, then everybody below the age of 25 without chronic illnesses and finally those above the age of 25 without chronic illnesses (STIKO 2009).

From the social anxiety theory point of view outlined above, this categorisation has two dimensions. The first and obvious one is that of managing bodies and risk. In defining the people most in need through various characteristics such as age and occupation, the problem of the emerging infectious disease becomes quantifiable. There are statistics and figures that can be consulted in order to estimate numbers of vaccines and hospital beds, which in turn creates targets for policy-making. The second dimension, closely linked to the first one but less obvious, is that of governing fear and anxiety. Through the defining of risk groups, the imagined community is divided into two halves. The two groups last named are defined negatively by not belonging to any of the other groups. This undefined 'mainstream' population appears less vulnerable than the other groups. Thus, it is a way of annihilating subjects of anxiety. If there are certain high-risk groups, it suggests that the others are not exposed to this risk in the same way and so have less reason to be anxious.

In a sense, mapping resonates with emotive knowledge, suggesting that most of the world succumbs equally to the power of the virus. Through the definition of risk groups, this power is countered by dividing societies into a smaller fraction of people who need to worry and a greater proportion of the population that needs to worry less, which corresponds to justifications of the unequal distribution of medical help. If it were only a problem of visualising the global threat through maps, the construction of risk groups seems an easy and obvious strategy to prevent social anxiety. In the German case, this was (unwittingly?) more successful than expected: most people avoided vaccination. But there is more to an emerging pandemic than maps, and it will be explained in the next section how other powerful emotives come into being and circulate.

The human and the non-human

Considering the threat of 'swine flu' and its immediate forerunner, the so-called 'bird flu', the apparent connection is the terminology. In both cases, the disease seems to stem from animals or – even worse – from an unlawful mixing of animal and human compounds. Whereas older pandemics do not make such a connection explicit in their names, many of them share this origin story. Ebola and HIV/AIDS are often connected to apes, SARS to chickens, and the great plagues of the early modern era with rats. Ebola and HIV/AIDS differ from the other pandemics mentioned, in the sense that they are placed within the narrative that explains the emerging infectious disease with the gap between an ancient past that still exists 'in the jungles' and the modern era of human civilisation. The other pandemics complicate this all-too-easy nature/culture divide. Pigs, chicken, rats, or for that matter pigeons and cows as well, are all part of the big modernising project of domesticating nature and engineering the environment (Davis 2006; Wallace 2009). It is there where the connection to risk society approaches are most obvious. The technological interferences that were intended to secure life and tame nature are at the same time creating new and unforeseen risks (Van Loon 2002).

Even if there are strong reasons to assume that 'swine flu' was already circulating in human bodies before the 'outbreak' in Mexico and the USA, the connection between the alleged 'patient zero' from the Mexican village of La Gloria, in the state of Veracruz, and the dangers of industrial livestock farming in the immediate vicinity, was too compelling to be overlooked by journalists.[2] As was depicted at the beginning of the pandemic, the origin of disease was the unhealthy proximity of masses of pigs and masses of people within an unhygienic setting, worsened through the industrialisation of farming where something has got 'out of the cage'. It is not very surprising than that the cover of the *Newsweek* issue dated 11/18 May 2009, entitled 'Fear and the Flu', showed a pig snout sticking out uncannily from a cage of metal bars.

All this resonates well with the above-mentioned anxieties about globalisation. Whereas many theorists of globalisation are interested mainly in the flows of people, information and goods, the increasing interconnectedness is more than that. There is not only a purely geographical type of interconnection to be followed, but also connections between various species and matters. The breakdown of boundaries concerns more than the boundaries between nation states (imagined or real); it also concerns the dissolution of boundaries between species. While this is not new and, as Bruno Latour (1993) suggests, was actually never the case but something that existed only within the imagination of a misguided enlightenment, it is only through the modern science of genetics that the porousness of boundaries between species has become a serious problem. Turning again to the work of Priscilla Wald (2000), we find that she diverts our attention not only towards those mappings that result in the well-known politically fractured representations of the globe, but also to the implicit mappings of the origins of viruses. Wald works through the various attempts at explaining the origins of HIV and the susceptibility or resistance of various social groups, highlighting the racialised bias of such endeavours. But even more literally, the ECDC (European Centre for Disease Prevention and Control) produced a slide show that contains one slide (#4) depicting the various genetic origins of the new H1N1 (A) virus commonly known as swine flu.[3] It shows two separate viruses: one is the North American H1N1 with mixed avian, swine and human lineages, and the other is the 'Eurasian' swine H1N1. They are believed to have merged into the new virus through the notorious 'viral reassortment'. All of these viruses are made up of various lineages that are ascribed geographical as well as species origins: classical swine North American lineage, avian North American lineage, human seasonal H3N2, Eurasian swine lineage.

Why does this information matter? Apparently it matters in that it also reinforces the notion of globality, i.e. the awareness of lives being interdependent on a global scale, inherent in the pandemic threat. It is the dangerous mixing of once locally isolated viral lineages together with those of different species that produces the global threat. Geographically dispersed natures, brought in contact through globalisation, threaten the global community. Not only contact between people who live far apart, but also contact between people and other species and matter – the non-human side of the world – is a powerful ingredient of anxiety in the pandemic age. The stranger as much as the animal and the mixing of viral strains become emotives of anxiety, and what is more, it is the notion of globality itself, encompassing the relationship between the human and the non-human, that turns the notion of the global into an object of anxiety.

Uneven geographies of global health security

Having traced some of the powerful conceptions that produce social anxiety, there is a further geographical aspect that needs attention. Up to this point I have treated the problem of pandemic anxiety from an American-Eurocentric perspective, and outlined some of the features of the outbreak narrative which readers from that background should be familiar with. The foregrounding of this perspective is not accidental, but rather a response to the increasing power this perspective wields over the rest of the world. The concept of global health security in particular has been pushed by 'the West' through the Global Health Security Initiative (GHSI) since the anthrax scare following the 9/11 terrorist attacks:

This Initiative was launched in November 2001 by Canada, the European Union, France, Germany, Italy, Japan, Mexico, the United Kingdom and the United States. The World Health Organization serves as an expert advisor to the GHSI. The GHSI was envisaged as an informal group to fill a gap for like-minded countries to address health issues of the day, such as global health security.[4]

While many countries of the Global North are increasingly able to monitor the waxing and waning of diseases within their own borders through ever more sophisticated means of surveillance and laboratory research, Ingram (2008b: 81) asserts that the 'surveillance gap' between developed and developing countries is widening. This is partly due to the fact that global public health surveillance has become integrated into the intelligence needs of the Global North, and that these security interests have taken the form of a 'biosecurity industrial complex' (Ingram 2008b: 82).

The term 'biosecurity' signals the emergence of a new politics built around human–non-human relationships since the late 1990s. Hinchliffe and Bingham (2008) discern at least three different areas in which this term is used: the management of the movement of agricultural pests and diseases, attempts to reduce the effects of invasive species on 'indigenous' flora and fauna, and, lastly, bioterrorism or 'the dangers of purposeful and inadvertent spreading of biological agents into the human population' (Hinchliffe and Bingham 2008: 1536).

But there is a misfit between intelligence needs expressed through concepts such as biosecurity or global health security, and the economic needs of the Global South. Instructive is the case of Indonesia, which stopped sharing virus samples in the wake of the avian influenza in 2007, sparking lengthy negotiations with the WHO:

> Indonesia's Minister of Health, Siti Fadilah Supari, has focused global attention on the fact that developing countries have supplied H5N1 virus to WHO Collaborating Centres for analysis and preparation for vaccine production, but that the resulting vaccines produced by commercial companies are likely to be unavailable to developing countries such as Indonesia. She called this system 'unfair.'
>
> At the same time, withholding viruses from WHO Collaborating Centres poses a threat to global public health security and the ongoing risk assessment for influenza, conducted by WHO Collaborating Centres.[5]

Developing countries seem to be being pulled into the intelligence needs of the North under the banner of 'global' security, whether they like it or not. But this pull rests on the firm boundary drawn between states that are threatened by the risk of viruses emerging from somewhere else and those that represent the threat and are thus also an object of anxiety: namely the Global South with allegedly poor levels of sanitation, hygiene and surveillance. Seen from this angle, swine flu was just another step for practising pandemic preparedness on a global scale, using data collected from the South in order to protect the North (cf. Sparke 2009).

Conclusions

This chapter began with a discussion of the conceptual links between anxiety and risk, stressing that both share notions of anticipation, the event, calls for action and the realisation of nothingness. It then moved on to the conversion of risk into anxiety through the very materials risk analysis produces. Moreover, the distinction between individual and social anxiety made it possible to register anxiety-inducing events without placing the individual bodily experience first, but the knowledge of the likelihood of nothingness that risk assessments activate. It was argued that social anxieties emerge through the disturbing qualities of an event, breaking down the routine of everyday life. Through the event, something 'new' enters the world that threatens subjects and is itself a threatening object. This collapse into subjects and objects of anxiety is the main divide addressed by reactions to the anxiety-inducing event, for instance public health agencies and other political institutions that seek to control the movements of subjects and to annihilate the objects of anxiety.

This task is complicated by the contagious qualities of the object of anxiety itself. It is not only the virus, for instance, that people fear, but the various representations of the threat, such as fatality rates and other statistics, maps, media headlines, animals or states. All of these objects can assume the quality of anxiety-inducing entities within a particular context, activating what I have termed 'emotive knowledge'. This is not only the knowledge that enables people to decipher something as threatening, but also the knowledge that even without being personally troubled, someone else may become agitated when encountering the emotives. Connecting these theoretical advancements with the agenda of the literature on geographies of fear, the case of pandemic threats such as 'swine flu' throws light on the various ways in which anxiety and risk are produced, imagined and negotiated.

Having identified three important dimensions of the risk-anxiety apparatus, all of them were explained within the practices of boundary-making. First, the inside world is separated from the outside world, through mappings that depict the emerging infectious disease as something 'other' that has found its way through the paradox processes of globalisation. Second, the boundary between different species such as animals and human beings was explored as another major concern in dealing with 'new' diseases. Third, the reinforcement of the boundary between the Global North and the Global South through the practices of global health security was discussed briefly.

The main issue at stake here is the reproduction of the boundary between risk and anxiety. The managerial, rational and quantifying approach of risk analysis works with and against the emotional, irrational and spontaneous approach represented by anxiety. In the first example, it was the recognition of the universal risk the virus presented that sparked social anxiety and was subsequently managed through the definition of risk groups. The second example showed how the 'culture of risk' struggles with the 'nature of anxiety' represented by various human–non-human connections on a global scale. The third example accessed the discourse of global health security of the Global North as the type of rational risk analysis that has its counterpart within the unruly and messy state of the Global South that becomes itself a major source of anxiety.

Having said that, there is no risk without anxiety and vice versa. The risk approach to modern and globalised ways of living suggests an entrepreneurial mode of governing, ordering and managing selves and others. By doing this it multiplies the very objects of anxiety it seeks to annihilate, thereby jump-starting the circulation of emotives on a global scale. Returning to its Global North logics, social anxiety is the awareness of something threatening that may lead to catastrophe and chaos, producing uncertainty and messiness in the present that can be exploited by various types of businesses and policies, from vaccine production to national security departments. The geographies of fear rest, so to speak, on the various forms of balancing risk and anxiety.

Notes

1   Available online at http://www.dailymail.co.uk/health/article-1036865/Inevitable-flu-pandemic-kill-75-000-Britons-50-million-worldwide-warn-Lords.html (accessed 25 February 2010).
2   See, for example, 'Schweinegrippe: Mediziner suchen nach "Patient null"', *Spiegel* online 29 April 2009, http://www.spiegel.de/panorama/0,1518,621932,00.html (accessed 25 February 2010).
3   'Evolution of the H1N1 pandemic'. Available online at: http://www.ecdc.europa.eu/en/healthtopics/H1N1/Pages/general_info.aspx (accessed 25 February 2010).
4   Available online at: http://www.ghsi.ca/english/index.asp (accessed 26 February 2010).
5   Available online at: http://www.who.int/mediacentre/news/releases/2007/pr09/en/index.html (accessed 26 February 2010).

7 Ungoverned territories

The construction of spaces of risk in the 'war on terrorism'

Conrad Schetter

Especially after the attacks on the World Trade Center and the Pentagon on 11 September 2001, discourses of security calling for the recognition of the global threat of international terrorism have gained importance and have significantly changed the global awareness of terrorism-related risks. The scope of the risks expected from this new 'era of terrorism' varies from small-scale attacks with, for instance, improvised explosive devices (IED) or suicide attacks, to large-scale attacks with proliferated nuclear, biological and chemical weapons. The 'likelihood of occurrence' (Renn 2008) of such terrorism-related risks has been difficult to assess so far, especially outside the OECD countries where terrorists seem to have the upper hand concerning knowledge of the relevant 'contexts for action' (Renn 2008).

Despite the often vague conceptualizations of the uncertainties connected to terrorism-related risks, they have featured very prominently in Western media in the past decade. This chapter focuses on the attempt to connect these risks to certain spaces. Especially, politicians and the media have repetitively used spatial references in order to locate the perils springing from terrorism geopolitically. Among the most prominent examples of spatialization of the risk of terrorism are the 'axis of evil' of the then US president George W. Bush, or the 'protection of Germany's security at the Hindukush' by the then German Minister of Defence Peter Struck.

In this chapter I will focus on the spatial concept of 'ungoverned territories' which has recently been invented to cope with the presumed terrorist threat. Hereby I follow the hypothesis that 'ungoverned territories' is a conceptual innovation in the 'war on terrorism' which suggests a strong connection between certain geopolitical contexts and terrorism-related risks. The initial assumption is that the connection between spaces and risk in the concept of 'ungoverned territories' is at least arbitrary, if not better understood as an attempt to legitimize political and military interventions. The 'rule of aggregation' (Renn 2008: 51) which the concept employs is predisposed to favour the available, military means for eliminating or reducing perceived risks. This chapter intends to show that not only the conceptualizations and selection of these risk-prone spaces called 'ungoverned territories' is questionable, but also that the devised strategies for countering these risks are mostly one-dimensional and bound to create new risks in an unending circle of violence. This contribution focuses on the discursive practices relating to 'ungoverned territories', and their suggestive power as to which spaces are prone to 'risk' – namely terrorism – with global effects; it cannot assess the risk exposure of particular spaces.

In order to make these connections visible, the development of the discourse, emanating from the US military and more recently also employed in the public media, will first be traced. Then the internal difficulties and contradictions of the concept will be analysed. Finally, the concept's potential political function is discussed. One overall aim of this chapter is to show how the spatial concept of 'ungoverned territories' has come to fit very well into the discussion of assumed terrorist threats and has recently even become paradigmatic for legitimizing interventionist politics.

Fragile states – locating the terrorist threat

The assumed terrorist threat is the starting point of the discussion about 'ungoverned territories'. However, agreeing on a definition of terrorism, much needed for qualifying risks as terrorism-related, has proven to be a significant problem (Balagandhara and de Roover 2010; Rodin 2004; Finlay 2009). The international community has not yet been able to define what structures, actors and activities should be subsumed under the term (Golder and Williams 2004). What is at the core of 'terrorism' escapes standardization as the term is often used with an inherent bias. Thus the Afghan case, for instance, shows that both NATO and Taliban refer to each other as 'terrorists'.

The vagueness of the term weighs heavily on the recent discussion of the 'war on terror'. Therefore, it is striking that – depending on the context – the terrorist threat is connected to different patterns of violent conflict: sometimes it is linked to 'rogue states' (Whiteneck 2005; Patrick 2006), then to the crisis of poverty and education in the 'South' (von Hippel 2009), to a deficit of democracy (McFaul 2005: 150), to cultural factors (Lewis 1994), or to the debate about 'empire' (Mallaby 2002).

A major thread of the discussion about the 'war on terror' links the terrorist threat to the debate about 'failed' or 'fragile states' (Rotberg 2003; Schneckener 2004, 2006; Crocker 2003).[1] Usually, this debate departs from Max Weber's definition of the 'ideal type' state, which – willingly or not – is a normative *ceterum censeo*, as it is based on an imagined ideal of order. According to Weber, the state is an institution that exerts authority over a bounded territory and its population. The state has the monopoly of violence, which is regarded as legitimate by the citizens. This monopoly of violence is the basis for further institutions of state authority: the monopoly of taxation, of making laws, decrees and regulations, which the citizens have to comply with, and the monopoly of punishment in the case of infringements of the law. The state is sovereign, which means that no other political authority supersedes it (Weber 1980 [1921]).[2]

The concentration on such an ideal of sovereign state apparatuses leads to negative definitions of all entities which deviate. When states cannot meet this standard, analysts search for attributes to describe the chasm between reality and ideal. Terms like 'eroding', 'weak', 'fragile', 'deformed', 'moribund', 'shadow', 'un-stately', 'decay', 'relative capability', etc., imply that the way in which the respective state is said to 'function' is located outside of the accepted normative model of the state and its relationship to society. Consequently, the functional view of the state as service-provider often leads to a descriptive vocabulary *ex negativo*, which stresses certain political risks. Political structures which contradict this normative definition are termed 'informal' or 'clientelistic' (Debiel *et al.* 2009).

Control of state territory is the main criterion within the 'failed states' debate. For instance, Ulrich Schneckener (2006) assesses the degree of 'statehood' primarily with respect to the ability of the state to control its territory and its borders, before he refers to several other criteria; this corresponds to the territorial monopoly of violence. The loss of such control is linked to the emergence of terrorist danger, a link which has recently been critically discussed (see Elden 2009). The hypothesis is that spaces devoid of state structures are especially prone to becoming spaces of risk; they can be used by terrorists as 'transit, withdrawal or flight spaces' (Schneckener 2006: 135–40) or as 'safe havens' (Lamb 2008). This line of argument not only marks the connection of functional spaces to certain anti-state actors, but means giving terrorism a particular place by localizing and territorializing this phenomenon (Takeyh and Gvosdev 2002). Especially, political decision makers often point to this spatial-causal connection of terrorism and weak states in order to explain deficits of security. In 2003, Joschka Fischer, the then foreign minister of the Federal Republic of Germany, perceived 'black holes of disorder' around the world, in which state structures have broken down and which destabilize whole regions through spillover effects (Lambach 2008).[3]

The 'ungoverned territories' discourse

Especially since 2007, the causal connection between space and state failure, as a factor facilitating the emergence of terrorism, has been categorized under a particular label, which has come to dominate the political discussion: 'ungoverned territories'. While the term has been used in political parlance for a couple of years, the RAND Corporation report prepared for the US Air Force entitled *Ungoverned Territories – Understanding and Reducing Terrorism Risks* (Rabasa *et al.* 2007) marked a new level of attention paid to the concept. The report identifies those territories which are regarded as dangerous to US security interests and run the risk of becoming hotbeds of terrorism. One year later the US Department of Defense (DoD) in cooperation with the US Government (USG) published the report *Ungoverned Areas and Threats from Safe Havens* (UGA/SH) (Lamb 2008). Since the publication of these two documents, to which I am going to refer continually, terms like 'ungoverned territories', 'ungoverned spaces' or 'ungoverned areas' have become part of the daily vocabulary of military and political discussions. Such terms have a clear purpose: they localize the diffuse threats that spring from the fear of terrorism linked to specific geographical spaces. Examples of the use of these terms can be found at the very top of US politics. The former secretary of state, Condoleezza Rice, has called wide areas of Pakistan 'ungoverned spaces' (Kumar 2008); President Barack Obama called the borderlands between Afghanistan and Pakistan 'vast, rugged and often ungoverned' on 27 March 2009 (Obama 2009). The US State Department, like the German federal government, bases its military mission in Afghanistan on the goal of preventing terrorism by controlling space: 'Afghanistan [should not] become the fallback space for international terrorists again' (Bundesregierung 2008: 5). The term is especially high on the agenda in the domain of strategy development for the military. Already in 2004, Admiral Jacoby, director of the Defense Intelligence Army, voiced the issue as follows:

> We are also increasingly concerned over 'ungoverned spaces,' defined as geographic areas where governments do not exercise effective control. Terrorist groups and narco-traffickers use these areas as sanctuaries to train, plan and organize, relatively free from interference. [...] I believe these areas will play an increasingly important role in the War on Terrorism as al-Qaida, its associated groups and other terrorist organizations use these areas as bases for operations.
>
> (Jacoby 2004)

Moreover, the term has recently found its way into key documents of US security policy: a whole chapter is dedicated to the term in the 'Global Strategic Assessment' of the International Center for Strategic Studies (Cronin 2009) and the 'National Defense Strategy', issued by the Pentagon, mentions the term four times. At one point, it says:

> Insurgent groups and other non-state actors frequently exploit local geographical, political, or social conditions to establish safe havens from which they can operate with impunity. Ungoverned, undergoverned, misgoverned, and contested areas offer fertile ground for such groups to exploit the gaps in governance.
>
> (US Department of Defense 2008: 8)

As these quotations show, 'ungoverned territories' have risen within just a few years to become a central guideline of US foreign policy in strategic and security studies and the military. The central claim behind the term is that those spaces which are supposed to be severe risks to the global order and the security of the USA – especially if they are used as safe havens for Islamist terrorists – can be localized (Lamb 2008; Cronin 2009).

Surprisingly, hardly any critical engagement with the term – despite its high political and military relevance – has emerged so far from the scholarly community (Clunan and Trinkunas 2010). Hence, my first intention now is to show the spatial essentialization suggested by the term 'ungoverned territories'. I will then illustrate how this term relates to the debate on interventionism.

What does 'ungoverned' mean?

Seen from a semantic perspective, the two studies issued by RAND and by the DoD/USG suggest a dichotomy between spaces defined as 'governed' and those defined as 'ungoverned'. In analogy to the failed-states debate, a state envisioned with ideal capacities ('governed') is contrasted with political structures, whose shortcomings can be deduced *ex negativo* ('ungoverned'). The RAND report in particular is based on an unquestioningly positive understanding of the state as the principal political power disseminating order, being at the same time faced with political risks. In a similar vein, Rabasa and Peters (2007a: 1) draw on medical terminology by describing states that meet the standards of the 'Western world' as 'healthy'. Consequently, 'ungoverned territories' must be seen as 'sick' and 'ailing'. The DoD/USG study expresses the qualities of 'ungoverned spaces' in slightly less pejorative terms, but still within the same framework, as 'inadequate governance capacities, insufficient political will, gaps in legitimacy, the presence of conflict, or restrictive norms of behavior' (Lamb 2008: 15).

Alluding to their antonymous relationship to the state, such an assessment insinuates that illegitimate and pre-modern social practices must predominate over 'ungoverned territories'. Both studies localize criminals, rebels and terrorists in 'ungoverned territories' (Lamb 2008: 15; Rabasa and Peters 2007a: 1). This underlines the impression that 'ungoverned territories' are inhabited by potential security threats. Moreover, it is striking to see how often the term 'tribe' is used to counter 'state' as pattern of order for 'ungoverned territories'. Zellin (2008) even sees a direct link between 'ungoverned territories' and tribal societies. The debate is in danger of falling prey to over-emphasizing tribalism, if pre-modern social practices are generally accepted as the dominant pattern of order or even prerequisite of 'ungoverned territories'. Such simplifying perspectives fail to take into account that even very remote areas experience 'multiple modernities' (Eisenstadt 1979) featuring diverging, yet partly overlapping societal structures and dynamics.

Furthermore, reducing the term 'governed' to its state dimension is at odds with the debate on governance which explicitly includes non-state actors. Besides, the possibility of a clear distinction between formal, state-based and informal and non-state-based spheres is taken for granted, even though research in the past decade (Chabal and Daloz 1999) has shown that the spheres of state and non-state institutions often overlap or mingle (and they may not be separable at all from the very start): phenomena like warlords, systems of patronage or corruption also occur in connection with state-rule, for they profit from an institutional bricolage, as formal and informal rules overlap (Reno 1998).

The term 'ungoverned' suggests that the state is generally the sole bearer of political legitimacy, which implies that non-state institutions and actors are generally illegal and pose uncontrolled risks to the global (state) order. Even though the UGA/SH report – seen from the local population's perspective – concedes limited legitimacy to non-state actors ruling in 'ungoverned territories', it views them as basically weaker and more fragile in comparison to state structures.[4]

Hence, the way in which the term 'ungoverned' is used implies an ideologically informed differentiation between effective states and ineffective 'ungoverned spaces'. The incapacity of governing – both studies converge in this point – depends on the degree to which private holders of force and criminal networks linked to terrorists and insurgents exist and can retreat to safe havens (Rabasa and Peters 2007a: 1; Lamb 2008: 17). Both studies often mention terrorists in direct connection with organized criminal networks, insurgents or warlords. Such a view denies the frequently observed connection between criminal networks and the state, or the potential involvement of the state in terrorism (Blakeley 2007).

Finally, the 'ungoverned territories' approach concentrates exclusively on the functionality of the state's monopoly of violence.[5] For instance, the RAND report defines 'ungoverned territories' as 'an area in which the state faces significant challenges in establishing control' (Rabasa *et al*. 2007: xv). Other key functions of the state, such as taxation, welfare and jurisprudential services, which are usually consulted for measuring political risks (Jarvis 2008), are eclipsed completely. Thus, the approach is in tune with proponents of a security-centred *Realpolitik*, especially following the Bush administration's missionary urge for 'democracy' (Etzioni 2007).

Defining the space of 'ungoverned territories'

Both studies clearly distinguish between state and non-state, or between legitimate order and assumed anarchy, but their discussion of spatialization is rather diffuse. For instance, they use different spatializations, such as 'territory', 'space' or 'area'. All these terms share the emphasis on the spatial component of governance: 'the degree of governance matters, but the particular way a place is governed matters more' (Lamb 2008: 4).

The use of the term 'territory' in this context is contradictory: following common definitions (Sack 1986), 'territory' refers to exactly fixated geodetic units, which are subject to political or societal control. The very politico-spatial processes of nation-state formation made 'territories' salient as political markers or containers (Giddens 1985; Ruggie 1993). As Stuart Elden (2009: 177) has recently put it:

> Territory matters because it is seen to provide the 'container' within which sovereignty is said to operate, because its extent limits what the state can do, and because its limits are the extent of the state.

However, by adding the adjective 'ungoverned' the RAND report questions the very central claim of control implicit to the term. So this is a contradiction in itself. Furthermore, using the term 'territory' together with the adjective 'ungoverned' suggests a clear-cut borderline between state territory and other 'territories', over which the state exercises, if any, insufficient control.

Thus, the term 'ungoverned territories' implies that spaces in which statehood is suspended can be exactly demarcated by geodetic boundaries (which would be an enormous advantage whilst fighting in them). According to this understanding state-controlled spaces can always be distinguished from spaces that lack state control. This image can be criticized from two perspectives: first, the exact localization of 'ungovernability' (Rabasa and Peters 2007a, 2007b) ignores the existence of hybrid or temporary spaces. Second, such a static, state-centric concept of space is not sensitive to findings of anthropological research showing that territorial thinking has often remained marginal in societies which have never been penetrated by the state (Foucault 2009). Thus, the RAND report completely denies the existence of cross-spatial networks, transnational movements and processes of globalization (Clunan and Trinkunas 2010: 7). These conceptual problems related to the term 'territory' have inspired the emergence of terms like 'ungoverned spaces' (Lamb 2008) or 'ungoverned areas' (Cronin 2009). Both terms add to the vagueness of the terminology of the debate.

The RAND report is permeated by faith in the territorial nation state. It coins the term 'counter-space' (to the territorial nation state), paralleling the portfolio of state-centric terms ('territory', 'ungoverned') *ex negativo* without permitting an alternative social structure on the conceptual level. The selection of spaces termed 'ungoverned territories' in the RAND report is also led by classic territorial state thinking. Thus, Rabasa *et al.* (2007) localize 'ungoverned territories' in the periphery of state control, such as border regions or in aerial or maritime transportation. This understanding is repetitively expressed in their case studies as well. The report lists the following 'ungoverned territories': the Arabian Peninsula, the maritime arch between Sulawesi and Mindanao, the East-African corridor, West Africa, the North Caucasus and several borders, such as between Afghanistan and Pakistan, Colombia and Venezuela, and Guatemala and Chiapas/Mexico, the Huallaga valley in Peru, the Darien gap between Colombia and Panama, the Golden Triangle (borderlands between Thailand, Vietnam, Laos and Burma), South Thailand and the region of the Great Lakes in Africa (Rabasa and Peters 2007a: 4). Other researchers have 'added' further 'ungoverned territories/spaces/ areas' to this list: the South-West of China (Zellin 2008), the Swahili Coast, coastal Somalia, the Gulf of Guinea (esp. the delta of the Niger river), the Sahel zone (North Mali, Darfur), and East Congo (Whelan 2006), the Lebanon, the triangle between Argentina, Brazil and Paraguay (The Economist 2009), the Gaza strip, Iraq, the Arctic (McGregor 2007), Transnistria and the Straits of Malacca (Cronin 2009). This mushrooming of 'ungoverned territories' underlines the difficulty of determining spaces which actually are 'governed'. Hence, this potentially endless list of 'ungoverned territories' supports arguments which contest that spaces can themselves be governed, and hold that the assessment of governance is subject to normative views.

According to such a normative perspective, 'ungoverned territories' are most likely to be localized in developing countries and thus appear as zones of risk external to the West. This comes as a surprise, since both the RAND and the UGA/SH reports identify border regions prone to intensive smuggling and illegal migration as 'ungoverned territories'. Due to intensive illegal migration and smuggling activities the borders of the EU and the USA should be counted as 'ungoverned territories', which only appears in a footnote in the RAND report (Rabasa and Peters 2007a: 4). A similar contradiction can be observed with regard to the density of population: on the one hand, 'rugged and remote areas' (McGregor 2007) are repeatedly mentioned as 'ungoverned territories'; on the other hand, agglomerations and megacities are named as spaces 'where terrorists can congregate and prepare for operations with relative impunity' (Jacoby 2004). Yet most spaces named as 'ungoverned territories/spaces/areas' are rural. At most, there may be reference to cities like Karachi or Sao Paulo (Rabasa and Peters 2007a: 4); European or American urban centres go unmentioned. In a footnote, the RAND report points to 'Muslim "ghettos" in some Western European cities as "ungoverned zones"' (Rabasa and Peters 2007a: 4). Thus, 'ungovernability' is also ascribed to culturally essentialized spaces. Or put differently: 'Muslim "ghettos"' now appear as spatial containers of security risks, which are singled out by religious markers; they seem to be territorialized states of exception (of 'ungovernability'), as enclaves (of disorder) in the ordered Western world. This outspoken reference to Muslim quarters in urban Western contexts could be read as meaning that the authors of the RAND report regard Muslims per se as standing outside any state's legal order and therefore as a risk to society. Therefore, the localization of 'ungoverned territories' does not reflect the gap in terms of development (West vs. 'Rest'), but – at least within the Western world – refers to a religious-cultural gap (Christians vs. Muslims).

In contrast to the enumeration of 'ungoverned territories', however, several authors contributing to the debate stress the de-bordering and de-territorialization of space (e.g. Whelan 2006; Cronin 2009). Following such approaches, recent publications distinguish between virtual and materialized spaces: cyberspace and global finances flows, for instance, are counted as belonging to the former (Lamb 2008: 25). In reference to these distinctions 'ungoverned spaces' has become an important term for the US Ministry of Defense's vocabulary (McGregor 2007).

Spaces of exception and politics of intervention

Present endeavours by American think tanks to issue a world map of 'ungoverned territories' can be understood as a new attempt at global geo-codification (Rose-Redwood 2006), i.e. mapping risks which threaten a global order based on nation states. In accordance with this understanding, Paul Hirst is right to argue that 'today we are not witnessing "de-territorialization", but the reverse' (Hirst 2005: 3). Thus in the past year think tanks have been busy identifying, naming and categorizing spaces of risk depending on the quality of the state's monopoly of violence. They detect spaces out of reach of state order, which then become exceptions to the global political order based on the sovereignty of territorially delimited states, and are identified as topographical zones of risk. Such geo-codifications construe not a temporary, but a permanent location of the state of exception, comparable to what Jörg Dünne calls 'inclusive exclusion' (2006: 379). Such activities gradually raise awareness of the project committed to spatially localizing 'the other' that seemingly is an outcast in the world of states.

The paradigm of 'increased security', propagated as a 'normal technique of governance' (Agamben 2004: 22), is employed to justify this state of exception.

The identification of states of exceptions accordingly questions the sovereignty of certain states with the intention of stabilizing the sovereignty-based international state system. Following Agamben, 'the contrast between norm and its application reaches the peak of its intensity' (2004: 47) during the state of exception. The identification of 'ungoverned territories' carries the corollary of casting doubt on the sovereignty of the assessed states. From the perspective of the analysts who claim to have supremacy of interpretation for naming 'ungoverned territories', those states fail to meet their prime task, i.e. the assertion of their monopoly of violence. The debate about 'ungoverned territories' therefore sets the scene for delegitimizing certain states and provides the ground for legitimizing external interventions. This chiasmic nexus is illustrated in core documents of US security and defence politics. For instance, the Global Strategic Assessment of the International Center for Strategic Studies reads as follows:

> If some states are unable to fulfill these obligations [...] there will be considerable pressure on others, whose people are targeted by terrorists enjoying sanctuary in ungoverned areas, to take matters into their own hands.
> (Cronin 2009: 103)

Additionally, the National Defense Strategy concludes:

> We will work with and through like-minded states to help shrink the ungoverned areas of the world and thereby deny extremists and other hostile parties sanctuary. By helping others to police themselves and their regions, we will collectively address threats to the broader international system.
> (US Department of Defense 2008: 8–9)

The then Secretary of Homeland Security, Michael Chertoff, mentioned on 1 December 2008 that 'risk must be managed in the "ungoverned space"'. Following this rationale, 'ungoverned territories' become spatial containers of exception. Thus, once the sovereignty of the respective intervened state is constrained, political and military interventions become legitimate (Gregory 2004). The novelty of the 'ungoverned territories' approach consists in the spatially limited, instead of complete, suspension of the state's sovereignty through military intervention or security operations. This modification appears to be a fine adjustment of intervention politics. Thus, the debate about 'ungoverned territories' has to be connected to an array of attempts to recalibrate (or even revolutionize) the relation between state sovereignty and intervention, such as the debates on 'Human Security', 'Responsibility to Protect' and other approaches in the general framework of 'Humanitarian Interventions' and 'New Humanitarianism' (see Duffield 2007; Schetter 2010): 'ungoverned territories' – as spaces of exception in a state-based world – are not only a novel approach to making interventions appear to be legitimate but also – please allow me the use of a medical comparison here – claim to help rectify aberrations through methods similar to minimally invasive surgery. Following this interpretation, Barry Zellin sees 'ungoverned territories' not only as a zone of risk to US security, but also as spaces of providence, in which the USA should act to maintain their global hegemony:

> The underlying tribal topology of these 'ungoverned territories' or tribal zones as I prefer to think of them presents numerous strategic opportunities for containing and/or rolling back communism (in China, Laos, and Vietnam), combating dictatorship and oligarchy (in Burma, Guatemala and southern Mexico; and the Andean highlands) and securing access to newly emergent natural resources (in the Arctic regions, Africa, Indonesia, the Philippines, and much of South and Central Asia).
>
> (Zellin 2008: 3)

'Ungoverned territories' are therefore places of exception, in which the interventionists' actions are not subject to the respective state's order. On the micro level, the practices of punishment and torture in camps like Guantanamo, Abu Ghraib or Bagram drastically display this state of affairs. Following Giorgio Agamben (2002), one can even argue that the inhabitants of 'ungoverned territories' become '*homines sacri*', whose life is reduced to mere naked existence: they are stripped of their rights on the one hand, but they are not worth being sacrificed on the other. Thus the conceptualization of 'ungoverned territories/ spaces/areas', as in the RAND and UGA/SH reports, serves as the territorial determination of a 'wild zone of power' (Buck-Morss 2003: 29), in which the state of exception is evident and which makes external intervention appear to be a legitimate means of 'remedy'. At least in the current US-military strategy in the border area between Pakistan and Afghanistan – as the most outstanding and most cited 'ungoverned territory' in the world – it can be observed that an entire population is treated as '*homines sacri*'. Here, the US-military approach changed from fighting terrorism by direct combat interactions to air strikes, which are launched by remotely operated unmanned drones. This approach is applauded as a new dimension of warfare which reduces casualties and even reduces 'collateral damage' due to finely tuned kinetic operations against assumed enemies. However, it is rarely mentioned what this kind of warfare means for the population living in such an 'ungoverned territory'. The population is no longer confronted with the momentum of a direct visible military force but continuously with an invisible one. In other words, the population is living under the continuous threat of air strikes that can happen anywhere and any time. As insurgents in Afghanistan and Iraq aim to threaten the feeling of security of the US Army and NATO by using improvised explosive devices and guerilla warfare, the US army threatens not only the insurgents, but the entire population of 'ungoverned territories' by drones.

Conclusion

The political dimension of the concept of 'ungoverned territories' illustrates the tendency of political think tanks and policy makers to make use of classical geopolitical coding in their endeavour to define a world order and its assumed exposure to risks (see O'Tuathail 1996). This approach follows the idea of making dynamic political and social phenomena comprehensible by relating them directly to particular topographical locations. Thus the geographical *locus* eventually becomes the intellectual place-holder for social or political phenomena. The assumed interconnection of the political and the spatial is turned upside down. Certain spatial figurations become attached to certain political qualities and are thus identified as severe risks to the global order. In the case of 'ungoverned territories' even an explanatory concept of what the world order looks like is grounded in a particular 'geographical imagination' (Gregory 1993). One reason for the conceptualization of 'ungoverned territories' might be that the – often unreflected – thinking in territorialized nation states and its geo-coded vocabulary still strongly guides the mainstream of political thinking.

From the perspective of theorizing political risks, much speaks in favour of connecting risks to certain modes of spatialization. In its etymology the term 'risk' already implies uncertainty of space and time. For political think tanks assessing risks it is a complex challenge to be accurate about the temporal and spatial predictability of risks: when and where to situate the risk? In this endeavour the territorialization of the subject appears to be much easier to operate than a precise forecast in time. This scientific *modus operandi* is deeply rooted in nineteenth-century philosophy of science, which tends to understand time as liquid and abstract, and space (especially in the form of a territory) as static and materialized (see Koselleck 2003).

In conclusion, the geo-coding approach visible in the concept of 'ungoverned territories' will keep its appeal as long as the security paradigm of the Western world is shaped by the fear of terrorist-related risks. For as long as the terrorist is seen as the enemy of the state-based world order, she/he can only be fought outside this order – which justifies, as Carl Schmitt (1922) put it, the 'state of exception'. Therefore, the debate about 'ungoverned territories' will not abate unless the causal connection between state erosion and terrorism-related risks is, at least partially, loosened. Hard political or military actions are not needed so much as a shift of perspective – e.g. by emphasizing new threats to security – in order to end the debate about 'ungoverned territories'.

The problematization of this connection opens up questions about coherency and the scholarly as well as political value of the concept. The progress that the concept promises with regard to terrorism-related risks turns out to be a self-fulfilling prophecy for further military interventions.

Notes

1　The dysfunctionality of states was, besides terrorism, a key concept for defining political risks in the past decade. Here, the political risk stems from a situation in which the exercise of power by the government is harmed, legitimate rule is undercut and political institutions are unable to operate (Milliken 2003).

2　Weber derived his conception of the state from European models and did not intend to apply it to political formations outside of Europe, nor did he pursue a generally universalistic approach.

3　Only a few scholars are sceptical of this connection between fragile statehood and terrorism. Ken Menkhaus (2007) uses the example of Somalia to illustrate that fragile states are hardly attractive to terrorists, as they lack communicative and logistical infrastructure.

4　A good indicator of the difficulty the UGA/SH study has in loosening itself from a state-centered framework of analysis is the assumption that the political arena is always structured by 'government'; political decision-making processes beyond 'government' are not even considered (Lamb 2008: 15).

5　The RAND report mentions the following criteria for assessing state governing capacities: penetration of society, monopoly of violence, border control, and the degree to which the state is subject to external intervention (Rabasa and Peters 2007b).

8 Spaces of risk and cultures of resilience

HIV/AIDS and adherence in Botswana

Fred Krüger

Opening the case: HIV/AIDS in Botswana and the problem of adherence

In 2009, almost 25 per cent of all adults in Botswana carried the HI virus. In recent years, HIV prevalence overall has been levelling off at around 17 per cent, and surveillance data show that HIV infections among young people under 25 years of age have been declining consistently (UNAIDS/NACA 2010; UNAIDS/WHO 2010). In the wake of the pandemic, however, mortality has increased and average life expectancy has decreased dramatically – in Botswana from approximately 70 years in 1990 to its lowest value of 36 years in 2004 (life expectancy at birth; UNAIDS 2006). Together with Swaziland, Botswana ranks highest in HIV prevalence of all countries worldwide (see Figure 8.1). After the introduction of a nationwide therapy scheme, the average life expectancy rose again considerably and is currently at c.54 years (UNDP 2009).

The recent upwards trend in life expectancy alone shows the huge impact the therapy programme 'Masa' has had on the demographic, and overall social, development in Botswana. The programme, which was started in 2002 and introduced on a nationwide scale in 2004, offers free lifelong antiretroviral treatment to all persons showing a certain HIV infection level or an AIDS-defining illness (Geiselhart and Krüger 2007). The scheme also involves widespread voluntary and routine testing as well as counselling activities, condom distribution, and social awareness and education campaigns. Approximately 90 per cent of all people eligible for treatment are actually enrolled in the programme, a figure which is well above the 80 per cent coverage recently defined by WHO/UNAIDS as the 'Universal Access' target (WHO/UNAIDS/UNICEF 2010). About 170,000 persons are currently receiving regular treatment. In sub-Saharan Africa, the 'Masa' programme is unique in its commitment, complexity and widespread impact – counselling and treatment are provided on a national scale and through the public health system and, despite addressing mainly biomedical aspects of the immune deficiency, they deeply influence everyday social processes on a wider scale. Its coverage and the fact that the scheme halted, and actually reversed, devastating mortality trends prove the programme's successfulness.

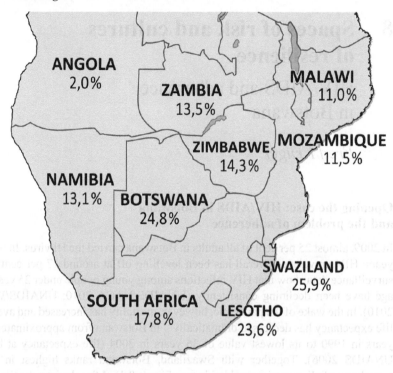

Figure 8.1 Estimated HIV seroprevalence among adults (15–49 yrs) in southern Africa in
2009
Source: UNAIDS/WHO 2010; Cartography: S. Adler 2011

With HIV and AIDS becoming a more and more omnipresent part of everyday life
in Botswana and elsewhere in sub-Saharan Africa, a wide array of literature has
covered multiple aspects of the evolution and social, cultural, economic or
political implications of the pandemic, let alone the medical backgrounds and
contexts. The basic biomedical aspects of HIV infections have been largely
disclosed (see for instance Bartlett and Gallant 2001; Cohen *et al.* 1999); here,
some interesting studies went beyond the mere medical context in recent years
and have touched for instance on access to prevention and care measures.[1] In
geography and the cultural and social sciences, a multitude of publications have
focused on aspects more or less closely related to the spatiality of HIV/AIDS –
often, however, without clearly framing such spatial everyday contexts.
Noteworthy in view of the concepts of risk and resilience touched upon in this
book are the studies compiled by Drescher (2007) and Drescher and Klaeger
(2006) on linguistic and communication patterns or works informed by medical
anthropology and development sociology (e.g. Rakelmann 2004; Gronemeyer
2005). Stillwaggon (2006), in her widely acknowledged book, draws on the
ecology of poverty in relation to AIDS from an applied economics perspective.
One of the first concise geographical contributions specifically focusing on Africa

was Barnett's and Blaikie's book on the impact of HIV and AIDS on livelihoods (Barnett and Blaikie 1992). While groundbreaking in its attempt to illustrate linkages between the pandemic and livelihood security (especially a potential increase, i.e. re-emergence, of famine induced by the decline of the rural workforce due to illness and sharply increasing mortality), the authors could of course only draw on assumptions and empirical findings available 20 years ago; in the meantime, quite a number of case studies have contributed to a much more differentiated, and less congruent, picture of the causes and effects of HIV and AIDS. Barrett (2007) for instance examines response measures to the pandemic, Schröter (2007) deals with solution concepts drawn up by national actors in Namibia, Ngigi (2007) looks into spatial patterns of AIDS in Kenya and Winkelmann (2010) studies social transformation and HIV/AIDS in Malawi, arguing from an actor-oriented perspective. All in all, such field studies, some of them indeed providing valuable insights into specific spatial and social processes related to HIV and AIDS, draw a rather disparate picture of the pandemic. Perhaps with the exception of Medical Geography,[2] there is still a lack of more conceptually oriented work which includes perceptions and constructions of threats and risk and could help to better assess and explain the complex nature of the cultural, social and spatial dimensions of HIV and AIDS.

Such insightful explanations are called for since HIV/AIDS therapy brings no cure, as there are currently no biomedical means to eradicate the HI-virus. In other words, an infection cannot be 'reversed'. Treatment is carried out by applying antiretroviral drugs (so-called 'ARVs') which suppress the virus (the 'viral load') and often lead to good recovery from the consequences of an infection, enabling people living with HIV/AIDS (PLWHA) to return to fully fledged access to and participation in everyday activities. Regular lifelong treatment with ARV drugs is administered through a so-called Antiretroviral Therapy, commonly referred to as 'ART', a term which is also used in this text.

The degree to which HIV-infected persons follow medical advice and stick to the prescribed taking of their antiretroviral medicines is crucial for both the efficacy of the ARVs and the effectiveness of the ART scheme. In fact, this so-called 'adherence' is a major factor for the long-term success of the whole therapy programme. Abandonment, or even short interruption, of the lifelong treatment may allow the highly mutable virus to rapidly develop drug-resistant quasispecies. Although various medication regimens have been developed in recent years, the spread of resistant viral quasispecies would have catastrophic consequences for the therapy schemes and, of course, the population in southern Africa. It is therefore of paramount importance to not only medically ensure concordance with treatment directions but also closely monitor the socioeconomic and socio-cultural conditions of adherence. After all, the preconditions for adherence, and the potentials of its success or failure, are not only deeply rooted in the medical sphere but also embedded in, and constituted by, socially and spatially disposed everyday practice.

It is the aim of this chapter, therefore, to shed light on the concept of adherence and how it is linked to broader conceptualisations of risk and resilience as social constructs. It is argued that an analytical framework that encompasses both risk and resilience may foster a better understanding of processes that sustain, or constrain, adherence. It is also important, however, to explain resilience concepts and draw attention to promising new, integrative conceptualisations which include ideas from various strains of the natural sciences, humanities and social sciences. Resilience, in geography and the social sciences, has often been seen as the flip side of vulnerability, the latter having received widespread academic attention in the last 20 years (Bohle 2002; Krüger 2003; Villagrán 2006; Watts and Bohle 1993). It will be shown in this chapter that a wider approach to resilience (and the social construction of 'risk' as such) is fruitful for gaining a deeper insight into everyday social practice in relation to dealing with threats and constraints such as HIV. Finally, spatial implications and their close linkages to risk-related social practice will be highlighted, calling for a truly transdisciplinary approach to risk and resilience analysis informed by, but not limited to, rationales from geography, social sciences, public health studies and psychology.

Adherence and everyday societal settings

Adherence cannot be taken for granted in all everyday situations. The 'Masa' scheme in Botswana therefore tries to secure adherence through an array of measures such as encouraging patients to find confidants who will assist in following the medication schedule or help whenever complications or side-effects become apparent. Also, clinics closely supervise dosage regimens and try to regularly ensure that the correct number of drugs be taken. Patients who have obvious difficulties, for whatever reason, in adhering to the antiretroviral regime receive intensified counselling. These measures have so far helped to minimise treatment interruptions or abandonments, but huge knowledge gaps remain when it comes to non-biomedical aspects of adherence (Hardon *et al.* 2006; IRIN 2004; Weiser *et al.* 2003).

Adherence is often used as a synonym for compliance and concordance. Compliance, however, refers to a more 'classic' hierarchical doctor–patient relationship, where physicians give treatment directions which patients are supposed to follow unchallenged (cf. Horne *et al.* 2005). Adherence stresses arrangements and agreements between physician and patient and describes the degree to which patients follow treatment regimens jointly agreed upon (Bell *et al.* 2007). Non-adherence can of course be intentional or non-intentional and have many different causes (forgetting or wilful ignoring of instructions, prescriptions which are too complicated to comprehend, occurrence of side-effects which have not been explained in advance, cost of prescribed medicine, lack of trust between patient and physician, etc.). As will be shown below, a large variety of more general societal factors can be crucial for (non-)adherence. Concordance accentuates communication patterns between patient and physician and stresses the importance of collaboratively designed treatment regimens. The aim of concordance is the establishment of a therapeutic alliance between the clinician and patient (Bell *et al.* 2007). Adherence, therefore, focuses best on how patients follow their prescribed treatment regimen under given individual circumstances and possible constraints in their societal and physical environments. This is why Horne *et al.* (2005) recommend using this term when it comes to describing how people keep up their therapy.

Successful adherence is dependent on factors far beyond the medical domain and mere epidemiological facts (see Kalipeni *et al.* 2004). On the individual level, patients must discipline themselves to take their medication regularly several times a day, and over many years. Also, having confidence in the biomedical explanation model of HIV and AIDS might be helpful. In a survey of the socio-economic impact of HIV and AIDS in Botswana conducted in 2005, we interviewed approximately 50 persons living with HIV/AIDS (Geiselhart and Krüger 2007; Geiselhart 2009). In the course of these empirical studies, one of our interview partners who had enrolled in the treatment scheme reported (through an interpreter):

> She likes them [ARVs], she gets them on time every day on eight o'clock in the morning and eight o'clock in the evening. [...] She said when she is out and the time for the ARVs is coming she is just feeling [it] that [her] time is near. 'I must go and get my pills.' [...] She has a watch and a radio, so she makes sure every now and then the battery is on, is ok. She never let it fail.[3]

On a group level, the social community needs to create an environment that supports sustained lifelong treatment. This social environment should tolerate, allow for and foster permanent treatment of a large part of the population, involving taking ARV drugs in private and in public as part of daily routines. Lifelong treatment of not just a few people but of a considerable portion of society must become a matter of course and, as such, be embedded into society. In other words, a *culture* of adherence will have to evolve that allows for a well-proven, widely understood and automatically accepted handling of HIV/AIDS treatment.

Some patients reported to us that they didn't dare to take their drugs at their workplace or during working hours, out of fear that their employer would identify them as 'sick' and therefore less fit for work, and lay them off. Recovery from acute symptoms that comes with successful medication sometimes leads patients to terminate treatment because they falsely believe they are permanently cured. There are also cases where ARV drugs are shared amongst family members who hope for relief from various ailments not related to HIV. Knowledge about the efficacy of ARV drugs is sometimes lacking or wilfully being ignored despite counselling efforts. The variety of reasons why adherence may be neglected is broad.

The analysis of adherence-related processes is thus closely linked to an understanding of normative societal factors and institutions. As the example of taking ARVs at the workplace shows, aspects of stigmatisation and discrimination also come into play (Geiselhart 2009). Before the therapy scheme was introduced, HIV and AIDS were always inseparably connected to traumatic experiences of illness and death. Many people in Botswana lost friends or family members. When the therapy programme was implemented, most patients had already experienced such traumatic events, or were suffering from ill health. With the treatment scheme's success, the horror of HIV is coming to an end as more and more people are being enrolled who have never had such a traumatic experience themselves. Medical professionals now fear that a crucial motivation factor for enrolling in the treatment scheme in the first place, or keeping up medication, is losing its importance: physicians from the Botswana–Harvard Partnership Program told us that they considered lack of personal traumatic experience to be an important factor in declining adherence.

Societal dealings with threats: danger space and risk space

When experience and knowledge, or a societal body of expertise, come into play it becomes obvious that matters of adherence are closely related to the ways a given society deals with contingencies, threats or stress. Adherence is thus action-oriented and embedded into the comprehensive context of risk-related day-to-day practice. Adequate actions and routines, i.e. everyday practices that are appropriate to tackling a social threat or challenge, require successful translation and interpretation of this threat and effective transformation of this interpretation into adaptation and coping (Krüger and Macamo 2003).

Assessment, interpretation and coping are, in fact, social actions concerning risk. Societal adaptation and coping achievements are, in turn, features of social resilience. Based on approaches to vulnerability, geographical development research has been increasingly informed by resilience concepts in recent years. Resilience, in the sense of 'adequate means to deal with the exposure to threats', is sometimes construed as the flip side of vulnerability. Other concepts interpret resilience as more than just the reverse of vulnerability, and stress notions of recuperative power and positive adjustment based on a learning process (Obrist 2010).

When we talk of resilience – and we hold the view that the establishment of a culture of adherence is one example of resilience – we must keep in mind that, as Obrist has aptly pointed out, it 'only exists in the context of potentially harmful change' (Obrist 2010: 279). It then follows that resilience, just like risk and vulnerability, is normative in that it represents the values and goals of those who define what actually constitutes resilience (ibid.). These values and goals are, in turn, embedded in larger social, economic, political or physical and, of course, spatial contexts: if we claim that adherence is currently the only way to avoid the long-term harmful consequences of HIV, then we already have a specific understanding of the nature of that threat (a biomedical phenomenon – physical context – which is transmitted from one human being to another – social and spatial context) and of the constraints of tackling it (social, political, economic and spatial contexts). This understanding is, of course, not undisputed. If we don't believe in a biomedical explanation but interpret the activity of HIV and AIDS as, for instance, the doing of evil spirits, our recommendations of appropriate counter-measures will be quite different. Meanings of resilience, and of risk and vulnerability for that matter, are either implicitly or openly negotiated in society (by experts as well as the general public; ibid.), but this does not necessarily lead to a unanimous understanding of resilience and of normative pathways towards more resilient social environments.

Such negotiations are social activities which aim to produce security and maybe, to a certain degree, reliability. Negotiation involves communication and the development of ideas concerning the borderline between danger and security (cf. Geiselhart *et al.* 2008). As a result, different imagined spaces evolve. Risk space is where security and reliability are negotiated and either achieved or missed. In risk space, resilience is created and associated day-to-day practices take place. Outside of risk space there is danger space (see Figure 8.2). From a sociological and geographical point of view, the perception of danger and the production of risk are preconditions for successfully coping with, adapting to, or avoiding (potential) hazards. Risk is calculated danger; the social construction of risk means turning contingencies into something accessible, assessable, measurable and manageable: into probabilities.

How efficiently a given society can manage dangers is dependent on the ways its population perceives and interprets these dangers and challenges, and whether the population finds appropriate means of adapting to, coping with or eliminating

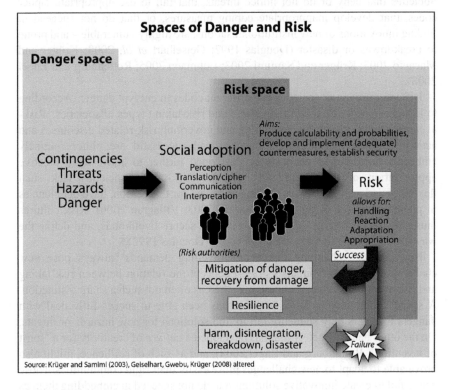

Figure 8.2 Spaces of danger and risk

these dangers. In short, for a social group to successfully deal with threats it must be able to articulate and address them. This means that dangers have to be socially adopted *and* translated into risk.

The translation process uses ciphers which must be understood by members of the threatened group, and must be interpreted and transformed into appropriate action. Only risk (as a calculated and translated danger/hazard) allows for adequate reactions which, if successful, reduce danger. The combined process of adoption and translation involves certain degrees of flexibility and creativity, i.e. an active examination of and engagement or involvement in the given threat. Rottenburg and Engel (2008)[4] go beyond the notion of mere adoption which they see as a more passive way for social actors to deal with (external) influences and changes: the authors claim that adaptation and creativity, in their dialectical relation to each other, are social capacities that may lead to (successful) translations of what they call 'travelling elements' and what we might call here, for the purpose of this text, external factors of contingencies, threats and stress.

Translation of dangers: risk, resilience and adherence as day-to-day social practice

Societies that deny or do not notice threats, that fail to use appropriate cipher codes, that develop inappropriate coping measures, or that do not succeed in finding innovations or new institutionalisations, are highly vulnerable – and prone to breakdowns or disaster (Douglas 1992; Geiselhart *et al.* 2008; Krüger and Macamo 2003; Krüger and Samimi 2003; Luhmann 2005; Rottenburg and Engel 2008).

Different groups or societies use different codes to encrypt danger. According to Douglas (1992), there are risk-averse and risk-taking types of societies.[5] Risk-averse groups are lively in developing and governing risk-related discourses and actions. Coping measures that have proved successful are either routinely embedded into danger adoption or developed further to allow for a creative appropriation of threat-mitigating actions. Risk-taking societies lack such flexibility and institutional embedding and may, for that reason, have deficiencies in preparedness (cf. Krüger and Macamo 2003; Villagrán 2006). Risk cultures thus play a vital role in maintaining safe and secure livelihoods, and define the way societies come to terms with insecurity (Douglas 1992).

New dangers, changing threats,or 'travelling demands' always pose new challenges. While in Douglas's (1992) concept the relation between risk taking and risk aversion is rather dichotomous, there is often not such a sharp distinction. A social community or individual that has been able to successfully deal with dangers for years may suddenly fail to find solutions for new hazards or threats. On the other hand, a society that has developed a *culture* of creativity (or a 'spirit of invention', Rottenburg and Engel 2008), and as such of resilience, might also prove able to adapt to new challenges more easily than rigid communities whose actors fail to create innovative solutions and do not succeed in embedding them as institutionalised practices into society.

It must also be noted that conceptualisations of risk-taking versus risk-averse action are not very clear in their usage of the term 'risk'. While in this chapter we understand risk as danger which has been calculated through a whole set of perceptions, negotiations and actions, the ideas of Douglas or Yates see risk rather as a chance/probability of a negative outcome. Negotiation and action as social practice are only implicitly touched upon.

The translation of danger into risk is crucial in order to avoid harm or disaster. It is here that communication processes come into play: are judgements based on local, i.e., traditional knowledge and perceptions or on external and/or scientific expertise? Which roles do different members of a social group play with respect to defining risks? Who perceives a threat as 'noteworthy'? Who discusses its harm potential, who decides about who should be informed and what action should be taken? Those who participate in decisions are not always those who have to bear the consequences of decisions made (Luhmann 2005). The presence or absence of legitimate and reliable 'risk authorities' is critical to the outcomes of reactions to threats. Creative, and as such resilient, communities will have found ways to establish institutionalised risk-handling regimes where social capacities and capabilities can be mobilised to find adequate solutions.

The example of adherence in Botswana makes this quite clear: on the grounds of a broadly socially accepted biomedical concept of the efficacy of ARV drugs, and of the necessity to take them without interruptions and lifelong, an effective risk-handling regime would foster adherence and concordance without the patients having to fear embarrassment or, for instance, having to legitimise themselves time and again for taking their drugs in public or at the workplace. In the case of Botswana, one such crucial risk authority has always been the government which has uncompromisingly declared war on HIV/AIDS: 'Let us deal with the HIV/AIDS epidemic as an emergency and respond with measures that a crisis deserves. Let us divert resources from military expenditure to fighting the HIV epidemic', former President Mogae announced over a decade ago (Geiselhart and Krüger 2007). While such commitment by risk authorities greatly enhances the chances that a culture of adherence will evolve, it is by no means a guarantee that a sustainable social practice for dealing with HIV/AIDS can be established. On a governmental level, an understanding of the necessity to act may well be present, but the 'true' devastation of HIV and AIDS occurs within social communities and family contexts, and it is here where creative resilience patterns must emerge. There are still huge knowledge gaps about what constitutes the conditions for such a culture of adherence, and it remains essential to examine 'cultural' explanations for people's behaviour and practices (cf. Cannon 2008).

Cultures of resilience: two approaches

An institutionalised mobilisation of social capacities of adaptation and creativity, i.e. a successful danger–risk translation which is embedded into society and allows for the appropriation of contingencies as a day-to-day practice, can be called a culture of resilience. The theoretical debates on resilience and how it relates to risk are currently fed along two major strands.

First, coming from a systems theory approach, representatives of the so-called 'social ecology' concept argue that transformations of the physical environment are socially determined and shaped (cf. Becker and Jahn 2006). In the context of intertwining societal and natural processes, disturbances become important that deflect or displace established societal relations to nature. These deflections or disturbances can be unexpected and erratic or anticipated, and they may, but need not be successfully buffered. An investigation into these processes includes notions of resilience and risk and their social negotiation, regulation and structuration (Felgentreff and Glade 2008; Müller-Mahn 2007; Obrist *et al.* 2010). Concepts of risk are here complemented by conceptualisations of resilience (in the sense of buffering or blocking of disturbances), which draw on ideas from ecosystems research and describe 'robustness' to changes and 'handling' of unexpected interferences. Folke (2006) underlines the adaptive capacity of ecosystems which he interprets as a major element of resilience. A system is resilient when it can tolerate and absorb disturbance 'without collapsing into a qualitatively different state that is controlled by a different set of processes' (Resilience Alliance 2011; see also Carpenter *et al.* 2001). In this context, self-organisation is seen as an integral part of resilient social-ecological systems.

It must be noted, however, that these notions and definitions of resilience are somewhat blurred in terms of both conceptualisation and terminology. Strictly speaking, processes described here as 'resilient' are not adaptive instances at all: adaptation transfers a system into a *new* status with altered structures and modified steering mechanisms instead of retaining the *same* controls on function and structure. With reference to systems theory, there is no sufficient differentiation between resistance and resilience. Also, despite the fact that social-ecological research attempts to focus on social systems and their 'added capacity of humans to anticipate and plan for the future' (ibid.), the aspects of negotiation, decision and action mentioned above have hitherto not been very explicitly addressed in systems analysis.

Second, the capacity to adapt and persist (and, in addition, to be creative) as a core element of resilience is more distinctly drawn upon in psychology. These approaches have only recently begun to inform research on risk in the social sciences and geography. Resilience is here explicitly referred to as the ability to negotiate contingent situations and find appropriate and sustainable solutions despite exposure to intense chronic stress or significant traumatic events. It is a positive and prospective adaptation performance on the basis of decision-making skills and competency which is achieved despite severe adversities (Luthar 2008, Norris *et al.* 2008). The emphasis of this approach to resilience is on protective-enabling factors (Obrist *et al.* 2010: 286). The role of people exposed to threats and stress is rather one of *actors* than of mere elements of a (social) system (McMurray *et al.* 2008). Especially in child development psychology, studies have been conducted that focus on how individuals and social groups perceive uncertainties, assess their own capabilities for dealing with uncertainties and finally embed adversities into their daily routines, or cope with them through the development of attitudes and values that help them to respond competently (Obrist *et al.* 2010).

Luthar *et al.* (2000) highlight the dynamic processuality of resilience which they term as thriving despite adversities, and stress two factors which are crucial in this process: exposure 'to significant threat or severe adversity' and 'the achievement of positive adaption despite major assaults on the developmental process' (ibid.: 543). Almedom and Tumwine (2008) complement the notion of response to adversity on the individual level by the capacity to anticipate and manage threats through social support on the family or community levels. These constructs are relevant for the geographical debate on risk and space because their notion of social capacity to deal with uncertainties and threats reaches far beyond the idea of 'coping' which is so dominant in classic vulnerability research. The creative ability to proactively mobilise resources or invent new means of protection, and have them embedded (institutionalised) into day-to-day practice, is a core element of a culture of resilience.

Based on Bourdieu's practice theory, and drawing on a number of empirical case studies on vulnerability and resilience in different development contexts, Obrist *et al.* (2010) suggest an analytical framework of 'multi-layered social resilience' where resilience is defined as

> the capacity of actors to access capitals in order to – not only cope with and adjust to adverse conditions (that is, reactive capacity) – but also search for and create options (that is, proactive capacity), and thus develop increased competence (that is, positive outcomes) in dealing with a threat.
>
> (Obrist *et al.* 2010: 289)

Adaptation and thus the strengthening of capacities take place in the form of an adequate and successful access to, and transformation of, economic, social and cultural capitals which then increases power-related symbolic capital. The authors point out that the ability to actually mobilise capitals varies according to the actors' position in the social field. Here, of course, the proximity to classic vulnerability concepts becomes evident. Still, the new framework reaches further in that the term resilience

> refers to learning from past experience, from one's own experience and from the stock of experience available in a community or society and thus encompasses acting before (ex-ante) not just afterwards (ex-post). Resilience thus involves planning, preventing, evading, mitigating, avoiding as well as coping with and reacting to challenging livelihood conditions. It refers to proactive capacities like capabilities to anticipate, change and search for new options.
>
> (Obrist *et al.* 2010: 290)

Why places and environments matter: constructed spaces of risk, resilience and adherence

How do these latest constructs relate to our conceptualisation of danger space and risk space above? To recall: we argue that the building of social resilience occurs in the domain of 'risk' as opposed to the sphere of 'danger'. Both the social-ecological constructs of 'robustness/regulation in times of interferences' or 'buffering of unexpected disturbances' and the psychological concept of 'proactive thriving despite adversities' are part of a translation process from contingencies to probabilities and reliabilities. Adaptation and creativity (and, as such, appropriation) take place within the domains of perception, communication and interpretation of dangers, and of the institutionalisation of (successful) handling. Again, we call these domains 'risk space' because it is here where complex social interaction related to danger and risk occurs. It is this complex dimension of the social that is 'space' (see Massey 2005). And it is here where resilience is negotiated and produced.

Here, then, lies the added value of including resilience concepts in their various dimensions when it comes to assessing and explaining crises brought about by factors such as HIV. Risk space and resilience space can be seen with the patient in the centre (after all, it is the individual who is most directly affected by the threat and burden of a potentially lethal infection) as well as being produced and construed, fostered and hampered by actors beyond the individual, i.e. social groups, the community, society. These notions of risk and resilience allow for an investigation into that individual's social setting, handling, acting and agency, and into patterns of communication, interpretation, negotiations, etc. of key actors and social groupings, under given internal and external conditions and foundations and their reshaping. The complexity of avoiding, or adapting to, individual infection *plus* intersubjective, societal (or, if we like, 'cultural') dealings with the pandemic constitute an institutionalised form of resilience (however loose or rigid, temporal or sustainable, subordinate, authoritative or powerful these institutions might be) which is embedded in the risk space.

In addition to this comprehensive concept of risk space we must acknowledge that there are concrete and measurable spaces, places and locations associated with the production of risk and resilience. Reverting to our example of HIV/AIDS and therapy adherence, one such place (on a national level) is Botswana. If we talk of institutionalised negotiations and handling practices, we mean social communities, groups or households and families in their roles as both institutional systems as well as societal spaces. If we talk of risk-taking versus risk-averse practices, these take place (sic) in locations: the HI virus is transmitted through social (bodily) interaction which is spatially positioned in certain locations, ARV drugs are (not) taken in certain locations (for instance the workplace in our example above), medical counselling occurs in specific spatial settings (e.g. the clinic or hospital), or the adequacy of measures to avoid virus transmission or promote adherence is discussed in certain socio-spatial environments (which might be anything from a living-room, a classroom, a television studio or parliament to an expert workshop or a church). In other words, what Obrist *et al.* (2010) term 'multi-layered' social resilience (household level, intermediate levels, (inter-)national levels) has very concrete spatial settings and platforms where risk communication and practice occur and are being influenced and transformed. Risk and adherence are thus spatially bound.

It is interesting to note that most studies on adherence or the lack of it follow 'Western' biomedical explanation models. Some authors do stress the imperative of an emic perspective and the importance of local (or 'indigenous') constructs of health and disease (Hardon *et al.* 2006). Cannon (2008) calls for a much stronger consideration of 'insider' beliefs when it comes to evaluating and explaining risk-related behaviour. On the other hand, these factors are often not emphasised in risk research on HIV/AIDS. This is all the more surprising as autochthonous social realities in southern Africa have already been widely investigated (for instance Gronemeyer and Rompel 2008; Korte *et al.* 2004; Rakelmann 2005; Rödlach 2006).

Also, adherence is largely centred around patients. Other actors and the socio-spatial environment receive little attention. It would be essential, for instance, to investigate the role of health professionals as carriers of different, and differing, belief systems. Sometimes, specific places (e.g. the clinic) are described with reference to their material configurations and infrastructural equipment (see for instance Hardon *et al.* 2006), but they are not identified as emotionally charged or otherwise appropriated spaces. Hence their meaning for adherence is not recognised: in which ways are specific social or physical spaces beneficial for the production of adherence, and how are they constructed to foster or constrain the successful negotiation of social resilience?

Risk-, resilience- and adherence-related daily practices are closely incorporated into interpretative systems of morality, ethics or spiritual beliefs; social ethics form an important basis for risk-related action and influence the social practices of inclusion as well as discrimination and stigmatisation in connection with HIV/AIDS and the therapy scheme. In Botswana, for instance, value and belief systems of society, and practices that derive from these, are subsumed under the concept of *Botho*. Botho (in Zulu referred to as *Ubuntu* and probably better known under this term), as a social 'contract' of respect, responsibilities, discipline and social harmony, ultimately governs whether and how people can talk about AIDS and disease, influences the negotiation of adherence patterns and regulates margin-alisation, social exclusion or inclusion of HIV-infected persons. On the other hand, AIDS (in terms of impact and transformation induced by the pandemic) may heavily influence Botho/Ubuntu as a bundle of social norms; this bundle is constantly redefined and renegotiated, and also underlies any rearrangement brought about by external influences, which makes it difficult to grasp its many variations and its dynamic social 'moulding'. As there is usually no written record of such moral judgements and creeds (they are lived, not put down in writing), it is extremely difficult to capture and assess them empirically. Serious academic examination of Botho only started in recent years, and studies on interlinkages between normative moral systems and AIDS-related social practice tread new ground (Gaie and Mmolai 2007; Metz and Gaie 2010; Osterndorff 2010).[6]

Our argument that the social logics of risk and resilience are framed by morality and value systems is, of course, deeply rooted in a cultural approach to risk analysis. What Cannon (2008) subsumes under the 'imperative of cultural understanding' has, in fact, two major implications for the enquiry into risk-, resilience- and adherence-related social processes:

1   Cultures of risk-production (i.e. adequate danger–risk translation) and creative adaptation (appropriation) of risk are *socially* bonded and it is thus essential to emphasise enabling factors that help to marshal adversities and produce resilience which is *embedded* into day-to-day practice. Geographical research should accordingly focus on the *social dimensions* of capacities which enable 'actors not only to cope with and adjust to adverse conditions (reactive), but also to create options and responses (proactive) that increase competence, and thus create pathways for mitigating or even overcoming adversity' (Obrist *et al.* 2010: 291).
2   Cultures of risk, and resilience and adherence for that matter, are also *spatially* bonded as different communities (through experience and social interaction) as well as different social settings will construct differing ('localized') appropriated spaces that may foster, or impede, the development of resilient environments. Geographical research will thus have to look into the material fabric of spaces and places as well as their actor-related social appropriation.

Conclusion: one context of risk but multiple spaces of risk- and resilience-related action and practice

Both the social and the spatial dimensions are inseparably intertwined. If we return to the topic of ARV treatment adherence in Botswana for a last time, one example can highlight this interconnection: let us assume for a moment that a social environment in Botswana has been created that allows AIDS patients to take their medication, whenever necessary, in public or at their workplace without fear of being discriminated against. Will these same patients be able to follow their treatment regimen at home? Might not the patient, for instance, want to share out his or her drugs to other ailing family members on the grounds of 'what helped me should help you, too', and then not have enough pills left for him- or herself? This does occasionally happen and can seriously compromise adherence and the treatment scheme's success. Let us further assume that the patient, after having taken his or her evening dose of ARV drugs, wanders out to meet some friends for a beer – or two or three ... A member of a self-help support group, when interviewed in the course of our field studies, pinpointed their peers' influence on treatment success (cf. Geiselhart 2009):

> Nowadays, there are no person who are dying. [...] More people are testing themselves, they know their status [...] People are on ARV, even if they are

not at our support group, they are on ARV. They have tested themselves, they know their status. [...] But the behaviour, was because these people who are on ARV, some are drinking – beers ... doing that thing. [...] I don't know, but me I go on encouraging them not to, if they are on ARV, to drink, to mix ARV and alcohol. But nowadays the situation is bad.[7]

We have here several spaces (the workplace or the home) and several different social settings (colleagues at work, the family, peers), but still the same, consistent problem of risk and resilience: the individual's adherence. We must therefore not assume that an individual's or group's risk and resilience remain unchanged in different spaces and social environments or, vice versa, that there is a single socially determined and charged risk space within one 'risk setting'.

In fact, we will often find a multitude of such risk spaces which are shaped and transformed by a multiplicity of social and physical influences and inter-connections. The approach to risk and resilience spaces outlined here has implications for geographical enquiry into risk-related social practice: it highlights the imperative to identify and understand these entangled layers of different social and spatial settings and practices and their impact on the negotiation and appropriation of contingencies and threats.

Notes

1   See Monjok *et al.* 2010 for linkages between poverty issues, fragile institutions and the success and failure of therapy schemes.
2   See the overview by Curtis and Riva 2010, to give just one example.
3   Interpreter's transcription, interview held 25 April 2005.
4   See also for instance Bhabha 1994; Loimeier *et al.* 2005.
5   See also Yates 1992.
6   See also Dilger and Luig 2010 on various aspects of morale and grief in the African HIV/AIDS context.
7   Keledi Mothemele, interview held 22 April 2005.

9 Risk as a technology of power

FRONTEX as an example of the de-politicization of EU migration regimes

Bernd Belina and Judith Miggelbrink

Today we are facing extreme and most dangerous developments of this paradigm of security. In the course of a gradual neutralization of politics and the progressive surrender of traditional tasks of the state, security imposes itself as the basic principle of state activity.

(Agamben 2002)

Analysing the external EU border from a 'security' perspective

This chapter looks at the ways in which risks are created and dealt with in the context of crossing the external border of the European Union. According to Michel Foucault (2007), risks can be understood as a technology of power emanating from the logic of security, which aims to establish social order and generates specific knowledge, based on calculations of risk. Risk, therefore, is understood as the necessary complement of security.

Two security discourses currently shape the relationships between risk, security and borders in the context of the European Union. Since 9/11 and the ensuing debate about the new international terrorism and ways in which states can deal with it, the trilogy of terrorism, organized crime and human trafficking has become a prime legitimizing force for the production of borders. This debate affects the specific form of the European border regime and appears to encourage re-bordering as a matter of course, following a phase of (apparent) de-bordering in the 1990s (Andreas 2003; Walters 2006). This legitimation, referring specifically to moments of endangerment, represents a sort of minimal consensus between the EU member states, which is the basis for the work of the border security agency FRONTEX.

The second discourse concerns the connection between security and the integration of new member states in the EU.[1] Issues of security have influenced and in turn been influenced by the process of European integration and the inevitable associated reordering of external relations (Kuus 2007), and not only since 9/11. This second discourse is also reflected in the border regime.

Both discourses shape social relations *through risk and space*, although the many interests involved mean that they are not free of contradictions.

It is the aim of this chapter to examine the social and power relations underlying the strategic co-production of risk and space, using the example of FRONTEX in the context of the border regime of the European Union. We argue that this complex is subject to a hegemonic process of *securitization* and is governed through this process. The deployment of security is directed towards the creation of future social relations, in that risks to be avoided are identified on the basis of knowledge of current conditions, and measures are derived to ensure the avoidance of these risks. In a process of securitization, events and potential events, institutions and measures, actions and persons are included in a scenario of threat and a need for *surveillance, control and prevention* based on it. The events and potential events are not abstract in nature but are named as *illegal migration*, thereby determining the focus of the production of knowledge through FRONTEX and the source of the (perceived) risks. This point of view is not given – it had to be established in specific social circumstances by actors with individual interests and for specific purposes. Risk, security and control form a field of interrelated practices, legitimations and techniques that support each other and are materialized in features such as territorial borders. Therefore these cannot be simply interpreted as a means of the production of security; instead, security as a discursive topos produces borders in a semi-natural way – because who could object to (more) security?

We will analyse the current arrangement of the three topoi in the Schengen border regime by discussing the logic of risk, security and securitization as abstract concepts in the second section, followed in the third section by reflections on the specific production of space by the EU border regime. In the fourth section we concentrate on the de-politicized character of the *assemblage* of control at the external EU border 'that combines concepts (e.g. risk), materials which it comprehends as "flow", scanners, codes, passwords, security professionals, gateways and databanks' (Walters 2006: 197).

Foucault on security, biopower and risk

A power technology perspective based on Foucault's understanding of security, together with a demonstration of the function of the concept of risk in conceptualizing and governing social relations, will make it possible to examine the relationships between state, society and the population, and to show how social order is created in terms of power technology and how spatial means (territory, border, scale) are utilized for this purpose. Foucault developed the arguments fundamental to our analysis in his lectures on *Security, Territory, Population* and *The Birth of Biopolitics* in 1977–79 (Foucault 2007, 2008). Together with *The History of Sexuality* (Foucault 1978), these lectures can be read as a reaction to the emerging criticism of the hitherto inadequate conceptualization of the state in Foucault's work in the 1970s (Gordon 1991: 4) and as a convergence 'with [...] Marxist positions' (Jessop 2007: 67).

The key term in Foucault's attempt to include the state within his approach is 'governing' (Lemke 1997: 150), which refers to the governing of the self as well as of others. Foucault identifies three different logics of power: the juridical logic which aims at domination within a territory by interdiction, the disciplinary logic which aims to (trans-)form subjects (Foucault 1975), and a third logic that aims at governing populations, referred to as the security logic: 'sovereignty is exercised within the borders of a territory, discipline is exercised on the bodies of individuals, and security is exercised over a whole population' (Foucault 2007: 25). In this logic, governing takes place 'at a distance' (cf. Garland 1996), because attempts to influence populations directly produce all kinds of unintended and counterproductive effects as a result of their natural complexity (hence: *bio*power).

Security logic as a way to conceptualize phenomena inserts them, first,

> within a series of probable events. Second, the reactions of power to this phenomenon are inserted in a calculation of cost. Finally [...] one establishes an average considered as optimal on the one hand, and, on the other, a bandwidth of the acceptable that must not be exceeded.
>
> (Foucault 2007: 20–21)

Governing in this logic is 'a matter of maximizing the positive elements [...] and of minimizing what is risky and inconvenient' (Foucault 2007: 34). The formulations 'probable events', 'calculation of cost' and 'minimizing what is risky' hint at the constitutive relevance of the notion of 'risk' in the logic of security. The notion of risk is central to this way of governing, as it makes it possible to operationalize it by enabling informed decisions about which changes in the 'regulation within the element of reality' (Foucault 2007: 69) will lead to what effects.

Regarding social phenomena as possible risks constructs a 'specific relation to the future' (Aradau and van Munster 2007: 97), as it makes things that are yet to come – apparently – calculable. By trying to identify future phenomena that exceed the 'bandwidth of the acceptable' (Foucault 2007: 21), possible future deviant individuals and subpopulations are identified in order to treat them in a preventive manner. This is especially evident in the field of criminal justice, where the ideal of preventing crimes before they are committed calls for the identification of future criminals and potentially criminal groups, situations and spaces (cf. Zedner 2007). Stepping back from this apparent solution to all social ills – who can oppose the avoidance of crime? – we have to remember that 'deviant behavior is behavior that people so label' (Becker 1963: 9). What risk analysis does, then, is to provide a new, technical, statistics-based and therefore seemingly neutral way to provide help in labelling certain deviant behaviors. The supposedly neutral, purely technical drawing of a line between normal and deviant is always political, because 'risk as an abstract technology is always shaped and given effect by specific social and political rationales and environments' (O'Malley 2008: 453), and 'may take a wide diversity of forms that reflect the purposes to which it is put and the assumptions on which it is based' (ibid.). In so doing, risk calculation constructs (categories of) individuals as potential wrongdoers and groups, situations and spaces as fostering deviance. Although individuals 'are no longer pertinent as the objective, but simply as the instrument, relay, or condition for obtaining something at the level of the population' (Foucault 2007: 65), it is individuals that are treated in a preventive manner, be it as members of a group or a category, as inhabitants of a 'risky' neighbourhood or citizens of a 'failed state'. Foucault's discussion of neoliberal thought as entailing the security logic (2008) shows *how* security is constructed, while making only passing reference to the questions of 'by whom' and 'why' (addressed, for example, by Harvey 2005). Focusing on national and international 'security' and tracing it back to the foundations of liberal thought, Neocleous argues that 'security' is 'a semantic and semiotic black hole allowing authority to inscribe itself deep into the human experience' (Neocleous 2008: 4).

Thus, in the Foucaultian tradition, 'risk' and 'security' are ways of conceptualizing social and other phenomena that are not 'risky' as such, but made governable by thinking about and treating them in a particular way. For Beck (1992), on the other hand, risk is both 'real' and at the same time socially defined. While emphasizing that 'risks and the social definition of risks are one and the same' (Beck 2009: 31), he also stresses that '[n]obody can deny' that many fears 'are founded on objective realities' (ibid.: 13). While Foucault emphasizes the way the 'security logic' developed in conjunction with modernity as a way of governing populations, i.e. as a logic of power and therefore something social, Beck situates the emergence of a 'risk society' in the second half of the twentieth century as a condition produced by unintended side effects of industrial modernization.

In opposition to Beck and in agreement with Foucault, we do not believe that the social production and definition of risks can be singled out as the sole driver of social change today – one that is laden with normative hopes for a 'cosmopolitan moment' (Beck 2009: 47–66). Foucault emphasizes that the three logics of power he identifies do not mark historic eras, but that all three are intertwined, and that what 'changes is the dominant characteristic, or more exactly, the system of correlation between juridical-legal mechanisms, disciplinary mechanisms, and mechanisms of security' (Foucault 2007: 22). This leaves room for social theory to explain how and why this happens. In Beck's notion of risk on the other hand, a social theory is implicit that regards all social processes as determined by the emergence of a risk society and that abstracts from central power relations (cf. Stork 2001).

Where Beck and Foucault agree, though, is that it is necessary to *analyse how phenomena are treated as risk*. Beck uses one of his many neologisms to describe this, the 'relations of definition' (Beck 2009: 30), referring to the social and power relations that are responsible for the treatment of social phenomena as risk. Our focus, following Foucault, is to show how these definitions are strategies of power in that they de-politicize phenomena, and to identify the role that the production of space plays within them. In the context of our subject matter, territorial strategies are especially important.

Territorial borders in the security logic

Foucault's treatment of space has been criticized for being based on a Newtonian conception of space as absolute space, rather than the production of space as a social process (Harvey 2007). Although he insists that 'problems of space are equally common to all three [logics of power]' (Foucault 2007: 26), he seems to restrict certain forms of space to each logic. While 'territory' is linked to the juridical-legal form of power and 'discipline structures a space and addresses the essential problem of a hierarchical and functional distribution of elements, [...] security will try to plan a milieu' (Foucault 2007: 35). We go beyond this treatment of space. Our argument is that the production of territories or territorialization strategies can represent a strategy of the security logic of power, for the very reason that governing at a distance is made possible by the production of space. To this end an understanding of territory as something that is produced strategically and practically is necessary.

As Agnew (2009) argues, the sovereign state in political science and beyond is usually equated with 'territory', and 'territory' with 'space'. If one understands 'territory' as just one form of socially produced space and territoriality as the process of its production, the latter can be defined as 'the attempt by an individual or group *(x)* to influence, affect, or control objects, people, and relationships *(y)* by delimiting and asserting control over a geographic area' (Sack 1983: 56). As a qualification it is necessary to add that 'territorial interests and projects [...] always have some substantive content' (Cox 2002: 10–11). Although Elden wants to approach territory 'as a topic in itself; rather than through territoriality' (Elden 2010: 811), we believe that his formulation of 'territory as technology' is compatible with our approach in that we also focus on the way territory is used in order to govern populations. We regard territorialization as a strategic means that is based on the drawing of spatial borders between an inside and outside. This can take place in the service of the security logic and in accordance with calculations of risk. With reference to our subject matter, at least three variants are possible.

First, the EU territory is part of the *rhetoric* to legitimize EU policies in the security logic. Since the Treaty of Amsterdam (1997),[2] the European Union has defined itself and its policies as aiming at the creation of an '*area* of freedom, security and justice' (our emphasis). Thus for the interior of the territory to be secure, following the spatial logic outlined above, it is necessary to make the external border secure.

Second, territorialization is used for the *classification* of people. In this respect,

> [t]o 'territorialize' means to assign 'identities' for collective subjects within structures of power, and, therefore to categorize and individualize human beings – and the figure of the 'citizen' (with its statutory conditions of birth and place, its different subcategories, spheres of activity, processes of formation) is exactly a way of categorizing individuals.
>
> (Balibar 2009: 192)

In order to classify people, the EU uses the territory-based categories of 'citizens of the Union', 'third state citizens', 'citizens of countries taking part in the

European Neighborhood Program', etc., who are granted 'stratified rights' depending on their country of origin (cf. Buckel and Wissel 2009). Issuing visas based on territorializing strategies means that 'place has now become an additional indicator of one's economic and political status' (Bekus-Goncharova 2008: 3).

Third, *policies* designed in the light of the security logic and based on risk assumptions are themselves practices of territorialization that aim at safeguarding territorial borders in the name of security. It is this third aspect that we will focus on in the following discussion of FRONTEX.

Governing, masking and producing risk: FRONTEX

The 'European Agency for the Management of Operational Cooperation at the External Borders of the Member States of the European Union' (FRONTEX) was 'created as a specialized and independent body tasked to coordinate the operational cooperation between Member States in the field of border security' (Council Regulation (EC) 2004). Its legal authority is based on Articles 62(2)a and 66 in Title IV of the Treaty of Amsterdam. These Articles do not explicitly call for the foundation of an agency – referring only to 'measures' to be taken by the Council 'in order to guarantee co-operation between the relevant departments of the member states' government authorities in these areas of the Title as well as the co-operation between these authorities and the Commission'. The foundation of FRONTEX was, however, a logical consequence insofar as agencies have been an instrument in widespread use for the implementation of intergovernmental and shared tasks in the European Union, which has been highly executive-oriented since its foundation (cf. Tohidipur 2009). In fact this is not the origin of FRONTEX. Instead, this agency has to be seen in the context of the co-operation between national security experts and ministers of the interior, which has been in place to fight terrorism since the 1970s and led to the foundation of the TREVI group of senior police and secret service agents in 1976.[3] The Maastricht Treaty provided a legal foundation for the 'co-ordinating committee composed of senior civil servants' which had prepared the Schengen Agreement and had participated in the preparation of 'compensatory measures' in security policy for the implementation of the single European market (Marischka 2007: 3). The work of the Strategic Committee on Immigration, Frontiers and Asylum (SCIFA, later SCIFA+) (ibid.: 3–4) also played a major role in preparing the ground for the foundation of FRONTEX. The Risk Analysis Centre (RAC) in Helsinki was also established on the basis of the work of this committee, and its director, Brigadier General Ilkka Laitinen, has been Executive Director of FRONTEX since May 2005.

Like other European agencies, FRONTEX is 'not among the administrative institutions provided for in primary legislation and therefore lacks a legal definition' (Fischer-Lescano and Tohidipur 2007: 1231). For many years now, however, such agencies have been used as an instrument for the provision of expert knowledge to process complex administrative tasks co-operatively and at multiple levels. Only since the 1990s have agencies acquired responsibilities and rights of a sovereign nature, serving to further the implementation of the single European market, and thereby blurring the originally clear(er) boundaries between the production of expert knowledge and political-sovereign functions (ibid.: 1232–4). FRONTEX belongs to this newer type of agencies which have 'outgrown the purely technical-regulatory construct' (ibid.: 1234) and has developed its own efficacy, which although it is discussed in political and academic circles continues to be more or less ignored outside these circles. Through FRONTEX the European border regime – in itself a highly political issue – has acquired a markedly de-politicized image due to no small extent to its specific organizational form as an *agency* (cf. de Boer 2010).

FRONTEX in the context of EU territorial policy

The position and functioning of FRONTEX can only be understood if it is borne in mind that the border regime defined as a common property in the *Schengen acquis* calls for co-operation among the executives of the member states in an area that is the classic defining moment of nation-state sovereignty, i.e. securing the border. A concerted regulation of the external border was always considered to be a necessary pre-condition for the establishment of a single European market, but 'suffers' from a lack of willingness to relinquish sovereignty. The establishment of the single European market, and especially the foundation of the European Monetary Union, led to a relocation of the economically relevant border functions to the external EU border, by means of which an entity called 'Fortress Europe' – a term that was originally part of military rhetoric during the Second World War – was organized in a highly selective manner. FRONTEX is part and parcel of the technical and institutional infrastructure that is supposed to guarantee this selectivity (Busch 2009: 9). In order to become a globally competitive geo-economic unit capable of rivalling the USA (cf. Altvater and Mahnkopf 2007), the four internal freedoms that are supposed to 'facilitate' mobility (Article 1 of the Treaty of Amsterdam) had to be established: the free movement of goods, capital, services and persons. As Narr (2009: 169–72) emphasizes, their status and quality as rights is determined by their concrete functioning in time and space. The introduction of EU citizenship, implemented by the Maastricht Treaty (1992), aims to create individual rights for persons accredited a specific status which is simultaneously denied to all non-EU citizens. This deepens the outward distinction between the two status forms, both legally and ideologically (cf. Balibar 2009). In this way an EU population is created, which represents a *governable* unit. This enables 'governing at a distance' in terms of the security logic of power.

The replacement of mostly bilateral border regulations with the attempt to produce a homogeneous ('harmonized') border regime can be understood as a territorial strategy in the sense of the expansion of a territory with unified norms. The Schengen Process became the instrument for the creation of a common territory with largely irrelevant internal borders and a unified external border. Its implementation was associated with a limitation of the sovereignty of nation states with regard to determining the regulations for crossing this border. Control over access to national territory – a classic defining moment of state sovereignty – has become the subject of political negotiation between the states and between state and supra-state EU authorities (Sassen 1998). In this way the creation of a territory is being pursued on the scale of the EU, a territory which is more than the sum of the territories of the individual member states because of its gradually established uniformity. At the same time the creation of a common external border is also – and herein lies the political difficulty – a re-scaling. For both territorialization and re-scaling hitherto remained incomplete. This was primarily because there is a marked horizontal differentiation between the member states along the lines of their individual interests (including diverging positions with regard to access to labour markets, refugee and asylum policy, relations with EU neighbouring states). This is reflected in the structure of FRONTEX. On the one hand FRONTEX is vertically integrated, in that it fulfils co-ordination functions for the member states, and – as described below – encourages standardization. However, on the other hand it is dependent on majority decisions on the part of the member states' representatives on the administrative board.

Thus the EU is a re-scaling and territorialization project, whose logic leads to the possibility of governing populations in the security logic of power through EU citizenship. This is especially apparent in the prominent status accorded to cross-border mobility within the EU. Discourses of control, surveillance and limitation have focused on the newly emerging common external border as both downside of and pre-condition for market-driven integration (Altvater and Mahnkopf 2007). Within these securitizing discourses, policies of migration and asylum have become a (highly) Europeanized topic in that they were communitized when they were transferred from the third (EC) pillar to the first pillar by the Treaty of Amsterdam (1997, Title VI, Article 62ff). In this context security has become the 'first principle of equal weight to "freedom of movement"' (Crowley 2003: 37), a process that began in the 1980s when migration increasingly became a central theme in 'policy debates about the protection of public order and the preservation of domestic stability' (Huysmans 2000: 756). Indeed, migration policy was the first field of common European policy to be wholly permeated by security discourses and technologies, even though it still continues to be made up 'of heterogeneous regulatory complexes within the European space of freedom, security and law' (Fischer-Lescano and Tohidipur 2007: 1221). It can even be argued that the process of communitizing has mainly been realized via policies against illegal migration, whereas it has slowed down in other fields. This might explain why FRONTEX concentrates on this issue which is on an undisputed common agenda. In factual terms this is not a common migration policy but rather a joint action against those forms of migration that have been made illegal and thereby placed in the sphere of criminal activity. In dealing with these, the antecedent organizations had already accumulated a fund of experience. As it poses a threat to the emerging community, *illegal migration* and the need to prevent it form the more or less explicitly legitimizing framework in all FRONTEX reports and programmes.

In the following three sub-sections we discuss the reasons why FRONTEX is a prime example of de-politicization through securitization.

FRONTEX as an institution – de-politicization I

While the agencies' original primary function was to provide expert knowledge for issues subsequently to be politically negotiated, and parliamentary control therefore appeared superfluous, FRONTEX is a politically active agency. However, it sees itself as 'the anchor stone of the European concept of Integrated Border Management, promoting the highest level of professionalism, interoperationability, integrity and mutual respect of stakeholders involved' (FRONTEX 2008: 9). FRONTEX thereby places itself in a central position in the implementation of a European border regime, but does this in the guise of a pure services agency meeting the expectations of its 'customers' (cf. FRONTEX 2009: 6, 9). The impression thus created that FRONTEX is an unpolitical community agency (and thus removed from corresponding debate) must, however, be controverted. First, FRONTEX's 'activities are "emergency driven" and a by-product of political pressures and strategies exercised by particular member states' (Carrera 2007: 9), and second, the European Commission 'exercises significant influence over the Agency' (ibid.). Its de-politicization is manifest in its weak parliamentary supervision. FRONTEX uses its status as an agency to portray itself as unpolitical, but is in fact a thoroughly political institution which is furthermore rapidly gaining in significance.

In practice, and although FRONTEX has no official operational power (cf. Rijpma and Cremona 2007: 20), it has already been deeply involved in the operational sphere. Also, the agency has acquired extensive authority to store, analyse and transfer data and to train border police. Furthermore, it can also be temporarily granted executive powers (Tohidipur 2009: 15).

FRONTEX is increasingly acquiring more far-reaching authority well beyond simple co-ordination between border security authorities of member states, and political strategies, calculations and interests influence the work of FRONTEX, with a discrepancy emerging between institutional legitimization and actual, entirely political activity. This is a form of de-politicization in the name of risk and security as it removes the matters at issue from political debate through its institutional form. The core of the de-politicization of FRONTEX's activities is to be found, however, in the form of its production of knowledge and the legitimizing semantics of risk.

FRONTEX and risk – de-politicization II

FRONTEX is concerned with 'possible events' and administers 'open series' which can only be 'controlled' by means of 'estimates of possibilities' (Foucault 2007: 35). This is a core element of the agency's current work that is the *standardization* of the border regime. Its current working programme contains detailed lists of training programmes for its executive bodies. Likewise, the member states are explicitly called to harmonize all relevant definitions in order to facilitate comparative analyses. Current recommendations for risk analysis demand '[n]ew indicators' which are supposedly essential for risk analysis, including for example 'passenger flows, visa issues and readmission'. They also call for indicators allegedly essential to the practice of border management such as 'assets available (staff and equipment)' (FRONTEX 2010: 25). Analysis and reactive capacities are already short-circuited here.

Given the fact that FRONTEX describes itself as intelligence driven, the complete absence of any definition of basic concepts and models is jarring but not surprising. The way that knowledge about risk(s) is produced and the concealed knowledge itself are always closely intertwined. As a consequence, the idea of risk on which FRONTEX's legitimization is built becomes necessarily the most safeguarded element when it comes to specific issues. While 'risk' is increasingly used to describe the object of what FRONTEX has been dealing with, any definition of these risks as well as the results of risk analyses have been covert from the beginning.

Even though (or perhaps because) 'risk analysis serves as the basis and "driver" of all operational activities' (FRONTEX 2008: 18), virtually no opportunity is given to examine the risk analyses and dossiers. This also holds for the Common Integrated Risk Analyses Model (CIRAM), which is considered to be the 'core' of FRONTEX (Marischka 2007: 7). Any description of CIRAM is a rather vague circumscription that highlights its overall and somewhat nebulous purpose – to avoid risk – enduing it with an aura of both secrecy *and* objectivity.

One main source for risk analysis appears to be incidents 'detected' along the external border, reported by the member states and evaluated and analysed by FRONTEX. Given that there is no further explanation of the term, 'risk' seems literally to emanate as a natural given from migration which is synonymous with *illegal* migration and is therefore treated in terms of 'detection of illegal border crossings', 'detection of illegal stays', 'detection of trafficking in human beings', etc. In an equally 'natural' chain of cause-and-effect, the number of 'detected' incidents in Italy and Spain is immediately followed by an enumeration of several 'joint operations' carried out in 2008, ensuring that action automatically follows a detected risk.

FRONTEX has to produce *relevant* knowledge because it is supposed to be the *authorized* entity. In order to do so, it presents a pseudo-scientific method: on the one hand it is academic according to the methods applied and their components – 'conceptual model, methodological toolbox, collection plan and indicators' (FRONTEX 2007: 16) – from which conclusions are to be drawn. This gives the results which are delivered to the relevant national border police authorities and EUROPOL, with a semblance of objectivity borrowed from the scientific idea(l) of producing *true* knowledge. On the other hand it is the complete opposite of true knowledge, as every single step from model conception to the final conclusion is completely beyond control, critical discussion and replicability. It is intelligence-driven knowledge. As such it is, from an epistemological point of view, the prototype of applied research with a small but significant difference to other forms of applied research: its object of reference is always an 'enemy' (Horn 2002: 173–74).

The benefit of presenting this type of clandestine knowledge as technical, apolitical knowledge about risks is that it opens the regulation of migration to political influences that are not democratically legitimized, without making this immediately apparent. By treating migration as a risk, calculated using secret/ intelligence knowledge, its regulation appears to be the opposite of what it actually is: a technical issue, which is de facto thoroughly political. This is the de-politicizing achievement of 'risk'. And there is more: when FRONTEX asserts that '[i]t is crucial to elaborate a common definition of risks at the border' (FRONTEX 2010: 25), it is the de-politicized concept of risk that becomes the moment of communitization – against the common enemy. At the same time the questions of 'by whom' and 'why' posed above should be borne in mind, i.e. questions about the 'relations of definition' (Beck 2009: 30) that must be posed concerning all risk definitions.

FRONTEX and space – de-politicization III

At the level of FRONTEX's operative activities, space becomes a means for calculation and control and reinforces the two forms of de-politicization already discussed here. Even though border-relevant functions have been de-aggregated and displaced from the border itself, the territorialization of migration control at the scale of the EU is central to the migration regime. It has quite rightly been pointed out that numerous surveillance and control measures – both in the Schengen and the US border regimes – take place both temporally and spatially before the 'actual' border crossing, and are therefore separated from 'the borders of the territory' (and furthermore 'in some cases, beyond the formal apparatus of the state') (Walters 2006: 193). Nonetheless, all such measures aim to regulate population by means of territorialization. The point is always who is permitted to be within the territory of the EU, and therefore involves an attempt 'to influence, affect, or control objects, people, and relationships by delimiting and asserting control over a geographic area' (Sack 1983: 56). This is the first de-politicization through space: by ignoring all reasons for the desired stay within the territory of the EU, its regulation becomes an apparently technical task, which can be approached through specific projects. This is especially obvious when the hard-fought process of migration and its regulation become maps showing FRONTEX deployments.

The second de-politicization through space results from re-scaling, i.e. from the fact that migration control takes place on the scale of the EU. FRONTEX's most urgent task is to act as the mechanism which co-ordinates the co-operation of the member states' authorities. In this context FRONTEX does not (yet) function so much as a fixed-scale organization, but rather as a 'networking engine' (Marischka 2007) whose activities connect military, police and other national authorities concerned with border regulation, as well as the 'offices of urban immigration departments' (ibid.: 4). On the face of it, this appears to work towards 'making nation state [...] controls more efficient' (ibid.), but in the long run aims at gradually subjecting the 'loosely connected national segments' (Hobbing 2005: 7) of the external border, currently supervised by numerous state authorities on the basis of a multiplicity of laws and regulations, to a unified modus of surveillance and control. This model is to be implemented on the scale of the EU and will be subject to (even) less democratic control than is currently the case at the level of the member states.

Beyond FRONTEX: risk calculation and space production in the light of a broader concept of securitization

The argument so far can be summarized thus: according to Foucault, the human subject exists in relations of production and meaning which can be defined and analysed as complex power relations. Space, the appropriation of space, is considered to be an indispensable medium for the exercise of power in this context. The logic of security aims to arrange things in such a way that they serve certain purposes, e.g. 'common welfare'. Space thereby becomes an instrument for changing circumstances in a specific way, and is always directed to an end in the future, to be derived from that which is currently 'the case'. The instrumental character of space with reference to the European Union has been identified as a territorialization strategy, for which the production of a border 'of its own' is essential. While Foucault's territory is defined as a space where rules apply in the legal mechanism of power, we understand territorialization as a spatial-strategic means for the production of security. The spatial strategies employed to this end are varied in their nature and are tied to institutions but are all based on the existence of territories: up-scaling, extra-territorial action and the categorization of individuals on the basis of citizenship status.

It is undisputed that such strategies involve dealing with risks arising from the crossing of borders by individuals, and the production of greater security *at territorial borders*. The theoretical perspective chosen here has succeeded in demonstrating two things: first, that security (and its obverse: risk) is not a situation to be produced (or prevented), but a topos which pervades practices and shapes them. As a power mechanism, security is not merely produced but is also productive. Thus it is to be expected that the logic of security not only controls the classic field of dealing with risks at borders, but also extends to other areas. With regard to the European Union, there is growing evidence that gives weight to the assumption that security is 'more than a subsidiary consideration that may justify pragmatic restrictions' to freedom (Crowley 2003: 37). When security is understood as a pre-condition for development (European Commission 2003: 2), the logic of security permeates the formation of the European Union. In particular the European Security Strategy provides numerous indications that the production of security will in future not be limited to preventive measures (e.g. repelling undesired 'illegal' migrants), but that increasingly measures will be taken by means of which the societies of the future – failing, weak, declining and dissolving states (cf. European Commission 2003) – will themselves be shored up or reshaped in the interest of their own security.

FRONTEX, it is possible to conclude, may currently be a major interface in up-scaling the regulation of a common external border, but could, bearing in mind the expansion of the logic of security, be (merely) an intermediate stage: in view of the increasing risk of proliferation, in the future 'the first line of defense will often be abroad' (European Commission 2003: 7). However, this will compound the problems concerning the legitimation of extra-territorial action already existing with regard to FRONTEX activities. This problem can be expected to gain significance in the future. Agamben's observation hereby also gains weight. If security becomes the 'sole criterion of political legitimation' (Agamben 2002), security itself will become an 'essential risk. A state which has security as its only task and source of legitimacy is a fragile organism; it can always be provoked by terrorism to turn itself terroristic' (ibid.).

Notes

1   Compare the European Security Strategy's programmatic and legitimizing statements: European Commission 2003.
2   See: http://eur-lex.europa.eu/en/treaties/dat/11997D/htm/11997D.html, accessed 9 June 2010.
3   TREVI stands for *Terrorisme, Radicalisme, Extrémisme et Violence Internationale* as well as for the first meeting place of the group, the Italian town of Trevi.

10 An impossible site?

Understanding risk and its geographies in Goma, Democratic Republic of Congo

Martin Doevenspeck

Introduction

Living in the east Congolese city of Goma is risky. The eruption of the volcano Nyamulagira, located about thirty kilometres west of Goma, in January 2010, reminded the global public that the region around Lake Kivu has not only been suffering from prolonged civil war for nearly two decades, but is also exposed to a multitude of natural hazards. The second active volcano in the province of North Kivu is Nyiragongo, situated eighteen kilometres north of Goma. The eruption of Nyiragongo in January 2002 destroyed large parts of the urban infrastructure, forced 400,000 people to flee and left 120,000 homeless. While there are many cities in the world that face the threat of volcanic eruptions, it would be hard to find another city that is simultaneously threatened by carbon dioxide emissions from volcanic fissures onshore, and huge quantities of explosive gases dissolved in the lake water, as well as normalisation of violent crime in the course of persisting armed conflict, and a deterioration of state institutions incapable of providing the population with security. However, this depressing outline of the city's multi-hazard environment should not obscure the fact that Goma also offers opportunities.

Two questions will illustrate my concern to understand risk and its geographies in Goma. First, how can we conceptualise risk in a society that obviously does not belong to the reflexive late modern ones in which scholars came up with risk theory to describe a certain stage in the development of these societies? Second, which spatial dimensions of the place-specific understandings of risk can be identified in such a precarious context with a high number of densely concentrated hazards? I argue that one way to find answers to these questions within an analytical framework that makes empirical findings accessible for a concep-tualisation of risk is to discuss Luhmann's distinction between hazard and risk (Luhmann 1993). Thus, I will scrutinise translations of hazards into risks and the spatial dimensions of these translations. The main objective of this chapter is not to contribute to the bulk of practice-oriented studies on the nexus between natural hazards and urban development in the Global South, which focus on disaster preparedness and urban planning (e.g. Pelling 2003; Wamsler 2007; Paul and Bhuiyan 2010). I am not primarily interested in providing the basis for new external interventions in the life worlds that I seek to understand. The central idea instead is to foreground emic understandings of dangers and risk, and spatialities linked to these understandings, in order to get an idea of how the concept of risk can be used to understand how people in Goma make sense of the exceptionally high number of hazards in their everyday life.

In the following two sections I will outline the analytical framework and the methodology. The analysis of the wider context of the case study will pay special attention to the development of Goma's ambivalent character as an 'impossible but inevitable city', as Lewis (2003) put it in his analysis of New Orleans. Then three empirical sketches of gas in Lake Kivu, volcanism and violent crime will be presented to discuss how far Goma's inhabitants translate dangers into risks and to illustrate the spatial dimensions of these translations. The chapter ends with a concluding discussion of the findings against the backdrop of the analytical framework and a more general outlook on studying risk in Africa.

Translating hazards: conceptualising risk and its spatial dimensions

Contemporary risk concepts are first of all applied to describing the particular development stage of modern or post-modern societies, as reflected in the title of Ulrich Beck's seminal book on reflexive modernity (Beck 1992). The key thesis of the *Risk Society* approach is that in advanced modernity the societal production of wealth is systematically associated with the societal production of risk. Therefore, the problem of wealth distribution is superimposed by conflicts that emerge from the problem of distributing scientific and technological risks. Modern society becomes reflexive as it addresses self-made risks. Though the reflexive modernisation approach (see also Giddens 1991) is only one of several important theoretical approaches to risk in the social sciences,[1] most of these approaches share more or less the same deep-rootedness, both philosophically and empirically, in the Western experience of the successful use of risk for economic progress in the modernisation process. Another commonality is that they broaden the perspective by referring to the social construction of risk, thus highlighting its mental and selective dimension. In this regard, Deborah Lupton (1999: 35) distinguishes epistemologically between realist, weak constructivist and strong constructivist approaches, according to the degree to which they accept that risks are objectively given. In the realist variant, as in probabilistic risk assessments, and also, although to a lesser extent, in rational choice approaches (see Jaeger *et al.* 2001), risk is real and objectively given. By contrast, constructionist approaches claim that risks are, above all, representations of people's experiences of a threatening reality that gel in societal debates on this reality.

However, since construction and selection implies agency, the concept of risk should be applicable to the study of human agency in general, be it in modern or allegedly pre-modern societies. As I am interested in the way Goma's inhabitants interpret and handle their situation, I draw on the translation aspect of Niklas Luhmann's constructionist approach, which particularly allows for human agency.

Thus, his distinction between hazard as a fact independent of human agency, and risk as the outcome of a decision by actors or society, emphasises the relevance of social action (Luhmann 1993). In this perspective, risks are socially constructed, since they are translated hazards based on calculation. Risk is therefore a relative category, linked to and determined by particular actors. To be clear: I do not claim that people in Goma are not exposed to concrete dangers. As Ian Hacking has stated: 'You might be a social constructionist about brotherhood and fraternity, but maintain that youth homelessness is real enough' (Hacking 1999: 6). I agree with this instructive critique of constructivist exaggerations and the claim that reality and construction do not inevitably clash. The Nyiragongo volcano, for instance, is very real, and visible from any place in the city, just as the wisp of smoke rising from its lava lake. And the materialities of the need for security and other obvious impacts of violent crime on the urban fabric give evidence of widespread armed crime and lawlessness in Goma. However, as Berger and Luckmann (1966) have shown in their sociology of knowledge, social reality is constructed in so far as people perceive and cope with it differently. The same holds true for risk, since one person's risk may be a danger for another. If one agrees with this assumption, then it can be assumed that even hazards are not objectively given, but are the outcome of a translation process, since one person's hazard may for another person be just a circumstance, a phenomenon that one is not concerned with. What is analytically interesting, and, as I seek to show, empirically approachable, is if, why and how circumstances are translated into hazards and into risks.

What does this focus on risk as translation mean exactly? To put it simply, I seek to understand how people think about the different sources of potential harm, what conclusions they draw for their everyday life and how this shapes their agency, with special emphasis on the spatiality of risk taking. The starting point of my approach is the observation that coping with the situation in Goma includes both interpretation and activities, and thus has both a mental and a physical dimension. Therefore, I argue firstly that individual translations are shaped by perceptions and evaluations of the situation. Secondly, I assume that the translation process involves media – e.g. images, actions, institutions and materialities – in which translations are inscribed and that have specific spatial dimensions, such as imagined places of safety, spatial perceptions or physical infrastructure of protection.

Breaking up the translation process into these three analytical and interlinked dimensions of perception, evaluation, and spatiality of coping (Table 10.1) forms the basis of the presentation and the analysis of the case studies, and should enable us to grasp how people in Goma create and select risks and how they deal with them spatially, thus how they make sense of the multiplicity of perils in their everyday life. Assertions regarding interpretations of the sources of danger and their relevance for people, as well as assumptions of how they actually deal with them, will serve to link the different cases, and to foreground both emic understandings and the spatiality of related risk-taking practices.

There are many different facets and understandings of these three analytical dimensions that cannot be covered entirely. By perception (of phenomena, hazards and risk) I understand the images people create of a specific source of potential harm. Since these perceptions are shaped by a multitude of factors, whether rooted in the individual's psychology or in the societal and cultural context, they cannot all be covered in this article (Slovic 1987; Rohrmann 1999: 4–11; Jackson *et al.* 2006; Wachinger and Renn 2010). Therefore I will mainly concentrate on three elements which several studies have shown to be constitutive for risk perception and which I consider to be empirically approachable: personal experience (Grothmann and Reussewig 2006; Plapp and Werner 2006; Miceli *et al.* 2008), social status (Short 1984; Chester *et al.*, 2002; Gaillard 2008) and trust (Frewer and Salter 2007; Paton 2008). Trust means both trust in second-hand information, and in organisations and institutions. In my analysis, I will try to cover both the source of the potential harm and the context.

With regard to perception and its evaluation, I do not refer to the specific module of a technical- and policy-oriented risk governance approach that seeks to contribute to science-driven risk management (e.g. IRGC 2009). Instead I study evaluations as personal judgements of the potentially harmful situation by focusing on three elements: estimations of personal exposure and vulnerability, of the seriousness of the situation, and of the chances of being exposed, based on individual and social values. Studying perception and evaluation is a way of understanding 'everyday or lay accounts of risk' (Mitchell *et al.* 2001: 219) and context-specific 'risk knowledges' (Lupton and Tulloch 2002). To foreground the characteristics of these emic perspectives, I will contrast the lay accounts with the way experts story the situation, drawing on scientific work and interviews with scientists and practitioners. In a final step, and for all three case studies, I will discuss what kind of potential agency people see for themselves, how they seek to implement their reasoning on exposure, vulnerability and potential benefits, how they act. Special emphasis is thus placed here on three specific spatial dimensions: spatial imaginations, spatial practices and their locatable materialisations. In this way, my attempt to link the two concepts of risk and space does not spatialise risk as a facet of the social, but enquires into the reciprocity of everyday practices of risk-taking and spatial configurations.

Table 10.1 Analytical dimensions of translation and operationalizations

Analytical dimension	Perception	Evaluation	Spatial dimension
Focused elements	Personal experience	Personal exposure and vulnerability	Imaginations
	Social status	Seriousness	Practices
	Trust	Opportunities of being exposed	Materializations

Methodological approach

How can the translation of hazards into risks and its spatial dimensions be approached methodologically? Basically, I argue that this needs to be done by studying how Goma's inhabitants talk about hazards and about coping strategies, and by observing what they actually do. To illustrate my argument I draw on empirical findings ranging from ethnographic to statistical data, gained using a mixture of methods. I conducted fieldwork in Goma and the Congolese-Rwandan borderland around Lake Kivu in the period 2006–2008. I worked in different parts of the city to collect the accounts of various segments of the population: wealthy traders, day labourers, long-time residents, migrants from the south, and war refugees who had fled from the hinterland. I talked with people who had experienced the 2002 eruption of Nyiragongo, and with others who had not. Furthermore, I had meetings with ordinary policemen and senior police officers, with heads of private security firms and chief security officers of the United Nations Organization Mission in DR Congo (MONUC). And I accompanied Goma Volcano Observatory (GVO) staff during surveillance trips to the volcano and its flanks, self-help groups during night patrols to protect their neighbourhood against robberies, or simply people during their different daily activities. The statistical data stems from a survey sample that consisted of 138 persons. The questionnaires included both closed and open questions on information, perceptions and experiences, and provided descriptive statistics to frame the analysis of the ethnographic data.

Goma, city of dangers and opportunities: introduction to the case study

Goma has always been a *lieu d'opportunité*, a place that offers economic opportunities. Founded as a small regional administrative and military post by the Belgian colonial rulers near the village of Mungoma, it developed from the beginning of the last century into a residence for white settlers who established vast farms on the fertile volcanic soils in the hinterland. By independence in 1962, the population had grown to about 40,000 people. The airfield was used for the export of mining products, but also for supplying the western parts of the country, and especially the capital Kinshasa, with staple foods, meat and cheese produced on the fertile volcanic soils. Intensive cross-border trade, investments in public infrastructure, and the city's functions as the administrative capital of the province of North Kivu led to high immigration rates and population increase. *Twanjingoma* is a well-known saying in the regional Swahili and means as much as 'let's go to Goma to have a peaceful and easy life'.

Population growth in Goma was amplified significantly by war and lasting insecurity in North Kivu from 1990 onwards, when ethnicised land conflicts in the rural areas pushed the first wave of refugees into the city (Figure 10.1). This flow of refugees has never been interrupted since then, and during the different episodes of armed conflict in the Kivu region Goma's population shot up from 170,000 inhabitants to an estimated 800,000 in 2009. However, this enormous influx cannot be solely explained by the city's shelter function; it also includes migrants who are attracted by the relatively high food security in Goma, and a new job market that is directly linked to the three most important features of the war economy: the massive presence of international aid organisations, mineral trade, and intensive – largely unofficial – cross-border trade in general (Büscher and Vlassenroot 2010; Mitchell and Garret 2009; INICA 2006). It is against this background of the city as a shelter in a war-torn region, but also relatively low living costs due to moderate food prices, and the various income opportunities linked to its location on the border and to the war economy, that one has to assess people's attitudes towards natural hazards and crime.

The invisible threat: gas in Lake Kivu

Lake Kivu's huge gas reserves were initially only of interest to the natural sciences because of the uniqueness of the physical and chemical composition of the lake water. However, when a lava stream flowed into the lake during the 2002 eruption of Nyiragongo, experts feared that the hot lava could have disturbed the stability of the lake, thus making a future gas outburst, similar to the one in Cameroon (Tietze 1987) even more likely (Lorke *et al.* 2004). A massive gas outburst could kill hundreds of thousands or even millions of people living on the shores of Lake Kivu, and around Lake Tanganyika, if a gas cloud floated in that direction (Kling *et al.* 2006). Probabilistic risk assessments conclude that such an extreme event is unlikely at the present time, since gas concentrations have not yet reached dangerous magnitudes. But this applies only if no significant disturbance occurs, such as a great heat input into the lake during a volcanic eruption, or an earthquake, events that are not unusual in the western branch of the African Rift Valley.

The close attention paid to gas accumulation in Lake Kivu in the media and by scientists (Tassi *et al.* 2009) is seldom if ever echoed in the accounts of the local population. During the survey it was not mentioned as a problem even once. However, if asked about it specifically, Goma's inhabitants show that they know about the gas and the potential dangers linked to it. There are three remarkable and intertwined characteristics of people's accounts of the gas issue. The first characteristic is that they mainly speak about the direct risks related to the gas.

> I only know that people are dying because of the gas and the gas makes that the lake swallows up people.[2]

People either speak about the risk of drowning because of gas bubbles in the water, as in this interview quote, or about the fractures emitting carbon dioxide that are associated with the Virunga volcanic system (Vaselli *et al.* 2002/2003). Very frequent on the entire northern shore of Lake Kivu, these dry vents are called *mazukus*, which means 'evil winds' in local Swahili. Since the 1990s, several people have died in *mazukus*, mainly migrants and refugees to whom the phenomenon was unknown.

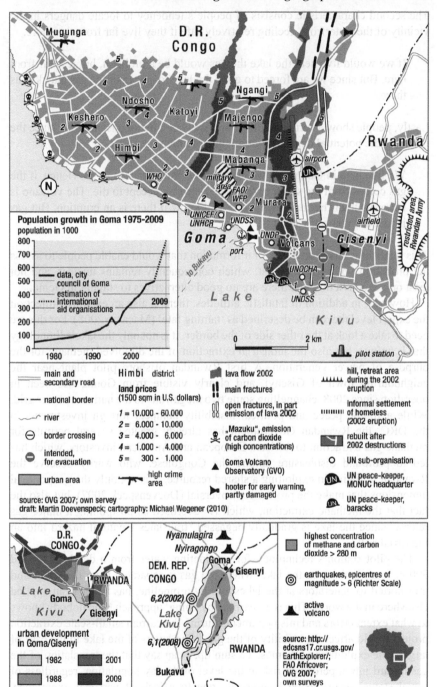

Figure 10.1 Goma: population growth, urban development and hazards

The second characteristic consists of people's tendency to locate dangers in the vicinity of the waterfront, feeling relatively safe if they live far from the shore.

> If we would live near the lake the gas would be a problem, but it is far from here. But since we are forced to go to the lake to get water the gas may kill us there.[3]

Lastly, people show a certain fatalism in respect of a major gas outburst, since the extent of the potential damage is unimaginably high.

> We live here in Goma and we do not have another place to go. Hence, if the gas comes from the south or from the north we accept to die. The volcano is better than gas because everybody will know if there is an eruption. But gas is like air, you can't see it.[4]

This fatalism is based on a lack of information that would enable people to assess the probability of a gas outburst, which consequently remains unclear, and not least on the conviction that there are no good alternatives to staying in Goma.

However, in addition to fatalistic attitudes, there is also an exciting project on the expert level that can be described as 'taming fate' (Macamo 2008). For this we need to take a look at the other side of the border. It is not only the lake's limnology that is unique, but also the industrial extraction of the dissolved methane for the purpose of power generation. A first Rwandan offshore pilot plant near the neighbouring town of Gisenyi, and clearly visible from Goma, has been in operation since 2008, channelling some two megawatts to the national power grid. While a fragile peace and political instability hampers foreign investments in the DRC, the Rwandan Government has already granted several permits for methane gas extraction to African, European and American investors, which has led to profound displeasure among the Congolese, who warily observe the Rwandan initiative in exploiting a shared resource. It is not only the geopolitical dimensions that make the project controversial (Doevenspeck 2007), but also the fact that the methane extraction, which is advertised as postponing a major gas release, since the lake is gradually degassed,[5] translates a natural hazard into an industrial risk.

The pilot station's technology for conducting water from a depth of around 300 m to a platform on the lake, where the gas is separated from the water and transported to generators at the lakeshore by a pipeline, has never been applied elsewhere in the world. This is a 'learning by doing' approach,[6] and nobody knows to what extent errors and misjudgements during the current small-scale extraction project would affect the stability of the gas-filled layers of the lake in the case of large-scale exploitation schemes. To sum up, I can say that the translation of the gas hazard into a perceived risk at the level of the lay population, regardless of social status, seems to be incomplete, due to a lack of personal experience, inability to see the relevance of the problem for everyday life, and poor information. Thus, evaluations are shaped by fragmented assessments of exposure and vulnerability, as well as of the seriousness of a potential gas outburst, and a possible gas outburst is consequently treated as an unavoidable blow of fate. This in turn leaves very few coping options, apart from shunning areas onto which the danger is projected. Something that one is not concerned with needs no coping strategy. In sharp contrast to this, the methane gas extraction project in Lake Kivu, even if primarily driven by economic interests rather than by considerations of risk reduction, could be viewed as a complete translation linked to very concrete practices of risk taking and the creation of new technological risks.

'It's our dangerous neighbour': narrating Nyiragongo

As a result of permanent volcanic activity on Lake Kivu's north shore, people are continually affected by creeping hazards, such as acid rain, endemic fluorosis, diarrhoea and other diseases due to polluted drinking water. However, in what follows I will concentrate on accounts of a new eruption of the Nyiragongo volcano, and in doing so I will again contrast lay and expert translations.

There are two reasons for this focus on eruption, and especially on lava flows into the city. First, because people in Goma are less exposed to volcanic emissions due to the prevailing wind directions, and second, because the 2002 eruption 'constitutes the most outstanding case ever of lava flow in a big town' (Favalli *et al.* 2009: 363), and together with the previous one in 1977 the only one worldwide 'in which people were directly killed by lava flows' (ibid.). During the eruption, lava flows from re-opened fractures of the 1977 event and from new ones in the immediate vicinity of the city's northern periphery inundated a third of the city (Komorowski *et al.* 2002/2003). What makes the situation in Goma so unique is the multitude of old and fresh potentially lava-emitting fissures, even within the urban area. Model-based recommendations to relocate the town or protect it by artificial barriers that would divert the lava flows (Chirico *et al.* 2009) generally provoke a shake of the head among the local GVO staff, who consider these technologisations of the volcanic hazard as being of academic value only.[7]

As in the case of the gas, people did not mention the volcano as a problem in respect of living in Goma. During the survey, two-thirds stated that they were afraid of Nyiragongo mainly because of potential economic losses, which reflects their personal experience. The majority of interviewees who said they did not fear the volcano explained their attitude by indicating that they are used to living with it. Both survey and interview data reveal that people often use the term 'neighbour' to describe their relationship with Nyiragongo. It is a scary and freakish neighbour, but its existence is inevitable …

> I don't fear the volcano any more. We were born and the volcano was already there. We grew up and the volcano was still there, and when we die it will remain.[8]

In contrast to the fatalistic attitude towards a gas outburst, the personal experience of former eruptions and also of the post-disaster reconstruction of the city, something unimaginable for many immediately after the event, seem to shape a certain defiance vis-à-vis a future volcanic crisis. People are fully aware of the seriousness of an eruption, as well as of their exposure and vulnerability to it, but they refuse to let it impose restraints on their life, let alone to abandon their homes in order to mitigate the disaster risk, as suggested in the above-mentioned study by Chirico *et al.* (2009). The same tendency appears in people's accounts of how they will react to a new eruption.

> The lava flows where it wants to. We can't do anything; we do not have any means to fight against the volcano. And as always we will flee to Rwanda and we will come back when the lava is cold.[9]

In 2002 more than 400,000 people sought shelter on the hills in neighbouring Rwanda, in an almost panic-free self-evacuation. Despite numerous reports of bad treatment of refugees in the interview data, and a general mistrust of a country that is deeply involved in the different wars in Eastern Congo, people mostly accept that with the volcano behind them and the lake ahead there are few alternatives to a border crossing.

There are at least two other prominent features of the way people translate the volcanic hazard into risk. The first one is a profound distrust of the institutions in charge of disaster preparedness. Though people usually refer to these institutions as *les volcanologues*, it is not so much the widely respected Congolese GVO staff that is targeted, but the showcase project of the United Nations Office for Project Services (UNOPS) in respect of risk management and awareness raising. Since at least 2006, there have been massive accusations against the project concerning misappropriation and embezzlement of funds that are openly discussed in local radio broadcasts.[10] Survey data show that scarcely more than 10 per cent of the interviewees had received information on what to do during an eruption from organisations in charge of risk management. Furthermore, there is still no consistent and coordinated concept of how to evacuate the city. This seems to be careless, since numerous roads that could serve as escape routes are still blocked by the 2002 lava, making self-evacuation much more difficult today.[11]

A further feature, similar to the gas issue, is what may be called imagined safe places. Interviewees are generally aware of the dangers during an eruption and they know about potentially eruptive fissures within the city. Nevertheless, many consider some parts of the town safer than others.

> We do not have any information out here. If we could live in the city centre we would be up to date and able to flee in time just as the others. But here we get no information.[12]

This is partly due to a perceived marginalisation in the peripheral districts, in a context where people have learned to appreciate hearsay in the absence of reliable 'official' information. As all rumours concentrate in the city centre (*en ville*), it is considered as being safer than other parts. After 2002, the idea of security was projected onto all parts of the city that were not affected by the lava stream. In particular, the western lakefront and Himbi district experienced a veritable construction boom, since many victims sold their properties in the badly hit city centre and built new houses in the western parts.[13]

As outlined above, Goma experienced a significant population growth even after the 2002 event. I do not know of any people who left the city because of the volcano, for victims weigh dangers against benefits.

> I lost everything in 2002 and I had only the clothes I was wearing. Believe me, I have the experience and I will be the first to flee. But for the moment I will stay in Goma. I have a house in Kisangani[14] too, but Kisangani is a bit remote. In Goma you have the border, there is business, trade, money.[15]

However, it becomes apparent that not everybody benefits from the opportunities Goma has to offer.

> The volcano is not more dangerous than the armed men in our forests. We are from a village close to Mweso, Masisi. There was always enough food but we had to flee from the war. Here in Goma we have to buy our food but we don't have money. Every day my husband tries to get a job but there are so many like us. As soon as there is peace in Masisi we'll go back.[16]

The options for displaced people with a rural background and without their own capital to start at least a petty trade business are very restricted, since the capacity of Goma's job market to absorb newcomers is far exceeded. During the survey, two-thirds mentioned that they were jobless, and only 6 per cent of those who stated they had a job had a formal employment contract. Hence, a large section of the population is exposed to the volcanic hazard without benefiting from the place-specific opportunities.

Compared to the incomplete translation of the gas hazard, people fully appreciate the seriousness of a volcanic crisis, in many cases due to their own experience. But risk perception is shaped by scepticism in respect of official disaster mitigation, and, though socially differentiated, by fate. Socially differentiated, too, is evaluation of the chances of being exposed, while all people are aware of their vulnerability. As shown in the previous section, the imagination of safe and unsafe places is part of the spatial dimension of translation. Another spatial dimension is mobility, since people have experienced that they can act during an eruption, namely by fleeing.

'Night-time visitors': the normalisation of violent crime

In a context of long-lasting state decline and prolonged civil war, it is not surprising that people do not bother so much about the rather abstract threat of suffocation in a gas outburst, or the possibility of losing their house and belongings through a new volcanic eruption. Both interview and survey data show that people's priority in everyday life is to cope with the lack of basic infrastructure and the dysfunction of public services such as water supply, schools, health services and, first and foremost, security. As the sun goes down, the city turns into a romping ground for criminals. About 40 per cent of interviewees stated that they were robbed once or even repeatedly during the night. Their depiction of these robberies follows a recurrent pattern: heavily armed men, often dressed in army clothes, break down the wooden doors of the houses with one of the big lava rocks that lie around everywhere. The 'night-time visitors' force the inhabitants to hand over their money and valuables, and then flee through the dark streets while shooting into the air to scare off potential pursuers. The loot may appear ridiculous, considering the weapons and the effort involved: maybe a couple of US dollars (East Congo's unofficial currency), mobile phones, a radio, or clothes and cooking utensils.

> They entered the house with a big stone you know. [...] They wore army trousers and shouted 'give the telephone, give the telephone, give money'. We said that we had nothing and so they took women's and children's clothes, a small radio and a sewing machine.[17]

Nearly all the people I spoke to had had such experiences themselves, or could tell stories about the experiences of neighbours and friends. There is no research on violent crime in the city, nor any reliable official statistics. However, a report by the Pole Institute (2009) on the security situation in Eastern DRC gives a depressing insight into the issue, listing eighty-two homicides in Goma between January 2007 and April 2008, while raising no claim to completeness. For the period August to November 2007, I recorded an average of six robberies per night and two murders per week.[18]

Lay and expert opinions on the source of this widespread insecurity and the culprits do not differ from each other.

> If the government would pay the army regularly, and guide and supervise them as is right and proper, we wouldn't have this problem. It's the soldiers, they are unpaid and undisciplined. At least they cooperate with the robbers. [...] If people see you change ten dollars in the market you must be afraid of being visited during the night.[19]

Just like this young woman from Mbanga South district, people blame the army personnel based in the city. During the survey, over 60 per cent of the interviewees accused the army of being the cause of insecurity. Hence, delinquency is directly linked to the heavy militarisation of Goma as a result of the war in North Kivu. In 2008, about 15,000 soldiers and their families lived under extremely difficult conditions in makeshift shelters distributed over the whole city, instead of being separated from the population in barracks. Mostly unpaid by the corrupt military command, the Kalashnikov became an important means of survival for many of them, as well as for the estimated 25,000 deserters and (former) members of various militias.[20] The frequency of robberies fosters a climate of mistrust, so that people avoid showing what they have in order to avoid being the next victim. Since the police are considered as a part of the problem,[21] people have developed several 'spatial' strategies of risk taking which can be clustered into three main practices: different forms of territorialisation, adjustment of personal mobility patterns, and the organisation of a cross-border routine.

Given the inability of state institutions to provide security in Goma, the most effective way of protecting one's house is to wall it in, to wire it and to 'buy shelter' from one of the private security providers. Prices for object protection and guaranteed armed intervention in the case of an attack vary between 250 and 370 US$ per month among the different private security companies. Since these companies are not allowed to carry weapons, they pay the police command to back up their response teams with armed policemen. Less wealthy house owners hire an armed policeman directly from the next police station to protect them from dusk till dawn. The 50 to 80 US$ that must be paid for this service are shared between the policeman and his superior. These detachments of policemen for the protection of private houses, banks and facilities of the international humanitarian organisations have two main consequences for the spatial configuration of safety within the urban fabric. On the one hand, there are many small islands of purchased security, which together form a comparably secure area in the city centre and in a westwards fringing band along the lakeside road lined with the most expensive residential areas in Goma, and on the other hand, there is a space that is totally unprotected by the police during the night, covering most of the rest of Goma. Popular districts such as Keshero, Ndosho or Katoyi, to name but a few, are left to take care of themselves and constitute veritable no-go areas for UN staff.[22]

> I am alone here and I am responsible for nearly 60,000 people. But I spend the night with my family in the barracks. So during the night there is no police at all in Mabanga. I used to have five officers but they were detached to protect some houses in Himbi. So what can I do? People are organising themselves into patrols to do our job. They are really brave.[23]

Abandoned by the state the inhabitants of some districts organise themselves and patrol in their neighbourhoods, assuring a minimum of protection for the population. Initially the municipality and the governor sanctioned this self-help, and voluntary policing seemed to be a successful deterrent. However, the project got in a crisis when gunmen wounded the first volunteers, who were only armed with machetes and sticks. Simultaneously some of the patrolling groups got out of control and established roadblocks where they intimidated passers-by and collected money from them.

Besides the spatially and temporally restricted zoning of security, the adjustment of individual mobility patterns to the situation is another spatial dimension of translation. Most attacks occur from dusk to midnight. Accordingly, most people try to get home by 7pm at the latest, leaving the city deserted. Moving around during the night was extremely risky for a long time, and people often call friends in the districts they want to go to in order to check the situation before crossing the city. People also regularly stay with friends during the night instead of taking the risk of walking home after nightfall or avoid stopping anywhere when they go by car.

> If you can't avoid going by car during the night don't stop, whatever you do, if persons in uniform challenge you to do so. You won't be able to tell the difference between police, army or gangsters. Even I can't. So it's better to flee like a gangster yourself than get robbed.[24]

Following this advice of a Congolese friend led me into a couple of critical situations, but also helped me to avoid potentially serious ones.

The third spatial dimension of coping with the risk of crime, which again is reserved for wealthier people, is to relocate to the neighbouring town of Gisenyi in Rwanda while continuing to work in Goma. The organisation of such a border-crossing routine is a temporal exit option; these commuters leave Goma in the evening to escape the prevalent insecurity and go back to join their families in Gisenyi.

> I live here [in Gisenyi], I have rented a house. Here I'm studying but every day I go to Goma for business. My life is in Goma, the only thing I am doing here is sleeping and I sleep well. […] There is a lot of insecurity in Goma and once we were raided in my house in Himbi. I feel safe now even if they want to control everything. But I don't care, I have nothing to hide you know. I like them; they know how to rule a country. But on the other hand, I feel pity for them. They are always scared.[25]

These mostly young Congolese have an ambivalent attitude towards Rwanda: they appreciate the efficiency and organisation of the Rwandans, while the omnipresence of control and surveillance causes disconcertion. However, for these people the decisive factor is that life in Rwanda, at least for them as Congolese, is much more predictable than in Goma.

Within the process of translating the crime threat into a risk, perception is shaped by lack of trust in public security institutions and a multitude of personal experiences, regardless of social status. Evaluation is marked by recognition of the seriousness of the problem and widespread exposure, whereas the degree of vulnerability is socially differentiated, as it is directly linked to the spatially and socially differentiated options of risk taking.

The risk of everyday life: conclusions

People in Goma expose themselves or are exposed to an extreme natural setting and the impacts of war for different reasons: no or few alternatives, no or little knowledge about alternatives, lack of economic means to go for alternatives, or expectations of gain, to name just a few. But what they have in common is that they live with these phenomena and translate them into hazards and into risks. By focusing on these translations, I have attempted to foreground both emic understandings of the precarious environment people live in, and the spatial dimensions of these translations, in order to get an idea of how people in Goma make sense of the exceptionally high number of hazards in their everyday life.

I have tried to show that the more concrete, the more relevant, a potential source of harm is for the everyday life of the city's inhabitants, the more profound is its translation into risk, shaped by perception and evaluation of the danger, and spatial strategies for dealing with it. The different depths of translation reveal social differentiation and a distinct contrast between the foreign expert and local lay accounts concerning what is risky in Goma. Based on a hegemonic interpretation of the nature of risk, and of what is needed for risk reduction, there are numerous reports on gas in Lake Kivu and volcanic activity as the output of relatively well-funded geoscientific research projects in the area. But there is a need for complementary social-science approaches to understanding how people really live with these hazards, and, perhaps even more importantly, which hazards are risks for them in the context of their precarious everyday lives. In this chapter I have focused on crime, while discounting other striking hazards for their livelihoods such as a dysfunctional water supply, health services and education system.

According to the different depths of translation, the spatial dimensions of risk in Goma involve socially differentiated practices, spatial imaginations and their locatable materialisations in the city. The empirical sketch of the crime problem shows that practices such as fencing and zoning, navigating the city according to a well-adjusted mobility pattern, and the organisation of border-crossing routines as an exit strategy, have shaped Goma's fragmented and highly dynamic urban riskscape. As a result, the urban fabric is traversed by materialisations of risk taking, apparent through road blocks, or the chain of islands of privatised security that form a kind of gated community through their spatial concentration, though in itself fragmented and heterogeneous. The social differentiation of practices linked to translation of the crime threat reveals that living in Goma is indeed risky. But it is not equally risky for everybody. This is in contrast to the gas and volcano hazards, where the probability of harm is equally distributed among all inhabitants. Though there are differentiated evaluations of the chances of being exposed to the volcano, the geographies of risk in this case mainly consist of spatial projections and ideas of risky places. However, here too, urban space is shaped by risk, since all new urban expansions towards the volcano in the north are considered as being riskier than others, and are therefore shunned by those who can afford to live in the city centre. Thus, what we can observe is that the accumulation of different types of dangers in the clearly delimited material urban space of Goma must be analysed by taking into account the ambiguous relationship between these tangible facts and the socially and spatially differentiated translation of dangers into risks. Depending on previous experience, social status, trust and assessments of exposure, vulnerability and seriousness, people in Goma perceive, evaluate and spatially translate dangers differently.

I will now return to the question raised at the beginning of this article concerning the problems associated with researching risk in a so-called pre-modern society. If we accept that risk research is also an attempt to understand the life worlds of people in precarious livelihood contexts, then it becomes clear what Elisio Macamo (2008: 258) means when he writes that Africa is an ideal empirical background for following a risk perspective: not necessarily to provide guidance for development experts or humanitarian intervention, but in order to reflect on the analytical dimensions of risk (such as spatiality) and to understand how people make sense of their everyday life by taking, avoiding and creating risks. Instead of solely interpreting interpretations as in discourse analysis within risk studies, it may be also rewarding to understand risk study as the study of human agency, and to do some empirical research that may advance our knowledge of certain analytical dimensions of risks. Moreover, the case of gas in Lake Kivu, and the beginning of gas extraction as an expert-dependent extra-societal project, shows that it is possible to add new aspects to risk research in Africa. This example shows the growing ambiguity of conceptualisations of risk in contemporary Africa. The predominant focus on vulnerability, natural hazards and coping strategies in alleged failed states should not be allowed to obscure the fact that core elements of the debate in Western academia, such as manufactured technological risks and the social construction of risk as symptoms of a reflexive modernity, are becoming increasingly important in African contexts, too. On the one hand, this development loosens a certain epistemological wedge that has resulted from making a distinction between concepts of risk in modern to late modern societies and those in the rest of the world, and on the other hand it leads to a complex coincidence of 'old' and 'new' empirical and epistemological objects of risk research.

Notes

1   For comprehensive overviews, see Renn 2008: 22–45 and Zinn 2008.
2   Interview with a widow who migrated from Bukavu to Goma in 2004; Katyoi district 19 March 2007 (all interview quotes translated from French or Swahili unless otherwise indicated).
3   Interview with a woman, native of Goma; Majengo district 10 March 2007.
4   Interview with a retired soldier of the Congolese army, in Goma since 1978; Majengo district 10 March 2007.
5   Several informal conversations with participants at the 'Workshop on the Lake Kivu Monitoring Program' in Gisenyi, Rwanda, 26–27 March 2007.
6   Interview with a European expert for the environmental monitoring of gas extraction at the pilot plant; Gisenyi 1 November 2008.
7   Several informal conversations with GVO staff, Goma.
8   Interview with a municipal administrator, Ngangi district 23 March 2007.
9   Interview with a bricklayer; Murara district 20 March 2007.
10 'They got the money but nothing had been done.' Interview with an executive employee of GVO, Goma 14 November 2007. The accusations were echoed during informal conversations with UNDP staff, Goma November 2007.

11 Interviews with an executive employee of GVO 18 November 2007, and with the head of the provincial commission for civil protection in North Kivu, Goma 22 October 2008.
12 Interview with a housewife; Ngangi district 11 November 2007.
13 Interviews with a building contractor, 20 November 2007 and the head of land registry office, 21 March 2007.
14 Third largest city in the DRC and a major inland port, about 1,000 km north-west of Goma.
15 Interview with a businessman, Murara district 20 October 2008.
16 Interview with a displaced woman, Katoyi district 21 November 2007.
17 Interview with a hotel employee, Majengo district 19 November 2007.
18 Own estimation, based on several informal talks with the head of the national police in Goma and officers of the UN police in October and November 2007 and October 2008, as well as on an interview with the head of KK Security, a private security firm, Goma 14 November 2007.
19 Interview, 8 October 2008.
20 Estimations made by officers of the UN civil police and by an officer of the United Nations Department of Security and Safety (UNDSS). Informal talks, March and November 2007, October 2008.
21 Over 70 per cent of the respondents described the police as corrupt and inefficient.
22 It is forbidden for employees of the UN to reside in these districts as they can't be protected there. NGOs are advised to avoid these areas. Informal talks with officers of the UN civil police, March and November 2007, October 2008.
23 Interview with the police commander of Mabanga South, 22 November 2007.
24 Informal conversation with a Congolese researcher, November 2007.
25 Interview with a Congolese student and shop owner, Gisenyi 13 March 2007.

11 Boundary-making as a strategy for risk reduction in conflict-prone spaces

Hermann Kreutzmann

Introduction

A systemic analysis of spatial political entities and their performance over time suggests that certain territorial systems fulfil a cycle from invention to maturity. State-making, nation-building and escape strategies (Scott 2009) could be arenas worth looking at in a time–space context of boundary-making. In specific cases the system tends to disaggregate and/or collapse (Lewin 2007), while new entities might emerge and be consolidated. The envisaged cycle incorporates certain properties and is influenced by a wide range of elements. The probability of failure seems to be a permanent challenge to such systems. Risk of collapse, shifting of boundaries, likelihoods of separatism and/or violent conflicts are often mitigated, modified and reduced by powerful actors through the implementation of administrative reforms and restructuring. In most cases the actors at the centre are perceived as setting an agenda that others have to accept. Enclosure and incorporation will be the fate of all participants in the case that state action pursues its goal of ultimate control. Beyond central control there are 'regions of refuge' (Beltran 1979) that follow their own rules and regulations. The creation of escape strategies and the search for regions of refuge can be seen as an attempt to reduce risk and to avoid conflicts with powerful actors. Escape strategies require migration and mobility. Other strategies to mitigate conflict-prone relations need to address internal conflict constellations and require imaginative solutions. Strained relationships between different actors result in a set of operations which modify spatial entities and their set-ups.

In an Asian context we can observe different effects of state-making and state evasiveness. Zomia (see Figure 11.1) – Inner Asian uplands – is an exceptional and unique case for the understanding of active strategies of risk reduction.[1] By 'keeping the state at distance' in a 'shatter zone' (Scott 2009), the inhabitants of Zomia have developed strategies of state prevention over time that have enabled them to be active players in the state-making process. In highly contested spaces of the 'Great Game', history followed different paths. Central Asia represents an arena in which administrative, political and spatial interventions and transformations based on European blueprints have shaped recent developments in state-making. The South Asian highlands form the northern border of the British Indian Empire and the southern extent of Russian and Chinese spheres of influence.

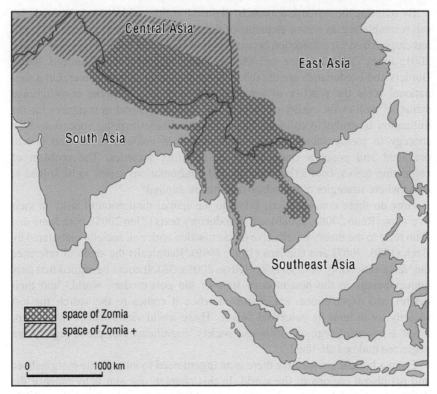

Figure 11.1 Zomia and Zomia+ in the Asian borderlands
Source: modified after van Schendel 2002:653 and Michaud 2010:188

Boundary-making in the Hindukush-Karakoram-Himalayan mountain arc was one of the prime activities in safeguarding and securing space at the threshold to a periphery where the prime objectives – adequate accessibility and cost-efficient administration – could not be achieved in order to contain local unrest. Imperial interests faded in the mountains, territorial neutralisation and indirect rule posed strategies of maintaining domination by excluding other spatial actors and containing competitors. Post-colonial nation states in a Central Asian setting are the outcome of Russian/Soviet, Chinese and/or British imperialism. Simplistic role models – such as the so-called 'two-nation theory' dividing India and Pakistan – for the creation of independent states resulted in grave and long-lasting tragedies that caused numerous victims and millions of refugees. Even in settings that on first sight seem to have been non- or semi-colonised spaces, such as Bhutan, Kashmir and Nepal, boundary issues prevail to the present day. After recently abolishing its monarchy, the former Hindu Kingdom of Nepal is a case in point illustrating the difficult transition to a broad-based system of parliamentary decision-making, and 'towards a federal Nepal' (Sharma *et al.* 2009). The pending administrative restructuring of Nepal is a prime example of a risky endeavour that incorporates all kinds of challenges for the stakeholders involved.

By adapting the systemic approach, territorial entities with changing boundaries can resemble arenas and/or elements of the system. Anthony Giddens (1985: 50) has emphasised the connection between nation states and borders (see also Cohen 2001; Jones 2010; Lamont and Molnár 2002; Migdal 2002; Rumford 2006). Borders and borderlands are the result of the formation of the former. On a sub-national scale the practice of granting autonomy and a special constitutional status, as well as the reality of indirect rule, are understood as measures for the mitigation of probable collapse. Province- and district-making appears to be a strategy to please stakeholders that originated in colonial times, and is still prevalent and poses a challenge in post-conflict societies. The problem of competing actors, conflicting interests and confrontations seems to be solved in cases where strategies of boundary-making are applied.

How do these considerations relate to the spatial dimension of risk? In their overview (Renn 2008a, 2008b) and introductory texts (Zinn 2008), both Renn and Zinn refer to the theory of reflexive modernisation and 'risk society' elaborated by Beck (1986, 2007) and Giddens (1990, 1999). Renn calls the arena of reference the 'meta-rationality of modernity' (Renn 2008a: 58). It could be argued that only human beings in the post-modern state or the post-modern world,[2] and their desires and expectations, are discussed when it comes to the search for lost security, or at least its perceived fading. These world views reflect only a part, albeit a powerful segment, of world society. Significant risk-prone regions are neglected and/or side-lined.

From a holistic perspective there is an urgent need to incorporate marginalised and peripheral regions of the world. In this chapter, our aim is to enhance the debate about social construction of space in relation to social construction of risk, by looking at boundary-making and the relevant discourses. In terms of boundary-making, we are interested in the discourses that stakeholders are engaged in when designing future political spaces. The social discourse on space allocation and control, the search for suitable administrative concepts, community-based negotiations concerning decentralised governance and the implementation of bounded territories function as indicators for group cohesiveness and the social constructedness of risk.

The chapter aims at providing a deeper understanding of socio-political 'riskscapes' by highlighting strategies of risk management in societies where external interests, colonial and post-colonial experiences, and unstable political conditions create the risk of the society becoming a 'failing state' in a socio-political environment where the nation state fulfils a different role than in affluent post-modern states (cf. Kreutzmann 2008b). In the concept of 'social amplification of risk' (Kasperson *et al.* 1988), where the 'social and economic impacts of an adverse event are determined by a combination of direct physical consequences interacting with psychological, social, institutional, and cultural processes' (Renn 2008b: 196), risk can be conceptualised as being socially constructed with reference to a detrimental event or hazard. The social amplification concept might be utilised for grasping 'social phenomena and for suggesting causal relations that can be investigated empirically' (Renn 2008b: 197). Keeping in mind that the perception and expectation of harm – even if not yet experienced – can trigger social action, it might be useful to test its applicability in respect to state-making and state evasiveness.

The cases introduced in the following sections can be positioned within a matrix (see Figure 11.2) that is constructed by an ordained time scale with historical reference points, from nineteenth-century developments to present-day events, and that is spanned between non-state and state positioning, ranging from state avoidance to state inclusion, in a spectrum spanning from evasion to enclosure. The cases presented have followed different developments that are related to boundary-making as a strategy of risk reduction. All path-dependent developments lead to enhanced modern statehood involving administration and bureaucracy, control and power that enable institutions to create boundaries serving the purpose of risk reduction.

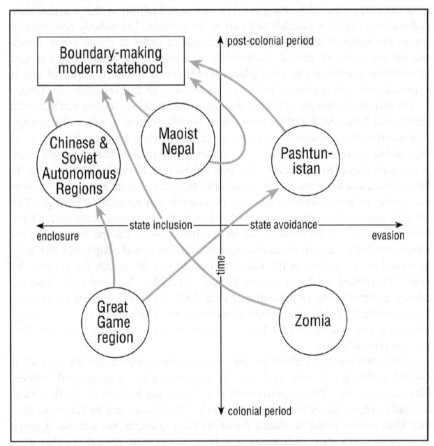

Figure 11.2 Boundary-making in path-dependent development

Colonial precedents and projections
Zomia – space for state evaders

In discussions of risk mitigation and avoidance there is always a suggestion of control mechanisms, early warning systems and optimising strategies. They refer to the stochastic systems and probabilistic approaches that trigger technical concepts and utilitarian strategies in economic concepts of risk (Renn 2008a). The technocratic approach easily disguises the fact that the nation state, regional organisations and international bodies might not be the most adequate institutions for addressing all kinds of challenges in risk contexts. The underlying assumption appears to be that a search for solutions needs to focus on existing administrative structures. In our special case of boundary-making as a strategy for risk reduction in conflict-prone spaces, physical and spatial stagnation seems to be one of the invariant categories. The setting is taken as given. Mobility within a nation state and within a region is possible and part of the solution. But nobody permanently leaves the space of administration and control in order to create a new abode outside the reach of central institutions. In contrast, the model requires that governance is extended to safer places within the structural set-up, and this is expected from administrative bodies and non-governmental organisations alike.

The historical example of Zomia challenges our thinking. Willem van Schendel (2002) and James Scott (2009) have drawn our attention to Zomia and a strategy that incorporates a search for security by means of state avoidance. The 'Art of Not Being Governed'[3] sensitises the reader to alternative strategies that were actively employed to avoid control by powerful actors, to evade administration by bureaucrats, and to create a space of security that served as an abode remote from the centres of power while voluntarily participating in economic exchange.[4] The struggle against the state was an act of risk reduction. Because these spaces have been shrinking by colonisation of the periphery – in Europe the enclosures movements of the nation states managed to transform local peripheries into fully governed areas, mainly in the nineteenth century – the search for security by spatial movement has become more difficult. In Africa, Asia and Latin America 'distance-demolishing technologies' (Scott 2009: 11) were applied by external actors during the colonial and imperial experiments. The technologies of railways and roads led to a significant loss of non-governed space, of which only few pockets remain today.

Administration and technology are two systematic approaches for expanding control within the frontier and creating boundaries for homogenised entities. Nevertheless, the Zapatista movement in Chiapas, the Berbers of North Africa, the Pashtun fortified settlements of Pakistan's Tribal Areas, and the Karen, Kachin and Shan armies in the Southeast Asian 'Golden Triangle' are witness of space defence and utilisation of 'regions of refuge' where state control is either non-existent or ineffective.[5] The active avoidance of state interference cost a high price that was readily paid in exchange for independence and non-domination in a more egalitarian environment than the state could provide.

The Zomian example seems to be a specific case for upland Southeast Asia, where physical barriers and technological challenges preserved a space that could be utilised in the described manner, because the investments needed to extend control and administration and to provide accessibility and regular exchange would have been too high. During colonial and imperial times, the creation of buffer zones and ungoverned spaces was a standard practice for keeping contenders at bay and for restricting sophisticated bureaucracy and state-of-the-art infrastructure to the valuable extraction zones close to the coast. Consequently, a lowland–highland opposition was perceived and realised, in which the mountainous highlands were considered as pagan peripheries, ungoverned spaces, marginal regions, buffer zones and remote valley societies, while the lowlands formed a contrast to these spaces in every respect.

The recent reinterpretation of active state evasion and out-migration to ungoverned spaces emphasises the risk of exploitation, over-taxing and enslavement. In the Southeast Asian context, the price paid for state avoidance and self-determined lifestyles was the replacement of paddy cultivation by swiddening and tuber cultivation, a reconfiguration of 'tribal' genealogies, and sometimes even refraining from the usage of certain languages and scripts (Scott 2009: 178–282). Here we find a case of actively becoming a 'people without history', although this statement rather contradicts Eric Wolf's (1982) intention. In other words we can state that the price people were willing to pay for avoiding interference by the colonial state was comparatively high.

The dichotomy of inclusion and exclusion survived into post-colonial times and posed one of the central challenges for Southeast Asian countries such as Burma, Thailand, Malaysia and Indonesia.

> in the second half of the twentieth century much of Zomia resisted the projects of nation-building and statemaking of the states to which it belonged. In these projects, uplanders were often excluded from discourses of citizenship, and cast in the roles of nonnationals, alien elements, or poachers of the state's forestry resources who could be redeemed only by assimilating to the lowland 'mainstream'. [...] All over Zomia, states implemented policies of population relocation, prevention of hill agriculture, land registration, logging, wildlife protection, dam building, watershed protection, and education in national languages, which led to new forms of competition and tension.
>
> (van Schendel 2002: 655)[6]

These observations prove to be valid for other upland–lowland contexts as well. In mountain regions of higher geopolitical interest, earlier attempts at control and inclusion were made. In the Central and South Asian highlands, long-term strategies and rivalries between powerful actors collided, and a different type of space control was applied. For our discussion of exposure to risk, a prime and prior example of ordering space and delineation of boundaries needs to be highlighted.

Great Game as the pretext for boundary-making

The Great Game between Russia and British India that finally led to the Asia Convention of 1907 is a case in point for the enhanced integration of remote mountain regions into state systems of control, and for the creation of buffer states such as Afghanistan, and pre-buffer zones such as the tribal areas of present-day Pakistan. Powerful actors – the superpowers of the time – engaged leading contemporary academics and diplomats to justify the expansion and incorporation of vast tracts of Central Asia into their empires. The spheres of influence were expanded in the direction of those of their respective rival. The intermediate spaces in the contested areas narrowed, and the 'people without history' (Wolf 1982) who lived there became victims of geopolitical designs, and the livelihoods of mountain agriculturists and pastoralists as well as their degrees of freedom were significantly affected. Remote spaces at the periphery were reinterpreted as the lost spaces of the 'people with history', where the pristine heritage and vernacular languages of the mainstream powers seemed to be rooted and where cultures were supposed to originate from.

In 1877, when Queen Victoria became the Empress of India, Russian diplomats and military strategists debated about the importance of Central Asia from a Russian perspective. Colonel M.J. Veniukoff vindicated 'the gradual movement of Russia in Central Asia' as 'the re-establishment of extension of the sway of the Aryan race over countries which for a long period were subject to peoples of Turk and Mongol extraction'.[7] Veniukoff advocates a diffusion theory in which he identifies 'the mountainous countries at the sources of the Indus and the Oxus to be the cradle of the Aryan or Indo–European race. From this birthplace our ancestors spread far and wide'.[8] After some deliberations about the spread of people, Veniukoff concludes that the Russian advances in Central Asia can be interpreted as

> this 'return' of part of the Slavs to the neighbourhood of their prehistoric home. [...] We are not Englishmen, who in India do their utmost to avoid mingling with the natives, and who moreover, sooner or later, may pay for it by the loss of that country, where they have no ties of race. [...] It is desirable that this historical result should not be forgotten also in the future, especially on our arrival at the sources of the Oxus, where we must create an entirely Russian border-country as the sole guarantee of stability of our position in Turkestan.[9]

The distinct interests and justifications put forward for the advance of these dominating powers contain on the one hand strategies of 'remigration' into an ancestral homeland, and on the other hand an exploitative interest in the wealth of Asia. Consequently, two types of colonies were created: Russian settlement colonies and British colonies of extraction.

Nevertheless, the commonalities between the two powers were discussed as well:

Possibly time will produce a radical change in the sentiments of the English, and then both great European nations will advance to meet the other in Asia, not with bitter suspicions and reproaches, but with confidence and benevolence as workers in the same historical mission – the civilization of the Far East. But will that time come soon? Russia, in any case, without awaiting it, must complete *her* mission: the occupation of the whole of Turkestan. This, unquestionably, will prove not disadvantageous in that respect as well, that it will force England to be more on her guard in other lines of universal policy, in which she is ever antagonistic to the views of Russia.[10]

British India and Russia were the players who gambled for influence in Central Asia. But this battle was not confined to regional control; it was a contest over world domination by imperial powers. Great Britain had already achieved maritime supremacy, and now one of the last and more important land-locked areas – Central Asia – came into focus.

In 1904 the geographer Halford Mackinder formulated his 'heartland theory', which is still one of the most influential texts for the geopolitical debate. Mackinder drew attention to Central Asia, stating that Tsarist regional dominance was linked to the Russian equestrian tradition from nomadic Asian backgrounds. From the safe retreat of the Inner Asian steppe regions, expeditions of conquest had started towards Europe, Persia, India and China. He described European civilisation as the result of a secular battle against Asian invasions (Mackinder 1904: 423). The naval predominance of Great Britain and imperial control of world trade had been modified through a shift in terrestrial traffic structures. The Russian railways were perceived as the successors of the equestrian mobile forces. Central Asia had become the arena of contest, the more so as a Russian-German and/or a Sino-Japanese alliance could contribute to a shift of world affairs to the 'heartland' of the Eurasian continent, which he perceived as a 'geographical pivot of history' (Mackinder 1904: 436). He predicted the transformation of Central Asia from a steppe region with little economic power into a region of prime geostrategic importance. Culture and geography would contribute to creating a key region.

Mackinder identified four adjacent regions surrounding the heartland of 'pagan' Turan in the shape of a crescent, and separated by religious affiliations: Buddhism, Brahmanism, Islam and Christianity (Mackinder 1904: 431). Similar ideas of a Central Asian 'heartland' or a pivotal role stimulated Owen Lattimore's perceptions in his book *Pivot of Asia* (1950). Keeping the experiences of the Second World War in mind, Lattimore drew a circle with a radius of 1,000 miles around Urumchi and identified Central Asia (see Figure 11.3) as a 'whirlpool' stirred up by 'political currents flowing from China, Russia, India and the Middle East' (Lattimore 1950: 3). By following the same Central Asian-centred approach, Milan Hauner shifted the centre in the 1980s to Kabul, drew a similar circle and identified a world of 'even greater contrasts' which 'touches upon the volatile and oil-rich region of the Middle East' (Hauner 1989: 7). The last statement has remained valid through the dissolution of the Soviet Union, Taliban rule in Afghanistan, and in the aftermath of 9/11 and the Iraq crisis. Ahmed Rashid

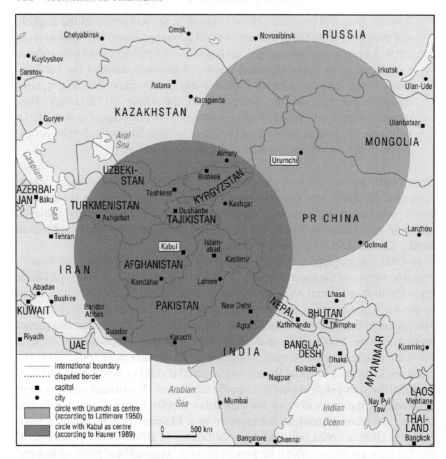

Figure 11.3 Urumchi and Kabul as centres of political instability
Source: topography based on UN 2004

(2000) subtitled his book on the Taliban 'Islam, Oil and the New Great Game in Central Asia', and this is only one of many references to the 'Great Game' in connection with contemporary geopolitical problems in the region. The presence of American and Russian troops at airports and along borders in Central Asia proves the continuing geopolitical significance of the region and its linkage to contemporary crisis zones. With the passage of time, Mackinder modified his theory under the impression of events during the First and Second World Wars and influenced the thoughts of Karl Haushofer and other geopoliticians of his time.

Boundary-making in Central Asian contexts – 'tribal areas' and buffer zones

How are boundaries constituted in a conflict-prone region? No safe spaces were left for montagnards and pastoralists or oasis dwellers and traders to evade these geopolitical designs in ordering space. The answer to the question of who benefits from risk reduction by boundary-making, and whose livelihoods are negatively affected, is largely determined by the makers.

Over long periods, borders and border-related territories were taken as spatial expressions of power and dominance, but recent debates have shifted towards the changing relations between borders and society (Delanty 2006; Kreutzmann 2008a; Rumford 2006). Present-day political and social change is embedded in border practices which have deep historical roots and far-reaching effects on the lives of the people concerned and diasporas. Communication, mobility and networks across borders, and the flow of goods and ideas are affected by boundary-making. At the same time, borders remain spaces of political dispute and territorial division in which different actors fulfil a variety of functions and defend their conflicting interests.

Political boundaries separating nation states are the result of developments and the 'making of a frontier' (Durand 1899). The second half of the nineteenth century up to the end of the First World War can be considered as the peak period of imperial intervention, the division of the world, and concomitant boundary-making. Contemporary debates by geographers, historians, politicians and diplomats focused on the philosophical interpretation of terms such as border, boundary and frontier. The implications for practice were discussed using terms such as 'stromstrich' and 'thalweg', which helped boundary commissions to negotiate on the ground of what their superiors discussed as 'natural' and/or 'scientific borders' in the 'Indian Borderland' (Holdich 1909). The debate ranged around the search for obvious solutions to enable colonial administrations to work on the ground.

The British explorer Ney Elias was in favour of the 'hill frontier' as opposed to rivers for separating spheres of influence. For him, border practice implies fathoming

> a possibility of coming to an arrangement with Russia on the subject, under which each party should keep the territory he now possesses. [...] the Afghans should consolidate the territory they now hold in these regions. For this purpose the three chief steps required are (1) to define the boundaries in every direction; (2) either to conciliate or thoroughly overawe the discontented inhabitants; (3) to make no embarrassing claims for more territory, but rather abandon old claims if more desirable boundaries can thereby be secured. They have a large tract of poor mountainous country divided into a number of petty provinces, the borders of which are still open to dispute. These provinces are inhabited by people who have little or nothing in common with the Afghans, and who hate them with the two kinds of which, taken together, make up perhaps the most intense form of enmity. They hate them with race hatred – both Tajik and Turk; and they hate them as conquerors.
>
> (Elias 1886: 71–2)

This statement by Ney Elias shows clearly that the prime interest was to define and separate in order to secure territory. In a second step, the affordable cost for the colonial power needs to be assessed, either in establishing indirect rule practices or controlling the people. Both steps are required to find the 'desirable boundaries', which he identifies as lying in the high mountain areas.

Information reported by Elias concerning Badakhshan and East Turkestan, the assumption confirmed by the Lockhart and Woodthorpe mission (Gilgit, Hunza, Chitral and Wakhan) that the northern mountains were unpassable for a large Russian army, and enquiries by Algernon Durand about the weakness of the Kashmiri administration on the Northern Frontier caused Mortimer Durand, the foreign secretary of the British Indian government, to formulate an active British boundary policy for the entire tribal belt between Dera Ghazi Khan in the south and Gilgit in the north (Durand 1888; Elias 1886; Lockhart and Woodthorpe 1889). Major elements of his plan were diplomatic agreements in respect of the conditions of power at the periphery of the Indian Empire, definition of the boundaries with Afghanistan as a buffer state, and avoidance of direct confrontation between Russia and British India. The cost factor is the guiding principle in finding appropriate measures for tackling the problems of boundary-making. Mainstream opinion about how to deal with desired territories was contested by some contemporary critics, who assessed the chances of survival in those conflict-prone regions that were likely to lose their status as a refuge. In numerous articles and commentaries in journals and in the London *Times*, Gottlieb Wilhelm Leitner, linguist, founder of the Oriental Institute at Woking and regular critical commentator of British imperial designs, challenged and strongly criticised the need for territorial expansion and bringing Britain's borders forward. He influenced the debates and became the self-appointed advocate of the affected mountain dwellers, whose survival conditions were at risk. In his opinion the narrowing of imperial boundaries would detrimentally affect the lives of local settlers, as he suspected them to be oppressed and subordinated to imperial demands. Discussions in political and diplomatic circles about the solution of the boundary issue were commented upon in a fierce critique of Britain's colonial policy in the Pamirs and Dardistan. Leitner kept the local people in mind and called for de-militarisation of the refuge space and autonomy of the ethnic groups in this region:

> The neutralization of the Pamirs is the only solution of a difficulty created by the conjectural treaties of diplomatists and the ambition of military emissaries. Left as a huge happy hunting-ground for sportsmen, or as pasturage for nomads from whatever quarters, the Pamirs form the most perfect 'neutral zone' conceivable. That the wanderings of these nomads should be accompanied by territorial or political claims, whether by Russia, China, Afghanistan, Kashmir, or ourselves, is the height of absurdity. As for Hunza-Nagyr, the sooner they are left to themselves the better for us, who are not bound to help Kashmir in encroaching on them.
>
> (Leitner 1891: 73)

Nevertheless, Leitner's adversaries, as the advocates of a 'forward policy', succeeded in their attempts to secure as much as possible for posterity during the

'Great Game'. Boundary-making became a major subject in diplomatic training and colonial administration. The Russian Empire designed its own blueprints for gaining control over vast tracts of Central Asia that were significantly modified by Soviet strategists and 'modernisers', thus further narrowing the space for independent lifestyles, utilisation and survival strategies.

Stalinist creation of autonomous entities – ethnicity as a factor of risk minimisation in territorial division

The colonial legacy in Middle Asia consisted of the Governor-Generalship of Turkestan, established in 1867, with its capital Tashkent, where the Turkestan Autonomous Soviet Socialist Republic (ASSR) was declared in May 1918. After the first Soviet government – the Council of People's Commissars, led by Lenin – had assured the emirates of Bukhara and Khiva complete independence and announced the abrogation of Tsarist privileges, their sovereignty fell victim in 1919 to the unified Turkestan front commanded by Frunse; after being finally taken by the Red Army, Bukhara and Khiwa were made into People's Republics in 1920. The de facto takeover of Middle Asian territories and their integration into the Soviet Union led to various administrative reforms, which started in 1924 and were largely completed by 1929.

To conform to the target of national and territorial delimitation and to counteract pan-Turkic movements, the Governor-Generalship of Turkestan was terminated with a view to creating eponymous or titular republics (see Figure 11.4), each ideally having a homogeneous national population.[11] The titular republics were created on the basis of complex boundaries drawn in deviation from the territories of the local rulers. Each eponym represents a dominant ethno-linguistic group that accounted for between two-thirds and three-quarters of the respective population at the time the titular republics were founded.

In the case of the ASSR of Tajikistan, demarcated within the SSR of Uzbekistan, there had also been a territorial dispute about the distribution of regions said to have a majority Tajik population. The national-territorial subdivision led to the creation of the Soviet republic of Tajikistan, which did not have a single important town.[12] Dushanbe (literally: Monday market), named Stalinabad from 1926 to 1961, was hastily upgraded from a market site to the capital city (General Staff India 1929: 51). As a result of this dispute, a sub-region, Khujand district, was separated from Uzbekistan when Tajikistan became an independent and equal Union Republic in 1929, but the most important urban centres of Tajik culture – Bukhara and Samarkand – were still not taken into account.

The unsatisfactory solution to the dividing up of nationalities – the Ferghana Valley became a symbol of the tripartite division of a rather congeneric area – was also linked to a border demarcation issue. The revision and restructuring of the Union Republics in 1929 resulted in administrative configurations that sometimes consisted of certain core areas together with outlier or enclave territories within other republics. Boundary-making in the Stalinist period created new territories and a legacy that has remained the cause of border disputes, irredentism and

Figure 11.4 Central Asian republics
Source: modified after Bregel 2003:97

mistrust until today and that significantly affects the diplomatic relations of the
independent Central Asian republics.

Within the Soviet republics created in this way, the titular nation played a
dominant role as the eponymous majority. An integral element of the nationalities
policy was the implementation of plans to establish standard languages and their
written forms, as well as research into the history of individual nations. In the case
of Tajikistan, the titular nationality included all Iranian-speaking groups, who
were then listed as members of the majority Tajik titular nation in subsequent
censuses. Vinnikov (1980: 81) sees the fact that the Pamir inhabitants (except the
Kyrgyz) were listed as Tajiks in censuses from 1959 onwards as evidence of their
assimilation and integration into the titular nation:

> Change in ethnic self-awareness is an important indicator of the depth of this
> process [...] virtually all the Pamir peoples called themselves Tadjiks by
> nationality, but where language was concerned they indicated their native
> tongues, which are widely used not only in home and family life but often on
> the job as well.

This line of argument does not correspond to official practice. In the *Spisok* (list) of villages compiled in 1932, the population of Gorno-Badakhshan is divided into Tajiks and Kyrgyz only (Uprawlenie 1932: 125–30). In territorial terms, however, the special status of the Pamir peoples was recognised, and the autonomous province of Gorno-Badakhshan was created, which was restructured and redivided several times in the course of administrative reforms.[13] This special administrative status reflects the regional disparities between the mountain agriculture of the Pamirs and the intensively cultivated lowland valleys of western Tajikistan (cotton production zone).

These disparities are recognisable in the terms used to differentiate topographic and regional features in combination with the ethnonym 'Tajiks'. In this way, the mountain or Pamir Tajiks were integrated into the community of the titular nation or were appropriated by it for the purpose of creating a republican identity: traditional contrasts in economy (high-mountain and oasis agriculture), language (East Iranian Pamir languages and West Iranian Tajiki) and religion (Ismaili and Sunni), and regions with few reciprocal exchange relations, were ignored in the name of a Tajik nation. Despite all Pamiri efforts to maintain their own cultural identity and their separate languages, Vinnikov (1980: 81) considers their inferior numbers – only about 3 per cent of Tajikistan's population – to be a further important factor leading to the amalgamation of all Tajiks. He cites additional evidence of the transformation process:

> the rapid building of socialism, particularly the construction of roads through formerly roadless country, the establishment of regular automotive and air communications, the founding of industrial enterprises, the transformation of agriculture, the triumph of the collective-farm system, and the cultural revolution, not only broke down the age-long isolation and backwardness of these areas but also made for tremendous progress in the socioeconomic and cultural development of all Cis-Pamir peoples, their economic, cultural, and ethnic convergence with the Tadjiks. [And quotes Monogarova 1972: 13–14] [...] all the Cis-Pamir peoples successfully acquired progressive features of the contemporary national culture of the Tadjiks, saturated with elements of regional Central Asian and general Soviet culture.
>
> (Vinnikov 1980: 80–1)

However, Rakowska-Harmstone (1975: 326) recognises more significant differences between mountain Tajiks (*Gornyje Tadjiki*) and plains Tajiks (*Dolinnye Tadjiki*) than between the latter and the Uzbeks, who had symbiotically shaped the Middle Asian oasis cultures of the now independent titular republics and the Ferghana valley. At the end of the 1920s, the national-territorial formation phase of the Middle Asian republics was more or less concluded, and the phase of the 'brotherliness of the peoples of the Soviet Union' (Eisener 1991: 54) began. On the foundation of the administrative and hierarchical entities thus created, the Soviet Union then began to restructure the basis of production, which had a permanent impact on existing social structures, the regional economic systems of the Pamir region, and its exchange relations. The example of the mountain dwellers in Tajikistan, and their incorporation into mainstream 'modern' culture and economy, represents a number of similar cases and is evidence of the process that led to a narrowing of the freedom of state evaders and creation of the riskscapes of our time. Contemporary riskscapes take their properties from a historic burden, from unsolved disputes and competing claims based on different interpretations and ancient references. These riskscapes bear substantial leverage and degrees of freedom for the creation of disputes by interested actors and stakeholders.

Post-colonial transformations of riskscapes

Pashtun irredentism

The contenders of the 'Great Game' in High Asia agreed to lay down boundaries in the comparatively sparsely populated regions of the Hindukush and Pamir. These borders were sometimes described as natural frontiers, scientific boundaries or dialect borders. The Durand Line of 1893 separating Afghanistan from British India/Pakistan epitomises such an effort and has continued to function as the symbol of colonial border delineation referred to as the 'dividing line' (Felmy 1993). In order to ensure the physical separation of two imperial opponents, international borders were laid down and Afghanistan was created as a buffer state. Local livelihoods and regional interests were neglected. The Pashtun settlement region was divided into two parts following an arbitrary line through the Hindukush ranges. The traditional migratory paths of seasonal nomads between the Central Afghanistan highlands and the Indus lowlands were intersected along the Hindukush passes.

   Numerous clashes between tribal groups and imperial troops in the borderlands characterised political relations along the frontier which served as a buffer belt on the fringe of the empire (Fraser-Tytler 1953). While the imperial designs of creating Afghanistan as a buffer state and the 'tribal areas' as a pre-buffer zone were immediately and for the time being fulfilled, the livelihoods of mountain farmers, pastoralists and traders became increasingly endangered and vulnerable. Every political crisis between Afghanistan and Pakistan affected their mobility patterns and freedom of movement. In addition to short-term conflicts, a long-term dispute developed into a crisis based on irredentism. This term describes the aspirations of interested ethnicity groups to regain control over territory that was forcefully taken away, but is still regarded as home to fellow members of the same 'ethnic group'.[14] The 'tribal areas' were side-lined and represented a true periphery within Pakistan.

   The strategy for coping with this situation was to create an autonomous zone of 'lawlessness' that was characterised by not applying constitutional rights, by continuing to adhere to colonial practices such as the 'Frontier Crimes Regulations'[15] and by introducing a form of indirect rule that was exercised by tribal leaders (*malik, sardar*) who were subsidised by the central government. The special legal status continues in these regions to this day, as they are administrated as Federally or Provincially Administered Tribal Areas (FATA or PATA). The movement of nomads (*kuchi*, *powindah*) and their herds now depends on bilateral political relations and has been restricted, but it has not totally ceased.

Continuing border disputes and conflicts such as the irredentist movement for 'Pashtunistan' are still alive, and one of the main squares in Kabul has continued to be named after this Pakistan–Afghanistan dispute during all the winds of change since the 1960s. The Afghan demand for a territory named Pashtunistan and consisting of the Pakistan North–West Frontier Province (NWFP) and Baluchistan (including the 'tribal areas') is a result of the imperial design that led to the creation of the Durand Line and the referendum at the end of British Rule in India. Pashtun representatives have taken these incidents as justification for their mobilisation of people for the cause of Pashtunistan. Imperial legacies and losses function as a measure of identity and supply the ideological platforms for charismatic leaders who mobilise their followership in order to rewrite history. Pashtuns of the Afghan–Pakistan borderlands have been described as the largest acephalous and/or segmentary society (Ahmed 1980; Sigrist 1994) on earth, but their livelihoods have always been at stake and have been gravely influenced by external interventions. Space for state evasion, as in the Zomian case, has been unavailable since boundary-making, so that different strategies were applied and different measures were taken to avoid the risk of being incorporated and dominated. Although van Schendel has expanded his Zomia+ (see Figure 11.1) westwards towards Central Asia and the Hindu Kush Mountains, it might be argued that the Pashtunistan case in the Pak–Afghan borderlands is contrasting the south east Asian experiences with 'state evasiveness' and subsequent developments. From an anthropological and human geographical point of view Michaud (2010:202) supports this observation. The Pashtun movements always played an independent role in their search for security within and without state control.

Post-monarchic Nepal – multiple designs for the future administrative set-up

The outcome of the Maoist-led insurgency in Nepal – the country in which the last Hindu monarchy was abolished – is a ubiquitous desire for a constitutional reform process. The informed public is currently debating an administrative reform that is aimed at risk reduction in light of a civil collapse. The case of Nepal reflects an important process that is related to the historical and contemporary cases presented above. In Nepal we find groups engaged in the search for state avoidance, strategies for enhancing autonomy and state evasion. In a remarkable effort, stakeholders with spokespersons for different models that all pretend to enhance security and provide federal protection have presented their priority solutions to transform the Nepal riskscape into a more peaceful administrative structure.

The threat of civil war is pending while more that 50 administrative models are being discussed to restructure the state into federal units, to promote devolution of authority and to rearrange the 75 districts of Nepal along ethnic, linguistic, political, economic and 'geographical' lines. All creators of models aim at 'resolving problems of socio-cultural disparity, enhancing ethnic/cultural identity with autonomy, and the right to self-determination' and/or 'addressing the challenges of development and achieving regional balance by promoting economic cooperation and preserving territorial integrity through decentralisation and devolution of power and authority' (Sharma *et al.* 2009: 34). The severity of instability and the threat of violent escalation cannot be underrated as contributing to enhancing risky conditions within the state. Nepal is faced with a situation where a society is trying to recover from the impact of a societal transformation, where political stakeholders are involved in power games to make the present society more resilient than the previous one, with a high expectation of loss, resulting in enhanced risk. Spatial boundaries of federal units and/or provinces reflect the aspirations of stakeholders. Even the naming of these units is highly controversial. In addition, minority groups claim their rights to territorial autonomy, sometimes overlapping significant spaces that will necessarily lead to conflict. The case of 'Federal Nepal' epitomises the conflict potential in boundary-making and its relation to riskscapes.

Conclusions

The cases of boundary-making over time presented here support the initial model of transformation (see Figure 11.2), which tends to indicate a certain path-dependent track of 'development'. The paradigm of 'modernisation' promises and suggests homogenisation in the realm of post-colonialism and state inclusion. The cases presented follow paths that proceed to this corner. Territories defined by boundaries represent two perspectives. The inner perspective highlights state penetration, while the outer defines excluded communities, individuals and infrastrucures. The majority of cases show that risk reduction seems to be an illusion. Spaces offering a certain degree of freedom are shrinking. In all cases, riskscapes and the vulnerability of the inhabitants are growing. The colonial roots are long and effective.

Classical interfaces in remote corners of spheres of influence are rapidly fading, as well as options for state avoidance. The Zomian example shows a strong transformation with small pockets of state evasion that are constantly negotiated. Pashtunistan is a region under threat as global interests focus on these 'tribal areas'. Maoist Nepal is a case showing how difficult it is to shape something new out of an existing system within international boundaries laid down two centuries ago. The 'meta-rationality of modernity' provides us with examples of nation states that are much stronger than were expected and were prevalent in post-modern contexts.

Notes

1   Willem van Schendel (2002: 653) defines Zomia as an 'area of no concern'. Zomia incorporates 'zomi', a term for highlander in a number of languages spoken in Bangladesh, India and Myanmar. It refers to contiguous upland regions located in China, northeast India, Nepal, Pakistan, Myanmar, Thailand, Cambodia, Laos and

Vietnam that can be interpreted as the result of the peripheralisation of upland regions and the neglect of mainstream powerful discourses.

2   The post-modern world is perceived in the framework of the categories proposed by Cooper (2002, 2003); for a critique, see Kreutzmann 2008b.

3   The title of Scott's book sets the stage for his 'anarchist history of upland Southeast Asia' (Scott 2009).

4   The active participation in exchange was based on an 'escape agriculture' that Scott (2009: 23) defines as aiming to 'thwart state appropriation' and which produced valuable and light-weight goods on the basis of swiddening and/or field-based crop farming. Cash crops such as poppy, herbs, etc. augmented necessary staples produced using subsistence practices.

5   The region of refuge concept was developed by Beltran (1979). He elaborates on the advantages and disadvantages of isolation (p. 25). His case study refers to Mexico; for recent developments, see Ocaña 2003.

6   For a supporting statement, see Scott (2009: 281–2).

7   Political and Secret Department Memoranda: The Progress of Russia in Central Asia by Colonel M.J. Veniukoff (translated from the 'Sbornik Gosudarstvennikh Zuanyi' 1877 (= IOL/P&S/18/C 17, p1).

8   Political and Secret Department Memoranda (= IOL/P&S/18/C 17, p1).

9   Political and Secret Department Memoranda (= IOL/P&S/18/C 17, p2).

10   Political and Secret Department Memoranda (= IOL/P&S/18/C 17, p22).

11   The Turkestan ASSR was therefore divided up into six sub-regions, the People's Republics of Bukhara and Khiva were split up and their respective populations were added to three of the six newly created administrative units. As a counterweight to the Turkic-language republics of Uzbekistan, Turkmenia and Kirghizia, the republic of Tajikistan was specially created for speakers of Iranian languages.

12   According to a report in the Izvestia newspaper in 1924, quoted by Eisener (1991: 30).

13   For details and further evidence, see Kreutzmann 1996: 161–70.

14   Irredentism is named after the 'terra irredenta' movement in the European Alps that claims to bring members of the same group back into the nation state.

15   The 'Frontier Crimes Regulations' of 1872 allowed colonial political agents to execute strong martial law-like measures without any judicial backing. After independence and up to today these regulations are valid in principle; see Kreutzmann 2008a.

12 Bethinking oneself of the risk of (physical) geography

Barbara Zahnen

Introduction

When physical geographers contribute to the field of risk research, they usually do so, and are generally expected to do so, as natural scientists. Unlike human geographers, their fields of expertise concern the natural system of the earth, and in this regard physical geography is indistinguishable from other earth sciences, such as meteorology, geology, hydrology, etc. Today, physical geography seems to be a hotchpotch of approaches belonging to such earth sciences, just as human geography seems to be a hotchpotch of approaches belonging to the social, cultural and economic sciences, applied to certain regions of the earth.

According to this view of geography and its two major sub-disciplines – a widespread, but questionable view – it must be far more difficult for physical geographers (and other earth scientists) than for human geographers (and other social, cultural or economic scientists) to make a genuine contribution to current *risk* research. In fact, it is due to the achievements and enhancements of risk research itself that it has become more difficult for physical geographers to make such contributions. There is more than one possible way to support this thesis.

One way would be to refer to the conceptual distinction between 'hazards' and 'risks': if – as Renn (2008a) suggests – a hazard refers to 'the potential of a technology, an event or an activity to cause harm to what people value', and 'a hazard becomes a risk if there is a likelihood that this potential is released in a way that it produces harm', so that 'without a chance of exposure a risk does not exist' (Renn 2008a: 50), one cannot do risk research without including questions concerning human behaviour and activities, that is without including questions which actually lie beyond the expertise of natural scientists.

A second, but related way to support the above thesis would be to draw upon the fact that within current risk research, approaches belonging to probabilistic risk assessment (PRA) – i.e. approaches preferred by the natural and technical sciences and their so-called 'positivistic' (Renn 2008a: 63) or 'reificating' (Bradbury 2009: 28), i.e. somehow objectivistic methodologies and epistemologies – fade from the spotlight, while approaches based on the methodologies and epistemologies of the social and cultural sciences step into it. In fact, any cursory glance at current journals of risk research, or *The Earthscan Reader on Risk*

(Löfstedt and Boholm 2009), show a strong dominance of contributions by social, cultural or economic scientists, or psychologists. And even if natural scientists are still strongly represented in journals or books concerning natural or environmental hazards, this field is also enriched by perspectives other than those of the natural or technical sciences (see for example Handmer 2009 and Moench 2009).

Before I mention a third way to support the thesis that it must be more difficult for physical than for human geographers to make a genuine contribution to current risk research, let me characterise the above-mentioned enrichment of both hazard and risk research by the human sciences by drawing on different meanings of the word 'potentiality' (and 'potential' or 'potentially' accordingly) which – at least implicitly – play a role in risk research: scholars in the human sciences do not only refer to potentiality in the sense of the capability of something to cause harm ('something' which according to Renn's terminology would be a technology, an event or an activity). Rather, they are additionally, and primarily, interested in potentiality according to the *contingency*, or indeterminedness, of ways of defining, dealing with or being involved in the potentiality of such harmfulness.

Yet, there is another layer of potentiality which implicitly or explicitly plays a role if one considers *natural* or *environmental* hazard or risk research: namely the potentiality according to contingent changes in the behaviour of the earth's natural system, or it's subsystems, regardless of which spatial and temporal scales these changes might pertain to, and whether these changes are triggered in an anthropogenic way or not. These potential changes (or potential 'events') refer to discontinuities or abrupt changes in the state of the earth's natural system or its subsystems, involving the destruction ('collapse') of previous equilibria, or so-called attractor states. They are *explicitly* investigated by natural scientists (in physical geography and the whole range of earth sciences) concerned with complex or nonlinear system dynamics.[1] As these changes *can* be regarded as 'something' potentially harmful,[2] but do not necessarily *have to* be regarded in such a way (as in the many 'pure' natural science papers that analyse the range of possible system behaviours), the study and discussion of the potentiality of such changes can be included in hazard and risk research, but also falls out of this context. But even if natural scientists do not necessarily have to think of hazard or risk research when studying the potentiality of changes in system behaviour, the reverse case applies: For as Pohl and Geipel (2002: 5) state, physical geographers associate the concept of natural hazards, and, by implication, also risks arising from natural hazards, with the potential of such 'collapses' in nature.

Accordingly, as Figure 12.1 shows, one can address a model of layered potentialities within natural or environmental risk research (i.e. risk research referring to the earth's natural system), consisting of the three following layers of potentiality that researchers have implicitly or explicitly focused on so far: the potentiality of contingent changes in system behaviour of or within the earth's natural system (layer 1), the potentiality of harmfulness of such changes (layer 2), and potentiality according to the contingency of ways of defining, dealing with or being involved in the potentiality of such harmfulness (layer 3). This model does

Layer 1: Potentiality of contingent changes in system behaviour of (or within) the earth's natural system	Dimension addressed by natural or earth sciences
Layer 2: Potentiality of harmfulness of such changes	Dimension addressed by natural/technical sciences within hazard or risk research
Layer 3: Potentiality according to the contingency of ways of defining, dealing with or being involved in this potentiality of harmfulness	Dimension addressed by human sciences within risk research

Figure 12.1 Model of different layers of potentiality that have been focused on in hazard or risk research referring to the earth's natural system

not only help to address a current view of how research undertaken by physical geographers or earth scientists can become part of hazard or risk research (be it risk research of the 'unfashionable' PRA style) – namely by involving the second layer of potentiality. It also helps to address how today's risk research can meet the standards of approaches developed by human scientists (of the social and cultural sciences as well as psychology) – namely by involving the third layer of potentiality. Thus, the model shows why human scientists have different expectations concerning how to speak about risks: while natural or technical scientists are used to working with layers 1 and 2, and express themselves accordingly,[3] it is by the inclusion of layer 3 that, for example, formulations like 'sudden and disruptive climate change – exploring the real risks and how we can avoid them' (the title of MacCracken and Topping 2008) become questionable. And although it might be conceded by human scientists that natural or technical scientists know that their results 'cannot be viewed as value-free or so-called objective reality',[4] it is the horizon of layer 3 according to which natural or technical scientists are criticised for undertaking some kind of 'reification of risks', especially by scientists representing a social constructivist point of view (like Bradbury 2009).

In this context, let me address the third way of supporting the thesis that it must be more difficult for physical than for human geographers to make a genuine contribution to current risk research. This third way refers to the fact that the practices of natural scientists can become an object of research of the human sciences, as in the field of science studies. And if risk researchers from the human sciences apply the perspective of layer 3 to the practices of natural or technical science risk researchers whose work focuses on layer 2, this can be regarded as corresponding to the situation of such science studies. One could say that layer 3 promotes an attitude correlating with some kind of *second-order observation* of risk research. Therefore, it is quite likely to happen that natural scientists (doing risk research) are confronted with human scientists (doing risk research) who believe to understand certain aspects of what the natural scientists do better than the natural scientists themselves. And to some extent, that cannot be denied.

However, this can give rise to the question of what it is that human scientists observing the practices of the natural scientists (doing risk research) are blind to themselves. A seemingly obvious way to answer this question would be to refer to the necessity of an even higher-order observation. The *subjects* observing would have to become the new *objects* of observation. In the following, however, I want to show a different way of dealing with traits of natural science research within the earth sciences which are missed by external observation (no matter of what order). These traits cannot be revealed by any 'approach' that remains bound to the subject–object divide. In fact, my chapter aims at:

- revealing traits of natural science research undertaken by physical geographers or other earth scientists, on the basis of being experienced in physical geography myself, but not in a mode of self-*reflection* (for reflection, in a strict sense, always remains bound to the subject–object divide);
- showing that revealing these traits allows us to understand in which way not only physical geography, but geography as a whole, due to its tradition (at least in the German-speaking area), can be understood as making a genuine contribution to current risk research concerning the earth's natural system;
- showing that this way of contributing to risk research is not only prior to or beyond a contradistinction or juxtaposition of natural and human sciences and their defined approaches or epistemologies (and corresponding views of geography), but also involves another form of potentiality, a more foundational potentiality, which should be included in the model of layered potentialities given in Figure 12.1.

Thus, as Figure 12.2 shows, what I want to do in the following is to unfold a foundational layer of potentiality that is worthwhile for geography as well as for risk research, and to present this foundational potentiality by its accessibility from the sphere of physical geography or earth sciences (layer 1), rather than from the sphere of explicit risk research as assigned to layers 2 or 3. Even if this means that there is a way to make a genuine contribution to current risk research from physical geography (and geography), it is still, in a sense, a 'difficult' way. However, this difficulty does not arise from some disadvantage or lack of expertise in comparison to human scientists. Rather, the difficulty arises from the fact that not only *what* is addressed in this chapter, but also *how* it is addressed, refers to a sphere of thinking, but also doing and being, which is prior to or beyond the contradistinction and juxtaposition of natural sciences and human sciences and their common and prevailing methodologies that we are all used to.

Bethinking oneself

The way the above-mentioned sphere will evolve in this chapter, but also – as I will show – in genuine contributions of geography to risk research, I deliberately

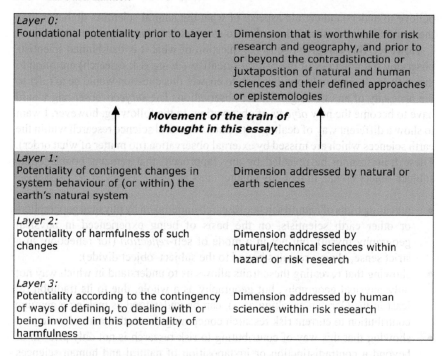

Layer 0: Foundational potentiality prior to Layer 1	Dimension that is worthwhile for risk research and geography, and prior to or beyond the contradistinction or juxtaposition of natural and human sciences and their defined approaches or epistemologies
Movement of the train of thought in this essay	
Layer 1: Potentiality of contingent changes in system behaviour of (or within) the earth's natural system	Dimension addressed by natural or earth sciences
Layer 2: Potentiality of harmfulness of such changes	Dimension addressed by natural/technical sciences within hazard or risk research
Layer 3: Potentiality according to the contingency of ways of defining, to dealing with or being involved in this potentiality of harmfulness	Dimension addressed by human sciences within risk research

Figure 12.2 Model of different layers of potentialities within hazard and risk research referring to the earth's natural system. Layers 1–3 are common fields of research by natural/technical scientists or human scientists. Layer 0 represents an additional, foundational layer of potentiality which is introduced in this essay and presented by its accessibility from the sphere of natural sciences (layer 1)

call by the archaic expression 'to bethink oneself (of something)'. I chose this expression as a reasonably apt translation of the German '*sich (auf etwas) besinnen*', in particular when thinking of Heidegger's usage of the verb '*sich besinnen*' or the noun '*Besinnung*',[5] and because several aspects of the expression make it possible to signify essential traits of the way in which the mentioned foundational potentiality can show itself.

One of these aspects is that the reflexive use of the word bethinking can be read as bearing witness of an attitude different from that of a subject/object divide: something is thought of, or considered, not as a distant object, but as something which emerges from a certain way of relatedness of someone to oneself. Another aspect lies in the fact that the expression 'to bethink oneself of something' sometimes is paraphrased by 'to cause oneself to consider something' or 'to bring oneself to consider something'. This is to be read here as bearing witness to some kind of *opening process* by which to consider something becomes possible in the first place. In fact, the mentioned attitude which is decisive for the issue and the form of this chapter is to be seen as being inherent in some kind of opening processuality. Furthermore, the expression 'to bethink oneself of something' implies the relevance of a certain kind of temporality. As will be seen, all these traits will play a decisive role in the rest of this chapter. Additionally, however, what will play a decisive role is 'sensing' and 'sense' (*Sinn*), and thus a field which manifests itself only in the German expression '*sich auf etwas besinnen*', but, unfortunately, not in any of its English translations. Therefore, in this chapter, 'bethinking' has to be understood as involving a kind of sensing and sense.

The fact that the train of thought of this chapter evolves by bethinking *myself* is reflected in various layers or features of my text, three of which are presented in the following.

First, it is already reflected in the question of how physical geographers can contribute to current risk research in a genuine way. The fact *that* this question is posed, and *how* it is posed and sought to be answered (namely in a movement from layer 1 to layer 0) can be understood as bearing witness of a process in which I bethink myself of (physical) geography – i.e. my profession, the field I am experienced in myself. In this process, physical geography will be reconnected to a sphere prior to or beyond the contradistinction of the human and natural sciences, and thus also human and physical geography. Thus, due to the opening process of bethinking which finds its expression in the train of thought of this chapter, my chapter acknowledges a distinction between these different branches of geography, but also transcends it (this also explains the brackets in the title of my chapter).

Second, it is also reflected in the fact that I see myself as being involved in a tradition which is sometimes called 'continental thinking' or 'continental philosophy', as distinct from 'analytic philosophy' which, very loosely speaking, is predominant – or at least used to be predominant – in the English-speaking world. In concrete terms, it is Heidegger's and Gadamer's philosophy – hermeneutic phenomenology or hermeneutic philosophy (rather than hermeneutics as a methodology) – which I also draw inspiration from. In fact, I understand the process of bethinking and revealing some foundational potentiality within geography and risk research as a hermeneutic way of *being* in science. As such a way of *being* cannot be thought of in terms of an epistemological subject/object divide, it also means the chance of an alternative to any kind of thinking which is torn between the 'objectivistic' side of risk research – which the natural and technical sciences are said to represent – and the 'constructivist' side of risk research – which focuses on the contingent and subjective act of taking risks by human beings, that is the role of individual or collective subjects, and in this sense can be said to be 'subjectivistic'.[6]

Third, bethinking oneself allows for contemplation of the language of one's science, in a way that is not restricted to explicitly defined terminology and concepts, but is open to the realm of everyday language, its implicit meanings and associations that inevitably steer and accompany our scientific activities and ways of expression. In this sense, it is especially the expression of 'creeping risks' (*schleichende Risiken*) that will play a decisive role later in this chapter – an expression which (at least German-speaking) physical geographers use when thinking of risks that emerge in a 'creeping' way: that is by very slow or hardly perceptible (natural) processes which – once they reach a critical point – could eventually lead to abrupt changes in system behaviour. Interestingly, involving this expression in the train of thought of this chapter will enable me to coalesce the two aspects mentioned above, i.e. aspects of research undertaken by physical geographers or other natural scientists concerned with natural phenomena of the earth, and some aspects of the central ideas of hermeneutic philosophy.

Earth's nature in the double sense, risks and the openness of the researcher

Let me come back to the first layer of potentiality introduced above (layer 1), and thus to nonlinear dynamical system theory. By focusing on identifying the conditions under which certain attractor states – which correspond to a certain kind of system behaviour – can be maintained or reached, studies of nonlinearity often raise expectations concerning the controllability of natural systems (as Thornes 2003: 138–39, discusses critically, using arguments developed from geomorphology).[7] That is, precisely because studies of nonlinearity try to *catch hold* of something apparently 'uncontrollable', something apparently random or chaotic, they mirror the wish to control nature themselves. However, as those scientists know best who are at home in nonlinear dynamical system theory, as well as being experienced in the complexity and time- and space-dependence of the earth's natural phenomena by fieldwork, total technological control of nature is just as impossible as the prediction of future natural processes in the earth system. Thus, despite, or contrary to, the wish to technologically exploit scientific knowledge, despite, or contrary to, the 'faith' (Baker 1988; Phillips 1999: 758) in the controllability of the earth's natural phenomena, scientists have learned both the *inevitable* limitations of such technology-driven knowledge and the contingent nature of natural phenomena at the same time. It is important to note that they have thus gained a kind of knowledge which is not technological or technologically utilisable: they have rather *come to a realisation*. Inasmuch as this realisation, or understanding, concerns the *nature* (i.e. the contingent nature) of the *natural* phenomena of the earth, it refers to 'the earth's nature' in a *double* sense. This is how I will use the expression 'earth's nature' in the following. It already hints at a certain ontological dimension of my train of thought which I will come back to later.

Before doing this, however, I want to stress two points which both touch the issue of risk and which are already implied by the above.

First, what is implied is that any scientific endeavour which results in representations of present or future states of the earth system, or some of its phenomena, means producing a risk: a risk which is not so much a risk of getting it wrong instead of right, as it is the risk of an *inappropriate reading* of such representations by those who do not know, or do not want to know, the unresolvable limitedness of science in light of the contingency of the earth's natural phenomena. This foundational limitedness cannot be resolved by calculating uncertainties or likelihoods, or similar efforts to fixate contingencies, that is: efforts to control uncontrollability. It eludes the *techniques* of science, even though it can be experienced by doing science.

The second implication touches the issue of risk in another way: what is implied is that it is science itself which confronts us with the fact that the earth's nature – in the double sense elucidated above – cannot only be said to be a permanent and unresolvable *hazard*, but also a permanent *risk*. In fact, it has to be stressed that at the basic level of the relation between human beings and the earth's nature in the double sense which is discussed here, the scientific distinction between 'hazards' on the one hand, and 'risks' on the other hand, becomes irrelevant. According to Renn's definition, the distinction between hazards and risks is a question of *getting into* a concrete situation of exposedness, and with respect to the example that Renn gives, namely the hazard of a toxic chemical substance (Renn 2008a: 50), it is reasonable to make this distinction. However, regarding the earth's nature in the double sense, the question is whether it is appropriate to suppose the possibility of being truly *out of*, or exterior to, a situation of exposedness *at all*. Strictly speaking, the answer to this question is in the negative. At least as long as human beings live on the earth, they will be exposed to its contingent nature, and therefore be 'at risk'. In spite of all efforts to control the (uncontrollability of) natural phenomena of the earth, they are always a hazard, or a risk, for us.

It is important to see that it is the scientific endeavour itself by which we can come to this realisation. This hints at the fact that the risk I am speaking of here is not to be understood solely as equivalent to the 'inherent risk' addressed by the United Nations Development Programme (2009: 230): an 'inherent risk associated with life on an unstable and still evolving planet' and which additional risks (i.e. the risk due to the industrial revolution and the risk due to global climatic change) can be 'compounded with' (ibid.). Rather, it is a risk that remains bound to the situation of the researcher, a risk that can affect, and change, the way the researcher works. Therefore, the above remarks do not amount to pessimism about, or even hostility to, earth sciences and risk research. They are intended neither to disqualify earth scientists from mastering their subject matter, nor to undo conceptual distinctions which scientists have made every effort to introduce in the first place. On the contrary, they help to reveal a certain forte of researchers.

In order to understand this, and how it is possible to take such a positive view of the experience of one's limitedness in the context of the earth sciences and risk research, we need to recognise that the risk due to the earth's nature is related to the unresolvable relationship between human beings and the earth's nature, and, therefore, to a way of *being* of human beings, but, *at the same time*, to the way this nature *is*. That is, such a notion of risk is ontological, not in the sense of an ontology that is subject to the subject/object divide, but in the sense of a *hermeneutic* ontology, or hermeneutic phenomenology, which emerges against the background of our experience of the inevitable and existential limitedness of us as human beings, but outreaches the being of human beings at the same time. Because of the outreaching nature of this experience, it corresponds to an attitude of openness, or to put it in a better way: it corresponds to a way of *being* in openness.

Because this openness is a way of being which emerges from an inevitable and foundational relation between human beings and the earth's nature, it is not constructable by scientific techniques, methods or approaches. But yet it is brought to bear in science. For even if this way of being in openness applies to all situations in which one *feels* or *senses* that one is at risk – prior to any cognitive evaluations[8] and scientific assessments, it is a special characteristic feature of the experienced researcher:[9] it is the experienced researcher who distinguishes himself or herself by not being fixated on what is already known, but by being open for the unexpected, or for that which has not been seen or anticipated before. This is a crucial point with regard to the question of a foundational potentiality that is prior to – or beyond – the potentialities which have been addressed in risk research so far, and it is also a good moment to come back to the issue of 'creeping risks'.

Creeping processes and the situational sense of the researcher

As I said earlier in this chapter, physical geographers tend to use the expression 'creeping risks' (*schleichende Risiken*) when thinking of risks that emerge due to very slow or hardly perceptible (natural) processes which – once they reach a critical point – could eventually lead to 'collapses' in nature, that is to abrupt changes of system behaviour within the earth system. In the usual context of the earth sciences, referring to such creeping processes would involve a statement about measurable or observable velocities, intensities or magnitudes of processes – and thus processes which are already known, processes which researchers are fixated on.[10]

When turning to a different kind of thinking, however, a thinking which is in tune with the realisation, and understanding, of the existential limitedness and openness introduced above, creeping has to be understood in a different sense. Rather than referring to something known and scientifically measurable or observable, one has to step back in order to see that creeping is a problem of perceptiveness and attentiveness (*Aufmerksamkeit*)[11] primarily. Against this background, the new question is: how is it possible that someone, by him- or herself, perceives hardly perceptible (*schier unmerkliche*) processes at all, although they could escape his or her attention? That is, I am referring neither to perceptibility in the physiological or technical sense, nor to the production of attention by the media, political undertakings, or other 'power-induced [...] influences and manipulations' and 'structural forces' (Renn 2008a: 61) which the social and cultural sciences concentrate on. Rather, what is interesting is the process of becoming perceptive and taking notice of something which, although it was overlooked before, suddenly catches the eye – a process which takes place in those moments during research in which the researcher's view changes and new possibilities present themselves.

In order to further discuss this process in its relevance to research that refers to changes in the behaviour of the earth's natural system (layer 1), but also in order to bring the issue of spatiality into play, I want to make use of the discussion of complex and nonlinear system behaviour. In concrete terms, I want to refer to the so-called panarchy model (Gunderson and Holling 2002), which – in the course of the discussion of complex systems – has also been reflected upon in physical geography literature (e.g. Dikau 2006; Slaymaker 2006; Thornes 2003). Presupposing a system of processes that is split up into a variety of processes on different spatial and temporal scales (smaller and faster ones, and bigger and slower ones), one purpose of the panarchy model is to illustrate the collapse of formerly stable states (or 'equilibria') due to linking mechanisms between such scales. Another purpose is to illustrate that any collapse is always accompanied by the chance of renewal. Furthermore, the model illustrates that the dynamics of such 'creative destructions' (Holling 2001: 396) can only be understood if the scales above and below are not disregarded, i.e. 'slow' processes of a longer persistence and bigger spatial extension, and recurring 'fast' processes of a shorter persistence and smaller spatial extension.

According to the panarchy model, it is these latter processes which 'revolt', i.e. which trigger the collapse of a formerly stable state. Because of this potential to trigger the collapses, and because of their short persistence and small spatial dimension, these processes can be thought of as an example of creeping processes meaning creeping risks. Dikau (2006), for example, taking up arguments by Thornes (2003) and Gunderson and Holling (2002), uses the expression of creeping (*schleichend*) processes in such a way, referring to creeping processes of soil erosion which create the conditions for the collapse of an ecological pasture system (which is assigned to a larger spatial and temporal scale). However, I would not want to rule out the possibility that abrupt changes in system behaviour could also be triggered by processes of a higher scale, i.e. relatively 'slow' processes of a longer persistence and bigger spatial extension. These processes could be called creeping with regard to their relative slowness.

Either way, when discussing such models not from the point of view of the natural sciences, but as a problem of perceptiveness or attentiveness, one has to be mindful of the fact that what is split up into a variety of different spatial and temporal scales in the panarchy model,[12] but also in common tables of geography textbooks, is not yet split up in the primary bodily experience in the field. Therefore, the actual challenge for the scientist in the field consists in becoming perceptive not only in respect of the different scales that are of relevance in certain situations, but also, and primarily, for their potential connectedness. To see 'creeping risks', to see the potential of abrupt changes in system behaviour (layer 1 in Figure 12.2) is grounded in the potential connectedness of different processes which, in an unresolvable way, is related to someone's potential to see this possible connectedness.

Obviously, such a potential must find expression in someone who experiences in a way that is not fixated on a natural phenomenon of a certain scale, but rather in an open way that allows the creeping processes to catch the person's eyes as being of relevance to the phenomenon of the scale the person was engaged with before. With some reservations, such a process of opening one's eyes can be described as a spiral movement starting from the larger scale (to which, for example, the pasture system is assigned), shifting to the smaller scale (which the creeping processes belong to and which is included in the larger scale), and back to the larger scale whose sense (*Sinn*) has become altered by the movement itself.

The reason why I describe the process in this rather artificial way is that it may help us to understand that, at these moments, the creeping processes resemble the key passage of a text in a hermeneutic sense: just as a key passage cannot be found – or show itself – *as such* without a reading of the text beforehand, and just as this key passage changes the sense – or the quality – of the text at the moment of its finding, to see creeping processes as creeping risks means to be involved in a situation which – due to its quality – allows the revelation of processes and their relevance – their qualitative situatedness – at the same time. Thus, to see creeping processes as creeping risks presupposes a qualitative, and open, situatedness that reveals another, and open, qualitative situatedness; it means a movement of *mutual foundation and the emergence of different layers of qualitative situatedness,* which is a quality in itself. In fact, this layered qualitative situatedness can be understood as a kind of situational sense which is neither just the sense of the 'subject' researcher, nor just the sense of the 'object' of research, but rather both – or beyond and prior to this divide. Thus, it is a sense in the double sense. And just as there are texts which can be read and experienced as a multi-layered phenomenon on the basis of such a situational sense, somehow conveying that there might be more layers to reveal,[13] the (natural) phenomena of the earth can also be experienced as a multi-layered phenomenon – open to further layers of experience.

Hence, someone's potential to see the potential connectedness of processes belonging to different scales is based on such a layered situational sense. Moreover, any notions of a 'multiscale character' or a 'spatio-temporal nestedness' of (natural) phenomena, and any representations, typical of geography textbooks, which split up (natural) phenomena of the earth by listing them according to different temporal and spatial scales, have to be understood as being based on the human being's potentiality to go through – or rather to live – the hermeneutic movement by which situational sense is altered and formed at the same time, so that a manifold layeredness, and situatedness, emerges. And if, as I said before, it is the experienced researcher who distinguishes himself or herself by not being merely fixated on what is already known, but by being open for the unexpected or for that which has not been seen or anticipated before, it is because he or she has gone through this movement again and again – thereby broadening and deepening his or her situational sense. In fact, I understand this situational sense to be an expression of the researcher's experiences and experiencedness; it is a kind of *tacit knowledge* (Polanyi 1966) that not only concerns *how* one sees the natural phenomena in one's mind's eye, but that basically guides the way in which one carries out one's scientific activities, the way one tries to understand the problem one feels confronted with, and thus also the way one moves in the field.[14]

Emergence of riskscapes within the earth sciences

If the situational sense discussed above enables someone to see the potential of some connectedness between processes belonging to different scales, and if – according to the panarchy model – such a connectedness means the potential of nonlinear system behaviour (layer 1 in Figure 12.2), it is now possible to come back to my thesis of a foundational potentiality which is prior to the potentialities considered in natural or environmental risk research so far (layer 0 in Figure 12.2). In fact, it is now possible to address this foundational potentiality as some kind of multi-layered situational sense which is as much a potentiality of the earth scientist, or physical geographer, as it is a potentiality of the studied landscapes, or layered natural phenomena of the earth. Taking into account that this foundational potentiality prior to or beyond any subject/object divide corresponds with the realisation, and understanding, of an unresolvable *risk* due to the earth's nature in the double sense which I discussed above, it is now even possible to link this foundational potentiality with the idea of an 'emergence of riskscapes'. In fact, within the context of earth sciences or physical geography, from the field-experience of its researchers, and prior to or beyond any *definitions* of risk as prevailing in either the natural and technical sciences or the human sciences (layer 1 and 2 of Figure 12.2), speaking of the 'emergence of riskscapes', as in the subtitle of this book, means speaking of the emergence of a qualitatively new layered situatedness due to the process of fulfilling, altering and forming such a foundational potentiality or situational sense. If earth scientists or physical geographers 'shape the emergence of riskscapes', they primarily do so when involved in this process – a process which is neither an act of social construction, nor an act which is subjected to a positivistic epistemology or objectivistic methodology.

To call attention to this process is not a purely academic endeavour. To think in such a way would mean to forget that the revelation of this process is linked to the realisation, or understanding, of the earth's nature in the double sense, i.e. to experience of the contingency of the nature of the earth which corresponds to a *basic* and *unresolvable* relation between human beings and the earth's nature. It would also mean to disregard *that* and *how* it is possible to let my revelation of some foundational potentiality become productive, or 'implemented', within earth sciences, and risk research.

The question of 'implementability' and the aspect of temporality

By considering how this realisation of a foundational potentiality and situational sense which concerns the layered natural phenomena of the earth can become productive, or 'implemented', I do not mean that it is possible to create a methodological manual, or instructions to scientists, telling them what they have to do in order to reach this level of, or rather being in, potentiality *for certain*. In fact, such a procedure would be doomed to failure, as it would preclude any being in openness. That is, what applies to the process of research in the earth sciences, or physical geography, applies to the question of how to let the above realisations become productive as well. In either instance, it would be counterproductive to be fixated on something in some way, blindly repeating former definitions, methodologies or approaches, as if it were legitimate in principle to ignore the fact that circumstances, and thus situations, alter. Instead, opening oneself to something, or aspects, one has overlooked before, to new ways of experiencing, and thus to revisions of sense by altering and forming sense at the same time (sense in the double sense as discussed in this chapter, beyond any subject/object divide), comes along with bethinking oneself of being in altering circumstances: circumstances – or situations – that alter themselves as much as they alter the person – or the sense of the person – who is bethinking him- or herself.

In these moments, time is not the time which physical geographers or other earth scientists usually refer to (see for example Ahnert 1996: 21–23). It is neither the time of 'physics', nor merely a 'historical' time of earth history. Both of these concepts of time are based on the Greek *chronos* and involve imagining time as an external framework into which things or events can be filed sequentially. Time as *chronos* therefore also refers to a measurable or countable time.

The time in which the hermeneutic experience takes place, however, can neither be measured nor described as a chronological sequence of events. Rather, the hermeneutic experience takes place in a time in which one forgets this external, sequential time. For without 'pausing' (*innehalten*) in the chronological sequence of events, at decisive moments which the Greek called *kairos*, it would not be possible to *re*-vise sense, and it would not be possible to become attentive and perceptive for something 'creeping', imperceptible or unnoted, for something 'which has been there without being there' before catching the eye, and for something that arises from, or corresponds to, some potentiality. Therefore, it is at these moments of *kairos* that any decisive change in the way one sees the spatio-temporal nestedness of the natural appearances of the earth, and that a corresponding emergence of riskscapes, takes place.[15]

Just as the collapses in nature which I discussed above cannot be determined (according to the panarchy model: the moments of creative destruction), the moments of *kairos* cannot be determined, planned and produced for certain either. However, it is possible to *raise the potential* for these creative moments in which new ways of spatio-temporal nestedness can be seen, and riskscapes can emerge, according to some foundational potentiality or situational sense. It is only in the sense of raising this potential that my revelation of some foundational potentiality and situational sense can become productive within the earth sciences and natural or environmental risk research.

Raising the potential – and the potential of geography in this regard

Here I will introduce four *interdependent* ways of raising the potential for moments of *kairos* as described above, none of which can be achieved in a technical and strictly methodological way.

One way is to leave the realm of external time, of *chronos*, with its fixed plans, intentions and methodologies, by being in a way which resembles experiencing art, involving what Gadamer (2006: 94) calls 'dwelling' (*Verweilen*) in view of an – astonishing – work of art. With respect to physical geography, this would mean dwelling on, and in, certain regions or places of the earth for the sake of these regions or places and their natural phenomena. Accordingly, dwelling is to be understood with respect to temporality *and* spatiality.[16]

Another way is to gain experience by seeing many different regions or spatio-temporal situations in their surprising and diverging otherness (*Anderheit*). For the more often one has been confronted with the ever-changing spatio-temporal nestedness and idiosyncrasy of natural appearances, so that one's situational sense is altered and formed again and again, the higher the complexity of the (tacit) knowledge that is formed by such experiences. In turn, this higher complexity increases the potential for such new experiences. In this respect, it is possible to draw a parallel with the neuroscientific discovery that any perception can be the more nuanced, the more diversified the neuronal structure of the brain (see Breidbach 2004: 58).

Furthermore, the potential can be raised not only by experiencing many different regions in their diverging otherness, but by being experienced in the difficulties and situations that arise when trying to describe this otherness and the region's specific spatio-temporal nestedness. Because in the struggle to find an *adequate* ('adequate' instead of 'correct' or 'true' in the sense of a binary logic) description, or representation, one has to pause (*innehalten*), leaving the realm of *chronos*, in order to experience the tension between previous descriptions and the new experience which goes beyond these descriptions. In my view, this is a geographic variant of Gadamer's concept of '*Sprachnot*' (lack of language), a kind of suffering one experiences when seeking the appropriate word, or when trying to articulate something that seems to elude language (see Gadamer 1995: 82–83, for one of many possible examples).

Last but not least, the potential for the creative moments of *kairos* concerning the spatio-temporal nestedness of natural appearances can be raised by being experienced in reading texts which don't just state facts, but bear witness to the author's hermeneutic experience in respect of the earth's phenomena, texts which implicitly show that they were produced out of this struggle to find an adequate description, or on the basis of the experience of a new kind of spatio-temporal nestedness in someone's mind's eye, i.e. texts which implicitly show that the author has gone through the movement of forming and altering some qualitative situational sense.

Even for someone not familiar with the history of geography, it should be comprehensible that the four ways outlined above touch very basic traits of the manifold historical tradition of the geographical endeavour. They are related to a complex of problems emerging from the practices of (geographical) expeditions and exploration journeys in past centuries, but also a complex of problems that were discussed in a theoretical way by geographers, particularly in the German-speaking area, and especially in the nineteenth century and first half of the twentieth century, concerning the form of geographical descriptions or representations and/or the idiographic character of geography. Interestingly, and related to the idea of idiography, what comes into play here as well is the notion of the 'spatio-temporally specific', which not only has a long tradition in geography, at least in the German-speaking area, but also turned up again recently in a discussion concerning the common base between human and physical geographers (see Massey 2001: 259).

However, by referring to a foundational potentiality and situational sense, the thoughts presented in this chapter illuminate these long-lasting and re-emerging theoretical discussions, and practices, in a new way. This possibility of a new way also shows itself when taking into account that the notion of a 'spatio-temporally specific' – be it of human phenomena, or of natural phenomena of the earth – can only be understood against the background of the ever-changing character of these phenomena, which also implies an ever-changing way of how these phenomena are spatio-temporally nested, or layered. Therefore, the notion of a 'spatio-temporally specific' – as a basic trait of geography – is implicitly linked, or linkable, to the idea of the earth's nature in the double sense and thus to my above thoughts. Accordingly, like 'risk', the tradition of the endeavour of geography, and the four ways of raising the potential for the creative moments in which new ways of spatio-temporal nestedness can be seen and riskscapes can emerge, can and have to be newly understood as expressing experiences, *and* experiencedness, emerging from the *unresolvable* relation of human beings to the contingent spatio-temporal variability of the (natural) phenomena of the earth, and thus as expressing a way of *being* in openness in the sense of hermeneutic phenomenology or hermeneutic philosophy (see above). And just as this way of being is prior to or beyond the subject/object divide, it is also prior to or beyond the dichotomy between human and physical geography.

Conclusions

It is beyond the scope of this chapter to elaborate on the far-reaching consequences that the insight we have just gained has for the subject of geography. However, what has found expression already in this chapter is that it is worthwhile – both for the subject of geography and for current risk research (and other fields of applications) – to (re-)understand the subject of geography in a way that has fallen into oblivion. This revised understanding refers neither to a geography which is nothing but the sum of different approaches in the natural and human sciences applied to certain regions of the earth,[17] nor to a geography that one would do justice to by characterising it as an endeavour steered by 'power-induced influences and manipulations' or 'structural forces', as social or cultural scientists engaged in science studies could assume. Rather, and primarily, geography is to be understood as a subject, or question, of *Bildung*,[18] referring to a kind of non-static, open and opening knowledge *and* attitude that can only be obtained by an indeterminable and interminable process of experiencing geography oneself and in a double sense: for what is acquired, and permanently altered and formed, is experience of the multi-layered and manifold (natural) phenomena of the earth, especially in fieldwork, *as well as* experience of our struggling endeavour to experience and to describe, or represent, these phenomena.

Against this background, let me answer the question, posed at the beginning of this chapter, of how (physical) geographers can contribute to current risk research in a genuine way. In order to contribute in a genuine way, we do not only have to bethink ourselves of fieldwork as a way of being in altering circumstances – or situations – that alter themselves as much as they alter us, our situational sense or foundational potentiality. We also, and primarily, have to bethink ourselves of being involved in a long tradition, and thus heritage, which *also* means the chance of altering circumstances. Opening ourselves to these altering circumstances of the heritage of geography can also raise the potential of the creative moments in which new ways of spatio-temporal nestedness can be seen, and riskscapes can emerge. If we – as geographers – want to contribute to risk research in a genuine way, broadening the ways of being alert to potentially harmful processes that human beings might face in future, it is not by adapting approaches of either the natural or technical sciences or the human sciences, or a combination of both, even if it makes sense to study these approaches. Rather, it is by bethinking ourselves, in a new and indeterminable way, of where we come from. Geographical risk research needs to take risks itself.

Notes

1   With regard to this explicitness, nonlinear dynamical system theory differs from more traditional approaches in physical geography or the earth sciences which refer to such changes rather implicitly (as stated by Phillips 1992b: 196, for geomorphology, but, in my view, this also applies to other fields of the earth sciences. See for example Phillips (1992a, 1992b, 2006) for short reviews of this development in geomorphology.

2   See for example the discussion of sudden and disruptive climate change in MacCracken and Topping (2008).

3   MacCracken and Topping (2008) contains several good examples referring to climate change issues.

4   As Bradbury (2009: 30) concedes for most PRA practitioners.

5   Note that Heidegger's 'Besinnung' or 'sich besinnen' is often translated as 'mindfulness', 'to be mindful of', as in Heidegger (2006). In the context of my chapter, however, which is *not* a treatise on Heidegger's philosophy and far from reaching the scope of his thoughts concerning the problem of 'Besinnung', I regard the translation 'to bethink oneself of something' to be less misleading and more helpful.

6   At the same time, it is also an alternative to Renn's suggestion how to 'solve' the problem of different notions within risk research – and also geography, i.e. to the suggestion of a 'case-specific combination of different methods' (Renn 2008b: 196) belonging to the various sciences that are involved in risk research. Note that there are other contributions to risk research which cannot be said to be torn between an objectivistic and a subjectivistic or constructivist approach to risk research *in every respect*, for example those concerning risks as feelings (Loewenstein *et al.* 2009). But even if *what* these contributions address appears to transcend the subject–object divide, *how* they address it or do their research usually remains caught in it.

7   Geomorphology proves to be a good example for this chapter, especially because its literature comprises reflections on the relevance and challenges of nonlinear dynamics for field studies.

8   This is where my chapter touches issues discussed by Loewenstein *et al.* (2009).

9   Note that – as a decisive feature of hermeneutic philosophy – the word 'experience' refers to both the *process* of experiencing as well as the *result* of such a process. The latter can be expressed by the word 'experiencedness'. With regard to the nexus between experiencedness and openness, see Gadamer (2004: 267–69).

10 Interestingly, a similar phenomenon can be found with regard to a psychological model of risk perception which Renn outlines in his review of interdisciplinary risk research (Renn 2008a: 56). Concerning 'insidious' or 'lurking dangers' and addressing the role

that scientific studies, and trust in scientists, plays in the public awareness with regard to the perception of such 'slow agents', this model also presupposes that the 'creeping' processes are known and have been taken into account by someone already – at least by the scientists who are supposed to facilitate the detection of insidious dangers. In this context, of course, it is legitimate to do this.

11 Note that the German word *Aufmerksamkeit* involves both a kind of perceptiveness and attentiveness. As shown by the verb *aufmerken*, it can also refer to the process of becoming perceptive or attentive. For a phenomenology of *Aufmerksamkeit*, see Waldenfels (2004).

12 See for example the graphical illustrations in Holling (2001: 397–98) or Slaymaker (2006: 14–15).

13 See Zahnen 2007 for a deeper discussion of the reading of 'texts' ('texts of nature', or texts written by geographers) within the context of physical geography, and the difference between a hermeneutic and a deconstructivist understanding of reading in such a context.

14 For a discussion of the necessity and creation of such a guiding tacit knowledge in earth sciences, see also Zahnen (2007, 2008). Referring to fieldwork in geology, Raab and Frodeman underline the *embodied* character of such knowledge which depends 'on the geologist's experiences in the world (2002: 73).

15 For a general discussion of the moments of *kairos*, see also Gadamer and Stappert (2002); for a discussion of such moments in the context of physical geography or geology, see also Zahnen (2008).

16 While the German word *verweilen* emphasises the temporal aspect of 'dwelling', the German word *wohnen* underlines the spatial aspect. However, both aspects of dwelling have to be understood in a philosophical sense. In this respect, see also Heidegger (1975).

17 With regard to the fragmentation of geography, see also Zahnen (2005, 2007).

18 The German word *Bildung* does not have an appropriate equivalent in the English language. Often translated as 'education', one tends to forget that it refers to a specific kind of knowledge that cannot be taught in a strict sense but rather has to grow by one's own experience and studies. This also finds expression in the fact that the word *Bildung* also means 'forming' or 'formation'.

13 Space and time

Coupling dimensions in natural hazard risk management?

Sven Fuchs and Margreth Keiler

Introduction

Extreme geophysical events, such as those which recently occurred in the U.S. (hurricane Katrina), Europe (floods), Myanmar and Haiti (tropical cyclone and earthquake), have focused the attention of the global community on susceptibility to natural hazards. Why has there been so little progress in our ability to mitigate and adapt to natural hazards? White *et al*. (2001) summarised this situation in an article with the title 'Knowing better and losing even more: the use of knowledge in hazard management'. One of the fundamental reasons for the lack of progress is the continuing separation of research on natural processes and social processes without considering interaction between these systems.

Taking into account that the international community as a whole is affected by considerable damage to infrastructure and property as well as loss of lives, the United Nations General Assembly designated the 1990s as the International Decade for Natural Disaster Reduction (IDNDR) (United Nations General Assembly 1989). Within the associated international framework of action, the objective of this decade was to promote concerted action in order to reduce loss of life, property damage and economic disruption caused by natural hazards, not only with a particular focus on developing countries, but also with respect to most developed countries. Initially, IDNDR was largely influenced by scientific and technical interest groups. However, a broader global awareness of the social and economic consequences of natural disasters developed as the decade progressed (White 1994; United Nations 2004). Based on this framework, which was continued by the International Strategy for Disaster Reduction (ISDR) (United Nations General Assembly 2000), the primary focus was shifted from hazards and their physical consequences to the processes involved in the physical and socio-economic dimensions of risk and a wider understanding, assessment and management of natural hazards. This highlighted the integration of approaches to risk reduction into a broader context between natural sciences and social sciences. The main challenge of risk reduction is rooted in the inherent connected systems dynamic driven by both geophysical and social forces: it is the need for an integrative risk management approach based on a multi-disciplinary concept taking into account different theories, methods and conceptualisations.

Space and time are two key factors when information on risk has to be assessed, since risk only emerges due to the physical overlap between hazardous events and elements at risk[1] and due to the temporal synchrony of such events and the exposure of elements at risk – which is a positivist approach rooted in the conceptualisation of risk common in the natural sciences and engineering. Taking the European Alps as an example, we will focus in the following sections on the spatial and temporal dimension of risk. We will show why such an approach prevailed with respect to applied natural hazard mitigation under the umbrella of institutional spatial planning in European mountain regions, and how this approach might be connected to the constructivist conceptualisation of risk common in the social sciences.

The concept of risk

Risk has been a focal topic of many scientific and professional disciplines as well as practical actions (e.g. Löfstedt and Boholm 2009). Consequently, a broad range of conceptualisations of the term exist that have as lowest common denominator the likelihood that an undesirable state of reality may occur as a result of natural events or human activities (Kates and Kasperson 1983). Undesirable states of reality are linked to damage, loss, or similar negative and thus adverse effects to those attributes valued by mankind (Crozier and Glade 2005). Although the possibility that something adverse might occur is appreciated, there is uncertainty as to when this potential will be realised. This inherently implies that people do make causal connections between the trigger of an event and the consequences. Therefore, this concept of risk is a construct which is directed towards potential future states of the studied system. Technically, these processes and situations that have the potential to bring about undesirable states of reality are referred to as a hazard, while this may have two different meanings: (1) the physical process or activity that is potentially damaging; and (2) the threatening state or condition, indicated by the likelihood of an occurrence of a given magnitude in a specified location and a specified period of time. Following the latter, and funnelling down from the latent danger to a specifically defined hazard setting, results in the concept of risk. The adverse effects can then clearly be linked to these settings, quantified by numbers and spatially separated by boundaries. The definition of risk contains three elements: (1) outcomes that have an impact upon what humans value; (2) the likelihood of occurrence; and (3) a specific context in which the risk may materialise (Renn 2008). Risk is materialised as the potential loss to the exposed system, resulting from the convolution of hazard and consequences at a certain location and during a certain period of time. From the perspective of the natural sciences, this relationship is regularly expressed by the risk equation which is conceptualised by a quantifying function of the probability of occurrence of a hazard scenario (p_{Si}) and the related consequences for objects exposed (c_{Oj}). The consequences can be further quantified by the elements at risk and their extent of damage (e.g. Fell *et al.* 2008), and specified by the individual value of objects j at risk (A_{Oj}), the related vulnerability in dependence on scenario i ($v_{Oj, Si}$), and the probability of exposure ($p_{Oj, Si}$) of objects j to scenario i.

$$R_{i,j} = f(p_{Si}, A_{Oj}, v_{Oj,Si}, p_{Oj,Si})$$

This quantitative definition of risk provides the framework for probabilistic risk assessment and has its roots in a spatial materialisation of risk: all parameters included in the risk equation have a two- and three-dimensional spatial dimension. This is operated in terms of a first-order observation (compare Pohl *et al.*, this volume), dividing space in endangered and safe areas. These areas are represented in maps and development plans, and are simultaneously taken into consideration in land-use planning.

Material aspects of risk versus social constructedness

The spatial materialisation of risk, even if conceptualised on different scales ranging from European (Commission of the European Communities 2007) to national and state levels has attracted criticism from scholars in the social sciences (Hoos 1980; Freudenburg 1988; Adams 1995), for the following reasons, as summarised recently by Renn (2008): first, what people perceive as an undesirable effect is related to their values and preferences, a fact which is not mirrored in the technical risk equation (Dietz *et al.* 2002). Second, the interactions between human activities and their consequences are more complex than average probabilities used in technical risk analyses are able to capture (Fischhoff *et al.* 1982; Zinn and Taylor-Gooby 2006). Third, the institutional structure of managing and controlling risks is prone to organisational failures and deficits that may increase the actual risk (Short 1984). Fourth, risk analyses cannot be regarded as an objective, value-free scientific activity (Fischhoff 1995), and values are reflected in how risks are characterised, measured and interpreted. Fifth, the numerical combination of magnitude, frequency and consequences assumes equal weight for the hazard component and the elements at risk. Consequently, no difference is made between high-consequence/low-probability and low-consequence/high-probability events, whereas people show distinct preferences for one or the other (Slovic 1987). Sixth, technical risk analyses can provide only aggregate data relating to large segments of the population and long time periods. Each individual, however, may face different degrees of risk depending upon the variance of probability distribution (Cullen and Small 2004). Moreover, cognitive psychologists and decision researchers have investigated the underlying patterns of individual perception of risk and identified a series of heuristics and biases that govern risk perceptions (Vlek and Stallen 1981; Slovic 1987). But studies on risk perception have clearly revealed that most individuals have a much more comprehensive conception of risk, including aspects of voluntariness, personal ability to influence the risk, familiarity with the hazard and so on (Slovic *et al.* 1982; Slovic 1987).

These findings from the social sciences have stimulated equivalent results within the geographical hazard community. It has been repeatedly argued that any natural hazard and resulting risk, and consequently any form of natural disaster is caused by humans and not by nature (e.g. Geipel 1992; Wisner *et al.* 2004), since any process operating in nature is only based on physical rules. Any damage due to natural hazards is thus the result of bad or false adaptation to nature, such as misdirected land use, improper development planning, inappropriate building techniques and materials, as well as lack of preparedness and insufficient awareness on the part of the people concerned (Dombrowsky 2002); these arguments are also used by scientists with respect to the so-called passive mitigation of natural hazard risk (e.g. ONR 2009). Obviously, the concept of risk is rooted in the interaction between society and the physical environment (Barrows 1923), which is a fundamental starting point of any (and therefore also geographical) research on natural hazard risk. Most scientists point to Starr's (1969) seminal article on social benefit versus technological risk as the beginning of quantitative risk analysis and the development of the risk paradigm (Cutter 2001). Yet antecedents are found much earlier, as summarised by Covello and Mumpower (1985) or Banse and Bechmann (1998).

Nevertheless, from a scientific point of view, dealing with undesired outcomes of natural events is rooted in spatial hazard assessment. The concept of space thereby refers to places where hazards are located, their distribution and regional patterns. These approaches have been further developed to cover the positivist concept of (materialised) risk, which includes the spatial analysis of (material) values at risk. In recent years, the assessment of vulnerability has emerged as a companion concept increasingly in the focus of the hazard community (Fuchs 2009). This shift from hazard to risk and vulnerability analyses and evaluation is, from a technical point of view, mirrored in the risk equation, where all parameters needed are combined as a functional relationship.

Space in the institutional dimension of natural hazard risk management

The concept of space, as introduced above, is inseparably bound to human actions within a region or an area, and is linked to any spatialised development activities. A sustainable use of mountain areas must include the analysis, assessment and management of natural hazard risk due to the relative scarceness of areas suitable for development activities. Taking countries in the European Alps as an example, only 38.7 per cent of the territory is suitable for such purposes in the Republic of Austria (Statistik Austria 2008). In Switzerland, 26 per cent of the territory is classified as non-productive, and approximately 68 per cent as suitable for agriculture and forestry purposes; only around 7 per cent is suitable for settlement and infrastructure purposes (Hotz and Weibel 2005). The historical shift of a traditionally agricultural society to a post-modern service-based society is reflected by an increasing usage of mountain areas for human settlement, industry and recreation. Accordingly, a conflict between human requirements on the one hand and naturally determined conditions on the other hand leads to an increasing concentration of tangible assets in regions exposed to natural hazard processes. This concentration is particularly observable with respect to agglomerations along the larger valleys of the eastern Alps and in the Alpine foreland (Bätzing 2002;

Fuchs and Bründl 2005). As a consequence, an increasing number of persons are exposed to natural processes, which are considered as natural hazards when they are likely to cause harm to human life or property. In recent years, public perception has been directed towards these issues due to the broad media coverage of events occurring in the Alps. However, the challenge of dealing with natural hazard risk in mountain regions is not a new one, as can be shown for the Republic of Austria, as an example of a densely populated mountain region in Europe.

In the Republic of Austria, strategies to prevent or to reduce adverse effects of natural hazards in areas used for settlement and economic activities can be traced back to the Middle Ages. Official authorities were first founded in 1884, based on the first legal regulations (Österreichisch-Ungarische Monarchie 1884). In the second half of the nineteenth century and in the early twentieth century, protection against natural hazards mainly consisted of implementing permanent measures in the upper parts of the torrent catchments to retain solids from erosion, as well as in the release areas of avalanches. These measures were supplemented by afforestation efforts at high altitudes. Since the 1950s, such conventional mitigation concepts, which were aimed at decreasing both the magnitude and the frequency of events, were increasingly complemented by more sophisticated technical mitigation measures. Before the 1970s, mitigation concepts were mainly aimed at the deflection of hazard processes into uninhabited areas, and watershed management measures as well as technical measures were implemented (Holub and Fuchs 2009). However, since structural mitigation inevitably has its limitations, passive mitigation was introduced in the 1970s, i.e. hazard zoning in the context of spatial planning (Stötter and Fuchs 2006) (for technical details, see Appendix). The overall aim of such passive prevention measures is to reduce losses without directly influencing the process by a spatial separation of process trajectories and values at risk.

Such a separation, which has been laid down in the respective legal framework in many Alpine countries (e.g. Republik Österreich 1975, 1976; Schweizerische Eidgenossenschaft 1991; Repubblica Italiana 1998), is based on the positivist approach of separating areas that are by definition safe, from those areas that are endangered. This separation is undertaken by using the spatial approach of a so-called design event with a defined frequency and magnitude. This approach refers to institutional and therefore collective efforts to translate public expenditures into priorities for area investment and according to principles of land-use regulation. As a result, there is a need for dividing space (defined as any location in first approximation) by distinct boundaries which have to be identified in terms of hazard characteristics, and to analyse how development sites are positioned in relation to the identified hazard threats. Position is here not defined as a geographical point, but in terms of the spatial characteristics of the built environment, such as the distance of elements at risk from the impact pressure threshold of the design event. By the normatively formalised act of delineating hazard zones, a spatial distinction is made between those areas that are – per legal definition – at risk and areas that are safe and therefore suitable for development activities. As a result, a difference is recognised between the acts of accumulating geographical facts and representing the spatial form embedded in these facts; and understanding the processes involved in analysing these facts (Golledge 2002): by intersecting the defined hazardous areas with values at risk, new information (on risk) is produced that is not directly a result of data gathering.

From an institutional point of view, the concept of risk, even if referred to as a construct of ideas with multiple facets, is the most suitable tool for defining such spatial characteristics, and drawing boundaries in the landscape that separate areas differently affected by hazards and, consequently, societal threats (Keiler and Fuchs 2010). As a result, spatially relevant theories about the location, arrangement and distribution of geographical phenomena and spatial interaction between both physical and human components of those phenomena are developed in order to understand human–environment interaction.[2]

Time in the institutional dimension of natural hazard risk management

The fundamental impetus for any form of risk management is an awareness of the threat, a notion of responsibility (which in the case of mountain hazards in Europe is regularly taken over by the political regulator instead of being borne by the individual, Fuchs 2009) and a belief that human action might reduce the risk (Crozier 2005). In the broadest sense, risk management options are developed to identify and assess risk, to prioritise appropriate mitigation activity for the reduction of risks found to be situated above a level of societal tolerability, and to lessen the effects of the underlying hazardous events. Elements at risk are essential within the concept of risk since 'a hazard is not hazardous unless it threatens something; [and] vulnerability does not exist unless some elements at risk are threatened *by* something' (Alexander 2004: 267, original emphasis). Apart from the restriction shown above which originates from a scientific approach, the concept of risk has a static component: when risk analyses are carried out, they only reflect the situation at a certain point in time, and for a given location with a distinct spatial dimension of scale.

However, risk changes over time. Due to climate change processes and the associated impact on the Alps (Keiler *et al.* 2010), magnitude and frequency will most probably slightly increase in the case of those processes where water is the driving agent (Solomon *et al.* 2007). On the other hand, technical mitigation measures aiming at a reduction of the spatial extent in the accumulation area have been implemented. However, socioeconomic developments in the human-made environment have led to spatial asset concentration and a shift in urban and suburban population in the Alps. Thus, the temporal variability of elements at risk is an important key variable in the assessment of risk.

Recently, conceptual studies related to the temporal variability of natural hazard risk have been carried out. These studies were focused on elements exposed to the risk of snow avalanches with respect to both the long-term and the short-term temporal evolution of indicators (Fuchs *et al.* 2005; Keiler *et al.* 2005, 2006). The principal method underlying these studies was the following

(Fuchs *et al.* 2004): the cumulative risk for the settlement area in the year 1950 was compared to the situation in the year 2000. Initially, the values at risk were quantified for the year 1950 (Figure 13.1a). In a second step, the values at risk relating to the year 1950 were recalculated on the basis of the reduced accumulation areas applicable in 2000 (Figure 13.1b). This represents the theoretical development of risk between the years 1950 and 2000 as it would have been without new buildings, but with the mitigation measures realised during that period. In a third step, the process areas of the year 2000 were intersected with the effective values at risk in the year 2000 (Figure 13.1c). This is the development of risk, resulting from the reduction in the accumulation areas on the one hand and the aggregation and expansion of buildings on the other hand. This procedure is theoretically applicable to any arbitrary time interval and shows the development of risk over time by following the risk materialisation approach.

Furthermore, owing to the requirement of economic efficiency of public expenditure on mitigation measures, there is a need for a precautionary, sustainable way of dealing with natural hazard phenomena, taking into account the values at risk (Fuchs *et al.* 2007). On the basis of these studies, the multi-temporal development of values at risk is fundamental with respect to spatially optimised mitigation measures.

The evolution of values at risk due to socioeconomic transformation in the European Alps varies remarkably on different temporal levels. Long-term changes are superimposed by short-term fluctuations, and both have to be considered when evaluating risk resulting from natural hazards.

Long-term changes are rooted in the significant increase in numbers and values of buildings endangered by natural hazard processes, and can be observed in both rural and urban areas (Fuchs *et al.* 2005; Keiler *et al.* 2006). In the urban areas studied, the total number of exposed buildings had almost tripled due to a remarkable shift in the category of residential buildings, while in the other categories the number of buildings was approximately unchanged (Figure 13.2a). A significant increase in number dated back to the 1960s and 1970s before the

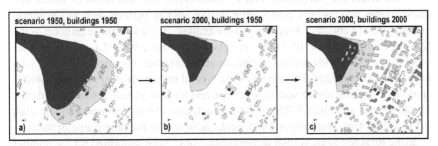

Figure 13.1 Temporal variation of both the hazard run-out area and the elements exposed to risk, taking the years 1950 and 2000 as an example. Dark grey represents the red hazard zone and light grey the yellow hazard zone. For principles of hazard mapping, see the Appendix.

Source: Fuchs *et al.* (2004: 265), with permission

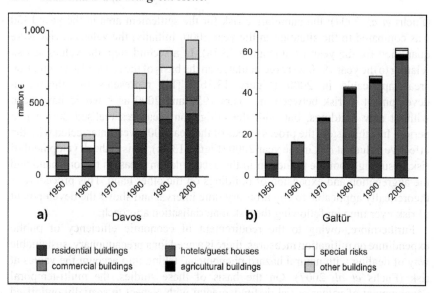

Figure 13.2 Temporal increase in number and value of elements exposed to the risk of
snow avalanches in Davos (Switzerland) and Galtür (Austria)
Source: Fuchs *et al.* (2005: 898), with permission

spatial regulation of land-use planning by hazard maps came into force (Fuchs and
Bründl 2005). In the rural test sites, the total number of endangered buildings had
increased by a factor of approximately 2.5, most of this increase being due to the
category of accommodation facilities, such as hotels and guest houses (Figure
13.2b, Keiler *et al.* 2006).

Short-term fluctuations in values at risk supplemented the underlying long-
term trend. Within the test sites, remarkable short-term variations of persons and
vehicles at risk were detected (Fuchs and Bründl 2005; Keiler *et al.* 2005). Results
from the urban test sites show that by subdividing the utilisation of hotels and
guest houses into months, peaks arose during holiday periods such as Christmas
and the end of February. According to the analysis in the avalanche bulletin of the
Swiss Federal Institute of Snow and Avalanche Research SLF, these periods
coincided closely with periods having an above-average occurrence of days with
high avalanche danger. This results from typical meteorological situations with a
stationary cyclone above northern Europe and an anticyclone above the Atlantic
Ocean (Fuchs and Bründl 2005). As a result, considerable amounts of snowfall
occur in the Alps, and temporal risk peaks arise within the time frame of weeks.

In the rural test sites, similar developments have been quantified for the number
of endangered persons by implementing a quantifying model. Over the entire
study period, the total number of endangered persons fluctuated by a factor of
almost six. Based on a fluctuation approach outlined in Keiler *et al.* (2005), strong
variations could be observed during the winter season as well as in the daytime
(Figure 13.3). The seasonal fluctuation was characterised by a strong increase in

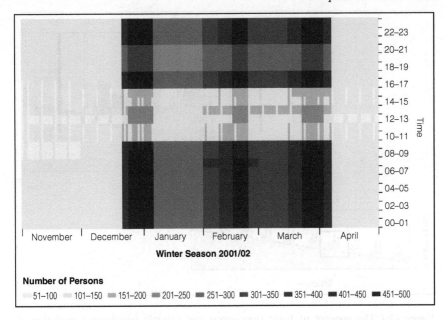

Figure 13.3 Temporal fluctuations in the number of persons exposed to snow avalanches in Galtür (Austria)
Source: Keiler *et al.* (2005: 55), with permission

the number of tourists at Christmas time and during the Easter travel season. The end of the winter season was highlighted by a sharp decrease in the number of persons to nearly the amount of the permanent population. Considering the diurnal fluctuation, the weekly structure could be easily followed. From the beginning of the winter season, these patterns were overlain by general movements of the tourists during daytime.

Hence, the evolution of values at risk due to socioeconomic transformation in the European Alps varies remarkably on different temporal and spatial levels. Long-term changes are superimposed by short-term fluctuations, and both have to be considered when evaluating risk resulting from natural hazards.

Long-term changes in values at risk could be regarded as the basic disposition (Figure 13.4). To reduce the risk resulting from this basic disposition, permanent constructive mitigation measures could be built and land-use regulations implemented. As a consequence, the basic risk could be reduced due to a spatial reduction of the process area. As pointed out in Fuchs *et al.* (2004) for an urban study area, the risk has decreased fundamentally since the 1950s, even if the values at risk in the municipality have increased. This development can be mainly attributed to the construction of permanent mitigation measures, and is strongly related to immobile values. Similar results were obtained for rural study areas (Keiler *et al.* 2006). However, extraordinary losses can be estimated if rare events with severe effects occur, because the delimitation of the respective process areas is based on defined design events.

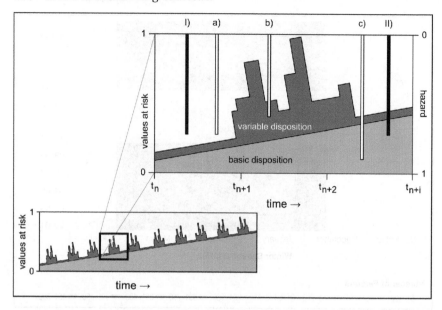

Figure 13.4 The concept of basic (long-term) and variable (short-term) evolution of elements at risk exposed to natural hazards

Short-term fluctuations in elements at risk supplement this continuing development of damage potential within a specific range. Thus, they can be considered as the variable disposition. To mitigate these fluctuations, temporal measures can be applied, such as evacuations or temporary road closures. Furthermore, because socioeconomic development differs within Alpine regions, studies of the long-term behaviour of values at risk contribute to the ongoing discussion of passive and active developing regions and suburbanisation (e.g. Bätzing 1993, 2002). However, if a potentially dangerous natural event occurs, it depends on the actual values at risk (basic and variable disposition) within the process area as to whether or not damage will be triggered.

Long-term as well as short-term variations in damage potential should be integrated into risk management approaches. In Figure 13.4, the significance of this for a consideration of dynamics in basic (long-term) as well as variable (short-term) damage potential is presented. As shown in example (a) for the period of time t_n, the event will not affect any values at risk, and thus, the level of risk reduction is sufficient. In example (b) for the period of time t_{n+1}, due to the high number of variable values at risk, damage will occur even if the event magnitude is moderate compared to event (a). As a result, passive and temporal mitigation strategies such as evacuation or road closures could reduce the variable damage potential to a critical level. In example (c) for the period of time t_{n+2}, basic and variable values at risk are affected by a process due to the large event magnitude. Thus, temporal measures are no longer sufficient for effective risk reduction. Consequently, active and permanent measures have to be undertaken. These examples clearly indicate the strong need for incorporation of dynamic assessments of elements at risk in community risk management strategies.

Apart from these issues directly applicable in operational risk management, the multi-temporal evolution of elements at risk results in significant institutional demands (Figure 13.4). In a certain period of time t_n, a natural event will not cause any losses since the run-out area of the respective design event does not overlap with elements at risk (example (I)). Due to the evolution of elements at risk, a natural event with comparable magnitude will be transformed into a hazard, since losses occur due to the increase in values at risk associated with a spatial expansion of elements at risk (example (II)) for the period of time t_{n+2}. The importance of considering such developments has recently been stated by Fuchs *et al.* (2004, 2005) and Keiler *et al.* (2005, 2006) for Alpine settlements; and this is of additional importance with respect to the discussion on climate change and possible variations in the frequency–magnitude relationship of events. As a result, variable risk management strategies taking into account this temporal and associated spatial evolution will be necessary.

Coupling positivist and constructivist approaches?

To manage natural hazard risk, a broader understanding of the concept of positivist (natural scientific) and constructivist (socio-scientific) approaches is needed in order to reduce losses resulting from hazardous events. Multiple conceptualisations of risk exist that show inherent differences in underlying theories due to sectoral disciplinary foci. If we look at the different roots of the multiple concepts of risk, it becomes apparent that only by a multi-dimensional approach can the overall aim of reducing natural hazards threats be achieved. Disciplinary approaches in risk assessment are linked with each other, leading to the conclusion that resulting structural, economic, institutional and social vulnerability are spatially inter-dependent and interacting within a complex coupled system (Werner and McNamara 2007).

As a result, disciplinary paradigms of risk research, such as the exclusive determinism of social standing or the sole dependence of resilience on economic risk transfer mechanisms is not sufficient to comprehensively explain susceptibility to mountain hazards in Europe. Starting with the destructive effect of an event, elements at risk will be damaged, which is linked to a positivist approach in risk research and materialised by a spatially explicit modelling of impacts on physical elements at risk. Depending on the institutional political setting of politics, e.g. the question of whether or not the loss occurred previous to elections, more or less public action will be undertaken in order to compensate affected people for the loss suffered. This compensation will in turn determine the economic vulnerability of the people concerned, and depending on the size of the financial losses, the people within a specific region will be more or less susceptible to such hazardous events. Natural systems, social systems and the built environment are spatially interconnected and therefore the separation of different types of risk is arbitrary. Human actions in mountain environments affect the degree of vulnerability and risk, which in turn shapes the possibilities of human action. More crucially, there are differences of approach between those that see natural hazard risk in terms of variations in exposure to hazards and those that concentrate on variation in people's capacity to cope with hazards (Few 2003). Studies of the former type tend to 'focus on the [spatial] distribution of some hazardous condition, the human occupancy of this hazardous zone [...] and the degree of loss (life and property) associated with the occurrence of a particular event' (Cutter 1996: 531). Studies in the latter tend to highlight the social construction of natural hazard risk or the socio-political process by which people are made vulnerable. Such different disciplinary concepts of risk, and associated paradigms of vulnerability, have at least two common elements that could be used in order to better evaluate the spatial dimension of risk in respect of mountain hazards in Europe. First, the concept of risk is based on the integrated assessment of human–environment interaction, which is a geographical approach based on a social-ecological perspective; and second, risk assessment should be based upon place-based spatial studies in order to be able to evaluate the impacts of adverse effects on the local or regional level. The challenge of moving from individual disciplinary views to an interdisciplinary analysis of risk by understanding the linkages and interactions between purely technical approaches and approaches based purely on the social sciences should be taken up. There is no doubt that elements at risk are highly susceptible if they are located in the run-out areas of mountain hazards: the risk of a specific location is triggered by the spatially distributed impact of any hazard, and affects the structural vulnerability of elements at risk. Structural vulnerability is complemented by economic resilience, the institutional framework and societal settings. A reduction of institutional vulnerability is essential in order to achieve a considerable reduction of societal susceptibility to natural hazard risk. One major step towards a more disaster-resilient society is information (Fuchs *et al.* 2009), highlighting the interaction between prevention and precaution, as well as creating incentives for loss-reducing actions on the local level in order to reduce susceptibility to natural hazards in Europe. As a consequence, technical as well as non-technical mitigation strategies continuously play a major role in reducing natural hazard risk.

To conclude, different concepts of risk have different roots, different methods and therefore different informative values. While scientific approaches are geared towards an improvement in the prediction of 'objective' risk resulting from natural hazards, constructivist approaches focus on societal-discursive decisions and processes in dealing with natural hazard risk. Integrating in a holistic way the contributions of the social sciences, natural sciences, politics and economics would by no means (at the present stage) result in one generally applicable integral method, but in a concept offering complementary results that might be combined with others for a deeper understanding of the spatial dimension of hazard and risk. Most probably, the positivist approach to risk assessment is necessary for the initial quantification of natural hazard risk, while thereafter constructivist approaches might be used to assess the societal effects of risk, and to develop appropriate management strategies (Egner 2008). Both positions need a theoretical foundation, a common language and a mutually adaptable abstraction, which is a major challenge for (geographical) risk research.

Appendix

To identify hazard zones, defined design events are used to estimate the spatial range and pressure distribution of the hazard processes. The methodologies applied therefore differ slightly between the Alpine countries, but the principle for drawing up hazard maps is similar; as described below for snow avalanche hazards in Austria (Republik Österreich 1975, 1976).

In Austria, red (dark grey in Figure 13.1) indicates areas where the expected pressure from avalanches with recurrence intervals T = 150 years exceeds a limit > 10 kPa/m². Yellow (light grey in Figure 13.1) indicates areas where pressure from avalanches with recurrence intervals T = 150 years is > 1 kPa/m² and < 10 kPa/m². Inside red areas, the construction of new buildings is legally forbidden. In yellow areas, particular regulations have to be considered with regard to the expected avalanche pressure, such as the reinforcement of walls on the hill side of a building. The spatial delimitation of hazard areas is thus based on a positivist approach, but is also a social construction based on legal regulations which are necessarily a result of engineering and political discourses.

Notes

1   Elements at risk are defined using a natural scientific approach, and include tangibles (the built environment, infrastructure lines and traffic corridors) as well as the population living in endangered areas (residents, commuters and tourists).
2   Here, environment refers to physical space and includes geomorphic processes and other spheres of physical geography, while human refers to anthropogenic activities in the studied region, such as the built environment and other spheres of human geography.

14 Making sense of the spatial dimensions of risk

Detlef Müller-Mahn, Jonathan Everts and
Martin Doevenspeck

Space matters, as Renn and Klinke affirm in their chapter on risk governance (Chapter 1). The spatial dimension is essential for the social construction of risk, including risk governance and moral judgements about risk taking and risk distribution. Space, the relation between risk and space, and the projection of risks into space are important for societal decision-making about which risks to take seriously, and against which risks to take precautions. However, analysing risk and space in conjunction with each other remains a major challenge; a challenge for which the discipline of geography is well equipped through its integrated perspective on social and physical space, as we will argue by way of concluding the present book.

Renn and Klinke (Chapter 1) point out that the understanding of space and its practical implications have changed in the transition from traditional risk management strategies to a broader and more comprehensive concept. While the established forms of risk management follow regulatory approaches that refer to the spatial dimension primarily as a means of orientation for risk assessments and measures to reduce risks, the more recent and broader approaches of risk governance expand their concern to questions of agency, institutions and participation, and therefore acknowledge the diversity of spatial perspectives of actors who become relevant in the process (Renn and Klinke, Chapter 1). This includes experts and lay people, risk managers and people at risk, their respective types of knowledge, personal concern and capacity, and finally, of course, their diverse understandings of 'space'. Conceptualizing space in risk governance therefore means to consider the multiple ways in which different social groups, stakeholders and experts relate their subjective risk assessments to a spatial framework (Hutter 2006, Renn 2008). In a way, the spatial dimensions of risk are as diverse as the number of different points of view on risk and space or 'riskscapes' (Müller-Mahn and Everts, Chapter 2). To sum up the overall argument of the present book, any meaningful and relevant risk research, communication and management practice needs to take the diversity and multiplicity of risk, space and riskscapes into account.

In a commentary piece on the 'spatiality of risk', human geographer Valerie November noted 'that no territory should be studied without considering all the risks it faces and that, on the other hand, no risk should be assessed without taking all its spatial dimensions into account. This spatial perspective is essential to appreciate the full complexity of links to other categories of risk' (November 2008: 1525). Likewise, the authors of the present book recognize the mutual relationship between space and risk: how space shapes risks and risks simultaneously shape space. Doubtlessly, the mutual relationship between risk and space is not easy to grasp in full. Suggested ways to achieve this aim include concepts and conceptual tools developed in the pages of this book, such as 'riskscapes' (Müller-Mahn and Everts, Chapter 2), the 'hybrid view of space' (Renn and Klinke, Chapter 1), 'warscapes' (Korf, Chapter 5), 'discursive understandings of space' (Weichhart and Höferl, Chapter 3), 'risk space' (Krüger, Chapter 8), 'translation of hazards into risks' (Doevenspeck, Chapter 10), 'layers of potentiality' (Zahnen, Chapter 12), the 'multi-dimensional approach to risk' (Fuchs and Keiler, Chapter 13), the 'system theory concept of risk' (Pohl *et al.*, Chapter 4) or 'border regimes' (Belina and Miggelbrink, Chapter 9; Kreutzmann, Chapter 11; Schetter, Chapter 7). Of course, the contributions to the present book cannot cover the entire spectrum of the spatial dimensions of risk. However, they draw the contours of a distinct geographic approach to the spatiality of risk. Instead of repeating the arguments elaborated in the preceding pages, we wish to use this concluding chapter to summarize distinct aspects of the geographical approach to risk which are key to our understanding and its implications for risk management and research practice.

Geography and the spatial dimensions of risk

Traditionally, geography has an exceptionally high stake in explaining the relation of humans to other physical elements in an attempt to provide an integrated perspective, combining insights from geography's two major sub-disciplines, human geography and physical geography (cf. Zahnen, Chapter 12). Whereas human geography tends to look at social and cultural processes, physical geography turns its gaze towards the biological, chemical and physical dynamics and how they play out in space and time. What links the two sub-disciplines is their shared interest in the spatial dimension and their decidedly spatial or geographical perspective. Although throughout the present book we may recognize from which geographical tradition each of the contributions stems, we can also see how the book as a whole offers an integrated perspective which relates the social and spatial dimensions of risk in insightful ways.

First, we can see how physical space and social space overlap in meaningful ways. For example, the ways in which societies organize flood risk management can be problematized from a physical geography perspective. Flood risk management is dependent on larger political bodies that are able to allocate and spend considerable amounts of money on projects such as building and maintaining dikes or polders. Thus, particular ways of managing floods often stop at political borders (see Pohl *et al.*, Chapter 4; Weichhart and Höferl, Chapter 3). But rivers do not respect administrative borders. Local risk management efforts can be thwarted by other flood prevention measures upstream or downstream. Any comprehensive risk analysis needs to take into account the risk created through the space constituted by the river, and the risk created through different territorial regimes of risk management. The quirky relationship between administrative space and natural space can in itself be an important source of risk (see Fuchs and Keiler, Chapter 13). Another important issue relates to the question of territorialization, which has recently become a major topic among human geographers (see Schetter, Chapter 7). Here, the focus is on political strategies that create borders, separating an 'inside' from an 'outside', in order to create governable societies and subjects (see Kreutzmann, Chapter 11). In a globalizing world of conflict and social inequality, the increasing emphasis on 'securitizing the border' has become the new doctrine for high-income nations and state-like conglomerates (Belina and Miggelbrink, Chapter 9). Thus, on the basis of the imagined spaces of who belongs inside a demarcated territory and who does not, physical space becomes reorganized with real consequences for those whose lives and welfare depend on their mobility. In other words, borders create security for some, but risk for others (Korf, Chapter 5; Doevenspeck, Chapter 10).

Second, the social and spatial dimensions of risk play out differently in different places. The ways in which risks are understood, identified and dealt with are related to place-specific characteristics, and to the people who live in the places concerned (see Doevenspeck, Chapter 10; Korf, Chapter 5). For example, researching the spatial inequalities of risk addresses the potential harm of different vulnerability approaches (Wisner *et al.* 2004; Scheuer *et al.* 2011; Cissé *et al.* 2012). In addition, the spatial perspective showcases the unequal distribution of risk. It helps to understand and document the spatial gap between those who are exposed to a risk and those who benefit from it, in order to grasp the complex and fragmented spaces that stretch in between and are perpetuated by these different groups (see November 2004). It is doubtful, for example, whether people living around Lake Kivu, on the border between Congo and Rwanda, will gain any advantage from the most obvious volcanic benefit, the methane gas dissolved in the lake (see Doevenspeck, Chapter 10). Cheap electricity generated by using the gas benefits first and foremost consumers far away who will not be affected by volcanic eruptions or gas outbursts. Geographers have been keen to stress that what is happening in the world does not take place on the head of a pin (Massey 1995: 49–52). Risks are unequally distributed and tied to locales, sites, places and particular landscapes (hence the term 'riskscapes' – see Müller-Mahn and Everts, Chapter 2). This has major implications for our understanding of risk. Contrary to Beck's (1992) claim, the shift from distributing 'goods' to distributing 'bads' has not democratized risk (Mythen 2005). Even many of the globalized modern risks have a location, and create uneven spatial risk configurations that have major consequences for some, while having virtually no effect on others – be it people who happened to live in the wrong 'landscape' in war-torn Sri Lanka (Korf, Chapter 5) or people who live near Lake Kivu on either side of the border between the Democratic Republic of Congo and Rwanda (Doevenspeck, Chapter 10).

Third, both the physical and the social spaces of risk production are of practical relevance. Any action targeted at reducing risk has to take into account the causes and mechanisms of processes in the material world, as well as perceptions, socio-cultural dynamics and how people react to potential threats. All the chapters in this book apply perspectives that are more or less constructivist in their theoretical background, i.e. they acknowledge that risk and space do not exist independently from human perception and agency. However, both risk and space are characterized by objective and subjective components, and both refer to material as well as imagined worlds. Consequently, an integrated analysis requires both physical and social concepts. Some argue, for analytical purposes and epistemological clarity, that these concepts must be kept separate (e.g. Renn and Klinke, Chapter 1; Pohl *et al.*, Chapter 4; Fuchs and Keiler, Chapter 13). However, realist and constructivist perspectives also complement each other when it comes to their practical application, for example in risk management. Fuchs and Keiler (Chapter 13) give an example of a pragmatic combination of perspectives in a study of the management of risks connected with natural hazards in the Austrian Alps, first presenting the physical dangers, and then exploring how they are socially evaluated. By studying the emergence of different concepts of flood management in Lower Austria, Weichhart and Höferl (Chapter 3) show how areas threatened by inundation are represented as 'the spatial manifestation of flood risk', and interpret this representation as 'discursively constructed social space'.

The geographical approach in the present book is characterized by these three aspects. Social space, present in administrative areas and bordered territories, does not exist independently from physical space. Their relationship determines the kind and number of risks people need to face. Second, any particular risk is not everywhere the same. Although many risks cross political boundaries, and some need to be considered as global, each risk plays out differently depending on the local context, producing social and spatial inequalities based on risk. Third, theoretical work brings together concepts from the natural sciences and the social sciences, since the geographic perspective must integrate elements from both the physical and the social world.

Implications for risk management ...

Against the backdrop of contradictory views of 'risky territories', Korf, and Müller-Mahn and Everts (Chapter 5; Chapter 2) use the metaphorical terms of 'warscapes' and 'riskscapes', respectively, to emphasize how humans make sense of and navigate through perilous territories and try to manage risk by avoiding uncertainties. They conceptualize these imagined landscapes as being shaped by contradictory relationships between risk and uncertainty, and between the views and strategies of different social actors. Landscapes of risk, and, even more tangible, landscapes of war, are real-and-imagined geographies based on individual and collective experience, tradition and knowledge. They reflect cultural norms, preferences, and symbolic meaning, but also contradictory representations of boundaries and contested territories. Contradictory represen-tations of space are a major source of uncertainty in these landscapes of risk, as Korf (Chapter 5) explains vividly in his case study of the warscape of the Sri

Lankan civil war. The army maintains the image of an ordered political territory with demarcated borderlines and checkpoints between what they refer to as 'cleared and uncleared' areas, so that there can be no doubt about which piece of land belongs to whom, whereas the realities of guerilla warfare and of the everyday life of the inhabitants are characterized by the fluidity of boundaries and control. This is a situation that Korf describes as the 'certainty of uncertainty'. For the people living in such a warscape, the uncertainty of their environment is the most difficult thing to tackle, i.e. the surprises and unexpected events resulting from being caught in the middle of fighting, whereas ordinary risks can be accommodated more easily.

Risk management is difficult under conditions of uncertainty. Decision makers come to ambiguous or contradictory conclusions about how to manage risky situations when the degree, time and place of a particular risk remain unknown and knowledge is incomplete. The capacity to localize risks in time and space is an essential prerequisite for risk governance. In other words, taking the spatiality of risk into account contributes to the reduction of uncertainty by translating it into risk. Decision-making as a form of deliberate risk-taking requires regulation of responsibilities, or, as Pohl *et al.* (Chapter 4) call it, of the 'ownership of a particular risk'. Risk management, according to Pohl *et al.*, aims at the identification of 'protection targets', which are defined by threshold values. Threshold values and their projection into space may be interpreted as tools to reduce uncertainty and translate it into risk.

As Renn and Klinke (Chapter 1) point out, risk management has to come to an understanding about 'how much uncertainty and ignorance the main stakeholders and public interest groups are willing to accept or to tolerate in exchange for some potential benefit'. The expected spatial extension of a risk is decisive with regard to who feels affected, and who does not. Risk management involves communication about questions of space, for example where impacts of an adverse event may be expected, how far-reaching these effects will be, which areas (and people living in these areas) are going to be affected, and how risky processes can be controlled. By referring to a spatial framework, measures to control risky processes can be coordinated and implemented efficiently. In addition, the monitoring of risky areas is important in order to avoid unexpected developments. The extent to which such uncertainty considerations are seen as significant or not largely depends on 'the shared meaning of spatio-temporal experiences' (Renn and Klinke, Chapter 1).

... and for research practice

Throughout this book, authors emphasize how risk is not only naturally given, but is also constructed by societies and social relations. One important tool is cartographic visualization of riskscapes or risk zones. These representations can have discriminatory effects, predefining those at risk and those who seem to live in a secure environment. This can have negative effects on either side, be it stigmatization of people who are seen as a risk to society, since they live in riskscapes (see Doevenspeck, Chapter 10; Belina and Miggelbrink, Chapter 9), or the dangerously soothing effect of making people believe they live 'on the safe side' (see Everts, Chapter 6; Krüger, Chapter 8). It is one of geography's strengths that it can construct and deconstruct cartographic imagery at the same time. While cartography can be used as a major tool for showing the geographical variation of risk and of those in need, its products are also a worthy instrument of critical interrogation, as they not only represent but also create space (e.g. Kreutzmann, Chapter 11). Although the chapters in this book do not directly refer to the nascent sub-discipline of 'critical cartography', many of them contribute to this promising new approach (see Kitchin and Dodge 2007; Crampton 2010).

Apart from the cartographical tool, other modes of visualization are important, too. For instance, the photograph is still highly valued as a way of viewing places. It is not just 'evidence' in the sense of showing what things look like 'in the field', but it is also a tool for empirical research such as mapping or interviewing. What picture we seem to have been compelled to make is a question for thorough analysis. The same applies to the question of what we have photographed and what we have left out. Moreover, photographs and other imagery should be critically interrogated, just as cartographic representations and the use (and possible abuse) of imagery within the construction and management of risk and riskscapes needs to be analysed (e.g. Everts, Chapter 6; Pohl *et al.*, Chapter 4; Fuchs and Keiler, Chapter 13).

Just as we have emphasized the multiplicity of risk factors and their spatial dimensions, there is not 'one' geographical method but a multitude of methodological approaches and tools. Mappings, statistics and questionnaires have been part of the geographical toolkit for a long time. So has (landscape) observation. More recently, qualitative methodologies have garnered more interest (see DeLyser *et al.* 2010). Some fine examples of open or semi-structured interview techniques, participant observation and ethnographic writing, and the powerful insights gained from using these methods, can also be found within the present book (see Korf, Chapter 5; Doevenspeck, Chapter 10).

We wish to conclude by expressing our gratitude to all the authors, who have contributed tremendously to our understanding of the spatial dimensions of risk. We hope that in compiling these chapters we can enrich current and future debates about the risks we face, and give some ideas regarding how we can deal with them, in research and in practice.

References

Chapter 1

Abels, G. (2007) 'Citizen involvement in public policy-making: does it improve democratic legitimacy and accountability? The case of pTA', *Interdisciplinary Information Science*, 13, 1: 103–16.

Aven, T. and Renn, O. (2009) 'The role of quantitative risk assessments for characterizing risk and uncertainty and delineating appropriate risk management options, with special emphasis on terrorism', *Risk Analysis*, 29, 4: 587–600.

Aven, T. and Vinnem, J.E. (2007) *Risk Management: With Applications from the Offshore Petroleum Industry*, Heidelberg/London: Springer.

Bender, H.F. (2008) 'Ergebnisse der Projektgruppe Risikoakzeptanz des AGS', *Gefahrstoffe – Reinhaltung der Luft*, 68, 7/8: 287–88.

Beierle, T.C. and Cayford, J. (2002) *Democracy in Practice. Public Participation in Environmental Decisions*, Washington: Resources for the Future.

Bickerstaff, K. and Simmons, P. (2009) 'Absencing/presencing risk: rethinking proximity and the experience of living with major technological hazards', *Geoforum*, 40, 2: 864–72.

Boholm, A. (1998) 'Comparative studies of risk perception: a review of twenty years of research', *Journal of Risk Research*, 1, 2: 135–63.

Brooks, H. (1984) 'The resolution of technically intensive public policy disputes', *Science, Technology, and Human Values*, 9, 1: 39–50.

Daft, R.L. and Weick, K.E. (1984) 'Toward a model of organizations as interpretation systems', *Academy of Management Review*, 9, 2: 284–95.

Feldman, M.S. (1989) *Order without Design: Information Production and Policy Making*, Stanford, CA: Stanford University Press.

Filar, J.A. and Haurie, A. (eds) (2010) *Uncertainty and Environmental Decision Making*, New York: Springer.

Frewer, L.J. and Salter, B. (2007) 'Societal trust in risk analysis: implications for the interface of risk assessment and risk management', in M. Siegrist, T.C. Earle and H. Gutscher (eds) *Trust in Cooperative Risk Management: Uncertainty and Scepticism in the Public Mind*, London: Earthscan, pp. 143–58.

Functowicz, S.O. and Ravetz, J.R. (1992) 'Three types of risk assessment and the emergence of post-normal science', in S. Krimsky and D. Golding (eds) *Social Theories of Risk*, Westport and London: Praeger, pp. 251–73.

Goldstein, J. and Keohane, R.O. (1993) 'Ideas and foreign policy. An analytical framework', in J. Goldstein, and R.O. Keohane (eds) *Ideas and Foreign Policy. Beliefs, Institutions, and Political Change*, Ithaca, NY: Cornell University Press, pp. 3–30.

Hagendijk, R. and Irwin, A. (2006) 'Public deliberation and governance: engaging with science and technology in contemporary europe', *Minerva*, 44, 2: 167–84.

Health Council of the Netherlands (2006) 'Health significance of nanotechnologies', *Publication No. 2006/06E*, The Hague: Health Council of the Netherlands.

HM Treasury (2005a) *Managing Risks to the Public: Appraisal Guidance, Draft for Consultation*, London: HM Treasury Press. Available online at: http://www.hm-treasury.gov.uk (accessed 11 June 2011).

HM Treasury (2005b) *Managing Risks to the Public: Appraisal Guidance*, London: HM Treasury. Available online at: http://www.hm-treasury.gov.uk/media/0/B/Managing_risks_to_the_public.pdf (accessed May 2011).

Horlick-Jones, T. and Sime, J. (2004) 'Living on the border: knowledge, risk and transdisciplinarity', *Futures*, 36, 4: 441–56.

Horlick-Jones, T., Rowe, G. and Walls, J. (2007) 'Citizen engagement processes as information systems: the role of knowledge and the concept of translation quality', *Public Understanding of Science*, 16, 3: 259–78.

HSE (Health and Safety Executive) (2001) *Reducing Risk – Protecting People*, London: Health and Safety Executive.

Hudson, K.L. (2006) 'Preimplantation diagnosis: public policy and public attitudes', *Fertility & Sterility*, 58, 6: 1638–45.

Hutter, B.M. (2006) 'Risk, regulation, and management', in P. Taylor-Gooby and J. Zinn (eds) *Risk in Social Science*, Oxford: Oxford University Press, pp. 202–27.

IRGC (International Risk Governance Council) (2005) *Risk Governance: Towards an Integrative Approach*, White Paper 1, O. Renn with an Annex by P. Graham, Geneva: IRGC.

Kahneman, D. and Tversky, A. (eds) (2000) *Choices, Values, and Frames*, Cambridge: Cambridge University Press.

Klinke, A. (2006) *Demokratisches Regieren jenseits des Staates. Deliberative Politik im nordamerikanischen Große Seen-Regime*, Opladen: Barbara Budrich Publisher.

Klinke, A. and Renn, O. (2001) 'Precautionary principle and discursive strategies: classifying and managing risks', *Journal of Risk Research*, 4, 2: 159–73.

Klinke, A. and Renn, O. (2002) 'A new approach to risk evaluation and management: risk-based, precaution-based, and discourse-based strategies', *Risk Analysis*, 22, 6: 1071–94.

Klinke, A. and Renn, O. (2010) 'Risk governance: contemporary and future challenges', in J. Eriksson, M. Gilek and C. Ruden (eds) *Regulating Chemical Risks: European and Global Perspectives*, Berlin: Springer.

Klinke, A. and Renn, O. (2012) 'Adaptive and integrative governance on risk and uncertainty', *Journal of Risk Research*, 15, 3: 273–92.

Klinke, A., Dreyer, M., Renn, O., Stirling, A. and van Zwanenberg, P. (2006) 'Precautionary risk regulation in European governance', *Journal of Risk Research*, 9, 4: 373–92.

Laudan, L. (1996) 'The pseudo-science of science? The demise of the demarcation problem', in L. Laudan (ed.) *Beyond Positivism and Relativism. Theory, Method and Evidence*, Boulder: Westview Press, pp. 166–92.

Lewin, R. (1992) *Complexity: Life at the Edge of Chaos*, New York: Macmillan.

Löfstedt, R.E. (1997) *Risk Evaluation in the United Kingdom: Legal Requirements, Conceptual Foundations, and Practical Experiences with Special Emphasis on Energy Systems*, Stuttgart: Center of Technology Assessment.

Löfstedt R. and Vogel, D. (2001) 'The changing character of regulation: a comparison of Europe and the United States', *Risk Analysis*, 21, 3: 393–402.

Luhmann, N. (1993) *Risk: A Sociological Theory*, Berlin: de Gruyter.

Marti, K., Ermoliev, Y. and Makowski, M. (eds) (2010) *Coping with Uncertainty. Robust Solutions*, Berlin and Heidelberg: Springer.

Merad M., Rodrigues N. and Salvi O. (2008) 'Urbanisation control around industrial Seveso sites: the French context', *International Journal of Risk Assessment and Management*, 8, 1/2: 158–67.

Nelkin, D. and Pollak, M. (1979) 'Public participation in the technological decisions: reality or grand illusion?', *Technology Review*, 6: 55–64.

Nelkin, D. and Pollak, M. (1980) 'Problems and procedures in the regulation of technological risk', in C.H. Weiss and A.F. Burton (eds) *Making Bureaucracies Work*, Beverly Hills: Sage, pp. 233–53.

OECD (Organisation for Economic Co-operation and Development) (2003) *Emerging Systemic Risks: Final Report to the OECD Futures Project*, Paris: OECD Press.

Pelling, M., High, C., Dearing, J. and Smith, D. (2008) 'Shadow spaces for social learning: a relational understanding of adaptive capacity to climate change within organisations', *Environment and Planning A*, 40, 4: 867–84.

Radandt, S., Rantanen, J. and Renn, O. (2008) 'Governance of occupational safety and health and environmental risks', in H.-J. Bischoff (ed.) *Risks in Modern Society*, Heidelberg and Berlin: Springer, pp. 127–258.

Reese, S.D., Gandy Jr., O.H. and Grant, A.E. (eds) (2003) *Framing Public Life: Perspectives on Media and our Understanding of the Social World*, Mahwah, NJ: Lawrence Erlbaum Associates.

Renn, O. (2008) *Risk Governance. Coping with Uncertainty in a Complex World*, Earthscan: London.

Renn, O. and Schweizer, P. (2009) 'Inclusive risk governance: concepts and application to environmental policy making', *Environmental Policy and Governance*, 19, 3: 174–85.

Renn, O. and Walker, K. (2008) 'Lessons learned: a re-assessment of the IRGC framework on risk governance', in O. Renn and K. Walker (eds) *The IRGC Risk Governance Framework: Concepts and Practice*, Heidelberg and New York: Springer, pp. 331–67.

Renn, O., Klinke, A. and van Asselt, M. (2011) 'Coping with complexity, uncertainty and ambiguity in risk governance: a synthesis', *AMBIO*, 40, 2: 231–46.

Rosa, E. (1997) 'Metatheoretical foundations for post-normal risk', *Journal of Risk Research*, 1, 1: 15–44.

Rouse, J. (2011) 'The chairman of the Joint Chiefs of Staff risk assessment system. Incorporation of the international risk governance council framework', Paper presented at the Annual Meeting of the Society for Risk Analysis in Salt Lake City, December 6, Washington, D.C.: Arete Associates.

Rowe, G. and Frewer, L.J. (2000) 'Public participation methods: a framework for evaluation', *Science, Technology and Human Values*, 25, 1: 3–29.

Stirling, A. (2003) 'Risk, uncertainty and precaution: some instrumental implications from the social sciences', in F. Berkhout, M. Leach and I. Scoones (eds) *Negotiating Change*, London: Edward Elgar, pp. 33–76.

Stoll-Kleemann, S. and Welp, M. (eds) (2006) *Stakeholder Dialogues in Natural Resources Management: Theory and Practice*, Heidelberg and Berlin: Springer.

Underdal, A. (2009) 'Complexity and challenges of long-term environmental governance', *Global Environmental Change*, 20: 386–93.

US Environmental Protection Agency (2009) *Potential Nano-Enabled Environmental Applications for Radionuclides*, Washington, D.C.: EPA.

van Asselt, M.B.A. (2000) *Perspectives on Uncertainty and Risk*, Dordrecht and Boston: Kluwer.

van Asselt, M.B.A. (2005) 'The complex significance of uncertainty in a risk area', *International Journal of Risk Assessment and Management*, 5, 2/3 and 4: 125–58.

WBGU (German Advisory Council on Global Change) (2000) *World in Transition: Strategies for Managing Global Environmental Risks*, Heidelberg and New York: Springer.

Wilkinson, C.F. and Lamb, J.C. (1999) 'The potential health effects of phthalate esters in children's toys. A review and risk assessment', *Regulatory Toxicology and Pharmacology*, 30, 2: 140–55.

Vos, E. and Wendler, F. (2009) 'Legal and institutional aspects of the general framework', in M. Dreyer and O. Renn (eds) *Food Safety Governance. Integrating Science, Precaution and Public Involvement*, Berlin: Springer, pp. 83–109.

Zahariadis, N. (2003) *Ambiguity and Choice in Public Policy. Political Decision Making in Modern Democracies*, Washington: Georgetown University Press.

Chapter 2

Adger, W.N., Lorenzoni, I. and O'Brien, K.L. (eds) (2009) *Adapting to Climate Change. Thresholds, Values, Governance*, Cambridge: Cambridge University Press.

Anderson, B. (2006 [1983]) *Imagined Communities. Reflections on the Origin and Spread of Nationalism* (rev. edn), London: Verso.

Appadurai, A. (2006 [1990]) 'Disjuncture and difference in the global cultural economy', in M.G. Durham and D.M. Kellner (eds) *Media and Cultural Studies. KeyWorks* (rev. edn), Malden, MA: Blackwell, pp. 584–603.

Aven, T. and Renn, O. (2009) 'On risk defined as an event where the outcome is uncertain', *Journal of Risk Research*, 12, 1: 1–11.

Beck, U. (1999) *World Risk Society*, Cambridge: Polity Press.

Bickerstaff, K. and Simmons, P. (2009) 'Absencing/presencing risk: rethinking proximity and the experience of living with major technological hazards', *Geoforum*, 40, 864–872.

Bloemertz, L., Doevenspeck, M., Macamo, E. and Müller-Mahn, D. (eds) (2012) *Risk and Africa. Multi-Disciplinary Empirical Approaches*. Beiträge zur Afrikaforschung 51, Berlin: LIT.

Boko, M., Niang, I., Nyong, A., Vogel, C., Githeko, A., Medany, M., Osman-Elasha, B., Tabo, R. and Yanda, P. (2007) *Africa. Climate Change 2007: Impacts, Adaptation and Vulnerability. Contribution of Working Group II to the Fourth Assessment Report of the Intergovernmental Panel on Climate Change*, M.L. Parry, O.F. Canziani, J.P. Palutikof, P.J. van der Linden and C.E. Hanson (eds), Cambridge University Press, Cambridge UK, pp. 433–67.

Conway, D. and Schipper, E.L.F. (2011) 'Adaptation to climate change in Africa: challenges and opportunities identified from Ethiopia', *Global Environmental Change*, 21, 1: 227–37.

Conway, G. (2009) *The Science of Climate Change in Africa: Impacts and Adaptation*. Grantham Institute for Climate Change. Discussion paper no.1.

FSNWG (Food Security & Nutrition Working Group) (2011) 'Emergency in the Horn of Africa. Famine declared in Somalia: Massive multisectoral response is critical', *Drought July 2011*. Available online at: http://www.disasterriskreduction.net/fileadmin/user_upload/drought/docs/FSNWG%20UpdateJuly2011%20110722Version13.pdf (accessed 12 July 2012).

IPCC (2007) 'Climate Change 2007: Synthesis Report', Valencia: IPCC.

Keen, D. (2008) *Complex Emergencies*, Cambridge: Polity Press.

Löfstedt, R. (2005) *Risk Management in Post Trust Societies*, Basingstoke: Palgrave/Macmillan.

Löfstedt, R. and Boholm, A. (eds) (2009): *The Earthscan Reader on Risk*, London: Earthscan.

Morello-Frosch, R., Pastor, M. and Sadd, J. (2001) 'Environmental justice and southern California's "riskscape": the distribution of air toxics exposures and health risks among diverse communities', *Urban Affairs Review*, 36, 551–78.

Müller-Mahn, D., Rettberg, S. and Getachew, G. (2010) 'Pathways and dead ends of pastoral development among the Afar and Karrayu in Ethiopia', *European Journal of Development Research*, 22: 660–77.

November, V. (2004) 'Being close to risk. From proximity to connexity', *International Journal of Sustainable Development*, 7, 3: 273–86.

November, V. (2008) 'Spatiality of risk', *Environment and Planning A*, 40: 1523–27.

November V., Penelas, M. and Viot, P. (2009) 'When flood risk transforms a territory: the Lully effect', *Geography* 94/3: 189–97.

November, V., Camacho-Hübner, E. and Latour, B. (2010) 'Entering a risky territory: space in the age of digital navigation', *Environment and Planning D: Society and Space*, 28: 581–99.

Renn, O. (2008) *Risk Governance. Coping with Uncertainty in a Complex World*, London: Earthscan.

Rettberg, S. (2009) *Das Risiko der Afar. Existenzsicherung äthiopischer Nomaden im Kontext von Hungerkrisen, Konflikten und Entwicklungsinterventionen*. Studien zur Geographischen Entwicklungsforschung, 35, Saarbrücken.

Rettberg, S. and Müller-Mahn, D. (2012) 'Human-environment interactions: the invasion of *Prosopis juliflora* in the drylands of Northeast Ethiopia', in L. Mol and T. Sternberg (eds) *Changing Deserts*, Cambridge: Whitehorse Press, pp. 297–316.

Schatzki, T. (1996) *Social Practices: A Wittgensteinian Approach to Human Activity and the Social*, New York: Cambridge University Press.

Schatzki, T. (2002) *The Site of the Social: A Philosophical Account of the Constitution of Social Life and Change*, University Park: Pennsylvania State University Press.

Schatzki, T. (2009) 'Timespace and the organization of social life', in E. Shove, F. Trentmann and R. Wilk (eds) *Time, Consumption and Everyday Life. Practice, Materiality and Culture*, Oxford: Berg, pp. 35–48.

Schatzki, T. (2010) *The Timespace of Human Activity: On Performance, Society, and History as Indeterminate Teleological Events*, Lanham: Lexington Books.

Schillmeier, M. (2011) 'Unbuttoning normalcy – on cosmopolitical events', *The Sociological Review*, 59, 3: 514–34.

Slovic, P. (2000) *The Perception of Risk*. London: Earthscan.

Slovic, P. (ed.) (2010): *The Feeling of Risk. New Perspectives on Risk Perception*. London: Earthscan.

Soneryd, L. (2004) 'Hearing as a way of dwelling: the active sense making of environmental risk and nuisance', *Environment and Planning D: Society and Space*, 22, 737–53.

Stirling, A. (2007) 'Risk, precaution and science: towards a more constructive policy debate. Talking point on the precautionary principle', *EMBO Reports* 8, 4: 309–15.

Sutherland, C., Scott, D., Brooks, S. and Guy, H. (2012) 'Lay knowledge of risk: exploring the "riskscapes" of South Durban communities', in L. Bloemertz, M. Doevenspeck, E. Macamo and D. Müller-Mahn (eds) *Risk and Africa. Multi-Disciplinary Empirical Approaches,* Wien: Lit Verlag, pp. 47–86.

UNICEF (undated): *Humanitarian Aid and Emergency Relief: Food Crisis in Sahel.* Available online at: http://www.unicefusa.org/work/emergencies/ (accessed 18 July 2012).

Wisner, B., Blaikie, P., Cannon, T. and Davis, I. (2004) *At Risk: Natural Hazards, People's Vulnerability and Disasters* (2nd edn), London: Routledge.

Zinn, J.O. (ed.) (2008) *Social Theories of Risk and Uncertainty. An Introduction.* Oxford: Blackwell.

Chapter 3

Agamben, G. (2008) *Was ist ein Dispositiv?*, Berlin: Diaphanes.

Ashlin, A. and Ladle, R.J. (2007) 'Natural disasters and newspapers: post-tsunami environmental discourse', *Environmental Hazards*, 7, 4: 330–41.

Bartels, D. (1974) 'Schwierigkeiten mit dem Raumbegriff in der Geographie', *Geographica Helvetica*, 2/3: 7–21.

Bauriedl, S. (2007) 'Räume lesen lernen: Methoden zur Raumanalyse in der Diskursforschung', *Forum Qualitative Research*, 8, 2: 1–86.

Bauriedl, S. (2009) 'Impulse der geographischen Raumtheorie für eine raum- und maßstabskritische Diskursforschung', in G. Glasze and A. Mattissek (eds) *Handbuch Diskurs und Raum*, Bielefeld: Transcript-Verlag, pp. 219–31.

Beck, U. (1986) *Risikogesellschaft: Auf dem Weg in eine andere Moderne*, Frankfurt a.M.: Suhrkamp.

Bickerstaff, K., Lorenzoni, L., Pidgeon, N.F., Poortinga, W. and Simmons, P. (2008) 'Reframing nuclear power in the UK energy debate: nuclear power, climate change mitigation and radioactive waste', *Public Understanding of Science*, 17, 2: 145–69.

Blotevogel, H.H. (2005) 'Raum', in Academy for Spatial Research and Planning – ARL, *Handwörterbuch der Raumordnung*, Hannover: Academy for Spatial Research and Planning, pp. 831–41.

Bourdieu, P. (1984) *Distinction: A Social Critique of the Judgement of Taste*, Cambridge: Harvard University Press.

Boykoff, M.T. (2008) 'The cultural politics of climate change discourse in UK tabloids', *Political Geography*, 27, 5: 549–69.

Boykoff, M.T., Frame, D. and Randalls, S. (2010) 'Discursive stability meets climate instability: a critical exploration of the concept of "climate stabilization" in contemporary climate policy', *Global Environmental Change*, 20, 1: 53–64.

Caborn, J. (2007) 'On the methodology of dispositive analysis', *Critical Approaches to Discourse Analysis Across Disciplines*, 1, 1: 115–23.

Collins, T.W. (2009) 'The production of unequal risk in hazardscapes: an explanatory frame applied to disaster at the US-Mexico border', *Geoforum*, 40, 4: 589–601.

Curry, M. (1996) 'On space and spatial practice in contemporary geography', in C. Earle, K. Mathewson and M.S. Kenzer (eds) *Concepts in Human Geography*, Lanham: Rowman & Littlefield Publishers, pp. 3–32.

Davidson, D.J. (2003) 'Risk in the redwoods: contending for normalcy in timber country', *Journal of Risk Research*, 6, 3: 253–66.

Diaz-Bone, R. (1999) 'Probleme und Strategien der Operationalisierung des Diskursmodells im Anschluss an Michel Foucault', in H. Bublitz, A.D. Bührmann, C. Hanke, A. Seier and R. Diaz-Bone (eds) *Das Wuchern der Diskurse – Perspektiven der Diskursanalyse Foucaults*, Frankfurt a.M.: Campus-Verlag: 119–35.

Egner, H. (2006) 'Autopoiesis, Form und Beobachtung – moderne Systemtheorie und ihr möglicher Beitrag für eine Integration von Human- und Physiogeographie', *Mitteilungen der Österreichischen Geographischen Gesellschaft*, 148: 92–108.

Fassmann, H. (2004) *Stadtgeographie I: Allgemeine Stadtgeographie*, Braunschweig: Westermann.

Feindt, P. and Oels, A. (2005) 'Does discourse matter? Discourse analysis in environmental policy making', *Journal of Environmental Policy and Planning*, 7, 3: 161–73.

Flyvbjerg, B. (1996) 'The dark side of planning: rationality and realrationalität', in S.J. Mandelbaum, L. Mazza, R.W. Burchell and B. Flyvbjerg (eds) *Explorations in Planning Theory*, New Brunswick: Center for Urban Policy Research, pp. 383–94.

Flyvbjerg, B. and Richardson, T. (2002) 'Planning and Foucault – in search of the dark side of planning theory', in P. Allmendinger and M. Tewdwr-Jones (eds) *Planning Futures: New Directions for Planning Theory*, London: Routledge, pp. 44–62.

Foucault, M. (1972) *The Archeology of Knowledge*, New York: Pantheon.

Foucault, M. (1978) *Dispositive der Macht*, Berlin: Merve.

Glaser, B.G. (1992) *Basics of Grounded Theory Analysis*, Mill Valley: Sociology Press.

Glasze, G. (2005) *Diskurs – Stadt – Kriminalität – Städtische (Un-)Sicherheiten aus der Perspektive von Stadtforschung und kritischer Kriminalgeographie*, Bielefeld: Transcript-Publishing.

Glasze, G. (2009) 'Der Raumbegriff bei Laclau – auf dem Weg zu einem politischen Konzept von Räumen', in G. Glasze and A. Mattissek (eds) *Handbuch Diskurs und Raum*, Bielefeld: Transcript-Publishing, pp. 213–18.

Glasze, G. and Mattissek, A. (2009) 'Diskursforschung in der Humangeographie: Konzeptionelle Grundlagen und empirische Operationalisierungen', in G. Glasze and A. Mattissek (eds) *Handbuch Diskurs und Raum*, Bielefeld: Transcript-Publishing, pp. 11–59.

Hajer, M. (1993) 'Discourse coalitions and the institutionalization of practice: the case of acid rain in Britain', in F. Fischer and J. Forester (eds) *The Argumentative Turn in Policy Analysis and Planning*, Durham: Duke University Press, pp. 43–76.

Hajer, M. and Versteeg, W. (2005) 'A decade of discourse analysis of environmental politics: achievements, challenges, perspectives', *Journal of Environmental Policy and Planning*, 7, 3: 175–84.

Höferl, K.-M. (2010) 'From the avoidance of hazards towards a risk culture – discourses on the governance of flood prevention within Austrian spatial planning'. PhD thesis. Vienna: University of Natural Resources and Life Sciences.

Holzheu, F. (1987) 'Die Bewältigung von Unsicherheit als ökonomisches Grundproblem' in Bayerische Rück (eds) *Gesellschaft und Unsicherheit*, Karlsruhe: Versicherungs-wirtschaft e.V., pp. 11–36.

Huffschmid, A. and Wildner, K. (2009) 'Talking spaces, locating discourses? Thoughts about a transdisciplinary ethnography', *Forum Qualitative Research*, 10, 3: 1–67.

IRGC (2005) *Risk Governance – Towards an Integrative Approach*, Geneva: International Risk Governance Council.

Jäger, S. (2006) 'Diskurs und Wissen – Theoretische und methodische Aspekte einer Kritischen Diskurs- und Dispositivanalyse', in R. Keller, A. Hirseland, W. Schneider, W. Viehöver and S. Jäger (eds) *Handbuch Sozialwissenschaftliche Diskursanalyse – Band 1: Theorien und Methoden*, Wiesbaden: VS Verlag für Sozialwissenschaften, pp. 83–113.

Jokisch, R. (1996) *Logik der Distinktion – Zur Protologik einer Theorie der Gesellschaft*, Opladen: Westdeutscher Verlag.

Jokisch, R. (1999) 'Technik und Kunst: Distinktionstheoretische Beobachtungen', in S. Weber (ed.) *Was konstruiert Kunst? Kunst an der Schnittstelle von Konstruktivismus, Systemtheorie und Distinktionstheorie*, Vienna: Passagen, pp. 47–118.

Kanonier, A. (2005) 'Naturgefahren im österreichischen Raumordnungsrecht', in Austrian Conference on Spatial Planning (ed.) *Präventiver Umgang mit Naturgefahren in der Raumordnung*, Reports of the Austrian Conference on Spatial Planning, 168: 81–114.

Keller, R. (1998) *Müll – die gesellschaftliche Konstruktion des Wertvollen*, Opladen: Westdeutscher Verlag.

Kewell, B. and Beck, M. (2008) 'The shifting sands of uncertainty: risk construction and BSE/vCJD', *Health, Risk & Society*, 10, 2: 133–48.

Klinke, A. and Renn, O. (2006) 'Systemic risks as challenge for policy making in risk governance', *Forum: Qualitative Social Research*, 7, 1: Art 33.

Kyrer, A. (2005) *Wirtschaft von A-Z. Das IV-Industrielexikon*, 2nd edn, Wien: Industriellenvereinigung.

Lange, H. and Garrelts, H. (2007) 'Risk management at the science–policy interface: two contrasting cases in the field of flood protection in Germany', *Journal of Environmental Policy and Planning*, 9, 3: 263–79.

Lange, H., Haarmann M., Wiesner-Steiner, A. and Voosen, E. (2005) *Projektbericht Klimawandel und präventives Risiko- und Küstenschutzmanagement an der deutschen Nordseeküste (KRIM) – Teilprojekt IV – Politisch-administrative Steuerungsprozesse (PAS)*. Available online at: http://www.krim.uni-bremen.de/endberichte/endbericht_tp4.pdf (accessed 18 May 2009).

Latour, B. (2005) *Reassembling the Social: An Introduction to Actor-Network Theory*, New York: Oxford University Press.

Lichtenberger, E. (1998) *Stadtgeographie: Begriffe, Konzepte, Modelle, Prozesse*, Stuttgart: Teubner.

Luhmann, N. (1990) 'Risiko und Gefahr', in N. Luhmann (ed.) *Soziologische Aufklärung 5: Konstruktivistische Perspektiven*, Opladen: Westdeutscher Verlag, pp. 131–69.

Luhmann, N. (1991) *Soziologie des Risikos*, Berlin: De Gruyter.

Luhmann, N. (1995) *Social Systems*, Stanford: Stanford University Press.

Luhmann, N. (1997) 'Die Moral des Risikos und das Risiko der Moral', in G. Bechmann (ed.) *Risiko und Gesellschaft*, Opladen: Westdeutscher Verlag, pp. 327–38.

Massey, D. (1985) 'New directions in space', in D. Gregory and J. Urry (eds) *Social Relations and Spatial Structures*, New York: St. Martin's Press, pp. 9–19.

Massey, D. (1991) 'A global sense of place', *Marxism Today*, 35, 6: 24–29.

Massey, D. (1999) 'Philosophy and politics of spatiality: some considerations. The Hettner-Lecture in Human Geography', *Geographische Zeitschrift*, 87, 1: 1–12.

Miggelbrink, J. (2002) *Der gezähmte Blick. Zum Wandel des Diskurses über 'Raum' und 'Region' in humangeographischen Forschungsansätzen des ausgehenden 20. Jahrhunderts*, Beiträge zur Regionalen Geographie no. 55, Leipzig: Institut für Länderkunde.

Popper, K. (1973) *Objektive Erkenntnis. Ein evolutionärer Entwurf*, Hamburg: Hoffmann und Campe.

Reichert, D. (1996) 'Räumliches Denken als Ordnen der Dinge', in D. Reichert (ed.) *Räumliches Denken*, Zürich: Verlag der Fachvereine, pp. 15–45.

Renn, O. (2008a) *Risk Governance – Coping with Uncertainty in a Complex World*, London: Earthscan.

Renn, O. (2008b) 'Concepts of risk: an interdisciplinary review – part 1: disciplinary risk concepts', *GAIA*, 17, 1: 50–66.

Schreiber, V. (2009) 'Raumangebote bei Foucault', in G. Glasze and A. Mattissek (eds) *Handbuch Diskurs und Raum*, Bielefeld: Transcript-Publishing, pp. 199–212.

Sharp, L. and Richardson, T. (2001) 'Reflections on Foucauldian discourse analysis in planning and environmental policy research', *Journal of Environmental Policy and Planning*, 3, 3: 193–209.

Spencer-Brown, G. (1969) *Laws of Form*, London: Allen & Unwin.

Stehr, N. and von Storch, H. (2000) 'Von der Macht des Klimas: Ist der Klimadeterminismus nur noch Ideengeschichte oder relevanter Faktor gegenwartiger Klimapolitik?', *GAIA*, 9, 3: 187–95.

Strauss, A.L. and Corbin, J.M. (1998) *Basics of Qualitative Research: Techniques and Procedures for Developing Grounded Theory*, London: Sage Publications.

Sturm, G. (2000) *Wege zum Raum. Methodologische Annäherungen an ein Basiskonzept raumbezogener Wissenschaften*, Opladen: Leske und Budrich.

Swartout, W. and Neches, R. (1986) 'The shifting terminological space: an impediment to evolvability', in American Association for Artificial Intelligence (ed.) *Proceedings of the Fifth National Conference on Artificial Intelligence*, Philadelphia: Morgan Kaufmann Publishers, pp. 936–41.

Taleb, N.N. (2007) *The Black Swan: The Impact of the Highly Improbable*, London: Penguin.

Thywissen, K. (2006) *Components of Risk – A Comparative Glossary*. Available online at: http://www.ehs.unu.edu/file.php?id=118 (accessed 25 April 2008).

Weichhart, P. (1999) 'Die Räume zwischen den Welten und die Welt der Räume. Zur Konzeption eines Schlüsselbegriffs der Geographie', in P. Meusburger (ed.) *Handlungszentrierte Sozialgeographie: Benno Werlens Entwurf in kritischer Diskussion*, Stuttgart: Steiner, pp. 67–94.

Weichhart, P. (2007) 'Risiko – Vorschläge zum Umgang mit einem schillernden Begriff', *Berichte zur Deutschen Landeskunde*, 81, 3: 201–14.

Weichhart, P. (2008) *Entwicklungslinien der Sozialgeographie. Von Hans Bobek bis Benno Werlen*, Stuttgart: Steiner.

Werlen, B. (1997) *Sozialgeographie alltäglicher Regionalisierungen. Band 2: Globalisierung, Region und Regionalisierung*, Stuttgart: Steiner.

Zierhofer, W. (1999) 'Die fatale Verwechslung. Zum Selbstverständnis der Geographie', in P. Meusburger (ed.) *Handlungszentrierte Sozialgeographie: Benno Werlens Entwurf in kritischer Diskussion*, Stuttgart: Steiner, pp. 163–86.

Chapter 4

Baecker, D. (2005) 'A note on space', *German Law Journal*, 6: 65–69.

Bahrenberg, G. and Kuhm, K. (1998) 'Weltgesellschaft und Region – eine systemtheoretische Perspektive', *Geographische Zeitschrift*, 87, 4: 193–209.

Bartels, D. (1974) 'Schwierigkeiten mit dem Raumbegriff in der Geographie', *Geographica Helvetica*, 29, 2/3: 7–21.

Carvalho, A. and Burgess, J. (2005) 'Cultural circuits of climate change in UK broadsheet newspapers, 1985–2003', *Risk Analysis*, 25, 6: 1457–69

Derrida, J. (1990) *Chora*, Vienna: Passagen.

DKKV (ed) (2003) 'Hochwasservorsorge in Deutschland. Lernen aus der Katastrophe 2002 im Elbegebiet', (=Schriftenreihe des DKKV no. 29), Bonn: Deutsches Kommitee für Katastrophenvorsorge.

Dikau, R. and Weichselgartner, J. (2005) *Der unruhige Planet. Der Mensch und die Naturgewalten*, Darmstadt: Primus Verlag.

Egner, H. (2008) 'Warum konnte das nicht verhindert werden? Über den (Nicht-) Zusammenhang von wissenschaftlicher Erkenntnis und politischen Entscheidungen', in T. Glade and C. Felgentreff (eds) *Naturkatastrophen und Soziale Katastrophen*, Heidelberg: Spektrum Akademischer Verlag, pp. 423–33.

Fichter, H. and Moss, M. (2004) 'Regionaler Institutionenwandel durch die EU-Wasserrahmenrichtlinie' in I. Dombrowsky, H. Wittmer and F. Rauschmayer (eds) *Institutionen in Naturschutz und Ressourcenmanagement – Beiträge der Neuen Institutionenökonomik*, Leipzig: Umweltforschungszentrum Leipzig-Halle GmbH, pp. 72–86.

Gedan, P. (ed.) (1905) *Immanuel Kant, Physische Geographie*, 2nd edn, Leipzig: Dürr.

Hard, G. (1986) 'Der Raum – einmal systemtheoretisch gesehen', *Geographica Helvetica*, 41, 2: 77–83.

Hard, G. (2003) 'Eine Raum-Klärung für aufgeweckte Studenten', in G. Hard (ed.) *Dimensionen geographischen Denkens. Aufsätze zur Theorie der Geographie, Band 2*, Osnabrück: Universitätsverlag Osnabrück, pp. 15–28.

Hubig, C. (1994) 'Das Risiko des Risikos. Das Nicht-Gewußte und das Nicht-Wißbare', *Universitas*, 49, 4: 310–18.

Japp, K.P. (1996) *Soziologische Risikotheorie. Funktionale Differenzierung, Politisierung und Reflexion*, Weinheim and München: Juventa.

Japp, K.P. and Kusche, I. (2008) 'Systems theory and risk', in O.J. Zinn (ed.) *Social Theories of Risk and Uncertainty. An Introduction*, Malden, MA: Blackwell Publishing, pp. 76–105.

Kieserling, A. (1999) *Kommunikation unter Anwesenden: Studien über Interaktionssysteme*, Frankfurt a.M.: Suhrkamp.

Klüter, H. (1986) *Raum als Element sozialer Kommunikation*, (=Gießener Geographische Schriften no. 60), Gießen: Geographisches Institut.

Klüter, H. (1994) 'Sozialgeographie. Raum als Objekt menschlicher Wahrnehmung und Raum als Element sozialer Kommunikation. Vergleich zweier humangeographischer Ansätze', *Mitteilungen der Österreichischen Geographischen Gesellschaft*, 136: 143–78.

Kuhm, K. (2000) 'Raum als Medium gesellschaftlicher Kommunikation', *Soziale Systeme*, 6, 2: 321–48.

Lefebvre, H. (1991) *The Production of Space*, trans. D. Nicholson-Smith, Malden, MA: Blackwell Publishing.

Lippuner, R. (2007) 'Kopplung, Steuerung, Differenzierung. Zur Geographie sozialer Systeme', *Erdkunde*, 61, 2: 174–85.

Lippuner, R. and Lossau, J. (2004) 'Geographie und Spatial Turn', *Erdkunde*, 58, 3: 201–11.

Luhmann, N. (1975) 'Einfache Sozialsysteme', in N. Luhmann (ed.) *Soziologische Aufklärung 2. Aufsätze zur Theorie der Gesellschaft*, Wiesbaden: VS Verlag für Sozialwissenschaften, pp. 25–47.

Luhmann, N. (1984) *Soziale Systeme. Grundriß einer allgemeinen Theorie*, Frankfurt a.M.: Suhrkamp.

Luhmann, N. (1990) *Political Theory in the Welfare State*, Berlin: de Gruyter.

Luhmann, N. (1993) *Risk: A Sociological Theory*, trans. R. Barrett, Berlin and New York: de Gruyter.

Luhmann, N. (1995) *Social Systems*, trans. J. Bednarz, Jr., Stanford: Stanford University Press.

Luhmann, N. (1996) *Die Realität der Massenmedien*, Opladen: Westdeutscher Verlag.

Luhmann, N. (1997a) *Die Gesellschaft der Gesellschaft*, Frankfurt a.M.: Suhrkamp.

Luhmann, N. (1997b) 'Grenzwerte der ökologischen Politik. Eine Form von Risikomanagement', in P. Hiller and G. Krücken (eds) *Risiko und Regulierung: soziologische Beiträge zu Technikkontrolle und präventiver Umweltpolitik*, Frankfurt a.M.: Suhrkamp, pp. 195–221.

Luhmann, N. (2000) *The Reality of the Mass Media*, Stanford: Standford University Press.

Luhmann, N. (2006) *Organisation und Entscheidung*, Wiesbaden: VS Verlag für Sozialwissenschaften.

Moss, T. (2004) 'The governance of land use in river basins: prospects for overcoming problems of institutional interplay with the EU Water Framework Directive', *Land Use Policy*, 21, 1: 85–94.

Olausson, U. (2009) 'Global warming–global responsibility? Media frames of collective action and scientific certainty', *Public Understanding of Science*, 18: 421–36.

Pohl, J. (1993a) *Regionalbewußtsein als Thema der Sozialgeographie. Theoretische Überlegungen und empirische Untersuchungen am Beispiel Friaul*, Kallmünz: Laßleben.

Pohl, J. (1993b) 'Kann es seine Geographie ohne Raum geben? Zum Verhältnis von Theoriediskussion und Disziplinpolitik', *Erdkunde*, 47, 4: 255–66.

Pott, A. (2007) 'Sprachliche Kommunikation durch Raum – das Angebot der Systemtheorie', *Geographische Zeitschrift*, 95, 1/2: 56–71.

Rhomberg, M. (2009) *Politische Kommunikation: Eine Einführung für Politikwissenschaftler*, Paderborn: UTB.

Seidl, D. (2005) 'The basic concepts of Luhmann's theory of social systems', in D. Seidl and K.H. Becker (eds) *Niklas Luhmann and Organization Studies*, Copenhagen: Copenhagen Business School Press, pp. 21–53.

Shen, X. (2009) *Flood Risk Perception and Communication within Risk Management in Different Cultural Contexts. A Comparative Case Study between Wuhan, China and Cologne, Germany*, Bonn: UNU-EHS.

Soja, E.W. (1989) *Postmodern Geographies: The Reassertion of Space in Critical Social Theory*, London: Verso.

Stichweh, R. (1998) 'Raum, Region und Stadt in der Systemtheorie', *Soziale Systeme*, 4, 2: 341–58.

Stichweh, R. (2001) 'Der Raum der Weltgesellschaft. Klassische Kriege, neue Konflikte: Das globale System der Nationalstaaten und die Frage der Gewalt', *Frankfurter Rundschau*, 2/3 October 2001: 18.

Stichweh, R. (2003) 'Raum und moderne Gesellschaft. Aspekte der sozialen Kontrolle des Raums', in T. Krämer-Badoni and K. Kuhm (eds) *Die Gesellschaft und ihr Raum. Raum als Gegenstand der Soziologie*, Opladen: Leske & Budrich, pp. 93–102.

Stichweh, R. (2008) 'Kontrolle und Organisation des Raums in Funktionssystemen der Weltgesellschaft', in J. Döring, and T. Thielmann (eds) *Spatial Turn. Das*

Raumparadigma in den Kultur- und Sozialwissenschaften, Bielefeld: Transcript, pp. 149–64.

Thrift, N. (2004) 'Movement-space. The changing domain of thinking resulting from the development of new kinds of spatial awareness', *Economy and Society*, 33, 4: 582–604.

Wardenga, U. (2002) 'Alte und neue Raumkonzepte für den Geographieunterricht', *Geographie Heute*, 23, 200: 8–11.

Young, O. (1999) *The Institutional Dimensions of Global Environmental Change. Science Plan*, Bonn: IHDP.

Young, O. (2002) *The Institutional Dimensions of Environmental Change. Fit, Interplay and Scale*, Cambridge, MA: MIT Press.

Chapter 5

Appadurai, A. (1996) *Modernity at Large: Cultural Dimensions of Globalization*, Minneapolis, MN: University of Minnesota Press.

Beck, U. (1986) *Risikogesellschaft*, Frankfurt a.M.: Suhrkamp.

Beck, U. (2007) *Weltrisikogesellschaft*, Frankfurt a.M.: Suhrkamp.

Bonss, W. (1995) *Vom Risiko: Unsicherheit und Ungewissheit in der Moderne*, Hamburg: Hamburger Edition.

Gaasbeek, T. (2010) *Bridging Troubled Water? Everyday Inter-ethnic Interaction in a Context of Violent Conflict in Kottiyar Pattu, Trincomalee, Sri Lanka*, PhD dissertation, Wageningen University.

Goodhand, J., Lewer, N. and Hulme, D. (2000) 'Religion, conflict and boundary politics in Sri Lanka', *Disasters*, 24, 4: 390–406.

Goodhand, J., Klem, B. and Korf, B. (2009) 'Religion, conflict and boundary politics in Sri Lanka', *European Journal of Development Research*, 21: 679–98.

Hoffman, D. and Lubkemann, S. (2005) 'Warscape ethnography in West Africa and the anthropology of "events"', *Anthropological Quarterly*, 78, 2: 315–27.

Hyndman, J. and de Alwis, M. (2004) 'Bodies, shrines, and roads: violence, (im)mobility, and displacement in Sri Lanka', *Gender, Place and Culture*, 11, 4: 535–57.

Jaeger, C.C., Renn, O., Rosa, E.A. and Webler, T. (2001) *Risk, Uncertainty and Rational Action*, London: Earthscan.

Knight, F. (1921) *Risk, Uncertainty and Profit*, Boston, MA: Hart, Schaffner & Marx.

Korf, B. (2004) 'War, livelihoods and vulnerability in Sri Lanka', *Development and Change*, 35, 2: 275–95.

Korf, B. and Fünfgeld, H. (2006) 'War and the commons: assessing the changing politics of violence, access and entitlements in Sri Lanka', *Geoforum*, 37, 3: 391–403.

Korf, B., Engeler, M. and Hagmann, T. (2010) 'The geography of warscape', *Third World Quarterly*, 31, 3: 385–99.

Lash, S. (2000) 'Risk culture', in B. Adam, U. Beck and J. van Loon (eds) *The Risk Society and Beyond. Critical Issues for Social Theory*, London: Sage, pp. 47–72.

Lubkemann, S. (2008) *Culture in Chaos. An Anthropology of the Social Condition in War*, Chicago and London: University of Chicago Press.

Mehta, L., Leach, M. and Scoones, I. (2001) 'Editorial: environmental governance in an uncertain world', *IDS Bulletin*, 32, 4: 1–9.

Nordstrom, C. (1997) *A Different Kind of War Story*, Philadelphia: University of Pennsylvania Press.

O'Malley, P. (2004) *Risk, Uncertainty and Government*, London: Glashouse Press.

Oslender, U. (2007) 'Geographies of terror and spaces of confinement: re-conceptualizing forced displacement with an anti-geopolitical eye on Colombia's Pacific coast region', paper presented at the AAG Annual Meeting, San Francisco, April 2007.

Renn, O. (2008) 'Concepts of risk: an interdisciplinary review. Part 1: Disciplinary risk concepts', *GAIA*, 17, 1: 50–66.

Spencer, J. (2003) 'A nation "living in different places": notes on the impossible work of purification in postcolonial Sri Lanka', *Contributions to Indian Sociology*, 37, 1/2: 25–47.

Thangarajah, Y. (2003) 'Ethnicization of the devolution debate and the militarization of civil society in North-Eastern Sri Lanka', in M. Mayer, D. Rajasingham-Senanayake and Y. Thangarajah (eds) *Building Local Capacities for Peace: Rethinking Conflict and Development in Sri Lanka*, Delhi: Macmillan, pp. 15–36.

Tuan, Y. (1978) *Landscapes of Fear*, Minneapolis: University of Minnesota Press.

Tulloch, J. and Lupton, D. (2003) *Risk and Everyday Life*, London: Sage.

Vigh, H. (2006) *Navigating Terrains of War: Youth and Soldiering in Guinea-Bissau*, Oxford and New York: Berghahn Books.

Vigh, H. (2009) 'Motion squared: A second look at the concept of social navigation', *Anthropological Theory*, 9, 4: 419–38.

Walker, R. (2010) 'Violence, the everyday and the question of the ordinary', *Contemporary South Asia*, 18, 1: 9–24.

Walker, R. (2012, forthcoming) *Enduring Violence and the Question of the Ordinary in Contemporary Sri Lanka*. Manchester: Manchester University Press.

Zehetmair, S. (2012) *Zur Kommunikation von Riskien: Eine Studie über soziale Systeme in Hochwasserriskio-management*, Wiesbaden: Springer VS Verlag.

Zinn, J.O. (2006) 'Recent developments in sociology of risk and uncertainty', *Forum Qualitative Sozialforschung / Forum: Qualitative Social Research*, 7, 1: Art. 30. Available online at: http://nbn-resolving.de/urn:nbn:de:0114-fqs0601301.

Chapter 6

Ali, H. (2010) 'Globalized complexity and the microbial traffic of new and emerging infectious disease threats', in T. Giles-Vernick and S. Craddock (eds) *Influenza and Public Health*, London: Earthscan, pp. 22–37.

Anderson, B. (2010) 'Security and the future: anticipating the event of terror', *Geoforum*, 41, 2: 227–35

Barbalet, J. (1998) *Emotion, Social Theory, and Social Structure: A Macrosociological Approach*, Cambridge: Cambridge University Press.

Beck, U. (1992) *Risk Society: Towards a New Modernity*, London: Sage Publications.

Beck, U. (1997) 'Global risk politics', *The Political Quarterly*, 68, B: 18–33.

Beck, U. (2008) *Weltrisikogesellschaft. Auf der Suche nach der verlorenen Sicherheit*, Frankfurt a.M.: Suhrkamp.

Bernstein, P. (1998) *Against The Gods: The Remarkable Story of Risk*, New York: Wiley.

Bickerstaff, K. and Simmons, P. (2009) 'Absencing/presencing risk: rethinking proximity and the experience of living with major technological hazards', *Geoforum*, 40: 864–72.

Burt, B.A. (2001) 'Definitions of risk', *Journal of Dental Education*, 65, 10: 1007–08.

Cabinet Office (Department of Health) (2007) *Pandemic Flu. A National Framework for Responding to an Influenza Pandemic*, London: Department of Health.

Collier, S. and Lakoff, A. (2008) 'Distributed preparedness: the spatial logic of domestic security in the United States', *Environment and Planning D: Society and Space*, 26, 1: 7–28.

Davidson, J. and Smith, M. (2003) 'Bio-phobias/techno-philias: virtual reality exposure as treatment for phobias of "nature"', *Sociology of Health & Illness*, 25, 6: 644–61.

Davis, M. (2006) *The Monster at our Door: The Global Threat of Avian Flu*, New York: Henry Holt.

Douglas, M. and Wildavsky, A. (1983) *Risk and Culture: An Essay on the Selection of Technological and Environmental Dangers*, Berkeley: University of California Press.

Fielding, R., Lam, W., Ho, E., Lam, T.H., Hedley, A. and Leung, G. (2005) 'Avian influenza risk perception, Hong Kong', *Emerging Infectious Disease*, 11, 5: 677–82.

Giddens, A. (1991) *Modernity and Self-Identity. Self and Society in the Late Modern Age*, Cambridge: Polity.

Heidegger, M. (2008 [1927]) *Being and Time*. (Translated by John Macquarrie & Edward Robinson, 1962). Malden (MA): Blackwell.

Hinchliffe, S. and Bingham, N. (2008) 'Securing life: the emerging practices of biosecurity', *Environment and Planning A*, 40, 7: 1534–51.

Hunt, A. (1999) 'Anxiety and social explanation: some anxieties about anxiety', *Journal of Social History*, 32, 3: 509–28.

Ingram, A. (2008a) 'Domopolitics and disease: HIV/AIDS, immigration, and asylum in the UK', *Environment and Planning D: Society and Space*, 26, 5: 875–94.

Ingram, A. (2008b) 'Pandemic anxiety and global health security', in R. Pain and S. Smith (eds) *Fear: Critical Geopolitics and Everyday Life*, Aldershot, Ashgate, pp. 75–86.

Jackson, P. and Everts, J. (2010) 'Anxiety as social practice', *Environment and Planning A*, 42, 11: 2791–806.

James, W. (1983 [1884]) 'What is an emotion?' in W. James (eds) *Essays in Psychology*, Cambridge MA, Harvard University Press, pp. 168–87.

Keil, R. and Ali, H. (2006) 'Multiculturalism, racism and infectious disease in the global city: the experience of the 2003 SARS outbreak in Toronto', *Topia (Canadian Journal of Cultural Studies)*, 16: 23–49.

Latour, B. (1993) *We Have Never Been Modern*, Hemel Hempstead: Harvester Wheatsheaf.

Lawson, V. (2007) 'Introduction: geographies of fear and hope', *Annals of the Association of American Geographers*, 97, 2: 335–37.

Nerlich, B., Brown, B. and Crawford, P. (2009) 'Health, hygiene and biosecurity: tribal knowledge claims in the UK poultry industry', *Health, Risk & Society*, 11, 6: 561–77.

November, V. (2008) 'Commentary. Spatiality of risk', *Environment and Planning A*, 40, 7: 1523–27.

Pain, R. and Smith, S. (2008) 'Fear: critical geopolitics and everyday life', in R. Pain and S. Smith (eds) *Fear: Critical Geopolitics and Everyday Life*, Aldershot: Ashgate, pp. 1–19.

Pelling, M. and Dill, K. (2009) 'Disaster politics: tipping points for change in the adaptation of sociopolitical regimes', *Progress in Human Geography*, 34, 1: 21–37.

Reddy, W. (1997) 'Against constructionism. The historical ethnography of emotions', *Current Anthropology*, 38, 3: 327–51.

Renn, O. (2008) 'Concepts of risk: an interdisciplinary review', *GAIA*, 17, 1: 50–66.

Sparke, M. (2009) 'From global flu to global health'. Available online at: http://globalhealthspace.blogspot.de/2009/05/from-global-flu-to-global-health.html (accessed 6 May 2009).

STIKO (Ständige Impfkommission) (2009) 'Mitteilung der Ständigen Impfkommission (STIKO) am Robert Koch-Institut: Impfung gegen die Neue Influenza A (H1N1)', *Epidemiologisches Bulletin*, 41, 12: 403–26.

Svendsen, L. (2008) *A Philosophy of Fear*, London: Reaktion Books.

Taubenberger, J.K., Reid, A., Lourens, R., Wang, R., Jin, G. and Fanning, T. (2005) 'Characterization of the 1918 influenza virus polymerase genes', *Nature*, 437, 6: 889–93.

Taylor, C. (1971) 'Interpretation and the sciences of man', *The Review of Metaphysics*, 25, 1: 3–51.

Tyrer, P. (1999) *Anxiety: A Multidisciplinary Review*, London: Imperial College Press.

Ungar, S. (2008) 'Global bird flu communication. Hot crisis and media reassurance', *Science Communication*, 29, 4: 472–97.

Van Loon, J. (2002) *Risk and Technological Culture: Towards a Sociology of Virulence*, London: Routledge.

Wald, P. (2000) 'Future perfect: grammar, genes, and geography', *New Literary History*, 31: 681–708.

Wald, P. (2008) *Contagious. Cultures, Carriers, and the Outbreak Narrative*, Durham: Duke University Press.

Wallace, R.G. (2009) 'Breeding influenza: the political virology of offshore farming', *Antipode*, 41, 5: 916–51.

Wilkinson, I. (1999) 'Where is the novelty in our current "age of anxiety"?' *European Journal of Social Theory*, 2, 4: 445–67.

World Health Organization (WHO) (2006) 'Epidemiology of WHO-confirmed human cases of avian influenza A(H5N1) infection', *Weekly Epidemiological Record*, 81, 26: 249–60.

World Health Organization (WHO) (2010) *H5N1 Avian Influenza: Timeline of Major Events*. Available online at: http://www.who.int/csr/disease/avian_influenza/2010_10_20_h5n1_avian_influenza_timeline_updates.pdf (9 November 2010).

Zinn, J. (2006) 'Risk, affect and emotion', *Forum Qualitative Sozialforschung / Forum: Qualitative Social Research*, 7, 1: Art. 29. Available online at: http://nbn-resolving.de/urn:nbn:de:0114-fqs0601293 (accessed 12 July 2012).

Chapter 7

Agamben, G. (2002) *Homo Sacer. Die Souveränität der Macht und das nackte Leben*. Frankfurt a.M.: Suhrkamp.

Agamben, G. (2004) *Ausnahmezustand*, Frankfurt a.M.: Suhrkamp.

Balagandhara, S.N. and de Roover, J. (2010) 'The saint, the criminal and the terrorist; towards a hypothesis on terrorism', *Journal of Political Philosophy*, 18, 1: 1–15.

Blakeley, R.J. (2007) 'Bringing the state back into terrorism studies', *European Political Science*, 6, 3: 228–35.

Buck-Morss, S. (2003) *Thinking Past Terror: Islamism and Critical Theory on the Left*, London: Verso.

Bundesregierung (2008) *Das Afghanistan-Konzept der Bundesregierung*. Berlin: Auswärtiges Amt. Available online at: http://www.auswaertiges-amt.de/diplo/de/Infoservice/Broschueren/AFGHKonzeptBuREG.pdf (accessed 1 October 2009).

Chabal, P. and Daloz, J. (1999) *Africa Works. Disorder as a Political Instrument*, Oxford: James Currey.

Clunan, A.L. and Trinkunas, H. (eds) (2010) *Ungoverned Spaces? Alternatives to State Authority in an Era of Softened Sovereignty*, Stanford: Stanford University Press.

Crocker, C. (2003) 'Engaging failing states', *Foreign Affairs*, 82, 5: 32–44.

Cronin, P.M. (2009) *Global Strategic Assessment 2009. America's Strategic Role in a Changing World*, Washington: Institute for National Strategic Studies. Available online at: http://www.ndu.edu/inss/index.cfm?secID=8&pageID=126&type=section (accessed 1 October 2009).

Debiel, T., Glassner, R., Schetter, C. and Terlinden, U. (2009) 'Local state-building in Afghanistan and Somaliland', *Peace Review*, 21, 1: 38–44.

Duffield, M. (2007) *Development, Security and Unending War*, Cambridge: Polity Press.

Dünne, J. (2006) 'Politisch-geographische Räume. Einleitung', in J. Dünne and S. Günzel (eds) *Raumtheorie*, Frankfurt a.M.: Suhrkamp, pp. 369–85.

The Economist (2009) *Fixing a Broken World*. Available online at: http://www.economist. com/world/international/displaystory.cfm?story_id=13035718 (accessed 1 October 2009).

Eisenstadt, S.N. (1979) *Tradition, Wandel und Modernität*, Frankfurt a.M.: Suhrkamp.

Elden, S. (2009) *Terror and Territory: The Spatial Extent of Sovereignty*, Minneapolis: University of Minnesota Press.

Etzioni, A. (2007) *Security First. For a Muscular, Moral Foreign Policy*, New Haven: Yale University Press.

Finlay, C.J. (2009) 'How to do things with the word "terrorist"', *Review of International Studies*, 35, 4: 751–74.

Foucault, M. (2009) *Geschichte der Gouvernementalität 1: Sicherheit, Territorium, Bevölkerung*, Frankfurt a.M.: Suhrkamp.

Giddens, A. (1985) *The Nation-State and Violence*, Cambridge: Cambridge University Press.

Golder, B. and Williams, G. (2004) 'What is "terrorism"? Problems of legal definition', *UNSW Law Journal*, 27, 2: 270–95.

Gregory, D. (1993) *Geographical Imaginations*, Oxford: Blackwell.

Gregory, D. (2004) *The Colonial Present*, Oxford: Blackwell.

Hirst, P. (2005) *Space and Power. Politics, War and Architecture*, Cambridge: Polity Press.

Jacoby, L.E. (2004) 'Current and projected national security threats to the United States', *U.S. Defense Intelligence Agency*, Senate Select Committee on Intelligence, 24 February 2004. Available online at: http://www.fas.org/irp/congress/2004_hr/022404jacoby.pdf (accessed 1 October 2009).

Jarvis, D. (2008) *Conceptualizing, Analyzing and Measuring Political Risk: The Evolution of Theory and Method*. Available online at: http://www.lkyspp.nus.edu.sg/docs/fac/ jarvis/Political%20Risk.pdf (accessed 16 July 2012).

Koselleck, R. (2003) *Zeitschichten. Studien zur Historik*, Frankfurt a.M.: Suhrkamp.

Kumar, A. (2008) *Pakistan's Ungoverned Spaces Pose Threat to South Asia*, Breaking News 24/7. 22 December 2008. Available online at: http://blog.taragana.com/n/ pakistans-ungoverned-spaces-pose-threat-to-south-asia-us-10396/ (accessed 1 October 2009).

Lamb, R.D. (2008) *Ungoverned Areas and Threats from Safe Havens*. Available online at: http://www.cissm.umd.edu/papers/files/ugash_report_final.pdf (accessed 1 October 2009).

Lambach, D. (2008) *Staatszerfall und regionale Sicherheit*, Baden-Baden: Nomos.

Lewis, B. (1994) *Der Atem Allahs. Die islamische Welt und der Westen – Kampf der Kulturen?*, München: DTV.

Mallaby, S. (2002) 'The reluctant imperialist: terrorism, failed state, and the case for American empire', *Foreign Affairs*, 81, 2: 11–12.

McFaul, M. (2005) 'Democracy promotion as a world value', *The Washington Quarterly*, 28, 1: 147–63.

McGregor, M. (2007) *'Ungoverned Spaces', 'Phase Zero' Planning and the US Military in Africa*. Available online at: http://londoncommons.ca/content/ungoverned-spaces-phase-zero-planning-and-us-military-africa (accessed 1 October 2009).

Menkhaus, K. (2007) 'Terrorist activities in ungoverned spaces. Evidence and observations from the Horn of Africa', paper prepared for the 'Southern Africa and International Terrorism' Workshop, Tswalu, South Africa, 25–27 January 2007. Available online at: http://www.thebrenthurstfoundation.org/Files/terror_talks/Terrorist%20Activities%20 in%20Ungoverned%20Spaces.pdf (accessed 1 October 2009).

Milliken, J. (ed.) (2003) *State Failure, Collapse and Reconstruction*, Oxford: Blackwell.

Obama, B. (2009) *Strategy for Afghanistan and Pakistan*. Available online at: http://www.cfr.org/publication/18952/ (accessed 1 October 2009).

O'Tuathail, G. (1996) *Critical Geopolitics*, Minneapolis: University of Minnesota Press.

Patrick, S. (2006) 'Weak states and global threats: fact and fiction?', *Washington Quarterly*, 29, 2: 27–53.

Rabasa, A. and Peters, J.E. (2007a) 'Lack of governance', in A. Rabasa *et al.* (eds) *Ungoverned Territories. Understanding and Reducing Terrorism Risks*, Santa Monica, CA: RAND Corporation, pp. 1–6.

Rabasa, A. and Peters, J.E. (2007b) 'Dimensions of ungovernability', in A. Rabasa *et al.* (eds) *Ungoverned Territories. Understanding and Reducing Terrorism Risks*, Santa Monica, CA: RAND Corporation, pp. 7–14.

Rabasa, A., Boraz, S., Chalk, P., Cragin, K., Karasik, T.W., Moroney, D.P., O'Brien, K.A. and Peters, J.E. (2007) *Ungoverned Territories. Understanding and Reducing Terrorism Risks*, Santa Monica, CA: RAND Corporation. Available online at: http://www.rand.org/pubs/monographs/2007/RAND_MG561.pdf (accessed 1 October 2009).

Renn, O. (2008) 'Concepts of risks. An interdisciplinary review – part 1: disciplinary risk concepts', *GAIA*, 17, 1: 50–66.

Reno, W. (1998) *Warlord Politics and African Society*, Boulder: Lynne Rienner.

Rodin, D. (2004) 'Terrorism without intention', *Ethics*, 114: 752–71.

Rose-Redwood, R.S. (2006) 'Governmentality, geography and the geo-coding world', *Progress in Human Geography*, 30, 4: 469–86.

Rotberg, R. (ed.) (2003) *State Failure and State Weakness in a Time of Terror*, Washington: Brookings.

Ruggie, J.G. (1993) 'Territoriality and beyond: problematizing modernity in international relations', *International Organizations*, 47, 1: 139–74.

Sack, R.D. (1986) *Human Territoriality: Its Theory and History*, Cambridge: Cambridge University Press.

Schetter, C. (2010) 'Von der Entwicklungszusammenarbeit zur humanitären Intervention. Die Kontinuität einer Kultur der Treuhandschaft', in T. Bonacker *et al.* (eds) *Interventionskultur. Zur Soziologie von Interventionsgesellschaften*, Wiesbaden: VS Verlag: 31–47.

Schmitt, C. (1922) *Politische Theologie*, Berlin: Duncker & Humblot.

Schneckener, U. (2004) 'Transnationale Terroristen als Profiteure fragiler Staatlichkeit', SWP Studie 18, Berlin: Stiftung Wissenschaft und Politik.

Schneckener, U. (ed.) (2006) *Fragile Staatlichkeit. 'States at Risk' zwischen Stabilität und Scheitern*, Baden-Baden: Nomos.

Takeyh, R. and Gvosdev, N. (2002) 'Do terrorist networks need a home?', *The Washington Quarterly*, 25, 3: 97–108.

US Department of Defense (2008) *National Defense Strategy*. Available online at: http://www.defense.gov/news/2008%20national%20defense%20strategy.pdf (accessed 1 October 2009).

von Hippel, K. (2009) 'Does poverty serves as a root cause for terrorism?', in S. Gottlieb (ed.) *Debating Terrorism and Counter-Terrorism. Conflicting perspectives on Causes, Contexts and Responses*, Washington: CQ Press, pp. 51–66.

Weber, M. (1980 [1921]) *Wirtschaft und Gesellschaft*, Tübingen: Mohr.

Whelan, T. (2006) 'Africa's ungoverned space', *Nacao Defesa*, 114, 3: 61–73. Available online at: http://www.idn.gov.pt/publicacoes/nacao_defesa/consulta/ND_101_120/NeD114_TeresaWhelan.pdf (accessed 1 October 2009).

Whiteneck, D. (2005) 'Deterring terrorists: thoughts on a framework', *Washington Quarterly*, 28, 3: 187 –99.

Zellin, B. (2008) 'Tribalism and the future of conflict', *The Culture & Conflict Review*, 2, 3: 1–5. Available online at: http://www.nps.edu/programs/ccs/Journal/Summer08/Zellin.pdf (accessed 1 October 2009).

Chapter 8

Almedom, A. and Tumwine, J. (2008) 'Resilience to disasters – a paradigm shift from vulnerability to strength', *African Health Sciences*, 8 Special Issue: 1–4.

Barnett, T. and Blaikie, P. (1992) *AIDS in Africa – Its Present and Future Impact*, London: Belhaven Press.

Barrett, H. (2007) 'Too little, too late: response to the HIV/AIDS epidemics in sub-Saharan Africa', *Geography*, 92, 2: 87–96.

Bartlett, J.G. and Gallant, J.E. (2001) *2000–2001 Medical Management of HIV Infection*, Baltimore: Port City Press.

Becker, E. and Jahn, T. (2006) *Soziale Ökologie. Grundzüge einer Wissenschaft von den gesellschaftlichen Naturverhältnissen*, Frankfurt a.M.: Campus.

Bell, J., Airaksinen, M., Lyles, A., Chen, T. and Aslani, P. (2007) 'Concordance is not synonymous with compliance or adherence [Letters to the Editors]', *British Journal of Clinical Pharmacology*, 64, 5: 710–13.

Bhabha, H. (1994) *The Location of Culture*, London and New York: Routledge.

Bohle, H.G. (2002) 'Vulnerability – editorial to the special issue', *Geographica Helvetica*, 57, 1: 2–4.

Cannon, T. (2008) 'Vulnerability, "innocent disasters" and the imperative of cultural understanding', *Disaster Prevention and Management*, 17, 3: 350–57.

Carpenter, S., Walker, B., Anderies, J. and Abel, N. (2001) 'From metaphor to measurement: resilience of what to what?', *Ecosystems*, 4, 8: 765–81.

Cohen, P.T., Sande, M.A. and Volberding, P.A. (eds) (1999) *The AIDS Knowledge Base. A Textbook on HIV Disease from the University of California, San Francisco and San Francisco General Hospital*, New York: Lippincott Williams & Wilkins.

Curtis, S. and Riva, M. (2010) 'Health geographies I: complexity theory and human health', *Progress in Human Geography*, 34, 2: 215–23.

Dilger, H.J. and Luig, U. (eds) (2010) *Morality, Hope and Grief – Anthroplogies of AIDS in Africa*, New York and Oxford: Berghahn Books Inc.

Douglas, M. (1992) 'Risk and danger', in M. Douglas (ed.) *Risk and Blame: Essays in Cultural Theory*, London and New York: Routledge, pp. 38–54.

Drescher, M. (2007) 'Global and local alignments in HIV/AIDS prevention trainings: a case study from Burkina Faso', *Communication & Medicine*, 4, 1: 3–14.

Drescher, M. and Klaeger, S. (eds) (2006) *Kommunikation über HIV/Aids*, Beiträge zur Afrikaforschung, 27, Berlin: LIT.

Felgentreff, C. and Glade, T. (eds) (2008) *Naturrisiken und Sozialkatastrophen*, Heidelberg: Spektrum Akademischer Verlag.

Folke, C. (2006) 'Resilience: the emergence of a perspective for social-ecological systems analysis', *Global Environmental Change*, 16, 3: 253–67.

Gaie, J. and Mmolai, S. (eds) (2007) *The Concept of Botho and HIV&AIDS in Botswana*, Edoret: Zapf Chancery.

Geiselhart, K. (2009) *The Geography of Stigma and Discrimination. HIV and AIDS-related identities in Botswana*, Studien zur Geographischen Entwicklungsforschung, 36, Saarbrücken: Verlag für Entwicklungspolitik.

Geiselhart, K. and Krüger, F. (2007) 'Die HIV/AIDS-Krise – Botswanas strategische Antwort als Vorbild?', *Geographische Rundschau*, 59, 2: 54–61.

Geiselhart, K., Gwebu, T. and Krüger, F. (2008) 'Children, adolescents and the HIV and AIDS pandemic: changing inter-generational relationships and intra-family communication patterns in Botswana', *Children, Youth and Environments*, 18, 1: 99–125.

Gronemeyer, R. (2005) *Living and Dying with AIDS in Africa. New Perspectives on a Modern Disease*, Frankfurt a.M.: Brandes & Apsel.

Gronemeyer, R. and Rompel, M. (2008) *Verborgenes Afrika – Alltag jenseits von Klischees*, Frankfurt a.M.: Brandes & Apsel.

Hardon, A., Davey, S., Gerrits, T., Hodgkin, C., Irunde, H., Kgatlwane, J. *et al.* (2006) *From Access to Adherence: The Challenges of Antiretroviral Treatment. Studies from Botswana, Tanzania and Uganda 2006*, Geneva: WHO Press.

Horne, R., Weinman, J., Barber, N., Elliott, R. and Morgan, M. (2005) *Concordance, Adherence and Compliance in Medicine Taking*, Report for the National Co-ordinating Centre for NHS Service Delivery and Organisation R & D (NCCSDO). Available online at: http://www.sdo.nihr.ac.uk/files/project/76-final-report.pdf (accessed 15 January 2011).

IRIN (2004) *Botswana: Interview with Dr Ndwapi Ndwapi, Director of Princess Marina Hospital's ARV Programme*. Available online at: http://www.plusnews.org/Report. aspx?ReportId=36726 (accessed 10 January 2011).

Kalipeni, E., Craddock, S., Oppong, J. and Ghosh, J. (eds) (2004) *HIV & AIDS in Africa: Beyond Epidemiology*, Maldon and Oxford: Wiley-Blackwell.

Korte, D., Mazonde, P. and Darkoh, E. (2004) *Introducing ARV Therapy in the Public Sector in Botswana*, Geneva: World Health Organization.

Krüger, F. (2003) 'Handlungsorientierte Entwicklungsforschung: Trends, Perspektiven, Defizite', *Petermanns Geographische Mitteilungen*, 147, 1: 6–15.

Krüger, F. and Macamo, E. (2003) 'Existenzsicherung unter Risikobedingungen – Sozialwissenschaftliche Analyseansätze zum Umgang mit Krisen, Konflikten und Katastrophen', *Geographica Helvetica*, 58, 1: 47–55.

Krüger, F. and Samimi, C. (2003) 'Risikoräume. Die Gefährdung von Lebensräumen und Lebenswelten', *Praxis Geographie*, 33, 11: 4–9.

Loimeier, R., Neubert, D. and Weißköppel, C. (2005) *Globalization in the Local Context – Perspectives and Concepts of Action in Africa. An Introduction*, Bayreuth African

Studies Online, 2. Available online at: http://opus.ub.uni-bayreuth.de/volltexte/ 2005/171/pdf/loimeier_komplett_27_07.pdf (accessed 15 January 2011).

Luhmann, N. (2005) *Risk: A Sociological Theory*, New Brunswick, NJ: Transaction Publishers.

Luthar, S. (2008) *Resilience and Vulnerability. Adaptation in the Context of Childhood Adversities*, Cambridge and New York: Cambridge University Press.

Luthar, S., Cicchetti, D. and Becker B. (2000) 'The construct of resilience: a critical evaluation and guidelines for future work', *Child Development*, 71, 3: 543–62.

Massey, D. (2005) *For Space*, London: Sage.

Monjok, E., Smesmy, A., Mgbere, O. and Essien, E. (2010) 'Routine HIV testing in health care settings: the deterrent factors to maximal implementation in sub-Saharan Africa', *Journal of the International Association of Physicians in AIDS Care*, 9, 1: 23–29.

McMurray, I., Connolly, H., Preston-Shoot, M. and Wigley, V. (2008) 'Constructing reslience. Social workers' understandings and practice', *Health and Social Care in the Community*, 16, 3: 299–309.

Metz, T. and Gaie, J. (2010) 'The African ethic of Ubuntu/Botho: implications for research on morality', *Journal of Moral Education*, 39, 3: 273–90.

Müller-Mahn, D. (2007) 'Perspektiven geographischer Risikoforschung', *Geographische Rundschau*, 59, 10: 4–11.

Ngigi, M. (2007) 'AIDS and the city – exploring the spatial characteristics of the HIV/ AIDS pandemic in Nairobi, Kenya', *Geographical Review of Japan*, 80, 2: 291–305.

Norris, F., Stevens, S., Pfefferbaum, B., Wyche, K. and Pfefferbaum, R. (2008) 'Community resilience as a metaphor, theory, set of capacities, and strategy for disaster readiness', *American Journal of Community Psychology*, 41, 1/2: 127–50.

Obrist, B. (2010) 'Editorial', *Progress in Development Studies*, 10, 4: 279–81.

Obrist, B., Pfeiffer, C. and Henley, R. (2010) 'Multi-layered social resilience: a new approach in mitigation research', *Progress in Development Studies*, 10, 4: 283–93.

Osterndorff, M. (2010) 'Sozialethik in Botswana', unpublished Master's thesis, University of Osnabrück.

Rakelmann, G. (2004) 'Die Integration von AIDS: Widerstreitende Körper- und Heilungskonzepte in Botswana vor dem Hintergrund der AIDS-Epidemie', *Palaver*, 10/2004: 35–50.

Rakelmann, G. (2005) 'Prozesse des Einzugs von AIDS in die botswanische Alltagswelt: Von einer allochthonen zu einer einheimischen Krankheit', *Curare*, 28, 2/3: 153–68.

Resilience Alliance (2011) *Key Concepts Adaptive Capacity, Resilience*. Available online at: http://www.resalliance.org (accessed 13 January 2011).

Rödlach, A. (2006) *Witches, Westerners, and HIV. AIDS and Cultures of Blame in Africa*, Walnut Creek: Left Coast Press.

Rottenburg, R. and Engel, U. (2008) 'Adaptation and creativity in Africa – technologies and significations in the production of order and disorder', unpublished proposal for the establishment of a DFG Priority Programme, Halle.

Schröter. S. (2007) *HIV/AIDS – Eine neue sozio-politische Herausforderung für Namibia*, Entwicklungsforschung – Beiträge zu interdisziplinären Studien in den Ländern des Südens, 1, Berlin: Wissenschaftlicher Verlag.

Stillwaggon, E. (2006) *AIDS and the Ecology of Poverty*, Oxford and New York: Oxford University Press.

UNAIDS (2006) *2006 Report on the Global AIDS Epidemic*. Available online at: http:// www.unaids.org/en/media/unaids/contentassets/dataimport/pub/report/2006/2006_gr_ en.pdf (accessed 13 January 2011).

UNAIDS/NACA (2010) *Progress Report of the National Response to the 2001 Declaration of Commitment on HIV and AIDS – Botswana Country Report 2010.* Available online at: http://www.unaids.org/en/dataanalysis/monitoringcountryprogress/2010progressrep ortssubmittedbycountries/botswana_2010_country_progress_report_en.pdf (accessed 13 January 2011).

UNAIDS/WHO (2010) *A Global View of HIV Infection.* Available online at: http://www.unaids.org/documents/20101123_2010_HIV_Prevalence_Map_em.pdf (accessed 15 January 2011).

UNDP (2009) *Human Development Report 2009 – Botswana.* Available online at: http://hdrstats.undp.org/en/countries/country_fact_sheets/cty_fs_BWA.html (accessed 16 July 2010).

Villagrán, Juan C. (2006). *Vulnerability: A Conceptual and Methodological Overview,* Bonn: United Nations University Institute for Environment and Human Security.

Watts, M. and Bohle, H.G. (1993) 'The space of vulnerability: the causal structure of hunger and famine', *Progress in Human Geography,* 17, 1: 43–67.

Weiser, S., Wolfe, W., Bangsberg, D., Thior, I., Gilbert, P., Makhema, J., Kebaabetswe, P., Dickenson, D., Mompati, K., Essex, M. and Marlink, R. (2003) 'Barriers to antiretroviral adherence for patients living with HIV infection and AIDS in Botswana', *JAIDS: Journal of Acquired Immune Deficiency Syndromes,* 34, 3: 281–88.

WHO/UNAIDS/UNICEF (2010) *Towards Universal Access – Scaling up Priority HIV/ AIDS Interventions in the Health Sector: Progress Report 2010,* Geneva: WHO Press.

Winkelmann, T. (2010) *Handeln im Zeichen von HIV/AIDS. Untersuchungen zu gesellschaftlicher Transformation im ländlichen Raum Malawis.* Entwicklungsforschung – Beiträge zu interdisziplinären Studien in den Ländern des Südens, 8, Berlin: Wissenschaftlicher Verlag.

Yates, F. (ed.) (1992) *Risk-Taking Behavior,* Chichester: Wiley.

Chapter 9

Agamben, G. (2002) 'Security and terror', *Theory & Event,* 5, 4: unpaged.

Agnew, J. (2009) *Globalization & Sovereignty,* Plymouth: Rowman & Littlefield.

Altvater, E. and Mahnkopf, B. (2007) *Konkurrenz für das Empire,* Münster: Westfälisches Dampfboot.

Andreas, P. (2003) 'Redrawing the line', *International Security,* 28, 2: 78–111.

Aradau, C. and van Munster, R. (2007) 'Governing terrorism through risk', *European Journal of International Relations,* 13, 1: 89–115.

Balibar, E. (2009) 'Europe as borderland', *Environment and Planning D. Society and Space,* 27, 2: 190–215

Beck, U. (1992) *Risk Society. Towards a New Modernity,* New Delhi: Sage.

Beck, U. (2009) *World at Risk,* Cambridge: Polity Press.

Becker, H. (1963) *Outsiders,* New York: Free Press.

Bekus-Goncharova, N. (2008) *Living in Visa Territory.* Available online at: http://www.eurozine.com/articles/2008-02-22-goncharova-en.html (accessed 3 November 2009).

Buckel, S. and Wissel, J. (2009) 'Entgrenzung der europäischen Migrationskontrolle', in H. Brunkhorst (ed.) *Demokratie in der Marktgesellschaft,* Baden-Baden: Nomos, pp. 385–403.

Busch, H. (2009) 'Eine besondere Wirtschaftsförderung: vom Militärisch- zum Sicherheits-industriellen Komplex?', *Bürgerrechte & Polizei/CILIP,* 94, 3: 3–13.

Carrera, S. (2007) *The EU Border Management Strategy. FRONTEX and the Challenges of Irregular Immigration in the Canary Islands.* Available online at: http://www.ceps.eu/book/eu-border-management-strategy-frontex-and-challenges-irregular-immigration-canary-islands (accessed 19 November 2010).

Council Regulation (EC) (2004) 'Establishing a European agency for the management of operational cooperation at the external borders of the member states of the European Union' (=No 2007/2004 of 26 October 2004), *Official Journal of The European Union*, L 349, issued 25 November 2004. Available online at: http://www.frontex.europa.eu/gfx/frontex/files/frontex_regulation_en.pdf (accessed 19 November 2010).

Cox, K. (2002) *Political Geography*, Oxford: Blackwell.

Crowley, J. (2003) 'Locating Europe' in K. Groenendijk, E. Guild and P. Minderhout (eds) *In Search of Europe's Borders*, The Hague: Springer, pp. 27–44.

de Boer, K. (2010) 'Frontex: Der falsche Adressat für ein wichtiges Anliegen', *Kriminologisches Journal*, 42, 3: 181–95.

Elden, S. (2010) 'Land, terrain, territory', *Progress in Human Geography*, 34, 6: 799–817.

European Commission (2003) *A Secure Europe in a Better World. European Security Strategy.* Available online at: http://www.consilium.europa.eu/uedocs/cmsUpload/78367.pdf (accessed 12 May 2010).

Fischer-Lescano, A. and Tohidipur, T. (2007) 'Europäisches Grenzkontrollregime. Rechtsrahmen der europäischen Grenzschutzagentur FRONTEX', *Zeitschrift für ausländisches öffentliches Recht und Völkerrecht*, 67, 4: 1219–76.

Foucault, M. (1975) *Discipline and Punish: The Birth of the Prison*, New York: Random House.

Foucault, M. (1978) *The History of Sexuality, Vol. I: An Introduction*, New York: Pantheon.

Foucault, M. (2007) *Security, Territory, Population: Lectures at the Collège de France, 1977–78*, Basingstoke: Palgrave Macmillan.

Foucault, M. (2008) *The Birth of Biopolitics. Lectures at the Collège de France, 1978–1979*, Basingstoke: Palgrave Macmillan.

FRONTEX (2007) *FRONTEX Annual Report 2006.* Available online at: http://www.frontex.europa.eu/gfx/frontex/files/justyna/annual_report_2006[1].pdf (accessed 26 February 2010).

FRONTEX (2008) *General Report 2008.* Available online at: http://www.frontex.europa.eu/assets/About_Frontex/Governance_documents/Annual_report/2008/frontex_general_report_2008.pdf (accessed 20 July 2012).

FRONTEX (2009) *General Report 2009.* Available online at: http://www.frontex.europa.eu/assets/About_Frontex/Governance_documents/Annual_report/2009/gen_rep_2009_en.pdf (accessed 20 July 2012).

FRONTEX (2010) *Programme of Work 2010.* Available online at: http://www.frontex.europa.eu/gfx/frontex/files/justyna/pow2010.pdf (accessed 19 February 2010).

Garland, D. (1996) 'The limits of the sovereign state', *British Journal of Criminology*, 36, 4: 445–71.

Gordon, C. (1991) 'Governmental rationality', in G. Burchell, C. Gordon and P. Miller (eds) *The Foucault Effect*, Chicago: University of Chicago Press, pp. 1–51.

Harvey, D. (2005) *A Brief History of Neoliberalism*, Oxford: Oxford University Press.

Harvey, D. (2007) 'The Kantian roots of Foucault's dilemmas', in J. Crampton, and S. Elden (eds) *Space, Knowledge and Power. Foucault and Geography*, Aldershot: Ashgate, pp. 41–7.

Hobbing, P. (2005) *Integrated Border Management at the EU Level.* Available online at: http://www.ceps.eu/book/integrated-border-management-eu-level (accessed 22 November 2010).

Horn, E. (2002) 'Secret intelligence. Zur Epistemologie der Nachrichtendienste', in R. Maresch and N. Werber (eds) *Raum – Wissen – Macht*, Frankfurt a.M.: Suhrkamp, pp. 173–92.

Huysmans, J. (2000) 'The European Union and the securitization of migration', *Journal of Common Market Studies*, 38, 5: 751–77.

Jessop, B. (2007) *Kapitalismus, Regulation, Staat*, Hamburg: Argument.

Kuus, M. (2007) *Geopolitics Reframed. Security and Identity in Europe's Eastern Enlargement*, New York and Houndmills: Palgrave Macmillan.

Lemke, T. (1997) *Eine Kritik der politischen Vernunft*, Hamburg: Argument.

Marischka, C. (2007) 'FRONTEX. Die Vernetzungsmaschine an den Randzonen des Rechtes und der Staaten', *IMI-Magazin*, 12/2007: 3–10.

Narr, W. (2009) 'Ein Ort für jeden Menschen in einer mobilen und globalen Welt', in Komitee für Grundrechte und Demokratie (ed.) *Jahrbuch 2009: Jenseits der Menschenrechte. Die europäische Flüchtlings- und Migrationspolitik*, Münster: Westfälisches Dampfboot, pp. 147–81.

Neocleous, M. (2008) *Critique of Security*, Edinburgh: Edinburgh University Press.

O'Malley, P. (2008) 'Experiments in risk and criminal justice', *Theoretical Criminology*, 12, 4: 451–69.

Rijpma, J.J. and Cremona, M. (2007) *The Extra-Territorialisation of EU Migration Policies and the Rule of Law.* Available online at: http://papers.ssrn.com/sol3/papers.cfm?abstract_id=964190 (accessed 10 February 2010).

Sack, R. (1983) 'Human territoriality: a theory', *Annals of the Association of American Geographers*, 73, 1: 55–74.

Sassen, S. (1998) 'Zur Einbettung des Globalisierungsprozesses: Der Nationalstaat vor neuen Aufgaben', *Berliner Journal für Soziologie*, 8, 3: 345–57.

Stork, V. (2001) *Die 'Zweite Moderne' – ein Markenartikel?*, Konstanz: UVK.

Tohidipur, T. (2009) 'Das Agenturwesen der EU', in Informationsstelle Militarisierung (ed.) *Frontex – Widersprüche im erweiterten Grenzraum*, Tübingen: Informationsstelle Militarisierung, pp. 14–16.

Walters, W. (2006) 'Border/Control', *European Journal of Social Theory*, 9, 2: 187–203.

Zedner, L. (2007) 'Pre-crime and post-criminology?', *Theoretical Criminology*, 11, 2: 261–81.

Chapter 10

Beck, U. (1992) *Risk Society. Towards a New Modernity*, London: Sage.

Berger, P.L. and Luckmann, T. (1966) *The Social Construction of Reality: A Treatise in the Sociology of Knowledge*, New York: Anchor Books.

Büscher, K. and Vlassenroot, K. (2010) 'Humanitarian presence and urban development: new opportunities and contrasts in Goma, DRC', *Disasters*, 34, 2: 256–73.

Chester, D.K., Dibben, C.J.L. and Duncan, A.M. (2002) 'Volcanic hazard assessment in Western Europe', *Journal of Volcanology and Geothermal Research*, 115, 3/4: 411–35.

Chirico, G.D., Favalli, M., Papale, P., Boschi, E. and Pareschi, M.T. (2009) 'Lava flow hazard at Nyiragongo volcano, D.R.C. 2. Hazard reduction in urban areas', *Bulletin of Volcanology*, 71, 4: 375–87.

Doevenspeck, M. (2007) 'Lake Kivu's methane gas: natural risk, or source of energy and political security', *Africa Spectrum*, 24, 1: 95–110

Favalli, M., Chirico, G.D., Papale, P., Pareschi, M.T. and Boschi, E. (2009) 'Lava flow hazard at Nyiragongo volcano, D.R.C. 1. Model calibration and hazard mapping', *Bulletin of Volcanology*, 71, 4: 363–74.

Frewer, L.J. and Salter, B. (2007) 'Societal trust in risk analysis: implications for the interface of risk assessment and risk management', in M. Siegrist, T.C. Earle and H. Gutscher (eds) *Trust in Cooperative Risk Management. Uncertainty and Scepticism in the Public Mind*, London: Earthscan, pp. 143–58.

Gaillard, J.-C. (2008) 'Alternative paradigms of volcanic risk perception: the case of Mt. Pinatubo in the Philippines', *Journal of Volcanology and Geothermal Research*, 172, 3/4: 315–28.

Giddens, A. (1991) *Modernity and Self-Identity*, Stanford: Stanford University Press.

Grothmann, T. and Reusswig, F. (2006) 'People at risk of flooding: why some residents take precautionary action while others do not', *Natural Hazards*, 38, 1/2: 101–20.

Hacking, I. (1999) *The Social Construction of What?*, Cambridge and London: Harvard University Press.

INICA (L'Initiative pour l'Afrique Centrale) (2006) 'Les dynamiques transfrontalières dans la région des Grands Lacs. Burundi, République Démocratique du Congo, Ouganda et Rwanda', unpublished.

IRGC (International Risk Governance Council) (2009) *Risk Governance Deficits. An Analysis and Illustration of the Most Common Deficits in Risk Governance*. Available online at: http://www.irgc.org/IMG/pdf/IRGC_rgd_web_final.pdf (accessed 21 November 2011).

Jackson, J., Allum, N. and Gaskell, G. (2006) 'Bridging levels of analysis in risk perception research: the case of the fear of crime', *Forum: Qualitative Social Research*, 7, 1. Available online at: http://www.qualitative-research.net/index.php/fqs/article/view/63 (accessed 21 November 2011).

Jaeger, C.C., Renn, O., Rosa, E.A. and Webler, T. (2001) *Risk, Uncertainty and Rational Action*, London: Earthscan.

Kling, G., MacIntyre, S., Steenfelt, J.S. and Hirslund, F. (2006) 'Lake Kivu gas extraction. Report on lake stability', Report no. 62721-0001, unpublished.

Komorowski, J.-C. *et al.* (2002/2003) 'The January 2002 flank eruption of Nyiragongo volcano (Democratic Republic of Congo): chronology, evidence for a tectonic rift trigger, and impact of lava flows on the city of Goma', *Acta Vulcanologica*, 14/15, 1/2: 27–62.

Lewis, P. (2003) 'New Orleans: the making of an urban landscape' (2nd ed.), Santa Fe, NM: Center for American Places.

Lorke, A., Tietze, K., Halbwachs, M. and Wüest, A. (2004) 'Response of lake Kivu stratification to lava inflow and climate warming', *Limnology and Oceanography*, 49, 3: 778–83.

Luhmann, N. (1993) *Risk: A Sociological Theory*, New York: De Gruyter.

Lupton, D. (1999) *Risk*, London and New York: Routledge.

Lupton, D. and Tulloch, J. (2002) 'Risk is part of your life: risk epistemologies among a group of Australians', *Sociology*, 36, 2: 317–34.

Macamo, E. (2008) 'The taming of fate: approaching risk from a social action perspective. Case studies from southern Mozambique', unpublished habilitation thesis, University of Bayreuth.

Miceli, R., Sotgiu, I. and Settanni, M. (2008) 'Disaster preparedness and perception of flood risk: a study in an alpine valley in Italy', *Journal of Environmental Psychology*, 28, 2: 164–73.

Mitchell, H. and Garrett, N. (2009) *Beyond Conflict: Reconfiguring Approaches to the Regional Trade in Minerals from Eastern DRC*. Available online at: http://www.resourceglobal.co.uk/documents/Beyond%20Conflict_RCS_CASM.pdf (accessed 21 November 2011).

Mitchell, W., Crawshaw, P., Bunton, R. and Green, E. (2001) 'Situating young people's experiences of risk and identity', *Health, Risk & Society*, 3, 2: 217–33.

OVG (Observatoire Volcanologique de Goma) (2007) *Les Mazuku et le gaz méthane dans le lac Kivu*. Goma. Unpublished report.

Paton, D. (2008) 'Risk communication and natural hazard mitigation: how trust influences its effectiveness', *International Journal of Global Environmental Issues*, 8, 1/2: 1–16.

Paul, B.K. and Bhuiyan, R.H. (2010) 'Urban earthquake hazard: perceived seismic risk and preparedness in Dhaka City, Bangladesh', *Disasters*, 34, 2: 337–59.

Pelling, M. (2003) *The Vulnerability of Cities: Natural Disasters and Social Resilience*, London: Earthscan.

Plapp, T. and Werner U. (2006) 'Understanding risk perception from natural hazards: examples from Germany', in W. Ammann, S. Dannenmann and L. Vulliet (eds) *RISK 21 – Coping with Risks due to Natural Hazards in the 21st Century*, London: Taylor & Francis, pp. 101–108.

Pole Institute (2009) *Est de la RDC: Le Crime Banalisé!* Available online at: http://www.pole-institute.org/documents/banalisation_mort%20REGARD%2023.pdf (accessed 21 November 2011).

Renn, O. (2008) *Risk Governance. Coping with Uncertainty in a Complex World*, London: Earthscan.

Rohrmann, B. (1999) *Risk Perception Research. Review and Documentation*, Arbeiten zur Risikokommunikation 68, Jülich: Forschungszentrum Jülich.

Short, J.F. Jr. (1984) 'The social fabric at risk: toward the social transformation of risk analysis', *American Sociological Review*, 49, 6: 711–25.

Slovic, P. (1987) 'Perception of risk', *Science*, 236, 4799: 280–85.

Tassi, F., Vaselli O., Tedesco, D., Montegrossi, G., Darrah T., Cuoco, E., Mapendano, M.Y., Poreda R. and Delgado Huertas, A. (2009) 'Water and gas chemistry at lake Kivu (DRC): geochemical evidence of vertical and horizontal heterogeneities in a multibasin structure', *Geochemistry, Geophysics and Geosystems (G3)*, 10: Q02005, doi:10.1029/2008GC002191.

Tietze, K. (1987) 'The lake Nyos gas catastrophe in Cameroon: cause, sequence of events, consequences', in W.H. Graf and U. Lemmin (eds) *Topics in Lake and Reservoir Hydraulics*, Lausanne: École Polytechnique Fédéral de Lausanne, pp. 93–98.

Vaselli, O., Capaccioni, B., Tedesco, D., Tassi, F., Salire, M.M. and Kasareka, M.C. (2002/2003) 'The "evil's winds"' (Mazukus) at Nyiragongo volcano (Democratic Republic of Congo)', *Acta Vulcanologica*, 14/15, 1/2: 123–28.

Wachinger, G. and Renn, O. (2010) *Risk Perception and Natural Hazards*. Available online at: http://caphaz-net.org/outcomes-results/CapHaz-Net_WP3_Risk-Perception2.pdf (accessed 21 November 2011).

Wamsler, C. (2007) 'Bridging the gaps: stakeholder-based strategies for risk reduction and financing for the urban poor', *Environment and Urbanization*, 19, 1: 115–42.

Zinn, J.O. (2008) 'Introduction: the contribution of sociology to the discourse on risk and uncertainty', in J.O. Zinn (ed.) *Social Theories of Risk and Uncertainty: An Introduction*, Oxford: Blackwell Publishing, pp. 1–17.

Chapter 11

Ahmed, A.S. (1980) *Pukhtun Economy and Society: Traditional Structure and Economic Development in a Tribal Society*, London: Routledge & Kegan Paul.

Beck, U. (1986) *Die Risikogesellschaft. Auf dem Weg in eine andere Moderne*, Frankfurt a.M.: Suhrkamp.

Beck, U. (2007) *Weltrisikogesellschaft. Auf der Suche nach der verlorenen Sicherheit*, Frankfurt a.M.: Suhrkamp.

Beltran, G.A. (1979) *Regions of Refuge*, The Society for Applied Anthropology Monograph Series 12, Washington: Society for Applied Anthropology.

Bregel, Y. (2003) *An Historical Atlas of Central Asia*, Leiden and Boston: Brill.

Cohen, E.S. (2001) 'Globalization and the boundaries of the state. A framework for analyzing the changing practice of sovereignty', *Governance*, 14, 1: 75–97.

Cooper, R. (2002) 'The post-modern state', in M. Leonard (ed.) *Re-ordering the World. The Long-term Implications of September 11th*, London: Foreign Policy Centre, pp. 11–20.

Cooper, R. (2003) *The Breaking of Nations. Order and Chaos in the Twenty-first Century*, London: Atlantic Books.

Delanty, G. (ed.) (2006) *Europe and Asia Beyond East and West. Towards a New Cosmopolitism*, London: Routledge.

Durand, A. (1888) *Report on the Present Military Position in Gilgit*, Simla (IOL/P&S/7/57).

Durand, A. (1899) *The Making of a Frontier*, London: Thomas Nelson & Sons.

Eisener, R. (1991) *Auf den Spuren des tadschikischen Nationalismus. Aus Texten und Dokumenten zur Tadschikischen SSR*, Ethnizität und Gesellschaft, Occasional Papers 30, Berlin: Das Arabische Buch.

Elias, N. (1886) *Report of a Mission to Chinese Turkistan and Badakhshan in 1885–1886*, Calcutta (IOL/P&S/20/A 27).

Felmy, S. (1993) 'The dividing line', *Newsline*, 5, 5/6: 72–78.

Fraser-Tytler, W.K. (1953) *Afghanistan. A study of Political Developments in Central and Southern Asia*, London, New York and Toronto: Oxford University Press.

General Staff India (ed.) (1929) *Military Report on Soviet Turkistan*, Simla: General Staff India.

Giddens, A. (1985) *The Nation-state and Violence. Volume Two of a Contemporary Critique of Historical Materialism*, Cambridge: University of California Press.

Giddens, A. (1990) *The Consequences of Modernity*, Cambridge: Polity.

Giddens, A. (1999) *Runaway World*, London: Profile Books.

Hauner, M. (1989) 'Central Asian geopolitics in the last hundred years: a critical survey from Gorchakov to Gorbachev', *Central Asian Survey*, 8, 1: 1–19.

Holdich, T.H. (1909) *Indian Borderland*, London: Methuen.

IOL/P&S/18/C 17: India Office Library and Records: Political and Secret Department Memoranda *The Progress of Russia in Central Asia by Colonel M. J. Veniukoff (translated from the "Sbornik Gosudarstvennikh Zuanyi"* [Collection of Governmental Knowledge] 1877

Jones, R. (2010) 'The spatiality of boundaries', *Progress in Human Geography*, 34, 2: 263–67.

Kasperson, R.E., Renn, O., Slovic, P., Brown, H.S., Emel, J., Goble, R., Kasperson, J.X. and Ratick, S. (1988) 'The social amplification of risk. A conceptual framework', *Risk Analysis*, 8, 2: 177–87.

Kreutzmann, H. (1996) *Ethnizität im Entwicklungsprozeß. Die Wakhi in Hochasien*, Berlin: Reimer.

Kreutzmann, H. (2008a) 'Kashmir and the northern areas of Pakistan: boundary-making along contested frontiers', *Erdkunde*, 62, 3: 201–19.

Kreutzmann, H. (2008b) 'Dividing the world: conflict and inequality in the context of growing global tension', *Third World Quarterly*, 29, 4: 675–89.

Lamont, M. and Molnár V. (2002) 'The study of boundaries in the social science', *Annual Review of Sociology*, 28: 167–95.

Lattimore, O. (1950) *Pivot of Asia. Sinkiang and the Inner Asian Frontiers of China and Russia*, Boston: Little, Brown & Co.

Leitner, G.W. (1891) 'Rough accounts of itineraries through the Hindukush and to Central Asia', *The Imperial and Asiatic Quarterly Review, N. S.*, 2: 243–48.

Lockhart, W.S.A. and Woodthorpe, R.G. (1889) *The Gilgit Mission 1885–86*, London: Eyre & Spottiswoode.

Lewin, M. (2007) 'USSR – making and breaking', *Le Monde Diplomatique*, English edition, December 2007 Available online at: http://badmatthew.blogspot.com/2007_12_01_archive.html (accessed 14 July 2012).

Mackinder, H.J. (1904) 'The geographical pivot of history', *The Geographical Journal*, 23, 4: 421–44.

Michaud, J. (2010) 'Editorial: Zoma and beyond', *Journal of Global History*, 5: 187–214.

Migdal, J.S. (ed.) (2002) *Boundaries and Belonging. States and Societies in the Struggle to Shape Identities and Local Practices*, Cambridge: Cambridge University Press.

Monogarova, L.F. (1972) *Preobrazovanija v Bytu i Kul'ture Pripamirskich Narodnostij*, Moscow: Nauka.

Ocaña, A. (2003) 'Die Rebellion der Unrentablen. Zur Materialität des neozapatistischen Demokratiebegriffs', *Das Argument*, 253: 829–34.

Rakowska-Harmstone, T. (1975) 'Tadzhikistan and the Tadzhiks', in Z. Katz, R. Rogers and F. Harned (eds) *Handbook of Major Soviet Nationalities*, New York and London: The Free Press, pp. 315–51.

Rashid, A. (2000) *Taliban. Islam, Oil and the New Great Game in Central Asia*, London and New York: Tauris.

Renn, O. (2008a) 'Concepts of risk: an interdisciplinary review – part 1: disciplinary concepts', *GAIA*, 17, 1: 50–66.

Renn, O. (2008b) 'Concepts of risk: an interdisciplinary review – part 2: integrative approaches', *GAIA*, 17, 2: 196–204.

Rumford, C. (2006) 'Theorizing borders', *European Journal of Social Theory*, 9, 2: 155–69.

Scott, J.C. (2009) *The Art of Not Being Governed. An Anarchist History of Upland Southeast Asia*, New Haven and London: Yale University Press.

Sharma, P., Khanal, N. and Tharu S.C. (2009) *Towards a Federal Nepal. An Assessment of Proposed Models*, Kathmandu: Himal Books.

Sigrist, C. (1994) 'Staatsfreie Zonen im Great Game', *Peripherie*, 55/56: 81–93.

United Nations (2004) *Asian Highway Route Map*. Available online at: http://www.unescap.org/ttdw/common/TIS/AH/maps/AHMapApr04.gif (accessed 3 May 2007).

Uprawlenie narodno-chozjajstwennogo uceta Tadz SSR. Sektor uceta naselenija i kul'tury (= Administration for Tajik SSR's economic statistics) (1932) *Spisok naselennych punktov Tadz SSR* (= List of inhabited settlements within the Tajik SSR), Stalinabad.

van Schendel, W. (2002) 'Geographies of knowing, geographies of ignorance: jumping scale in Southeast Asia', *Environment and Planning D: Society and Space*, 20, 6: 647–68.

Vinnikov, J.R. (1980) 'National and ethnographic groups in Central Asia as reflected in ethnic statistics', *Soviet Sociology*, 19, part 1/2: 27–52, part 2/3: 74–97.

Wolf, E.R. (1982) *Europe and the People without History*, Berkeley, Los Angeles and London: University of California Press.

Zinn, J.O. (ed.) (2008) *Social Theories of Risk and Uncertainty. An Introduction*, Malden MA: Blackwell.

Chapter 12

Ahnert, F. (1996) *Einführung in die Geomorphologie*, Stuttgart: Ulmer.

Baker, V.R. (1988) 'Geological fluvial geomorphology', *Geological Society of America Bulletin*, 100, 8: 1157–67.

Bradbury, J.A. (2009) 'The policy implications of differing concepts of risk', in R. Löfstedt and A. Boholm (eds) *The Earthscan Reader on Risk*, London: Earthscan, pp. 27–42.

Breidbach, O. (2004) 'Über die neue und neuronale Ordnung von Welt – Ein Beitrag zur Neuronalen Ästhetik', in O. Breidbach and G. Orsi (eds) *Ästhetik – Hermeneutik – Neurowissenschaften*, Münster: LIT, pp. 51–66.

Dikau, R. (2006) 'Komplexe Systeme in der Geomorphologie', *Mitteilungen der Österreichischen Geographischen Gesellschaft*, 148: 125–50.

Gadamer, H.G. (1995) *Hermeneutik im Rückblick*, Gesammelte Werke 10, Tübingen: Mohr-Siebeck.

Gadamer, H.G. (2004, [1975]) *Truth and Method*, London: Continuum.

Gadamer, H.G. (2006) 'Bildkunst und Wortkunst', in G. Boehm (ed.) *Was ist ein Bild?*, München: Fink, pp. 90–104.

Gadamer, H.G. and Stappert, B.H. (2002) 'Kairos – Über die Gunst des Augenblicks und das weise Maß', *Sinn und Form*, 54, 2: 149–60.

Gunderson, L.H. and Holling, C.S. (eds) (2002) *Panarchy. Understanding Transformations in Human and Natural Systems*, Washington: Island Press.

Handmer, J. (2009) 'Adaptive capacity: what does it mean in the context of natural hazards?', in E.L.F. Schipper and I. Burton (eds) *The Earthscan Reader on Adaption to Climate Change*, London: Earthscan, pp. 213–27.

Heidegger, M. (1975) 'Building dwelling thinking', in M. Heidegger (ed.) *Poetry, Language, Thought*, New York: Harper & Row, pp. 145–61.

Heidegger, M. (2006) *Mindfulness*, trans. P. Emad and T. Kalary, London: Continuum.

Holling, C.S. (2001) 'Understanding the complexity of economic, ecological, and social systems', *Ecosystems*, 4, 5: 390–405.

Löfstedt, R. and Boholm, A. (eds) (2009) *The Earthscan Reader on Risk*, London: Earthscan.

Loewenstein, G.F., Weber, E.U., Hsee, C.K. and Welch, N. (2009) 'Risk as feelings', in R. Löfstedt and A. Boholm (eds) *The Earthscan Reader on Risk*, London: Earthscan, pp. 113–50.

MacCracken, M.C. and Topping Jr, J.C. (2008) *Sudden and Disruptive Climate Change. Exploring the Real Risks and How We Can Avoid Them*, London: Earthscan.

Massey, D. (2001) 'Talking of space-time', *Transactions of the Institute of British Geographers NS*, 26, 2: 257–61.

Moench, M. (2009) 'Adapting to climate change and the risks associated with other natural hazards: methods for moving from concepts to action', in E.L.F. Schipper and I. Burton (eds) *The Earthscan Reader on Adaption to Climate Change*, London: Earthscan, pp. 249–80.

Phillips, J.D. (1992a) 'Nonlinear dynamical systems in geomorphology: revolution or evolution?', *Geomorphology*, 5, 3/5: 219–29.

Phillips, J.D. (1992b) 'The end of equilibrium?', *Geomorphology*, 5, 3/5: 195–201.

Phillips, J.D. (1999) 'Methodology, scale, and the field of dreams', *Annals of the Association of American Geographers*, 89, 4: 754–60.

Phillips, J.D. (2006) 'Deterministic chaos and historical geomorphology: a review and look forward', *Geomorphology*, 76, 1/2: 109–21.

Pohl, J. and Geipel, R. (2002) 'Naturgefahren und Naturrisiken', *Geographische Rundschau*, 54, 1: 4–8.

Polanyi, M. (1966) *The Tacit Dimension*, New York: Doubleday.

Raab, T. and Frodeman, R. (2002) 'What is it like to be a geologist? A phenomenology of geology and its epistemological implications', *Philosophy & Geography*, 5, 1: 69–81.

Renn, O. (2008a) 'Concepts of risk: an interdisciplinary review – part 1: disciplinary risk concepts', *GAIA*, 17, 1: 50–66.

Renn, O. (2008b) 'Concepts of risk: an interdisciplinary review – part 2: integrative approaches', *GAIA*, 17, 2: 196–204.

Slaymaker, O. (2006) 'Towards the identification of scaling relations in drainage basin sediment budgets', *Geomorphology*, 80, 1/2: 8–19.

Thornes, J.B. (2003) 'Time: change and stability in environmental systems', in S. Holloway *et al.* (eds) *Key Concepts in Geography*, London: Sage, pp. 131–50.

United Nations Development Programme (2009) 'A climate risk management approach to disaster reduction and adaption to climate change', in E.L.F. Schipper and I. Burton (eds) *The Earthscan Reader on Adaption to Climate Change*, London: Earthscan, pp. 229–48.

Waldenfels, B. (2004) *Phänomenologie der Aufmerksamkeit*, Frankfurt a.M.: Suhrkamp.

Zahnen, B. (2005) 'Fragwürdigkeit und Eigensinn der Geographie', *Geographische Zeitschrift*, 93, 4: 201–20.

Zahnen, B. (2007) 'Lesen, Zeitlichkeit und das Geographische der Physischen Geographie', *Geographische Zeitschrift*, 95, 1/2: 72–90.

Zahnen, B. (2008) 'Das implizite Wissen der Erdwissenschaftler. Ein Beitrag zur Ästhetik und Geschichtlichkeit Physischer Geographie', *Berichte zur Deutschen Landeskunde*, 82, 2: 173–90.

Chapter 13

Adams, J. (1995) *Risk*, London: Routledge.

Alexander, D. (2004) 'Natural hazards on an unquiet earth', in J. Matthews and D. Herbert (eds) *Unifying Geography. Common Heritage, Shared Future*, London: Routledge, pp. 266–82.

Banse, G. and Bechmann, G. (1998) *Interdisziplinäre Risikoforschung. Eine Bibliographie*, Opladen: Westdeutscher Verlag.

Barrows, H. (1923) 'Geography as human ecology', *Annals of the Association of American Geographers*, 13, 1: 1–14.

Bätzing, W. (1993) 'Der sozio-ökonomische Strukturwandel des Alpenraumes im 20. Jahrhundert', *Geographica Bernensia*, 26: 1–156.

Bätzing, W. (2002) *Die aktuellen Veränderungen von Umwelt, Wirtschaft, Gesellschaft und Bevölkerung in den Alpen*, Berlin: Umweltbundesamt.

Commission of the European Communities (2007) *Directive 2007/60/EC of the European Parliament and of the Council of 23 October 2007 on the Assessment and Management of Flood Risks*, Brussels: European Commission.

Covello, V. and Mumpower, J. (1985) 'Risk analysis and risk management: a historical perspective', *Risk Analysis*, 5, 2: 103–20.

Crozier, M. (2005) 'Management frameworks for landslide hazard and risk: issues and options', in T. Glade, M. Anderson and M. Crozier (eds) *Landslide Hazard and Risk*, Chichester: John Wiley and Sons, pp. 331–50.

Crozier, M. and Glade, T. (2005) 'Landslide hazard and risk: issues, concepts and approach', in T. Glade, M. Anderson and M. Crozier (eds) *Landslide Hazard and Risk*, Chichester: John Wiley and Sons, pp. 2–40.

Cullen, A. and Small, M. (2004) 'Uncertain risk: the role and limits of quantitative assessment', in T. McDaniels and M. Small (eds) *Risk Analysis and Society: An Interdisciplinary Characterization of the Field*, Cambridge: Cambridge University Press, pp. 163–214.

Cutter, S. (1996) 'Vulnerability to environmental hazards', *Progress in Human Geography*, 20, 4: 529–39.

Cutter, S. (2001) *American Hazardscapes*, Washington: Joseph Henry Press.

Dietz, T., Frey, R. and Rosa, E. (2002) 'Risk, technology, and society', in R. Dunlap and W. Michelson (eds) *Handbook of Environmental Sociology*, Westport: Greenwood, pp. 329–69.

Dombrowsky, W. (2002) 'Flußhochwasser – ein Störfall der Vernunft?', *GAIA*, 11, 4: 310–11.

Egner, H. (2008) *Gesellschaft, Mensch, Umwelt – beobachtet*, Stuttgart: Franz Steiner Verlag.

Fell, R., Corominas, J., Bonnard, C., Cascini, L., Leroi, E. and Savage, W. (2008) 'Guidelines for landslide susceptibility, hazard and risk zoning for land-use planning', *Engineering Geology*, 102: 85–98.

Few, R. (2003) 'Flooding, vulnerability and coping strategies: local responses to a global threat', *Progress in Development Studies*, 3, 1: 43–58.

Fischhoff, B. (1995) 'Risk perception and communication unplugged: twenty years of process', *Risk Analysis*, 15, 2: 137–45.

Fischhoff, B., Slovic, P. and Lichtenstein, S. (1982) 'Lay foibles and expert fables in judgments about risk', *The American Statistician*, 36, 3: 240–55.

Freudenburg, W. (1988) 'Perceived risk, real risk: social science and the art of probabilistic risk assessment', *Science*, 242, 4875: 44–49.

Fuchs, S. (2009) 'Susceptibility versus resilience to mountain hazards in Austria – paradigms of vulnerability revisited', *Natural Hazards and Earth System Sciences*, 9: 337–52.

Fuchs, S. and Bründl, M. (2005) 'Damage potential and losses resulting from snow avalanches in settlements of the canton of Grisons, Switzerland', *Natural Hazards*, 34, 1: 53–69.

Fuchs, S., Bründl, M. and Stötter, J. (2004) 'Development of avalanche risk between 1950 and 2000 in the municipality of Davos, Switzerland', *Natural Hazards and Earth System Sciences*, 4, 2: 263–75.

Fuchs, S., Keiler, M., Zischg, A. and Bründl, M. (2005) 'The long-term development of avalanche risk in settlements considering the temporal variability of damage potential', *Natural Hazards and Earth System Sciences*, 5: 893–901.

Fuchs, S., Thöni, M., McAlpin, M.C., Gruber, U. and Bründl, M. (2007) 'Avalanche hazard mitigation strategies assessed by cost effectiveness analyses and cost benefit analyses – evidence from Davos, Switzerland', *Natural Hazards*, 41: 113–29.

Fuchs, S., Spachinger, K., Dorner, W., Rochman, J. and Serrhini, K. (2009) 'Evaluating cartographic design in flood risk mapping', *Environmental Hazards*, 8, 1: 52–70.

Geipel, R. (1992) *Naturrisiken: Katastrophenbewältigung im sozialen Umfeld*, Darmstadt: Wissenschaftliche Buchgesellschaft.

Golledge, R. (2002) 'The nature of geographic knowledge', *Annals of the Association of American Geographers*, 92, 1: 1–14.

Holub, M. and Fuchs, S. (2009) 'Mitigating mountain hazards in Austria – legislation, risk transfer, and awareness building', *Natural Hazards and Earth System Sciences*, 9: 523–37.

Hoos, I. (1980) 'Risk assessment in social perspective', in Council on Radiation Protection and Measurements (ed.) *Perceptions of Risk*, Washington: National Council on Radiation Protection, pp. 57–85.

Hotz, M.C. and Weibel, F. (2005) *Arealstatistik Schweiz*, Neuchâtel: Bundesamt für Statistik.

Kates, R. and Kasperson, J. (1983) 'Comparative risk analysis of technological hazards (a review)', *Proceedings National Academy of Science USA*, 80, 22: 7027–38.

Keiler, M. and Fuchs, S. (2010) 'Berechnetes Risiko. Mit Sicherheit am Rande der Gefahrenzone', in H. Egner and A. Pott (eds) *Geographische Risikoforschung. Zur Konstruktion verräumlichter Risiken und Sicherheiten*, Franz Steiner Verlag, Stuttgart, pp. 51–68.

Keiler, M., Zischg, A., Fuchs, S., Hama, M. and Stötter, J. (2005) 'Avalanche related damage potential – changes of persons and mobile values since the mid-twentieth century, case study Galtür', *Natural Hazards and Earth System Sciences*, 5: 49–58.

Keiler, M., Sailer, R., Jörg, P., Weber, C., Fuchs, S., Zischg, A. and Sauermoser, S. (2006) 'Avalanche risk assessment – a multi-temporal approach, results from Galtür, Austria', *Natural Hazards and Earth System Sciences*, 6: 637–51.

Keiler, M., Knight, J. and Harrison, S. (2010) 'Climate change and geomorphological hazards in the eastern European Alps', *Philosophical Transactions of the Royal Society of London. Series A: Mathematical, Physical and Engineering Sciences*, 368: 2461–79.

Löfstedt, R. and Boholm, Å. (2009) *The Earthscan Reader on Risk*, London: Earthscan.

ONR (2009) *Schutzbauwerke der Wildbachverbauung – Begriffe und ihre Definitionen sowie Klassifizierung, ONR 24800*, Wien: Österreichisches Normungsinstitut.

Österreichisch-Ungarische Monarchie (1884) *Gesetz, betreffend Vorkehrungen zur unschädlichen Ableitung von Gebirgswässern*, RGBl 117/1884.

Renn, O. (2008) 'Concepts of risk: an interdisciplinary review – part 1: disciplinary risk concepts', *GAIA*, 17: 50–66.

Repubblica Italiana (1998) *G.U. n. 134/1998: DD. LL. 11 giugno 1998, n. 180. Misure urgenti per la prevenzione del rischio idrogeologico ed a favore delle zone colpite da disastri franosi nella regione Campania*, Gazzetta Ufficiale della Repubblica Italiana, 134.

Republik Österreich (1975) *Forstgesetz 1975*, BGBl 440/1975.

Republik Österreich (1976) *Verordnung des Bundesministers für Land- und Forstwirtschaft vom 30. Juli 1976 über die Gefahrenzonenpläne*, BGBl 436/1976.

Schweizerische Eidgenossenschaft (1991) *Bundesgesetz über den Wald*, SR921.0.

Short, J. (1984) 'The social fabric at risk: toward the social transformation of risk analysis', *American Sociological Review*, 49, 6: 711–25.

Slovic, P. (1987) 'Perception of risk', *Science*, 236, 4799: 280–85.

Slovic, P., Fischhoff, B. and Lichtenstein, S. (1982) 'Why study risk perception?', *Risk Analysis*, 2, 2: 83–93.

Solomon, S., Qin, D., Manning, M., Chen, Z., Marquis, M., Averyt, K., Tignor, M. and Miller, H. (2007) *Climate Change 2007. The Scientific Basis: Contribution of Working Group I to the Fourth Assessment Report of the Intergovernmental Panel on Climate Change*, Cambridge: Cambridge University Press.

Starr, C. (1969) 'Social benefit versus technological risk', *Science*, 165: 1232–38.

Statistik Austria (2008) *Dauersiedlungsraum, Gebietsstand 2008*. Available online at: http://www.statistik.at/dynamic/wcmsprod/idcplg?IdcService=INSERT_ INDEX&WEBSITESEC=1545&RURL=/web_de/statistiken/regionales/ regionale_gliederungen/dauersiedlungsraum/index.html&Language=de (accessed 17 July 2012).

Stötter, J. and Fuchs, S. (2006) 'Umgang mit Naturgefahren – Status quo und zukünftige Anforderungen', in S. Fuchs, L. Khakzadeh and K. Weber (eds) *Recht im Naturgefahrenmanagement*, Innsbruck: Studienverlag, pp. 19–34.

United Nations (2004) *Living with Risk. A Global Review of Disaster Reduction Initiatives. Vol. 1*, Geneva: United Nations.

United Nations General Assembly (1989) *International Decade for Natural Disaster Reduction*, United Nations General Assembly Resolution 236 session 44 of 22 December 1989, A-RES-44-236.

United Nations General Assembly (2000) *International Decade for Natural Disaster Reduction: Successor Arrangements*, United Nations General Assembly Resolution 219 session 54 of 3 February 2000, A-RES-54-219.

Vlek, C. and Stallen, P.-J. (1981) 'Judging risks and benefits in the small and the large', *Organizational Behavior and Human Performance*, 28, 2: 235–71.

Werner, B. and McNamara, D. (2007) 'Dynamics of coupled human-landscape systems', *Geomorphology*, 91, 3/4: 393–407.

White, G. (1994) 'A perspective on reducing losses from natural hazards', *Bulletin of the American Meteorological Society*, 75, 7: 1237–40.

White, G., Kates, I. and Burton, R. (2001) 'Knowing better and losing even more: the use of knowledge in hazards management', *Environmental Hazards*, 3, 3: 81–92.

Wisner, B., Blaikie, P., Cannon, T. and Davis, I. (2004) *At Risk*, London: Routledge.

Zinn, J. and Taylor-Gooby, P. (2006) 'Risk as an interdisciplinary research area', in P. Taylor-Gooby and J. Zinn (eds) *Risk in Social Science*, Oxford: Oxford University Press, pp. 20–53.

Chapter 14

Beck, U. (1992) *Risk Society: Towards a New Modernity*, London: Sage Publications.

Cissé, G., Koné, B., Bâ, H., Mbaye, I., Koba, K., Utzinger, J. and Tanner, M. (2012): 'Ecohealth and climate change: adaptation to flooding events in riverside secondary cities, West Africa', in K. Otto-Zimmermann (ed.) *Resilient Cities. Cities and Adaptation to Climate Change. Proceedings of the Global Forum 2010*. London and New York: Springer, Dordrecht Heidelberg, pp. 55–67.

Crampton, J. (2010) *Mapping. A Critical Introduction to Cartography and GIS*, Chichester: Wiley-Blackwell.

DeLyser, D., Herbert, S., Aitken, S., Crang, M. and McDowell, L. (eds) (2010) *The SAGE Handbook of Qualitative Geography*, Los Angeles: SAGE.

Hutter, B.M. (2006) 'Risk, regulation, and management', in P. Taylor-Gooby and J. Zinn (eds) *Risk in Social Science*, Oxford: Oxford University Press, pp. 202–27.

Kitchin, R. and Dodge, M. (2007) 'Rethinking maps', *Progress in Human Geography*, 31, 3: 331–44.

Massey, D. (1995) *Spatial Division of Labor. Social Structures and the Geography of Production,* 2nd edn, New York: Routledge.

Mythen, G. (2005) 'From 'goods' to 'bads'? Revisiting the political economy of risk', *Sociological Research Online*, 10, 3. Available online at: http://www.socresonline.org.uk/10/3/mythen.html (accessed 15 July 2012).

November, V. (2004) 'Being close to risk. From proximity to connexity', *International Journal of Sustainable Development*, 7, 3: 273–86.

November, V. (2008) 'Commentary: spatiality of risk', *Environment and Planning A,* 40: 1523–27.

Renn, O. (2008) *Risk Governance. Coping with Uncertainty in a Complex World*, London: Earthscan.

Scheuer, S., Haase, D. and Meyer, V. (2011) 'Exploring multicriteria flood vulnerability by integrating economic, social and ecological dimensions of flood risk and coping capacity: from a starting point view towards an end point view of vulnerability', *Natural Hazards,* 58, 2: 731–51.

Wisner, B., Blaikie, P., Cannon, T. and Davis, I. (2004) *At Risk: Natural Hazards, People's Vulnerability and Disasters*, 2nd edn, London: Routledge.

Index

For Product Safety Concerns and Information please contact our
EU representative GPSR@taylorandfrancis.com Taylor & Francis
Verlag GmbH, Kaufingerstraße 24, 80331 München, Germany